W9-ATS-880

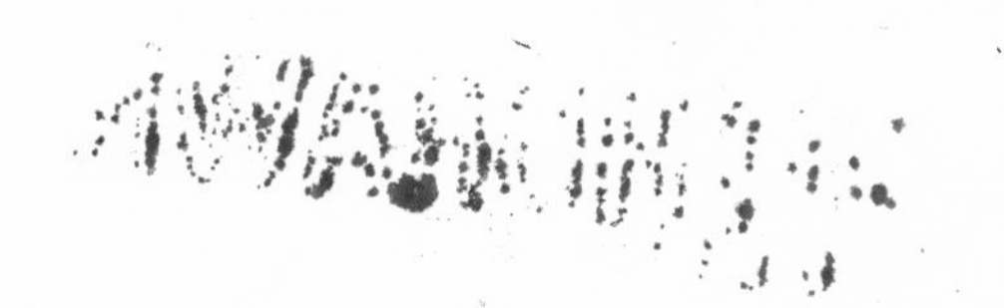

# IN THE BEGINNING WAS THE DEED

# In the Beginning was the Deed

## *REFLECTIONS ON THE PASSAGE OF FAUST*

◆

HARRY REDNER



UNIVERSITY OF CALIFORNIA PRESS

BERKELEY · LOS ANGELES
LONDON

University of California Press
Berkeley and Los Angeles
California

University of California Press, Ltd.
London, England



Printed in the United States of America

1 2 3 4 5 6 7 8 9

Published with the assistance of the
Monash University Publications Committee

**Library of Congress Cataloging in Publication Data**

Redner, Harry.
In the beginning was the deed.

Includes bibliographical references and index.
1. Civilization, Modern, 1800—
2. Philosophy. I. Title. II. Title: Faust.
CB428.R43 901 81-16090
ISBN 0-520-04435-5 AACR2

# CONTENTS

# DEDICATION

*I dedicate this book to the memory of my Fathers*

*Dov Redner (1908–1941)*
*Joachim Bernstein (1914–1978)*

If every philosophy contains within itself a hidden autobiography, as Nietzsche insists, then it is true that this work, too, is autobiographical. I have not written about anything that I have not experienced at least in thought, if not in life. My main motive in writing this work and in trying to make sense of our time has been to make sense of my life. May it be of help to others in doing the same. That is, ultimately, the only justification for the existence of this book, for anyone who now sets pen to paper with thoughts of publication must in all honesty ask himself whether his writing is really necessary, much as during the last great war people were exhorted to ask themselves, "Is this journey really necessary?" I leave it to my readers to decide—if they are patient enough to get to the end—whether this journey we have undertaken together has been worth making.

The journey for me has not been fast or easy. I have labored on this work for many years under diverse circumstances and in many places. The work itself underwent many revisions, altering its shape and form repeatedly, though the theme that was the initial inspiration remained constant from start to finish. Thomas Mann, when he had finished his *Doctor Faustus*, went on to write *The Story of a Novel* recounting the writing of the novel; I should also like to go on and write *Reflections on Reflections on the Passage of Faust,* but I know that such an involuted self-reflection would be unlikely to interest anyone else. A purely private struggle in what is to outward appearances an uneventful stretch of life cannot possibly be conveyed short of attempting a novel oneself, and that is beyond my powers.

All the while I was working on this book, my wife, Jill Redner, was working on her Shakespeare study "The World's Body Anatomized," and this acts as a kind of silent commentary on my work. What each work owes the other is now impossible to untangle, so many a thought was thought through together. It is likely that if we had not so kept pace on our journeys neither work would ever have been finished.

Even after this book was finished, however, the journey did not end.

It would be gratifying to be able to record that many welcomed it with open arms, but such was not the case. It is all the more gratifying, therefore, to be able now to acknowledge the few without whose help the book would surely have had to wait much longer to be read.

It was a stroke of sheer good luck that this work came to the attention of Norman Jacobson at a crucial point in its peregrinations. In attempting to convey my thanks to him perhaps I may repeat the words used by Ernest Becker in the acknowledgment he makes to this exceptional man in *The Structure of Evil*: I, too, have found his "generous encouragement, which extended even to points of view he may not have agreed with personally"—so characteristic of him—invaluable and indispensable. To John Pocock, who may well agree with even less in the book, I owe, nevertheless, thanks for a sympathetic reading and many useful comments. To the anonymous reader for the University of California Press who advised me on revisions, I wish to convey my belated appreciation. To my editor Alain Hénon and his assistant Cynthia Deno, who trusted their judgment with a "peculiar" work, I can only say that I hope the book will prove a vindication of their efforts. It is many years now since Gershon Weiler read the first version of the work and he may well not recognize what has become of it, but I should like him to know that his encouragement then helped to make the transformation possible. During all those years I have been helped by the impeccable secretarial services of Mrs. Joy Smith, whose calm demeanor has been as soothing as her clear typed pages. Finally, if the book is judged free at least of the errors that are avoidable it is in no small measure due to the countless touches of tactful and scrupulous copy-editing by Jane-Ellen Long.

To my department and its founding chairman, Rufus Davis, I owe thanks for congenial working conditions and for the periods of study-leave during which most of the book was written. I take this opportunity to acknowledge that this book was published with the assistance of the Monash University Publication Committee.

# PRELUDE

It seems I have written a book that librarians will find difficult to catalogue correctly—one that will not fit comfortably into any of the pre-established compartments neatly labelled as history, philosophy, literature, politics, music, or sociology, though it draws on all of these. It may even strike the reader as a chimerical, impossible kind of book, one that ought not to exist in an age of specialization but which, nevertheless, like some monster from a fabulous bestiary or like Morgenstern's *Nasobem,* "came not from any annual, encyclopedia or manual/ But on its nose strode out direct from my poetic lyre." It is in any case an old-fashioned book, which some may even see as harking back to ancient models of the Book: the book of the world, the book of time, the book as a repository of everything on a topic—as if exhaustiveness were even imaginable in this age of "exploding" knowledge! My topic, however, is so far from being antiquated that it has not as yet had time to age; nor have we as yet developed adequate models in which to accommodate it. Because it is so unprecedented and daunting it compels a recourse to the oldest forms, to those apocalyptic writings where the latest and last go back to the first. I begin, therefore, where I am not alone in fearing we may very well end.

The book is haunted by the twin presences of Auschwitz and Hiroshima. These two symbolic names are no longer news, yet they define for us the essential reality of our contemporary world, which began with this monstrous twin event. It is one of the grimmer ironies of history that at that very moment the perpetrators of the first were being tried and condemned by those who were preparing the second; it was almost as if the crime were being unknowingly passed on from the accused to the accuser, and, in being passed on, magnified from a relatively local level to a potentially universal dimension. Auschwitz and what it symbolizes was largely a European crime, even though the rest of the world has here and there shown itself ready to repeat it; together with the other European crimes of that period, such as the Gulag, it brought about the suicidal self-annihilation of the strictly European phase of modern civilization that had till then dominated the world. (Not altogether a bad thing, some who suffered this domination will even now say, since it freed the colonial world from the yoke of Europe.) Simultaneously but not coincidentally, at that point the world fell under the thrall of Hiroshima, under whose ever-darkening mushroom shadow, taken for a widening umbrella of safety, more and more of the world chooses to place itself. This, then, is our present time, an in-between time between one holocaust past and another in the offing.

In the last few years the world has been moving closer to rather than further away from this possibility. At such a moment one can no longer pretend that one can go on with intellectual business as usual. The possible disaster that is approaching is not some inhuman sideshow which threatens from the outside but has inherently nothing to do with the humane activities thinkers and writers are engaged in at such a seeming remove from the centers of power where the means of annihilation are being readied. Rather, the unthinkable deed and the deed of thought are rooted in the very same activities of the present age; they are both expressions of a common condition. The full realization of the horrendous truth has so far been hidden from the minds of most of us, and this book represents one attempt to bring this truth into the open, to exemplify the changed nature of intellectual activity that has ensued on the entry of the world into this new perilous state. And it in no way holds itself exempt from or above what it exemplifies.

Anyone who thinks it possible to write a book in the old sense in such a time, to measure the realities of this age in the old way so as to make thought fit life, has failed to appreciate the radically changed nature of human reality. Time no longer flows in its old continuities and writing cannot rely on the security of time to conserve and convey its message. One speaks of libraries where books might be preserved, of catalogues and subject matters, of authors and titles, but one does so largely out of ingrained habit and professional presupposition; one knows that libraries are no longer repositories safe from the ordinary ravages of time, and that the life of a book cannot be expected to be any longer than the life of a man. So no one can hope to write for a future that is itself uncertain or try to address coming generations who may not come. Everything that is done, it seems, can now only be done for the present alone. Bereft of any sense of permanence—which past ages used to call immortality—all present writing is caught in the constraints of this contracted time-span, and none can hope to escape from it. This should help to explain why the topic of this book has to be self-reflective, for the book has become a problem for itself, one it must confront within itself.

There is one thing a book can still try to accomplish in reflecting back on itself—something that goes beyond itself. For trapped in the present we are, nevertheless, compelled to think about the past, we want to know what has brought us to our present pass. We want to know not merely in order to understand but also in order to act. And we can only act if we do indeed live and think in the present and can free ourselves from that of the past which blinds us to our present predicament. Much of life and thought as it is still carried on now is based on the assumption that Auschwitz and Hiroshima never happened, or if they did, then only as mere events, far away and long ago, that need not concern us now. Few have fully realized that these events have grown to monstrous proportions and become unconscious symbols of ourselves, that they have changed us utterly, and that all our thinking needs to be made to register this change for otherwise it will be, strictly speaking, out-of-date, an anachronism no matter how up-to-the-moment it may seem. The fashionable is in this respect always already passé.

To account for this progression from the past to the present I have reused two earlier categories, Progress and Nihilism, much as one might recycle old materials from the lumber room of the history of ideas. I have reinvoked them not because I believe in their accepted significations but because it is always better to try to rework an old, familiar idea than to build up a new one *ex nihilo*. Progress and Nihilism in the way I use them no longer mean what they meant before; they are redefined to make them appropriate to the present, but nevertheless so as to maintain connection with the way they were used in the past. The same holds true for many of the other old ideas, themes, and forms of the book.

No attempt has been made to write extensive histories of these ideas in a scholarly spirit, though a few brief sketches of the previous meanings of Progress and Nihilism have been provided in passing. These are meant only to serve as a background to the relatively new meaning these old terms have assumed in the present. We now see the reality of Progress very differently from the way it was seen by those in the recent past who were actively intent on furthering it. Looking back over that progressive striving, we now realize that it meant the furtherance of Technology, Subjectivity, and Activism, the dominant trends of modern European expansion. These three terms are also old ideas that need to be rethought and reapplied. The same holds—even more so—for the word Nihilism, which is no longer to be recoiled from with aversion and horror and contrasted to Progress. We now know that Progress and Nihilism belong together, and that the latter is no mere unfortunate side effect of the former which might somehow or other be avoided. On the contrary, the book attempts to show that some of the most daring achievements of mankind in the modern age are part and parcel of its Nihilism. But to show this a firm distinction needs to be drawn between different qualities of Nihilism, and in particular between destructive and annihilatory Nihilism. The former constitutes a liberating force of some potential even while the latter brings us ever closer to utmost ruin through physical annihilation or technological dehumanization. The relationships between the two forms of Nihilism, as well as that of Progress to Nihilism in general, constitute the fundamental issues on which the fate of the times depends. This is the theme of the world-historic drama which we have sought to reenact by recollecting the well-known dramatic symbols of Faust and Macbeth.

Once again, there is nothing new in conceiving of human action on the dramatic metaphor and of composing a book on this conception. Many thinkers from Heraclitus onward have availed themselves of the dramatic metaphor, and even in our own day one of the leading thinkers on the dangers of technology, Mumford, insists that "man's existence in all its dimensions is perhaps best understood in terms of the theater, as a drama unfolding in action" *(Pentagon of Power,* "Epilogue").[1] Drama as a metaphor specifically for history has also become quite conventional since Vico, Herder, and Hegel. What has had to change drastically is the kind of drama we can now conceive history to be. For us that drama can no longer be expected to have the assured classical form of beginning, middle, and end; instead, a new and revised dramatic rendering is called for. Even our choice of Faust as the leading dramatis persona has, one might say, become a hackneyed bill of fare on the stage-boards of the history of thought; Spengler, for one, it might be assumed, had done that play to death. But our Faust is not Spengler's, it is not the "soul" of European culture or a spirit of its times; ours is the literary Faust as he actually appears in the plays carrying his name, above all the dramatizations of Marlowe, Goethe, and Mann—it is not a mythological Faust. The coupling of Faust and Macbeth is perhaps the only wholly unprecedented move to which we can lay claim, though even for that there are intimations in Alfred Weber's aptly named *A Farewell to European History,* written at the same historic moment as Thomas Mann's *Doctor Faustus* in response to the same events, the twin horrors of Auschwitz and Hiroshima.

What interest us in this book are Faust's three epochal appearances, the first at the end of the Renaissance, the second at the start of our modern era, and the third in our own time. Is this last appearance of Faust also in some way decisive? That is what we need to find out, but first we shall need to learn who and what is Faust. Right from the start he is the philosopher-scholar dissatisfied with his knowledge, and so he ever remains the dissatisfied self-conscious intellectual. This self-consciousness is raised to a higher power with every new appearance, for every new Faust reflects back on all the past forms of his former selves. Thus, Marlowe's Faustus reflects self-consciously on the first naive Faustus of the chapbook; and Goethe's Faust reflects back on these earlier two, indirectly, via the puppet-play Goethe witnessed as a child, and directly, through his reading of Marlowe in old age. Mann's Faust is almost the utmost in self-consciousness, for in its historical sweep all the previous selves of Faust are present together in layer upon layer of themselves. The passage of Faust is a self-reflective one, for each Faust looks back on all the previous Fausts, and what he sees in looking back down his passage, as in a hall of mirrors, is reflection on reflection of himself. (For a brief sketch of the story of Faust see Appendix I.)

Faust is above all the self-reflective, intellectual individual. The further he progresses the more his self-consciousness turns back on itself, until it threatens to become a paralyzing self-preoccupation. Trapped in itself, his consciousness spirals around the void inside him and is seized with a suicidal vertigo when it looks down into that yawning abyss of nothingness. It is in this predicament that every Faust turns to his Devil for succor. The negative principle seems the only firm ground in the hollow of nothingness for those intellectuals unwilling or unable to save themselves by a *sacrificium intellectualitatis* which will deliver them but also deliver them over to humdrum safeties. By refusing normal salvation, then, is Faust inevitably damned? The answer to this question becomes more and more ambiguous as salvation and damnation lose their absolute distinctness. The distinction between what is of God and what of the Devil is no longer so clear to us as God and the Devil repeatedly change and change places in what they stand for. Accompanying each Faust there is a changed Devil, but the Devil, too, maintains his identity from Faust to Faust. Similarly, the terms of the Deed on which Faust is willing to sell his soul also change, yet there is a continuity in what each Faust wants in return.

What Faust wants reflects closely the demands of each age, just as the turning to the Devil reflects the crisis of each age. And each crisis is brought on by the previous demands being satisfied but not satisfying—the Devil sees to that. Thus, each Faust negates the previous Faust, to be himself negated in his turn, the whole passage forming a dialectic of negations seemingly without end. The first Faust has the longing of the humanist Renaissance intellectual for knowledge, power, and life as desire. Only the Devil can provide him with these, for each entails a transgression, a breaking of the limitations imposed in its wisdom by Christian doctrine and Church teaching: curiosity, pride, and lust are deadly sins that arise from the most dangerous of human needs, those that most need to be curbed. The next Faust goes one better: already he looks on such dangers with ironic, amused contempt. He is, after all, a child of the Enlightenment; for him knowledge, power, and desire have nothing to offer—he has tasted them and found them wanting. The crude satisfactions of worldly living are tasteless and meaningless. But what is there that can give savor to life? Once more the Devil must enter to save Faust from the life-rejecting impasse into which his thought has pushed him. Paradoxically, in seeking to lead him through sin to perdition the Devil also succeeds despite himself in leading him back to active life, to the Deed and its inherent meaning as ever-creative activity. Life in its very progress leads on, and Man drawn on by love moves higher and higher. The final Faust deliberately and destructively takes it all back, cancels the ideal of human progress, which has taken him only to intellectual desiccation and barbaric violence. His sharp intellect sees through all the idealistic illusions of development and formal perfection dear to bourgeois art; but his intellect is sterile—without the Devil's help he cannot break through his impasse. Only from the Devil can he get that destructive power, the daemonic inspiration for a real break-through. The break-through is simultaneously a complete break-down; it is the end of Faust and all that Faust has been. Yet, there is a hint in Mann's book that somehow it is not the end of everything. In the very sound of the tragic lamentation, the requiem for modern life, do we not hear a note of hope, a distant echo of the resurrection? Will Faust somehow be reborn? Or is this merely the last of Faust's self-deceiving self-reflections?

And what of this present reflection on the passage of Faust—is that but another twist in the spiral of deepening self-consciousness? Is it the dead end of the passage of Faust, or is it the way to a new opening? Is it itself a Faust, or a valedictory to Faust, a closing commentary on a finished text? More than the literary death of Faust is involved in answering this question: also at stake is the possible death of Man himself. And the two are not unrelated.

Faust is the self-conscious thinker—in traditional terms, philosopher—right from the start, from the first words of his first speech: "I have, alas, studied philosophy." In the end, the last Faust is also a musician; he is the composer Adrian Leverkühn of Mann's book. Music, as we shall show, accompanies the Faust drama from start to finish, and it is, therefore, in a literal sense melo-drama. The form of this book follows the trajectory from Faustian philosophy at the beginning to Faustian music at the end. There is, as will appear, an inherent and close relation between philosophy and music. In between these major concerns the other main topics of the Faustian passage will progressively unfold Act by Act and scene by scene.

The first Act begins with Faust's epochal pronouncement "In the beginning was the Deed," for Faust's first act is the Deed, the meaning of which this Act explores. This Act also introduces another key Faustian thematic attendant on the Deed, that of Language. The second Act carries this further beyond the bounds of philosophy, and seeks to show how the reconception of Language on the basis of the Deed also extends to a rethinking of Man, Time, and Nothing in modern thought, culture, and science. Man as the doer of the Deed is a very different kind of agent from that envisaged by any ordered and static conception of human nature which gives Man a fixed place in the scheme of being; the Time of development and Progress is also different from the times of mutability and corruption or of static quasi-spatial representation of the preceding periods; lastly, the Nothing of modern Nihilism is no longer the nothingness of chaos, void, or despair, but a new active sense of reduction through the voiding of meaning. At the same time we also seek to bring out the contradictions and antinomies to which all such Faustian thought is prey and which in each case brings on a nihilistic Macbethan reaction. The dialectical play of these contradictions will give the whole Act its "musical," "quasi una fantasia," character. The third Act is further removed from such playful dialectics of ideas and closer to the concreteness of actual deeds, that is, closer to the disciplines of history and sociology. In this Act an historical analysis of Progress and its relation to Nihilism is undertaken. This does not cease to be dialectical, but in this instance the dialectic is that of the equivocations of Progress, of how it visibly presents itself in history and what it latently shows itself to be; to show this we expose the duplicities of Technology and Technocracy, Subjectivity and Subjectlessness, Activism and Inactivity. The last Act brings the drama to the end of Faust as this is dramatized in the three key Fausts of literary history. In each case we seek to explicate what the end holds in store for each Faust. This brings us finally to the very end of the Faust thematic itself, to the conclusion of the Faustian epoch of European history. This complex drama of progression and end, which we refer to as the passage of Faust, must conclude with the death of Faust.

The death of Faust is symbolically a "murder," for this is the new symbolic form the "deed" has assumed in our time. Murder in a new and unprecedented guise as the "deed without a name," referred to literarily in *Macbeth,* is the literal meaning of the final annihilating deed, which also cannot be fully conceived or named. The death of All is beyond our thinking grasp, and in that sense alone is it unthinkable. This is a new dimension of death that no age had previously encountered. Auschwitz and Hiroshima have opened up to us a new death. To try to speak this death, to devise a language for this new reality of death, is the primary concern of this book.

# EPILOGUE IN HEAVEN

## I

Death has always been the object of man's contemplation. It has been called the "muse of philosophy." "Man contemplates death in order to bring forth life," said Spinoza. That thought itself springs from philosophy, which has traditionally been understood as the love of wisdom in the knowledge of how to die. From Socrates, its martyred hero, onward down the ages, this has been the perennial topos of philosophy. It was re-evoked by Boethius and by Montaigne—"that to philosophize is to learn how to die"—eventually to be handed into our safekeeping as a commonplace made meaningless by repetition. And as in our time death itself has come to lose its sting for us, so has the thought of death ceased to act as a spur to philosophizing.

The death that the tradition invoked is, of course, the death of the single man, the individual, and what it asked him to contemplate was his own most certain demise. All men are mortal, Socrates is a man, therefore . . .—that first syllogism of logical thought rationally deduced the death of its hero Socrates, as if to bring death itself within the scope of reason. It inescapably forced on each individual the logical conclusion that he too must die, a conclusion it invited him to accept calmly, with reason, just as Socrates had done. Logic and death were at one in all traditional philosophy until they came apart in our time. "All men are mortal" was not just a general proposition but the fundamental truth to be contemplated by every individual, and it always meant that each individual must test in himself his own mortality and so prove himself to be a man. *Morior ergo sum* is an earlier, unspoken, and more fundamental way of demonstrating existence than *cogito ergo sum*, for the thought of death is more basic to philosophy than the thought of Thought. Humanity was more inextricably bound to mortality than to rationality. It was granted that what is common to all men is their human mortality, which is both the severance of men from each other—for in death each man is alone—and at the same time their union in a conjoined lot—for in death all men are one.

It is almost as if to make up to the individual for forcing on him the knowledge of his own death that traditional thought has tended to cultivate a compensating counter-theme. All men are mortal, therefore Man is immortal: because all men must die, the species Man is imperishable. That was another—unspoken—syllogism of traditional thought and it meant that not only is the species being of man, the human essence, indestructible, but also that mankind itself will continue to live. Indeed, men must die so that Man may live, for only by dying can individuals hand over their lives to others in the race; literally, the succession of generations is pictured as a relay race in which the torch of life is kept alight as it is passed from one runner to the next. That is, of course, a pagan, classical image, but there is something analogous to it even in our religious tradition when it conceives of the passing of generations: "one generation passeth away, and another generation cometh: but the earth abideth ever." Only doctrinal theological thinking could permit itself the hope of an end of Man and the conclusion of the agony of human mortality, for as it derived death from sin, so it could foresee an end to death in Man's ultimate redemption. Even so, it is only in this eschatological sense, in which Man is translated into a higher state of being, that the end of Man is contemplated—not as a threat but as a promise that really amounts to a most comforting reassurance that Man is immortal and that the ultimate life of Man, even beyond this earthly term, is within God's care. In short, both on religious premises and on humanist ones the immortality of Man, the human race itself, is affirmed. Man is immortal because life itself cannot die: it will forever follow death, just as death follows it. The balanced succession of life and death will continue for perpetuity or till "kingdom come." It has taken all the discoveries and uncoveries of our time first to weaken and then to destroy that assurance.

We now know that Man, too, is mortal. We know it not only as a theoretical scientific possibility but as an imminent practical fact. We know it now because only in our time has Man acquired the practical capacity to annihilate himself. The species can now achieve that which before was only open to the individual: to effect its own willed extinction. "To be or not to be," that is still the question, but only now does it put Man as a whole in question. And just as that question loomed so large for the individual because he could make his quietus with a bare bodkin, so it looms large for Man because it, too, can now be consummated—with somewhat more sophisticated instruments. Death becomes more real when suicide is within reach, for the race as for the individual.

It is this new death that calls on us to philosophize even when the old call can no longer be heard. We are now impelled to contemplate, not our own deaths alone, but the death of Man, and are driven to speculate on the meaning of that—*sub species nihilitatis*. But can it really be called philosophizing? Has it anything in common with the old contemplation of individual mortality? Will it eventually provide us with new knowledge of our own death as well? Whatever one chooses to call it, it is also a thinking in the face of death, but a death that has hitherto been unthinkable, for no previous thought could countenance that death as a real possibility or fear it as a threat. Neither humanist nor religious thought could entertain it: for the former, Man is the measure of things; for the latter, he is God's creature. In neither case can Man do away with himself by simply committing suicide; Being itself and the very order of the universe would be against it. Hence, it is a thought that is fundamentally unthinkable in traditional thought.

What, then, is the "thinking of this unthinkable" to be like now? What kind of Man must it think of who would be capable of committing the ultimate deed? It is clear that in the face of that new possibility our whole notion of Man must become utterly different to any traditionally entertained. Our thinking can no longer afford the naive innocence of believing that such a Man—capable of doing that to himself—is impossible. Such a comforting but credulous innocence will have to be abandoned. Man must eat a second time of the tree of knowledge so as to know the worst about himself: "to know / By the worst means the worst" (*Macbeth* III.iv).

But what is the worst? It is easy enough to think of a nuclear holocaust engulfing the globe. That is not unthinkable. Men think it all the time, without really believing it; they toy with it intellectually, even plotting and planning how to derive the most profit to themselves from such a threat or how to limit it to acceptable proportions. That is how we have made it thinkable. But behind our superficial thoughts and rational words the blind unspoken terror is always there; we know it in our nightmares, in our insecurities and anxieties, in the hectic rush of our everyday lives when we live for today in the dim awareness that there may be no tomorrow. And even when we are publicly confronted with the stark reality of our situation and are made to fear it together, even then this public fear is only a surrogate for the real personal terror. The public fear obfuscates the root anxiety, for that is the product of other threats of annihilation than merely the obviously visible and thinkable one of nuclear holocaust. It feeds on fears of other modes of annihilation as well, ones that have a personal bearing on individual existence, so that they have partly fused with but also partly supplanted the old *timor mortis*. It is this confused compound-fear that modern thought must try to untangle.

It is apparent to us now that Man can be annihilated in many more ways than simply that of physical extermination. It suffices merely to reduce the state of men's being to a point below which it is recognizably human. Again, recent history has given us ample practical demonstrations of such possibilities, for just as the A-bomb experiment on Japan showed what was possible on a global scale, the Gulag Archipelago and the Final Solution were relatively small-scale experimental demonstrations of the feasibility of similar final solutions to the problem of Man. Again, these "holocausts" have become contemporary clichés, words to be conjured with or to be solemnly evoked on ceremonial occasions; their reality has been eroded and their deeper truth is being evaded. Nevertheless, the fear remains. That is obvious from the avid way in which men consume such visions and previsions of annihilation in fiction. Scaremongering is now a profitable branch of the literary industry. Serious thought is lacking, and anyone who wishes to think and speak seriously risks being confused with the peddlers of doom.

The holocausts we have so far experienced are the highly visible manifestations of a barely visible process that has now been going on for some centuries, a passage in history whereby Western Man first constructs for himself and then adapts himself to a complex, impersonal system known too simply as Technology. It is from the invisible, nihilistic aspects of Technology that the holocausts we have so far seen derive. (Of course, Technology alone is not responsible for these horrific historic events—other, more immediate causes initiated them as well—but it is the root cause without which nothing so momentous could have happened.) This being so, it is in the negative secret workings of Technology, rather than in any of its specific open manifestations, that the greatest danger lies. For Technology is the new *logos* of *technē* that has come into the world, in direct succession through numerous translations of the initial logic of the Socratic syllogism that began by stating that "All men are mortal." It is as if logic itself had in all its tortuous ratiocinations for over two millennia merely progressed from that first premise to the final conclusion that "Man is mortal"; and, as if not satisfied with that theoretical demonstration of pure reason, it had striven to put it to the test in deeds and actually devised the means to bring its conclusion into effect. That logic, which in the beginning had sought to triumph over the death of the individual, in the end seeks to triumph in the death of Man. As, according to Heraclitus, everything begins in accordance with the Logos, so, according to Heidegger, everything may end in accordance with Techno-logy.

But the danger of Technology does not lie in the tools and machines men invent to serve their purpose; these are in themselves not harmful, and most are indeed beneficial. It lies, rather, in the systems of organization and control and the schemes of meaning and significance that derive from the ensemble of men and machines that is the complex of Technology and which impose themselves on mankind even against its conscious will and desire. Men have devised a way of systematically dominating, controlling, and disposing of all things, which in the first place was directed against Nature but which they now find is also turning on themselves and depriving them of their human nature. In the already accomplished fate of the animals, men are beginning to see a distorted image of what they can do to themselves. They can make themselves irrelevant, if not redundant, to their own schemes and so dispose of themselves. The computer is the new symbol of this future Technology and cybernetics is the new way of organizing the world. Technology aims at transformation of the world into a computerized and self-regulating mechanism and of human society into a functional system that is part and parcel of this organized world. As Ellul makes clear, this does not mean that men are transformed into robots; on the contrary, they appear freer in their movements than ever before—seemingly, less constrained.[1] But they can only move within the limits prescribed by the overall system, which are defined as the tolerance necessary for the functioning of the technological "machine." Hence, Man becomes a *homo ex machina,* a purely functioning being. A man can change from one function to another, perhaps with greater flexibility than that of any artificial machine, but as a functioning unit he begins to approximate asymptotically to the mechanical contrivance. When the difference between them has diminished to the point of legal status alone, then the point of no return will have been reached: Man will have attained his dead end.

Such a development is already appearing in one of the greatest feats of Technology ever devised: the conquest of outer space. The astronaut has become the symbol of a new "man," one no longer bound to the earth, who with the aid of his life-support system can open up new opportunities of human habitation in all the reaches of the solar system, and even beyond. Man, it seems, is about to liberate himself from his earthly nature and embark on an expansion into space itself, with no visible limits to his accomplishment. That is the new glorious adventure promised us, which, seemingly, can lead from Man almost to Superman. But looked at from another side, it can also appear as a process of transforming Man into No-man. For the astronaut is also a symbol of one who is totally integrated into a technological system. All his organic and mental functions are harnessed to the engineering device: his body is hooked up to machines that control its organic activity, and his mind to computers that leave him with only a very narrowly prescribed area of decision-making. Each of his functions or activities is harnessed separately: he becomes a man who is decomposed into his various functioning processes. From this point of view the astronaut is the unfortunate guinea-pig of a new experiment: that to decompose Man.

One may imagine a technological system in which human beings and all human relations, including all social relations, become in an analogous manner decomposed—a situation in which there are no stable "bodies," identities, or relations of any kind. Out of the decomposed "spare parts," as it were, one may imagine purely ephemeral identities being re-composed as the system requires them. Just as a character in a film is sometimes made up of parts of real human beings—one man's torso and another man's hands, one man's speaking voice, another's singing voice, the movements of one close up, another in the distance—so there might be non-human "beings" similarly made up of the spare parts of those who might have been human. It is not necessary in this context to imagine actual organ transplants or any other such simple technological games; it is merely necessary to suppose that no one is anything in himself but that each is only the temporary function he performs, and that these functions are the sole relations. Thus, the temporary task-force or working-team together with its machines and controlling devices might be the only unit of identification. Men would become nothing in themselves. There would be no reason not to use them or misuse them as the purely objective situation demands. Such a total technological system that decomposes and re-composes everything would spell the end of Man in a way even more insidious than that of any holocaust so far devised. It ought to be the task of sociologists and other social scientists to tell us to what extent such "ideas" are already being realized or prepared for in practice.

But why dwell on such morbid thoughts? Why "pursue conclusions infinite of easy ways to die" (*Antony and Cleopatra* V.ii)? Why speculate on the infinite modes possible for the death of Man? Surely not simply as a mental exercise because it has never been done before? It was never done before because it was neither possible nor necessary, but not to do so now would be to succumb unknowingly to whatever imposes itself as a necessity. A novel Death has emerged—and it merges with and even displaces the old death of the individual in our fears. It has to be thought through if it is to be avoided. Hence, to persist with the old thoughts of death would be suicidal in a new way. To dwell in their comforting consolations of God or Nature or History or Humanity would be to be oblivious to the greater threats that dispense with these. A new thought—which we might provisionally still call philosophy—should give up all the old securities and begin with the most extreme of possibilities as its founding logic: Man is mortal, we are men, therefore. . . . We do not as yet know the conclusion of this new syllogism, for we do not as yet understand what the first two premises mean. What does it really mean to say: "Man is mortal"? So far we have merely touched on the simple sense of technological death. But is that all? It is at this point that a "post-philosophy" begins its task.

## II

Let us begin by realizing that the concept *Man* can no longer be the mere abstraction it was. All the abstract definitions of *Man* as a certain kind of human nature or human essence or species-being or existence, or any other definition supplied by traditional philosophy, were representative of a pre-modern state of human society. Men's notion of *Man* was defined abstractly because men themselves had as yet no concrete sense of being men together: human societies were separate and dispersed, so men could only see each other as belonging to the same abstract, general species *Man*—and sometimes hardly even that, for barbarians and slaves were seen as barely men. Today, however, such abstract notions of *Man* are becoming increasingly anachronistic, at least partly because men are aware of themselves as belonging together to the one global society that is modern civilization. The old divisions are nearly at an end: the various races, societies, civilizations, cultures, and religions are no longer creating their separate histories, but share the single history of global civilization. Is this the end of prehistory and the prelude to true History—or to something quite other? Whatever else it may imply, it does mean that Man has discovered his hitherto dispersed and hidden unity and realized his oneness in a practical way. This is why the historical threat that exists today is a threat to mankind as a whole, for mankind is at one in a shared common fate—and a common end. It is, in other words, now possible to conceive an end to Man, a thing that was, in thought as well as in practice, impossible before. The discovery of the oneness of Man is at the same time the discovery of Man's mortality. This double discovery makes it possible, and necessary, to destroy all the old abstract definitions of *Man,* for man does not need to be defined abstractly when his concrete historical being is available, for the first time, to be studied in practice: *Man* now is all that men do and have done together.

Here we strike a peculiar paradox, one that would not have existed under the old philosophical dispensation. Formerly it was possible to define *Man* in such a way that it would have been easy to go on to say what the death of Man would amount to. If such and such is Man's essence, then it is easy to state, for example, that the death of this essence, as Heidegger puts it, is ipso facto the death of Man. If Man is *zōon logon echon,* then the dispersal of that logos is the end of Man. If rationality is the human essence, then it is not difficult to specify what the loss of rationality would be like for all men. Similarly, if the human essence is Spirit or Subjectivity or Freedom or Consciousness, or if Man is a creature of God having a definite place in the scheme of things, or even if man is *Existenz,* then it is also possible to specify exactly what it would be to lose this essence or status. It would have been easy to state it as an abstract possibility, though not really to think it as something that is actually possible or to specify how it might become actualized. By contrast, in modern thought where it is possible to think how, in practice, Man may end himself, it seems impossible to state in the abstract what Man must lose if he is to cease being Man. If *Man* cannot be defined in any such abstract way, then one cannot definitely say what Man's mortality would amount to. The peculiarity of this paradox is precisely this: the old philosophies that could specify what is *Man* could not conceive of Man's mortality, whereas a new philosophy that conceives of Man's mortality cannot specify what *Man* is.

How is this dilemma to be avoided? Not by offering some new definition of Man, but, on the contrary, by recognizing that no fixed definition of Man is possible. Nietzsche speaks of Man as "an animal not yet determined" (*ein noch nicht festgestelltes Tier*), but the paradox of this is that it is precisely a definition of Man as indefinable. Man is the being who is indefinable to himself, though ever liable to give himself definitions. Man constitutes himself in his self-understanding and being by placing himself within some system of thought or action or society, and seemingly fixing his nature once and for all, only to cancel that system, de-constitute himself, and begin all over again. Man is a self-cancelling, self-denying being, one who is always becoming something without being anything. No matter where Man may seek to locate himself—with Gods or with beasts, with mind or with matter, in Ideas or structures—he can never remain at rest there, for any such placement is only due to himself. No sooner is he there than he finds himself a stranger, ill at ease and needing to escape.

Man is a problem to himself: he can never be what he is, but he cannot *not* be something. Man is a perverse nature in Nature that frets, vexes, and torments itself. His is an unstable contradictory being that hops about like the grasshopper to which Mephistopheles likens him, for he is also the opposite of everything he is. Man is forever divided against himself, forced into forming oppositions within himself, for whatever he is he can only be this by denying and repressing other equally valid potentialities of his being. Thus he forms himself in opposition to himself, and so continually acts against himself. He is an "O without a figure" (*King Lear* I.iv), the zero figure that is nothing in itself but can multiply itself to infinity and be the sum of all things. Man is a nothing that is a bounded infinity, both empty in itself and fulfilled with All.

If Man were finally to be one definite thing, he would cease to be Man. If it were possible once and for all to define Man, then what was so defined would no longer be Man. That is the gist of the bet between God and the Devil over Faust. If Mephistopheles can fix Faust, identify him, make him content with being "something," if he can make him satisfied with what he is and willing to rest content with it, then he will have him—and Man will be damned. For Goethe such damnation was unthinkable, for everything in his scheme of Nature was against it. Man had to be himself and so he had ever to deny himself. And, according to Goethe, as he did so Man would rise toward his goal of ever greater perfection.

We now know just how elusive, and delusive, that goal can be. We know that Man can indeed "damn" himself. The ultimate possibility of his perverse being, as both everything and nothing, is that he can make himself become "something." That is perhaps his ultimate perversity: that Man who has the potential to be anything has also the potential not to be Man any longer, precisely by abandoning that potential and *defining* himself. This is the ultimate limit of human potentiality: that Man can unmake himself by determining to make himself once and for all. Thus it is that Man has the paradoxical power to contradict even his own contradictoriness: the indefinable being can define itself, the "O without a figure" can figure itself as an O.

Previously we had asked how, in a modern philosophical thought that is aware of itself as unable to define *Man,* it is possible to state the conditions of Man's mortality. Then it appeared that either there is something that is *Man,* some human essence which, once lost, would mean the end of Man as Man, or *Man* is indefinable, in which case there is no way of stating what would need to be missing for Man to cease being Man. The first alternative is historically impossible in present philosophy; the second alternative appears to involve a conceptual impossibility, as we have just seen. However, we may now have a way out of this dilemma, in the perverse possibility that Man who is indefinable can nevertheless define himself and so cease to be Man.

Before proceeding further, we should note that as a purely formal answer this is subject to the charge that it tacitly relies on the very impossibility it was devised to counter: in using it we may seem to be re-invoking, surreptitiously, yet another merely abstract notion of *Man*. For if we define Man by his indefinability do we not appear to endow him with a negative capability that is only the obverse of the positive capabilities it supplants? As if, for instance, we were simply arguing that he is not "essence" but "changeable essence," or if not "essence" then "existence"—or not an irreducible "something" now but an irreducible "nothing." The formal answer must be given specificity if it is to avoid that charge; it must demonstrate that it is concerned not with Man as an abstraction but with mankind in its concrete, practical, social, and historical specificity.

So let us first specify the formal answer in terms of a human capacity that fulfils these requirements: the universal involvement of men with language. What we have formerly defined as Man's capacity to be other than he is, is at least partly a product of men's dependence on language. It is in their language that men realize themselves and become whatever they specifically happen to be. It is also by means of their language that they change themselves. As long as language retains its potentiality for change, so long can men go on changing with it, define and undefine themselves, and so remain men. And all language so far has been changeable. Sometimes, as with us in the West, it has indeed been volatile, though more frequently language is conservative and changes by such small degrees as for this to be barely visible to those within it, or only visible in retrospect to those outside it. Like the men who use it, language has the potentiality of always being other than it is. In every language order, which is a seemingly unalterable system of meanings, there are hidden—suppressed and repressed—meanings that are capable of disrupting, finally of breaking up, the rigidity of that order. In every mode of speech and discourse there are "silences" that will surface and destroy the speech or discourse, thus forcing language to change. In this way language carries out a dialectic of self-contradiction. In short, the locus of Man's formal indefinability is to be found in these propensities of language, for it is by means of language that men define themselves, and as language changes their self-definitions become inadequate, are destroyed, and have to be created anew.

This process of changing self-definition is prompted by another universal involvement of men: their concern with death and with time. Men have always deployed their language so as to develop a conception of death in relation to time. One might even go so far as to say that men have devised language ultimately for the purpose of knowing death and time, though to say this is not to neglect all the other more practical and social explanations of the role of language. Men's concern with death and time has so far been a concern with individual existence. Death has always meant the death of the individual and time the lifetime of the individual leading up to death. The preoccupation of the race has in that sense been an individual one, and language has always provided a common meaning for what is ultimately a common but individual destiny. These concerns of men with language, time, and death are dependent on one another. Without language time could not be articulated as a temporality of tenses, and death, too, could have no meaningful reality. Alternatively, without the knowledge of death there would be neither language nor time. Behind the need to speak is the need to know death in words, and behind the felt remorseless flow of time is the sense of its destination to its end. In Language, Time, and Death, men maintain their humanity. If they were to abandon these concerns they would cease being men.

This provides a way of giving specificity to the formal answer to the paradox of Man's indefinability in relation to his mortality. If men were to cease concerning themselves with their time and death, if their language provided no meanings for such concerns, then they would no longer be men, regardless of what else they might be. They would then have nothing to do with our human condition, becoming as strange and incomprehensible to us as are Martians in popular imagination. In that sense Man must be the guardian of Language, Time, and Death, for if he were to abandon his care for them he would abandon himself. But this can also be put the other way, that Language in its provision of meaning for Time and Death holds Man in its safekeeping. Language has within itself the power to annihilate Man just as surely as any mechanical means. As Wordsworth said, "Language, if it do not uphold, and feed, and leave in quiet, like the power of gravitation or the air we breathe, is a counter-spirit, unremittingly and noiselessly at work, to subvert, to lay waste, to vitiate, and to dissolve."[2]

There are, indeed, many concrete sociological signs that some of the languages currently available to us are capable of precisely such workings. They are gradually eroding our inherited bodies of meaning concerning time and death, exposing them as mere facts and so rendering them meaningless: partly because these languages are registering the impact the new technologies of the body itself are having on the meaning of death, which as a biological event can now in principle be postponed indefinitely, so that there is no such thing any more as a natural lifetime or end; partly because they are themselves the agents of a new technology of language.

The new technologies of information, of the computerized storage and control of data, of communications networks—these are modes of a new functioning of language, of language at the point where it ceases to be human language. Such systems of exchanges of messages and of controlled noise are no longer within the province of human speech. They are not merely "formal languages" operating outside the more humane "natural languages"; they are systems of communication that annihilate human language. They do so by evacuating from language its inner core of "silences," the rich context of hidden meanings that are the tacit and implicit significations unspecifiable in any formal language. As more and more of language is formalized to make it conform to the requirements of computers and other devices of the communications network, so ever-wider areas of language are denuded of their silences, turned into controllable calculi and effectively wiped out. And when silence goes, with it goes the whole potential for language change, the power for constant renovation of language; for change in language is the outcome of the "silent" play of the inner contradictions, the oppositions, the suppressions and repressions within the unspecified and unspoken divisions in, as it were, the "unconscious" of language. When all language is finally fully formalized it will no longer change, no matter how much it permutes itself. It is to this final end-state that some of our languages are tending. And, in becoming a prisoner of his own devised modes of communication, Man is faced with the threat of himself becoming a product of his own productions. That is also the general formula for restating in specific terms the formal possibility of Man's annihilation, without recourse to any notions of Man's essence. If men became the products of their own productions, they would define themselves and become something definite, and so cease being men. The process of men producing themselves as products is that of producing themselves as something and so reducing themselves to nothing. In a totally technological world of production that formal possibility would be realized. What such a world would be like can now be stated with some degree of sociological and historical specificity, as Ellul does in his account of technology, which he sees as the Faustian "bet of the age."

It would be a world in which history came to an end, for time would no longer be meaningful. There would neither be the meaning of a lifetime nor of a single pregnant moment; all time would be a mere succession of events like the random events in nature, one no more significant than any other. These events could only recur on a treadmill of repetition ringing the changes on chance permutations. This mechanical "eternal recurrence" would constitute a world become a predetermined game with no inherent ends, a game for which men devised the rules and one which they put into play, but in which they would become inextricably trapped. Not even death could free one, for there would be no real end in death, only a drawn-out sinking into oblivion.

The very fact that men are so confident of themselves as producers, that they see themselves as creators of themselves and their world, makes it all the more likely that they will become trapped in their own productions. It is, in principle, impossible to say with scientific certainty that this will happen. Not even a science of futurology could make such a prognostication. Science can only extrapolate from present trends to future ones provided there are no unforeseen changes. But so long as men remain human they have the power to change themselves so as to invalidate any scientific projection. All one can say is that if present trends continue unaltered then mankind will approach closer to some kind of death of Man. Anything more definite is either only speculation or a moral stand based on one's commitments, attitudes, and predispositions in faith. There are those who by their faith in Man are predisposed to predict that everything will turn out well, despite all. Others, however, will insist that such a belief only grants an illusory false comfort. Still others may be skeptically resigned or may approach the question with ironic humor. The attitude taken to speculations of the final outcome matters less than how it is understood and what people are prepared to do about it.

III

It is perhaps the supreme irony of world history that we modern men have come to our present impasse, and to the conclusion that Man is now mortal, precisely by having acted on the premise of Man's immortality. The story is well known of how we Europeans launched ourselves on an unparalleled drive for power, which we called Progress. First in the name of religion, then civilization, and finally in the name of Humanity itself we subjugated the earth to serve our interests. All other societies and cultures were crushed or exterminated or forced to engage with us in our race of Progress; eventually, perhaps, some of them will even outdistance us. All the material and human resources of nature were put at our disposal to be transformed in accordance with our sovereign will. This willed thrust of power was justified in the name of an unlimited future of Man. Human expansiveness seemed endless, and so Man seemed immortal. It seemed that time itself would expand forever and so generate Progress of its own accord. The ceaseless, insatiable, unlimited onward striving of Western Man became the very definition of the human quest. And the figure of Faust, as it was popularly understood, became the prime symbol of Man.

After two centuries in pursuit of this quest of Man's immortality we have been brought to the brink of the one absolute limit to all human striving: the death of Man. Modern Man prided himself on being an overreacher, a breaker of all limits. He transgressed all the restrictions tradition had devised to hold Man in check: the ban on curiosity was lifted, all mysteries were probed and exposed; the ban on speech and thought was lifted, nothing need be silent anymore; the ban on feeling and action was lifted, nothing is absolutely forbidden and nothing is impossible. God is dead, all is permitted. And each new transgression was wonderfully vindicated, for through each such crime extraordinary new powers were won. Amazing achievements ensued: the old miracles of faith were trifling in comparison with the new miracles of knowledge. And at each demonstration of this there was a renewed exhilaration of freedom and enhancement of power. Eventually the feeling took over that there were no limits to be encountered ever. Progress seemed endless because it need never stop, and Man was immortal because he need never come to his end.

Only now has a strange kind of reversal occurred: this very striving for immortality in the unlimited has turned back on itself and established a new kind of limitation, one that men as individuals have always known as the limit of their striving—death. But now it is a new Death of a horror hitherto totally unknown, a new bound at the "promised end" (*King Lear* V.iii). What is individual death in the face of this new nothingness? And just as the limit of what any man can achieve is set for him by what he may do to himself in the process—ultimately, that he may kill himself—so, too, the limit of Man is set by what mankind may do to itself in its Progress—ultimately, that it may annihilate itself. The bound of Man is not prescribed by some logos, necessity, natural law, or higher will external to himself. It is inherent in Man's very Deed itself, by how its consequences rebound back on it, or, in the jargon of technology, by the principle of feedback.

Progress, which for some time appeared limitless because it seemed endless, has now finally revealed itself as indeed without any end, for it goes nowhere and achieves nothing. Or, more precisely, Nothing is exactly what it does achieve. It realizes a kind of nothingness never known before, the correlate of the new death of Man that it has revealed. That new nothingness is also familiarly known by the clichéd name of nihilism, and it thereby remains unknown. We do not know what Nihilism is; we barely begin to get a glimmer of understanding of it when we see it as an inextricable, hidden counterpart of Progress—a dark, silent absence within its enlightened, clamoring presence, an absence in the depths of Progress that is only now beginning to surface and show itself as having been its real inner presence all the time. It is the heart of darkness within the light of the world which the light knows not of, and which by its very illumination it cannot know. Nihilism is the shadow of Progress—but we might also see it the other way, that Progress is the luminous image of Nihilism. Whichever way we see it, it remains undeniable that Progress and Nihilism belong together. We ourselves belong to the one as soon as we belong to the other, so in fact we are bound to both. We can reject our darker side of Nihilism as little as we can reject our brighter side of Progress. Progress gave birth to us as modern men; it has made us what we are. We can as soon deny it as we can deny ourselves, and being brought into being by Progress we are delivered over into Nihilism, which is as much part of us as the other is. Any talk of overcoming Nihilism only makes sense insofar as it also speaks of overcoming Progress. And in the face of the present overwhelming dominance of Progress it is more than likely that most of it is merely idle talk.

The power of Progress is everywhere preponderant, and it is preponderant precisely because Progress is the supreme source of power. Men could never have dreamt of the powers that modern Progress would make available to them; it is now literally true that "all that moves between the quiet poles is at their command" (*Faustus* I.i). The diversity, extent, and scope of these powers are encyclopedic. Starting with the famous Encyclopédie of Diderot, encyclopedias have been magic books in which all such powers are named and codified and from which they can be conjured. They are the new testaments of the last will of Man. They might well become Man's last will and testament, his final deed, if the powers they contained were to expand to the point where they gained a momentum and will of their own. It is in terms of power that one can see at its simplest the workings of the dialectic of the Deed of Progress. The more power that Deed unleashes, the harder it becomes for men to control it and the more it begins impersonally to control them. Men are already in a multiplicity of ways becoming the victims of their own power: the most powerful systems of production, organization, authority, information, therapeutics are already so strongly entrenched that the idea of dispensing with them or radically altering them has become increasingly a utopian dream. These institutional powers are gradually developing an impersonal will of their own and imposing it on men. The enlightened facade of Progress as subserving Man is slowly being folded up, revealing a grimmer structural skeleton.

If men were to succeed in physically annihilating themselves it would be because their own power proved too much for them. The orthodox theological verdict on such a fate would be that Man, in his vain arrogance, did not keep within his limits and finally transgressed a fatal limitation prescribed for him in the limited capacities of his own being. As Samuel Johnson said, "That every being not infinite, compared with infinity, must be imperfect, is evident to intuition; that whatever is imperfect must have a certain line which it cannot pass."[3] If men were to annihilate themselves, then, on this view, it would be because they passed that line. That would seem no great event in a universe where disasters are an everyday occurrence. A theologian might even now insist that if such a thing were to happen it would still hold true that "The gods are just, and of our pleasant vices/Make instruments to plague us" (*King Lear* V.iii). But if that were so, then "As flies to wanton boys are we to th'gods,/They kill us for their sport" (IV.i). Or, as Dr. Johnson said ironically, "These hunters whose game is man have many sports" and "as we drown whelps and kittens, they amuse themselves now and then sinking a ship, and stand round the fields of Blenheim or the walls of Prague, as we encircle a cock-pit."[4] But what is the heavenly amusement at a Blenheim or Prague in comparison with the slaughter-fields of modern history? And what divine sport would be afforded by a nuclear first strike? If the gods who could tolerate the disasters of old seemed to men like infernal monsters beyond human comprehension, then what is one to think of gods who would permit the catastrophe of the death of mankind itself? Can there be gods of such depravity? The joke of Man's cleverness has now turned on the gods themselves and is laughing them out of existence. If Man can commit suicide then there can be no gods, for the gods require men even more than men require the gods. The thought of a universe of laughing gods without men as the butt of their joke is itself too ludicrous to entertain. God died at the moment when Man sensed for the first time that he himself was mortal.

And if God is dead, if there is no infinity or perfection in comparison with which Man is finite, imperfect, and therefore limited, then what of the theological answer that Man will only annihilate himself when he transgresses a fatal limitation? Even if there were such a limit, Man could not know it nor could he be guilty of transgressing against it. A god might know it, but no man can, for, as Hegel said, to know a boundary is already to overstep it. Since we cannot know what our limits are, we cannot know when we are about to approach a fatal limitation. There are those who say that Man is unalterably bound to his matrix, the earth, and that he will never be able to sever that umbilical bond and escape completely, no matter how far he gets in his interplanetary travels. On this view, then, Man has an earthly nature, one that limits him to his earthly origins. One might call this view an ecological cosmic conservatism, and it is clearly a modern secularized version of the orthodox theological conservatism. The objection to both is the same: there is no way its proponents can know that this is the limit, since they cannot have been beyond it.

There is a sense, then, in which Man can in principle never know his own ultimate limits, for to know them he has to go beyond them, and to go beyond them is already to transcend them. In that sense Man can have no limits at all. Once again, that is merely a formal answer which tells us nothing about Man's self-transcendence in practice and the practical determinations and circumscriptions by which it might be limited. Unless it is correctly understood as a strictly conceptual formal point concerning what can be known about Man's ultimate limits and whether any such limits can ever be determined, it will give rise to the illusion that there are no limitations whatever on Man, or that Man will always continue to transcend himself, or that he will move upward forever. This Faustian illusion, which Goethe anticipates but does not himself fully share, is one of the ideal forms of the ideology of Progress. It presents Man as completely free to attain to whatever he strives for. But Man is not free in that absolutely unlimited way, for he is hemmed in by all kinds of constraints determining him. These do not arise out of any determinate general essence or human nature but out of the conditions of human existence that can be given exact specificity in material, social, and psychic terms. However, knowing these determinations does not mean that one knows Man's inherent limitations, what is the scope of his self-realization, what he can and cannot become. It does, however, mean that one knows that Man is not completely free, unconstrained, and unlimited. Man, in other words, cannot be Faust forever.

Freud perhaps more than anyone else taught us this humbling lesson in specifying the psychic constraints operating in Man, and he delivered it at a time when the worst features of historical progress were not nearly as apparent as they are now.

> It may be difficult, too, for many of us to abandon the belief that there is an instinct towards perfection at work in human beings, which has brought them to their present high level of intellectual achievement and ethical

> sublimation and which may be expected to watch over their development into supermen. I have no faith, however, in the existence of any such internal instinct and I cannot see how this benevolent illusion is to be preserved. . . . What appears in a minority of human individuals as an untiring impulsion towards further perfection can easily be understood as a result of the instinctual repression upon which is based all that is most precious in human civilization . . . and it is the difference in amount between the pleasure of satisfaction which is demanded and that which is actually achieved that provides the driving factor which will permit no halting at any position attained, but in the poet's words "ungebändigt immer vorwärts dringt."[5]

The poet is Goethe but the words are spoken by Mephistopheles, who would have mockingly appreciated Freud's rather reductive diagnosis of the Faustian striving. But regardless of whether Freud is right in that respect, it must be granted him that the Faustian impulse is a culturally conditioned one that can now only be persevered in at increasing risk. There is one final limitation that threatens even unlimited Progress: the possibility of universal death. Death, the inevitable limit of individual human striving, also functions as a limit on Man's striving. According to Freud, all life is contracted to death; the individual lifeline is an asymptotic curve converging to that limit point—"The aim of life is death," he said. Life is a detour on the way to death, but each man finds his own way there, for "the organism wishes to die only in its own fashion."[6] Death, the ultimate limit, does not, however, come only at the very end of life. It is always there within life itself as the force that drives man to his limit. Death is inherent in life as the *Thanatos,* which, according to Freud, is the instinct of aggression and self-destruction that is an inherent part of man's psyche. Again, regardless of whether one concurs with Freud's theory of instincts, there is no denying that death is a force in life for aggression and destruction. It is this death in each man that takes its silent revenge on Man when, as Faust, he is presumptuous enough to believe himself immortal and assumes there to be no limit to his own growth toward perfection.

For Freud there is a limiting psychic economy in men that makes it impossible for Man simply to progress indefinitely to ever-greater heights. All the achievements of civilization take a heavy toll on men's psychic well-being, for every such advance is bought at the cost of the suppression of one kind of instinct or another, and this incurs a psychic debt that will eventually have to be paid with interest. In particular, the drives of aggression are suppressed by being held in check in civilized society. At first they are liable to turn inward on the self and make men suicidally inclined, but if opportunity offers they are ready to spring outward again and be projected onto others, and the more they are repressed the more violent will their eventual outbreak be. The specific outbreak of aggressive violence for which Freud sought to account was, of course, the carnage of World War I after a century of peace and progress that seemed to be heading toward elimination of major European wars. The shock of that outrage, as well as the new clinical experience of war trauma, led Freud "beyond the pleasure principle," and eventually to seek a diagnosis of the "discontents" of civilization itself. Once again there is room for disagreement as to whether it is precisely this psychic economy that needs to be invoked to account for the first and most manifest of the disasters of modern Progress, and even whether civilizations in general are prone to such collective bloodletting. Nevertheless, Freud has drawn attention to the potential for destruction and annihilation in what is seemingly the tamest and most peaceful of human animals: the law-abiding man of modern society. Whatever the full psychic explanation for it may be, it is undeniable that modern men have shown little hesitation in exterminating each other, as World War II amply demonstrated. And what is even more daunting is that modes of doing away with one another short of outright killing—modes ranging from character assassination to the imposition of psychic death through a denial of any opportunities for growth—are being practiced with increasing severity against decreasing protest. Such trends toward mass annihilation reveal the present inroads of death in society and are the early intimation of a possible future death of Man. That death is the limit of history itself. This does not mean that history is limited or that Man is historically fixated, that his development is bounded or that beyond a certain point it must exhaust itself and come to an end. But it does mean that, as in all processes of growth, the historical development of Man can only proceed by going through many critical passages, transformations inevitably involving contradictions that could be fatal. Modern Man is in a stage of transformation involving such contradictions in their severest and most dangerous forms, where a failure to overcome them will spell utmost disaster.

Freud was one of the first to have understood why Man is mortal.[7] Taking that as his first premise, he thought through anew all the traditional and modern conclusions about Man. The whole notion of Man underwent a revision in his theories that we still find it difficult to understand or to accept. He implicitly devised a new syllogism which is utterly terrifying to us, despite all that we have seen and suffered since: Man is mortal . . . therefore Man is a murderer. What the intermediate premises are that link the first with the conclusion is something we still do not fully understand, but the argument seems intuitively right; it was an argument Shakespeare dramatically enacted in his most terrifying play, *Macbeth*. Perhaps to come to understand the argument of that play will enable us also to understand the argument of Man's culpability. All that we know now are some of the mediating steps Freud had outlined: that in the first place each man's unconscious desire to kill is directed against himself, and what makes him so dangerous is that in order to continue living he has to project that desire away from himself onto others. The potential suicide becomes a potential homicide. This suicidal desire in Man can always be invoked by making him aware of his own mortality; as a man deeply realizes he must die, he perversely wants to do away with himself. That is the case of Hamlet.

Macbeth's case is the complementary one of a man who comes to realize that he must die at the very moment and in the very act of his murdering to empower and enrich his life, and whose every effort to evade that death-realization in further murders only extends it and enforces it on him. Shakespeare through his art forces that death-realization upon us, too, as does Freud in a very different way. Both impress on us that so long as Man is mortal he will remain a potential suicide and homicide. This is why the pious hope that in some unimaginable future Man may transcend himself and cease being such a danger to himself is doomed to disappointment—on the ground that if ever Man ceased to be mortal he would cease to be Man. Of course, there is no logical reason for predicting that Man will continue to be Man: he may become something more than Man—or something less.

It is this latter possibility that concerns us now. The present danger of the mortality of Man derives ultimately from the universal mortality of men. Men are mortal . . . therefore Man is mortal: that is a long historical argument which it would be too tedious, but not in principle too difficult, to substantiate. For one thing, it would involve us in the whole psychology of warlike activities, of how men's need to kill each other is socialized and institutionalized as war, and then the history of all the wars till the present cataclysmic ones which, it would seem, strive to fulfill themselves in the death of Man. And war is but one of the connecting threads: punishment, power, authority, discipline are others. If one were to follow that line of reasoning to the bitter end one would have to conclude finally that not only is Man mortal but that Man will most certainly be dead, and that very likely soon.

Yet, paradoxically, there is also a much more hopeful syllogism to be formed on the same premises but with a different conclusion, one that at first seems a complete nonsequitur: Men are mortal . . . therefore Man is mortal . . . therefore Man need not be dead. Here we strike upon what is perhaps the very ultimate in human perversity: that Man will live so long as men are mortal. How are we to understand this last absurdity of the human species? Put at its simplest and most obvious it is as follows: as long as men insist on remaining mortal and dying their individual deaths, so long will they resist the living death of non-being to which all the powers of annihilation are subjecting them, and just so long will they desperately struggle against those powers, thereby keeping Man alive. They will summon up the anger to fight against their dehumanizing fate so long as they still need to suffer the protracted human process of dying, for only that assures them of still being alive. Once that ceased, men would be living dead, mere functioning corpses striving to annihilate every living thing about them so as to reduce it to their own state of nothingness. The anger of violated human death speaks loudest in protest against the creeping death of inhuman annihilation. And that anger has behind it all the energy of death's destructiveness. It is precisely that still-human destructiveness that is the last resort against the dominant, already inhuman, annihilation, carrying in itself the power for a radical break from the present slide into the abyss of sheer empty nothingness.

To say such a thing will appear shocking to those still deeply dedicated to the humanist values of nature, life, creativity, human kindness, and goodness. These are the values that spring from the uncorrupted human heart. Unfortunately, this is not an argument in which the heart can have its reasons that reason knows not of, for one can as little follow one's heart in this issue as one can depend on pure reason. One can, perhaps, assuage some of the heart's outrage at the seeming inhumanity of these hard words by explaining that they are only directed against a soft humanism, that the destructiveness being appealed to in the final resort is not simply the opposite of the heart's creativeness. For the destruction that is the simple opposite of creation now belongs to annihilation. If one is going to speak of destruction, it must be in a completely new sense that supplants both creation and its opposite. Both God's creation and the Devil's destruction belong to the old traditional philosophy. The secular modern versions of it that speak of human creativity, self-realization, the life-force and their opposites, destructiveness, alienation, the death-drive, are also now the remainders of an inadequate mode of thought. At their best, they belong to a Faustian thought whose ideal form is still very touching and beautiful to behold, but which is no longer adequate to cope with present grim realities.

At their worst, however, such Faustian ideals are now part of the ideology of Progress. Faust had always been closely associated with Progress, but only late in the day did he betray himself to become an ideological apologist for it. The present ideologies of pseudo-creativity, unthinking life, hedonistic happiness, purely subjective freedom and non-conformity, and all the other idols of the present marketplace are themselves unthinking servants of the very things they denounce in the name of their so-called humanistic values. Their incessant demands for radical change in accordance with their "liberating" proposals only facilitate the inroads of Technology into hitherto inaccessible areas of life. That is the new memento mori in the midst of the modern Arcadia of life's plenty. New ways of death are prepared for men even as they think they are pursuing a *dolce vita nuova.* They succumb to them as soon as they become oblivious of their own death. It is this death that can no longer be assumed as inevitable, but must be safeguarded by each individual as his own.

IV

*Morior ergo sum.* Until the newly encroaching changed meaning of death, this might have been thought as indubitable a truth as *cogito ergo sum.* Just as one cannot doubt one's thought without thinking—and so being—so, too, one could not know one's death without dying—and so also being. The fear of death could no more be denied than the doubt of thought, and so long as one feared, one was. Men lived in fear; they lived through a dying fear. Dying was, indeed, their indubitable guarantee of living: "I am dying, and I will be dead, therefore I am now alive"—that was the unspoken reasoning in all men's thoughts, their raison d'être. This is why until very recently mortality could be taken as part of the definition of humanity. "All men are mortal" was not just an inductive, empirical generalization confirmed by many, many instances: it was the basic truth of humanity. An immortal was a god or a devil; he could not be a man. It is true that beasts also die, and this is why men always felt closer to them than to either gods or demons, but they die without that fear and knowledge of death accompanying all their lives. Theirs is an innocent, happy death, whereas man's death was tormented and guilty since it was a protracted dying process lasting the whole of a lifetime, for no sooner was a man born than he began to die. Beasts also die, but man was the only dying animal. He was that far sooner than he was a rational animal, and in dying man lived as no animal can live.

> All the time you live, you steal it from death: it is at her charge. The continual work of your life, is to contrive death: you are in death, during the time you continue in life: for, you are after death, when you are no longer living. Or if you had rather have it so, you are dead after life: but during life, you are still dying: and death doth more rudely touch the dying than the dead, and more lively and essentially.[8]

And it is precisely because death touched the living more lively and essentially that they knew themselves to be more alive; it touched them to the quick and roused their sensitivity of living. In the midst of death they were alive.

Death no longer touches men in the same rude way. It is as a direct consequence of this fact that *morior ergo sum* is no longer such an indubitable truth. It has been put in question, just as, for different reasons, the Cogito has. Death, which still seemed certain in Freud's time, has now become uncertain. It has become a highly problematical notion; what it is for the individual to die is now no longer a clear-cut thing, and it is certainly not a clear and distinct idea. One reason for this is that death no longer occurs very often as a natural unavoidable cessation; its onset can now be postponed almost at will, and in principle it could be put off forever. Technological progress has made of dying a controllable physiological process in which the individual undergoing it is uninvolved; he is kept alive or allowed to go under at the behest of physicians and lawyers. He can no longer prepare himself for that last moment of truth and submit to it as a fatality beyond human intervention. His death is no longer his own—except, perhaps, when he deliberately chooses it in suicide.

But the effects of technology are merely the most obvious manifestations of the new meaninglessness of death. This is being brought about even more decisively in language through the dissolution of all the old meanings with which it had been endowed. Stripped of these meaningful coverings, the facts of death appear bare, and all the more horrifying in the emptiness of their clinical sterility. As such a physical fact, death is only a pointless biological event. As a natural event death had always been endowed with meaning in human language. The need to endow death with meaning is indeed one of the hallmarks of humanity. No society, culture, or civilization prior to our own has ever failed to give death a meaning in its language by way of myths, stories, ceremonies, cults, mysteries, as well as by the much more sophisticated means of theology, philosophy, speculation, and reason. In this respect one could say that Man makes his own death, for it is not of itself a meaningful event—the facts of dying and death are outside human signification; as mere facts they are pointless, they signify nothing. In making his death, man makes himself as well; for if men were to cease endowing their end with meaning then their lives, too, would become an aimless process.

It is not fully correct to say that modern civilization is stripping death of any meaning; rather, it is imposing on death a highly rational, scientific meaning which in the last resort is purely physiological. Death as a physiological process is no simple natural event but as complex a function as are the machines required to control it. This highly rational meaning acts reductively, simplifying death to a new kind of nothingness of sheer physical generality. It acts as if it were a logical solvent, dissolving all the old encrusted meanings, freeing death from all the ancient grime of horror, mystery, guilt, evil, dread, and hope. Hence, it is the logic of a kind of reductio ad absurdum arguing away as absurd all the prior religious and humanistic meanings. The religious conception is absurd, since in most religions death is conceived of as a change of state from one mode of being to another, but as the very idea of distinct modes of being is made impossible within any modern rational thought, the idea of a changed mode of being is equally impossible. Similarly, the humanist sense of death as an utter and absolute extinction of being is made absurd, since without any opposition of being to non-being there can be no extinction of being. In the absence of either religious or humanist meanings death is now without terror, serenity, hope, despair, or tragedy; it is without significance as an end. It is a mere cessation of life-powers that is either instantaneous, fast, or slow.

However, Death is still active within modern history despite the official ideologies that seek to talk it away. All the old fears and irrational thoughts of death are still here, only suppressed and made unconscious and so made all the more irrational. The anxieties we all feel are partly symptomatic of that. If it were possible completely to eradicate the old *Angst* even from the unconscious, if men's psyches were sanitized even of the Thanatos, then men would be completely deprived of death—and, at the same time, of life. Theirs would be an unliving subsistence. However, men are still alive in their bodies if sometimes no longer so in their minds, for it is that body which they cannot control or know about that carries their unconscious selves, and in it death is still an agonizing presence. The body persists in its own life and death when the mind merely functions as a recording and calculating instrument. The body persists in the mortal torments of dying while it is still finding its own way to death. But now the body suffers in silence, blind and unaided by the seeing "I" of consciousness, or thrashes about in bitter conflict with a hostile self. Out of that conflict come many of the psychic maladies with which contemporary men are afflicted. If ever all men became "sane" and "well" it would be a sure sign that the death struggle was over and that their bodies, too, had finally expired.

If ever that were to take place, it would constitute the cessation of all individuality and lead inexorably to the death of Man. Then it would no longer be indubitably true that *morior ergo sum* or even that "All men are mortal," for merely expiring is no guarantee of either being or being human in any meaningful sense. But if it were no longer a fundamental truth of humanity that "All men are mortal," then the seemingly perversely irrational but nevertheless life-ensuring syllogism that "All men are mortal . . . therefore Man is mortal . . . therefore Man need not be dead" could no longer be relied on. Instead, there might ensue the killing syllogism: "Men are no longer mortal . . . therefore Man is dead."

Once again, it must be stressed that this is mere logical, formal argumentation; it tells us nothing substantive about how the inference is to be drawn from the total meaninglessness of individual death to the inevitability of the death of the race. The following may serve as a simple outline of the logical sequence of steps involved in that inference. If individuals were totally deprived of their own deaths then their whole bodily being would be deadened. These inert bodies, without even an unconscious, would reflect a total breaking-up or decomposition of the psyche. A decomposed body would be a functioning corpse operating on mechanical reflexes alone, not acting but twitching, yet still armed with a deadly rational mind. The design of such walking corpses on any living thing would be to make it dead like themselves, and their designs on each other would be mutual petrification: to keep each other permanently in a state of death.

To what extent are human bodies becoming deadened? To what extent are individuals being deprived of their own death? To what extent, therefore, is the death of Man being prepared? These are precise sociological, psychological, and historical questions, not mere existential speculations. To provide a tentative answer to them we must briefly look once more into the practical workings of Progress. Even before our modern civilization has succeeded in completely controlling the death of the individual, it has succeeded in largely cheating him of a meaningful life. It extracts from the individual his life-forces and energies, his labor-power, his intellectual and creative capacities, his needs and desires, his character traits, and it utilizes them for its own productive and reproductive processes. A hidden hand seems to be operating in the world economy of society, imposing an inverse law to the effect that the more Man progresses the more each individual man regresses. To exploit the individual fully the ideologies of Progress inculcate pseudo-doctrines of life that teach one to live solely for life and be unmindful of death. The only allowed meaning of life is in devoting it to its work of Progress. As one of the great apologists of Progress, Emile Zola, declared:

> Work! Consider, gentlemen: work forms the only law of the world. Life has no other purpose, there is no other reason for existence, we all come into being only in order to do our share of the work and then vanish.[9]

Such encouragements to work and inducements to lead a useful life are actually enticements to make use of one's life for ends not one's own. For once a man's usefulness is over, his life is over. Society forces him to retire and die in his spare time, waiting for organic death to complete the social sentence he is already under. But even before that end, each man has already carried out some of the sentence upon himself, has already had to partially deaden himself so as to make himself useful to the objective work-process that requires him eventually to subject his life to itself in toto. Thus social progress is bought at the expense of individual life. Though seemingly caring for him, the forces of production are really totally indifferent to and unconcerned with the individual. All systems of production, whether they be material, intellectual, or cultural, allow only for fungible roles that any replaceable standard man can be used to fill. As far as these systems are concerned, the individual is redundant.

If men as individuals do not count then there is no reason why collectively they should live or die. Any system that dehumanizes them individually is bent on pushing them to their collective annihilation. What we have called the death of Man is that annihilation in its varied modes, each of which is also an end of history in a fixation of time. Men deprived of their individual death become, unbeknownst to themselves, the agents of their collective suicide. Feeling themselves already dead as individuals, they would in unconscious resentment be determined to consummate their own death in the death of all. The man whose own life is as nothing to him hates himself and all that is about him, and is all too ready to project this hatred onto others. This is why the pitiful victim of dehumanizing Progress is capable of being a murderer of unparalleled dimensions. "I am not alive, so nobody else is alive either; let everyone else die!" That is the absurd logic which is nevertheless a psychic truth inherent in the logic of absurdity. And given that mutual annihilation need not be a physical killing, men are all too ready to perpetrate it on each other or blind themselves to its occurrence. As the old restraints of religion, morality, tradition, culture, humanism, and rational enlightenment progressively weaken, there will be less and less to inhibit these perverse psychic impulses from taking their due course.

It is a necessary feature of the logic of Progress that it hide its own conclusion from the knowledge of men. The ideology of Life serves to lull men into a false sense of well-being and security. And the very fact that in most non-Western societies men are desperately struggling for the first fruits of Progress, and that we all sympathize with them and wish to help them, as we must, to attain our own levels of material welfare, also hides from us the truth that when we are all as well-off as each other we shall all be much worse off together. Solving their more immediate problems must not blind us or them to the danger that we will then share.

V

Responsibility for speaking the real truth of Progress falls in the first place on the modern European individual. After all, it is he who is also responsible for bringing about that against which he now speaks. So he speaks out of guilt. His culpable speech is thus as much confession as it is denunciation. The individual as Faustian intellectual is particularly responsible for the ideas of Progress. Right from the start, during the Renaissance, before modern Progress was even envisaged, he had already acted on the fatal formula that knowledge is power, and for that power he was willing to sell his soul. Much later, at the inauguration of modern Progress, the newly rearisen idealist Faust envisaged Progress as development; he conceived it in its sublime and most ideal form and so followed it as his way to salvation. Later that was vulgarized into the ideology of Progress according to which Man too would find his salvation in upward expansion. Too late did Mann's Faust heed Nietzsche's warning about the illusion of Progress, discover his mistake, and seek to take back the Faustian ideal; too late did he desperately strive to warn his fellow men, and dying leave them his confession as a last testament. O, the sly cunning of history that Faust's Deed of will leaves him only his will to deed!

The surviving European individual has already outlived himself—his time is up, he is "really dead" as far as the world is concerned. Notwithstanding this, when he can no longer do anything he can still think and speak. "In the period of his decay, the individual's experience of himself and what he encounters contributes once more to knowledge, which he had merely obscured as long as he continued unshaken to construe himself positively as the dominant category."[10] We now understand very well why European individuality is not the dominant category, even though individuality in its most basic form as singleness does seem an irreducible category of human existence. We know in general terms that "the individual owes his crystallization to the forms of political economy, particularly those of the urban market."[11] This means that modern European individualism is deeply implicated in the economic forms of capitalism and the cultural forms of the bourgeoisie. Much of the culpability of the modern individual stems from that relationship, and he, too, must suffer much of the fate of the bourgeoisie. Nevertheless, the surviving European individual is a witness against the bourgeoisie and has a task to perform in the demise of the bourgeoisie.

The individual can now only exist as a survivor. His must be a reduced being, stripped of all outward ornamentation. For the thinking individual the inference to be drawn is "I think, therefore I am not," thus negating the Cogito that originally gave birth to his own subjective being. For thinking is precisely that which now leads him into non-being: into isolation, solitude, silence, and non-entity. But in this situation he has a chance of realizing that even more fundamental *principium individuationis*: *morior ergo sum.* And what he comes to realize is that as survivor he is already dead, that his is a post-mortem being, and that what he speaks and writes is already an *opus posthumus*: "he can jot down what he sees among the ruins, for he sees different and more things than the others; after all, he is dead in his own lifetime and the real survivor."[12]

It is precisely because he is himself thus "dead" that he can know death and strive to preserve and pass on this knowledge to others, for, ultimately, the ruins he writes about are his own, and it is his own ruined self that he is jotting down: the story of the dissolution and liquidation of the European individual. Mankind, if it paused to consider the fate of the individual, might realize the similar fate awaiting it. Of course, mankind's survival is not tied to that of the exotic cultural product, the unique individual, for humanity does not consist in individuality, and though every human being is individual in the sense that it is single, from this it does not necessarily follow that it is individualized. Yet it is precisely the unique individual who, knowing himself doomed, can speak "a message of despair from the shipwrecked"[13] to mankind at large. But in order to speak the individual must survive. Thus, surviving defines his whole mode of being. St. Paul's injunction to the early Christians in the catacombs, to live as if they were not living, is one that needs to be revised for those now living "underground": to live as if they were still living. Theirs can only be an "as if" life: as if the individual still had a place in the world, as if serious life and thought were still possible, as if what one thinks and writes were for others and not solely for oneself, as if the effort to survive and speak were not rapidly becoming pointless, as if it could make some difference to the future. . . .

The individual is not alone in his "as if" presuppositions: to some extent, everyone has to lead an "as if" life. To lead normal lives, all men have to live as if the dangers and threats they know very well are real were somehow not fully serious. In this way they have to repress all the fears which, if openly acknowledged, would paralyze them. The irony is that it is precisely this attitude of self-induced oblivion to danger that on the one hand makes everyday normal life possible, which on the other is an agent responsible for that very danger. It is partly because most people insist on leading at least a normal private life (and who would take it upon himself to blame them?) that the abnormality of the public situation as a whole persists: as in economics, where the normal pursuit of private advantage by everyone can lead to the abnormality of public chaos for all, so in every other sphere of life is to be found this phenomenon of restricted personal sanity being directly responsible for an overall insanity. Could anyone try to dissuade ordinary people from clinging to something secure, from desiring a normal "as if" life at least in their spare time? They can only go on as if life would go on forever as it always has, as if children could be brought into the world as always, as if the human generations would blossom and fall like the leaves on the tree of life forever, as if humanity were an inherent part of the nature of things: "As long as the sun and moon are above / As long as the bumblebee visits a rose / As long as rosy infants are born . . . ."[14]

However, we have just said that the individual also acts on such "as if" assumptions; is he, then, any different? If there is a difference it is merely this: that the individual should know that his "as if" is only a necessary "life-lie," no certainty or security but a mere assumption without which his survival would be impossible. His is a Pascalian wager that an individual life is still possible that, no matter what the odds *against,* he must stake everything *for,* since only through that wager does he have any chance of survival. This is the only possible version of the Faustian wager, since there is no adversary with whom to play for higher stakes.

Is there anything to safeguard the individual, despite his very different "as if" assumptions, from contributing to the likelihood of disaster just as much as the normal man? What are the dangerous consequences likely to be brought about by the individual's very fact of survival? There are dangers inherent in his speech, precisely when he knows he is speaking the truth. To speak the truth of their situation to people at large, to warn them of what can ensue on their pursuit of normality, would be to endanger them even further. Not only would it then appear as if one were intent on depriving them of the last vestiges of their life, of their last glimmer of hope, but it would also appear that these truths were lies and their opposites the real truths, and so one would only succeed in enabling them to succumb all the more readily to the real lies one was speaking to warn them against. The individual cannot simply speak the truth as he sees it but must take the effects of his own speech into account.

One way to guard against this danger is to speak in a guarded way. This is in any case inevitable since the individual's speech is concealed, for his is a lonely, private discourse. And, fortunately perhaps, when speaking in this way the danger of his speech for others is considerably mitigated by the fact that few will understand him. The truth that he has to tell cannot, strictly speaking, be told in any of the public languages now current, but only in one or another of the languages of privacy. For the statements he has to make are meaningless in the presently available public languages. In the functional languages of technology, how is one to say to people that their bodies are growing numb and that they're not fully alive? In the professional languages of medicine and law, how is one to say that people can be dead before they are professionally certified as such? In the languages of positivist ideologies, how is one to say that Progress leads to nothing? And finally, in the still conserved old languages of religion, morality, and philosophy, how is one to say that Man is mortal, that nothing in the world guarantees his being, and that the question no longer is that of Man's salvation but of his very survival?

All languages presuppose their own fundamental truths, and once the truths of a given language are questioned and revoked the whole of that language is put in doubt and can no longer be freely used. For example, just as in the languages of faith God cannot be denied or even seriously questioned, so too in the languages of Progress it is Progress itself that has that status. Now, what the individual as survivor has to say questions all the fundamental assumptions of the languages of Progress: it puts in doubt the reasonableness of rational development, the logicality of positivistic logic, the morality of the ethic of work. And in so doing it threatens to destroy them and seriously to disturb the rationalizations of Progress. What he has to say can no longer be admitted in public, for it too forcibly threatens the whole present public realm of discourse.

It is for these reasons that the individual's speech must be couched in a language of privacy. Usually it cannot even be literally speech but must be a mode of writing, for the activity of writing is a communicating in private, most frequently to someone unknown, who reads in private what was written in private. Such modern writing is a speech-form in which can be told truths that the public cannot afford to admit. For such a speech there must be a language of privacy, one based on the founding truths of individual survival: the truths of solitude, silence, and the knowledge of death. Only someone who knows and shares these truths will be able to enter into a language of privacy and engage in its discourse. An individual, private discourse is like a secret communication engaged in by those in the know, who in their own private experiences find a common code that is the language in terms of which they can decode the specific messages received. It is, therefore, a discourse beset by problems that are like those of secret, written communication: the uncertainties and ambiguities of meaning, mistranslations, misunderstandings, the impossibility of establishing a stable sense, and so forth. So how is such a language of privacy to be developed in the first place? It cannot be done by publicly fixing meanings. On the contrary, it can only be done by privately unfixing the available public meanings, so that those who enter into this activity of language-destruction come to understand each other when they are doing it and thus develop their own counter-language. It is in the nature of the case that this should be a private language.

But why engage in such a perverse activity? Why speak at all? Why not remain in total silence? As Kafka realized, for the surviving individual silence is the ultimate temptation, even more compelling than the song of the sirens, that is to say, more tempting even than music. The challenging question "Why speak?" is, however, the same as the question "Why survive at all?" Many an individual has proved himself unable to sustain that challenge, and beginning with a *sacrificium intellectualitatis* in his speech ended by making a *sacrificium individualitatis* in his being as well. However, the individual trying to lose himself in the impersonal crowd finds no communal warmth, only a more intense loneliness that is no more bearable by being unaware of itself, and is aggravated to the point of imposing self-oblivion. What choice is there, then, other than to try to survive as an individual? In any case, it is hardly a matter of choice: those who must must, and those who do not have to will not.

The ethical problems of speaking as a survivor have many psychological correlates, for the individual is prey to fatal, psychological reactions inherent in survival. He will tend to feel either that he has no right to survive or that he alone has the right to survive and is justified in so doing. In the first case he will feel guilty for having survived, somehow responsible for the demise of those who did not. In the second case he is liable to think of himself as special or unique, endowed with the qualities that alone justify survival; he might, for example, believe himself to be on some extraordinary mission. At the very worst he may even come to desire the death of those whom he survives, so as to continue as survivor. Canetti has explored at length this potentially disastrous tendency of survivors to make victims of others in place of themselves; this is particularly true of survivors as rulers.[15] But even those survivors who are the victims of the worst excesses of modern paranoiac rulers are themselves liable to lapse into all kinds of perverse reactions. It has been said of an extremely talented individual, the Polish writer Tadeusz Borowski, who survived Auschwitz, that "he assuaged his guilt for surviving when so many others had gone under by identifying with the evil he described"[16] (after the war he became a Stalinist and eventually committed suicide). It is also possible to react to the fact of survival perversely in the opposite way and take the guilt on oneself, assuming the role of universal scapegoat and becoming perpetually a victim. The psychological burden of being a surviving individual even in the peaceful conditions of democratic society, though far less extreme, is no less acute. Hence, such an individual has much to learn from those who survived under the most arduous conditions of totalitarianism and in constant peril of bodily annihilation. A man like Solzhenitsyn has much to tell us about living in our world.

Those survivors who have returned from the dead know best how one is to survive in death. They are the individuals who have realized the indelible truth of *morior ergo sum* as if it were inscribed in their very flesh, and what they speak and write is a transcription of that truth into a language that is private to them because it derives from the utmost sufferings of their bodies. Frequently these sufferings are altogether beyond expression, experiences in the face of which even the language of art gives out, experiences that put in doubt the very capacity of artistic expression. Art as aesthetic order, or as moral significance or as human creativity and expressivity, is quite incapable of accommodating the truth of what modern survivors have experienced, and it is certainly incapable of reconciling us to it. If this truth is to be spoken at all, it can only be in a language that breaks all the humane assumptions of the languages we have inherited in our traditions.

Every individual is a survivor, even if only of a painless, but also ruthless, onslaught on his individual identity. To have come through is a miracle of survival. For every individual it is difficult to speak and write; there is never a language at hand in which to express what he knows. Speech is a painful struggle to articulate something that defies every known language. Yet, that effort to speak must be made. It is an effort on behalf of mankind, not just a personal indulgence, for, as if from the other side of the grave, the individual who is himself doomed sees all the better the threat facing mankind as a whole. His speech is like a testament from the dead to the living. In its very incomprehensibility it serves as a mute warning, like the apparition of a ghost that "bodes some strange eruption to our state" (*Hamlet* I.i).

## VI

As might be expected, not all individuals speak with one voice, nor do they all see their task as anything like the one outlined here. Not all are even committed to the thought of *Man*. On the contrary, there are those who put in doubt the whole notion of *Man*; they make it their undertaking not to praise *Man* but to bury him. A new anti-humanist movement emanating from France has now spread throughout the intellectual world. First under the nom de guerre of structuralism and, since that structure fractured, divided into numerous parties each invoking its own shibboleth, frequently informed with a political message, the various proponents of this movement have all spoken out against the idea of *Man*.

They began by calling for the "death of Man" to follow from the "death of God," and have gone on to "deconstruct" the Ego. For good or ill what they are advocating deserves to be taken seriously, for theirs is a movement partly based on, and intended to carry forward, the critiques of European individualism and humanism already begun by Marx, Nietzsche, Freud, and Heidegger. This new movement is also expressive of the optimistic hopes of a humanity beyond humanism, particularly as that is prefigured in Marx and Nietzsche. It strives to break out of the narrow ethnocentricity of European civilization, particularly in its bourgeois forms, and to break through to the wider humanity of other races and even of primitive peoples. It is also a movement designed to place the humanities on much sounder scientific and linguistic foundations than those of the ideal humanisms hitherto current. In the name of that radical design it speaks of dissolving and even killing *Man*. Not only do these thinkers already look back on the End of Man, but some, most notably Derrida, already look forward in the same spirit as Nietzsche to the advent of the "Superman." Derrida exults in his future coming: "His laughter will break out towards a return which will no longer have the form of the metaphysical repetition of humanism. . . . He will dance, outside of the house, this 'aktive Vergesslichkeit', this active forgetfulness [*oublience*] and this cruel [*grausam*] feast is spoken of in 'Genealogy of Morals'."[17]

Unfortunately, this "gruesome feast" may be no mere metaphor, and what is consumed in it may be much more than the mere idea of *Man.* The, on the whole, necessary and even laudable theoretical anti-humanism this intellectual movement promotes lends itself also to subversion by and conversion to the ends of dehumanization for which the end of Man is a literal reality, not just a figure of speech. In the light of that reality it becomes doubtful whether the expectations inherent in a theoretical "death of Man" are any better founded than the prior hopes of humanism.

However, a critique of the old humanism and individualism is a necessary undertaking for the individual himself, as Adorno put it when speaking of modern art: "The inhumanity of art must triumph over the inhumanity of the world for the sake of the humane."[18] Something similar holds true for modern thought. But what is the inhumanity of thought, where is it to come from, and what are its chances as against the inhumanity of the world? The inhumanity of modern thought is invested in its effort to destroy the humanist illusions of Progress—ultimately, because they are a betrayal of humanity itself. The humanists, in aligning themselves with Progress, surrender themselves to its collective life and deny their own life and death. Even Faust, that most ideal figure of Progress, acts as an accomplice in its denial of death—not because, as orthodoxy has held against him, he is unmindful of the end, but because he is mindful of the end only as an end. He puts off death to the very end of his life. This is a misconception of death that orthodoxy itself fostered insofar as it, too, consigns death merely to the end, and localizes it in the last moment of life, "the dying moment." Humanism takes the orthodox conception as its starting point and goes on to deny death altogether. If death has no reality in this life except at the end, if it is merely the end of life and so outside the bounds of life, then it has no reality at all, for only that which is in life is real. Hence the early-modern humanist Faust can offer the Devil his soul with mocking insouciance because "Of the beyond I have no thought" (*Faust,* "Faust's Study").

In the civilization of modern Progress that unconcern becomes absolute. Progress bases itself on the immortality of Man, on his continual expansion to fulfil himself and so fill the universe, without any foreseeable end. To achieve this immortality of Man, Progress has to exclude death by relegating it to the private sphere of the individual, which is of no concern to itself. Death is granted no public acknowledgment, becoming purely a private possession, the last thing a man can call his own.

But death is not so easily denied; suppressed in one form, it reappears in others that are far more horrific. Many of the symptoms of Nihilism are new manifestations of a denied death. The root of Nihilism is the nothingness of death: the emptiness, futility, oblivion, destruction, and annihilation that are the inroads into life of a suppressed death-consciousness. Eventually life is completely evacuated of its own substance and is taken over by death. The more men as individuals are deprived of their own death, the more is the whole of mankind threatened with a collective inhuman death beyond its own comprehension. Man is made mortal all the more as death is denied. That is Death's ultimate revenge on the life fostered by Progress. The death that is denied reality by men realizes itself behind their backs as the coming reality of Man. The nothingness that is made nothing of makes a Nothing of its makers.

Death has always been a presence in life, a protracted process of dying simultaneous with living. Yet, that dying had to be consciously realized in life and the deaths of those who were already dead had to be sustained in the lives of those who were still living. If death were to be once more readmitted into life, if men became once more aware of themselves as inherently mortal, then the blind grasping for a life without death might be halted and the suicidal life-pursuit of Progress might be revoked. But how can modern men realize their mortality? What meaning can death be given in modern life? These are not questions to be answered but challenges to be acted upon. All that is clear is that men must begin by recognizing the reality of a new kind of death: the possible death of Man. From now on this possibility will never leave Man, who is irrevocably mortal.

Faust is no longer the most fitting symbol of Man capable of suicide. The Faustian question of Man's salvation has given way to the much grimmer one of Man's survival. The "metaphysical pact" has indeed been called off, the great wager of God and the Devil has been replaced by Man's Pascalian gamble of himself. The Faustian drama of the struggle of light and dark, good and evil—an historical passage going back to the origins of the world religions—has now finally been concluded. If the original Zarathustra was the prophet who raised the curtain on that moral drama of the universe, then Nietzsche's Zarathustra brought it down again. The drama of human destiny is now a play of hazards in which Man himself is at stake. Freud, who realized that Faust's time was up, sought for a more mythic, classically tragic figure to replace him.

Having looked into the horrors of the psyche he saw there the patricidal symbol of Oedipus. In terms of that symbol Freud could frame and bear his tragic sense of human futility with stoic resignation. For us, in our more nihilistic mood, neither tragedy nor stoicism is any longer meaningful. We need a symbol closer to our untragic sense of nothingness. Who better than Macbeth, for whom life became "a tale/Told by an idiot, full of sound and fury/Signifying nothing." As Alfred Weber said after the last great war, "Whole peoples, whole ages may succumb to the fate of Macbeth."[19] Might we not go further now and ask whether Man himself may not succumb to the fate of Macbeth?

Macbeth, however, does not displace Faust as our dramatic symbol of Man but merely complements him. He, like Faust, is caught, in the beginning, between the opposing values of religious orthodoxy and humanism but, unlike Faust, he is eventually forced by the dramatic workings of the play to realize a knowledge of death that is beyond either of the contending traditional conceptions. Initially, Macbeth is prepared to relinquish the hereafter for the here and now; like Faust, he too wants success, defined in terms of the power "Which shall to all our nights and days to come/Give solely sovereign sway and masterdom" (*Macbeth* I.v), though for Macbeth this sovereign sway is life-power and the kingship is its most fitting symbol. However, that "to come" proves to be the rub. Success here and now is less than fully satisfying; it demands the "succession" in the name of which it was itself sought and without which it is as nothing, for it is only in succession that Macbeth can hope to find the human immortality which alone compensates him for the spiritual immortality he has sacrificed. Not granted succession, he soon finds himself "here, but here, upon this bank and shoal of time," unable to "jump the life to come," trapped in the finality of his present moment and brought face to face with the futility of his "deed without a name" and with the emptiness of the limited span of his lifetime. He comes to look forward to nothing but death, his own finally, and that of all those he murders on the way to it. In this condition—unlike Faust, whose life-term is one of guaranteed satisfactions—Macbeth finds his life-term one long self-tormenting realization of his own death-sentence.[20]

In this dramatic situation Shakespeare can press on us a new and startlingly horrifying death-knowledge. Macbeth it is who makes "strange images of death"—apparently "Nothing afeared of what thyself didst make" (I.ii). Nothing is, however, precisely that of which he is afeared in making those "strange images"—just as we are, who have made some even stranger images of death for ourselves. It is true that

Macbeth is the murderer whereas most of us, like the people of Scotland, are potential victims of murder, but that in itself does not altogether separate him from them or from us, for his is, at least initially, the kind of murder in which the murderer is both killer and killed. In killing Duncan Macbeth knew he had committed a crime against his own life, murdered his humanity, and so should have died himself also: "Had I but died an hour before this chance, / I had lived a blessed time; for from this instant / There's nothing serious in mortality" (II.iii). From this instant his continued life can only be described as post mortem: his is the condition in which a man becomes intimate with death while still marginally living. And it is in this respect that his extreme condition is analogous to our own, existing as we do "post mortem" as survivors of the death of our individuality. It is, furthermore, an analogy that has historical as well as existential implications, for just as his next victim Banquo actually comes back from the grave as Death to usurp Life's place at the banquet of men, so, too, has today's gruesome feast of Progress been invaded by the secret presence of an insidious Death, and evacuated of real life. In the end, when life is merely death's shadow and when death itself is no longer real, when it all "signifies nothing," then is Macbeth's final state the closest ever imagined in literature to a condition of modern Nihilism. And yet, even in that ultimate situation Shakespeare's drama is able to read in that nothingness a signification of Nothing. It is to this that we must turn to read a sense of the significance of our own time and of the Nothing of our Nihilism.

Faust and Macbeth are our twin presences. They have been entwined ever since they originated at about the same time and place. Their passage in subsequent times was, however, very different. Faust went on expanding himself from one figuration to another, for each Faust translates himself forward into the next, so that the whole passage of Faust is a series of self-reflections in which each successive Faust reflects on all the previous ones. These reflections seem to expand to infinity, but actually, as we shall see, they are contracted to a limited end. Macbeth, by contrast, is fixed and frozen forever in his one moment of time, the moment of his blow that is the "be-all and end-all—here." He never changes. He never moves. His is the last dying moment. Nevertheless, as we shall also eventually see, the Faustian movement and the Macbethan moment are but one and the same time. They both define our time, which is both the expanding movement of Progress and the stock-still moment of Nihilism. We can realize this identity of time if at the end of the passage of Faust we rerun it, as it were, backward. Our static Macbethan moment is this inverted passage of time compressed into one final moment that is fixed and capable of enduring forever. Thus our second passage of reflection simply reflects the first negatively. Even though it begins at the end of the first, it does not begin again; in it there is nothing new, only another repetition of the old.

This is why Macbeth does not displace Faust, why he does not make a new beginning for Man, why he does not really introduce a new figure of Man or of human civilization. How could he—can there be a civilization based on murder? His monstrous presence simply reveals itself in the shadow at the end of the passage of Faust, at that moment of turning when Faust's Deed becomes the "deed without a name." And if we look back from that turning on Faust's passage, we see that the shadow has followed Faust's progress right from the very start. Faust and Macbeth are the light and dark facets of one historical image, an image of enlightenment and obscurity. It is the image of our historical duplicity, the doubleness of Progress and Nihilism.

But before we can come to that end, we must first begin at the beginning. What was there in the beginning? We know that it is Faust who begins. But what does he begin with? To know that, we do not go back to his very beginning, but catch sight of him in medias res, in the very middle of his passage, precisely at that passage where he first tries his hand at translation.

# ACT I

---

## *FAUST THE PHILOSOPHER*

◆

## SCENE I
### *Word, Thought, and Deed*

'Tis writ, 'In the beginning was the Word.'
I pause, to wonder what is here inferred.
The Word I cannot set supremely high:
A new translation I will try.
I read, if by the spirit I am taught,
This sense: 'In the beginning was the Thought.'
This opening I need to weigh again,
Or sense may suffer from a hasty pen.
Does Thought create, and work, and rule the hour?
'Twere best: 'In the beginning was the Power.'
Yet, while the pen is urged with willing fingers,
A sense of doubt and hesitancy lingers.
The spirit comes to guide me in my need,
I write, 'In the beginning was the Deed.'[1]

I

It has often been remarked that with these words there opens a new, a modern period in European history: the Faustian. Faust is our symbol of modernity, and with him there occurs a Faustian "revolution" which inaugurates our modern age. It is significant that in the original these are German words; "Germany . . . whose evil and destructive energy is so much responsible for all our progress,"[2] as the author of an English Faust said. Germany, too, is the nation which not only gave birth to Faust, but also seemingly took his fate as its own. Thomas Mann, the author of a modern *Doctor Faustus,* saw this fate as symbolic for the whole course of German history, even down to the traditional end. In his Faust, Mann incorporates and reflects on the whole Faustian tradition; hence, his is the final reflection on the passage of Faust. He reaches back beyond Goethe's Faust, beyond Marlowe's Faustus, to Spiess's chapbook legend of the Reformation period, and even beyond that to the real, living Faustus himself, the originator of his stories. To Mann, Faust symbolizes not merely Germany, not even modern Europe alone, but the whole of Western mankind.[3] Spengler has taken the symbol in that sense; however, he has assigned it, ultimately on racial grounds, to what might be called Aryan Christianity and has excluded it from the original Hebraic-Hellenistic-Latin Christianity of the Roman empire. That he allots to a "Magian" civilization, as distinct from the Western, to which he assigns a special essence or "soul" he calls "Faustian." It is, of course, highly questionable whether civilizations have such cultural "souls" and even more questionable whether the Christian spirit can be split up into two such separate "souls" much against its own teachings and traditions.

Our central focus in this work is on Goethe's *Faust,* for that is when the drama begins to matter historically. However, we do go back from that to its earlier origins, as far as literary history and traditions permit. Only since Goethe has Faust become the fundamental myth of modernity; it had no such role prior to Goethe, though it was well known as a folk legend and the dramatic tradition stemming from Marlowe's first dramatic realization was never lost, as is wonderfully attested by Rembrandt's print. That is more or less how Alfred Weber treats the symbol in his brief valedictory to the history of Europe.[4] As an historic symbol Faust might be stretched back to the waning of the Middle Ages, but his central locus remains modern.

"I have, alas, studied philosophy"—Faust's very first, weary words tell us much of his initial significance. It is to him that we must first look for a symbol of modern philosophy. He might be called the first modern philosopher, and his decisive pronouncement might be considered the first word, and perhaps also the last word on the subject: "Im Anfang war die Tat." Symbolically considered, these words stand at the head of a new, largely German-speaking philosophy which they may be said to inaugurate. They come at the end of a passage of translation in which Faust gives a new rendering of the original from the Gospel of St. John, "In principio erat logos," which he first reads out of the New Testament in Luther's German version as "Im Anfang war das Wort." He proceeds to give a different translation, not an alternative literal rendering but a figurative transformation, for he derives from it his own new beginning. The new modern philosophy, which this move symbolizes, starts with the same beginning, and it, too, arrives at its *principium* or *archē* by translating the traditional original words of philosophy so as to transform them into itself. It deprives the old words of their traditional meanings; in so doing it destroys those meanings and the philosophies that depend on them, in particular the two chief traditions of metaphysical philosophy, the original Greek and the classical European. Modern philosophy denies the Reason of metaphysics and Rationalist epistemology, the two main variants of Western rationality, by translating away the two words on which they depend, the "Logos" and the "Cogito," respectively.

Again, symbolically considered, something of this significative transformation is prefigured in Faust's translation. What specifically dissatisfies Faust is the Logos as the "Wort" because he "cannot set [it] supremely high," and the "Sinn" (Thought) because, as he asks, "Does Thought create and work?" And here it must be recalled that the German *Sinn* is also sense, meaning, mind, and understanding—all of which are to be found in various English translations. He next lingers on the notion of *Kraft* ("Power"), which momentarily seems to him nearly right, and following that lead the "spirit" impels him finally to its outcome, the *Tat* ("Deed"). What would have happened if he had succumbed to his "will to Power" is one of the unanswerable questions of literature and history. Perhaps at that time the Power and the Deed were so close as to be indistinguishable. Faust decides on the more concrete Deed, and he declares emphatically, "Im Anfang war die Tat." With these words the fatal formula is pronounced and the whole dynamic course of dramatic action and historical Progress is unleashed.

How is it that Faust gets to his Deed? He naively imagines that he is urged to it by the "creative spirit," but Goethe and we know better. We know by the restive growling of the dog that is with him in his narrow study what dark forces he is invoking, and from where the inspiration comes to lead him to that fatal Deed. We know, too, what backward, winding by-ways and side-ways of thought led Goethe to the modern Deed. Behind this Deed there is a long, somewhat heretically tainted, hermetic tradition of the *Actus purus* and *Energeia,* an underground stream of active and creative philosophy flowing beneath the orthodox ground of the metaphysics of the Logos and the Cogito. Goethe, like Faust, had dabbled in the book of Nostradamus and many other arcane Renaissance magi (among them Paracelsus, Boehme, and Bruno), for whom, as for Faust, the word is an act of power and potency. After the Renaissance the hermetic stream flows on barely noticeably in Spinoza, Vico, and Swedenborg right through the Rationalist European landscape, until Goethe and the German Idealists begin to drink from it. The sources of this stream can be traced as far back as Plato and Aristotle and the Alexandrian theology of Philo (*dabeir* means "word" and "deed" in Hebrew—a crucial ambiguity where the word of God is concerned), through neo-Platonic theories of pure actuality or Energeia as pure creation, through the complex elaboration of the Johannine Logos as the active and creative Word of God incarnate, all of this often mixed with the hermetica of Hermes Trismegistus and eventually with the lore of the cabbalists and alchemists. So it was quite a witches' brew of ideas that Goethe was concocting, but out of these emerged the magic potion that brought about a rejuvenated Deed.[5] That Deed is as unlike any older Actus as young Faust dedicated to a life of action is unlike the old Faust of magic words, cabbalistic signs, books, and cobweb. The modern Deed has nothing to do with hidden potencies, virtues, essences, and matters: it is primarily Man's creative or productive activity.

And just as the old Actus was not completely lost but was translated into the Deed, so, too, the Logos and the Cogito were not completely lost to modern thought. Under the impact of the Deed they too underwent translations and reemerged completely transformed—indeed, scarcely recognizable. "Bottom thou art translated," says Quince on seeing Bottom with the ass's head.[6] Perhaps the ancient Greek sages would react with similar astonishment if they could perceive what we have managed to do with their Logos, and the Rationalist, classical philosophes might be no less surprised to see what has happened to their Cogito; only the poets understood metamorphoses. Though not altogether a poet, Nietzsche, too, understood very well that that newly translated ass is no mere rustic innocent or holy fool but a new world beyond good and evil. "What hidden wisdom is it that He weareth long ears and ever sayeth only Hee-haw—Yea, and never Nay? Hath he not created the world in His own image, that is, as stupid as may be?—But the Ass replied Hee-haw—Yea!"[7] However, at the moment when Faust utters the fatal formula of his opening Deed it is not an ass but a little poodle-dog that is translated. The dog that had attached itself to Faust's side on his promenade with Wagner, at the moment when he invoked the intermediate spirits hovering between heaven and earth, now in his study begins to whine and growl restively, in response to the new commitment Faust has made. When Faust has it trapped within the magic sign of the pentagram, it seeks to escape by transmogrifying into a monster the size of a hippopotamus. When Faust controls that, too, with his spells, it turns into a mist, out of which finally the Devil in person, as Mephistopheles, steps from behind the stove. Mephistopheles, who understands only too well the significance of Faust's translation, mocks him as "one who gives the Word its lowest rate," who "only the depths of life will contemplate" ("Faust's Study"). It is in these terms that, in the next scene, Mephistopheles broaches his challenge, offering "quests never ending, action and joy"—which is, of course, the Devil's travesty of what Faust is after. Faust, after his great curse of despair, wants to reexperience life to discover what it may have to offer, what it can possibly amount to that is worthwhile. So with a bravado born of desperation, Faust takes up Mephistopheles' challenge and the fateful wager is sealed in blood.

This wager is already implicit in Faust's turning to the Deed, for the Deed is also a deed: a compact contracted for a fixed time. And Mephistopheles, the spirit of Denial, is also the active force that spurs Man on, as the Lord declared in the Prologue. Thus, in the first place, the Deed is continuing and continuous activity in time, an ever ongoing passage of progress in time. It promises indefinite expansion of time with no limit: "a work-filled eternity," as Mann's Devil was later to call it, promising his Faust free time, full time, time with no visible end. And yet, as we know from the very beginning, that end must come, for the Deed is also a deed that is contracted in time and so must contract time. The passage of Faust will shrink in its very expansiveness; it will converge to its limit and come to its end, and indeed end with the passage of Faust. Faust will pass—from the beginning this is written into his Deed. We merely need to read his opening passage to get that unwritten intimation of the full text of time. But at this starting point the end of the passage is still a long, long way off, barely to be thought of or reflected on, as the Devil insists.

Meanwhile, let us return to the Deed at hand—for that is really what it is: a deed of the hand. It is Faust's fist that shatters the old "beautiful world" into fragments and sends the ruins hurtling into Nothing, as the hovering spirits, Mephistopheles' minions, lament sorrowfully in wraithlike lyrics. But in bringing Faust to this destructive act Mephistopheles in effect saves him. That is the Lord's irony in the divine scheme of things, and of this Mephistopheles himself is bitterly aware. He saves Faust from the despair into which he had sunk by first turning him to the translated Deed and rousing him from his spiritual lethargy in provoking him to the destructive act of cursing the world as he knew it. To tempt him then into seeking to re-create the world follows almost as easily as creation must follow on destruction—or so it seemed to Goethe.

At the high point of the passage of Faust, Goethe could take a benign, cosmically comic view of the Faustian progress. For Thomas Mann, coming at the end of the passage, things seem to have turned out rather differently, but even he in the end seeks to vindicate the Faustian Deed in a larger scheme of things. For Mann, in the end everything will turn out well, despite Man. Perhaps that is the ineradicable meaning of the Faustian thematic. Every Faust declares paradoxically to his Devil: "In this, thy Nothing, may I find my All!" (*Faust* II.I.v)—and invariably he does, be it at the cost of his own damnation. Goethe's Faust, as we saw, turns to the spirit of Negation to save himself from the nothingness of his life. He, as it were, seeks salvation from nothingness in Nothing. And that is possible because Mephistopheles, cynical rationalist that he is, is nevertheless conceived of along Idealist lines, as Negation and Nothing at one and the same time. Insofar as he is Negation he is the necessary negative moment of activity in the upward dialectic of the Progress of time; insofar as he is Nothing he is the annihilating principle in the reduction of time to the Void. This very duplicity of the Devil works to Faust's advantage and enables him ambiguously to find his All in Nothing.

The dream of winning All from Nothing has persisted ever since. This Nothing is what the philosopher Jacobi, Goethe's friend, called for the first time by that ominous name of nihilism. Jacobi's famous letter to Fichte (written during the period when Goethe was struggling to complete *Faust,* Part I), he concludes with these words: "Truly, my dear Fichte, it would not annoy me if you, or anyone, were to call chimaerism what I oppose to Idealism which I stigmatize as Nihilism." He accuses Fichte, in other words, of seeking to build his All out of Nothing, of trying, out of the nothingness of his own subjectivity, to build up the whole world. Later on Stirner was expressly to say in the words of the English Bible: "I have laid my case on Nothing," for he, too, builds his world out of his solitary Ego, and so founds his All. As we shall eventually see, in Nietzsche's case it is much more complicated, and rather different, for Nietzsche provides us with our first truly modern definition of Nihilism. Nevertheless, he, too, in some basic respects "insists on the Mephistophelean prospect," as one critic puts it; like Faust he descends into the Abyss of Nothing to come back with All, "and yet not to despair, and yet to glorify, indeed to transfigure existence—this is the goal of Nietzsche's desperate strategy."[8] Finally, even Heidegger seeks to win Being out of the jaws of the essence of Nothing, as he tells us: "The clear courage for essential dread guarantees that most mysterious of all possibilities, the experience of Being. For hard by the essential dread, in the terror of the Abyss, there dwells awe"[9]—and essential dread, as he goes on to say, "is this Nothing."

Whether in fact this Faustian quest can succeed is one of the central questions of modern thought. Out of the Nothing that is the Nihilism of our time, can we at least extract Something, if not All? And that is not merely a question for philosophers. Or is it, rather, as Lear retorts, that "nothing will come of nothing"? That grimmer prospect, too, must be contemplated. At the end of Faust we shall have to take another signification of Nothing into account as well, but we are not yet ready for that. Let us in the meantime stay with the philosophers and hear what they have to say about Faust's Deed.

II

One of the most startling and seemingly paradoxical consequences of the Faustian Deed is that it provoked a return to words. What makes it less odd is that the words it invoked are nothing like what words had ever been before: these are words conceived of as Language in a quite new signification. Modern thought owes to the Deed its discovery of Language in the modern sense, perhaps the most fundamental and far-reaching discovery it has made. Language so understood is not words as *logoi,* it is not rational discourse, it is not logic, it is not the signs and signatures of the world, it is not the theological Verb, it is not a hidden text or a lost trace, it is not Idea or essence or nature, it is not the universal or name by convention—it is not anything in terms of which signification or meaning had ever been conceived before. On the centrality of Language to all of modern thought a modern philosopher has this to say:

> Today we are in search of a comprehensive philosophy of language to account for the multiple functions of the human act of signifying and for their interrelationships. How can language be put to such diverse uses as mathematics and myth, physics and art? We have at our disposal a symbolic logic, an exegetical science, an anthropology and a psychoanalysis and, perhaps for the first time, we are able to encompass in a single question the problem of the unification of human discourse. The very progress of the aforementioned disparate disciplines has both revealed and intensified the dismemberment of that discourse. Today the unity of human language poses a problem.[10]

This unity and dismemberment of modern Language corresponds exactly to the unity and dismemberment of modern Man, also due to the "progress" of his disciplines, which now discipline him. It is a situation of the greatest danger, one in which the fragmentation or dismemberment could easily turn into an annihilation or decomposition of the kind to which we referred earlier. However, a man of Ricoeur's deep religious faith can also see possibilities and hopes for Language, and so presumably for Man as well, in this situation of "apparent distress," as he puts it.

> The situation in which language today finds itself comprises this double possibility, the double solicitation and urgency: on the one hand, purifying discourse of its excrescences, liquidate the idols, go from drunkenness to sobriety, realize our state of poverty once and for all; on the other hand, use the worst "nihilistic," destructive, iconoclastic movement so as to *let speak* what once, what each time, was said, when meaning appeared

> anew, when meaning was at its fullest. Hermeneutics seems to me to be animated by this double motivation: willingness to suspect, willingness to listen, vow of rigor, vow of obedience. In our time we have not finished doing away with *idols* and we have barely begun to listen to *symbols*. It may be that this situation, in its apparent distress, is instructive: it may be that extreme iconoclasm belongs to the restoration of meaning.[11]

All this may well be. But only someone able to "listen to symbols," someone who can still hear the Logos in its original purity, would maintain that these meanings will be restored despite the ravages of Language, or precisely because of them. In this seemingly unlikely source we once more stumble upon the Faustian quest to extract All from Nothing: from "the worst 'nihilistic,' destructive, iconoclastic movement" Ricoeur seeks to arrive at the original word, "to let speak what once, what each time, was *said,* when meaning appeared anew, when meaning was at its fullest"—from emptiness of meaning he hopes miraculously to recover fullness. That miracle hermeneutics is to accomplish. However, might one not ask how anyone is to believe in the meaningful original word at the very moment when it has been nihilistically emptied of meaning? When Language is the "tale full of sound and fury, signifying Nothing" can it also signify everything?

Once more, like Mann's narrator Zeitblom, we have, in our nervous eagerness, run ahead of ourselves, exposed issues that should not have come till much, much later, like a clumsy composer who reveals his themes before he is ready to develop them. We return to our first subject, the Deed, Language, and modernity, but this time giving it an orderly exposition and development. This time we refer to Foucault, an author with the opposite predilections and hopes, to tell us what the upsurge of Language meant for the onset of modernity. Foucault makes that the breaking-point (*rupture*) separating what he calls the classical from the modern *epistemē*:

> At the beginning of the nineteenth century, [words] rediscovered their ancient, enigmatic density; though not in order to restore the curve of the world which had harboured them during the Renaissance, nor in order to mingle with things in a circular system of signs. Once detached from representation, language has existed, right up to our own day only in a dispersed way: for philologists, words are like so many objects formed and deposited by history; for those who wish to achieve a formalization, language must strip itself of its concrete content and leave nothing visible but those forms of discourse that are universally valid; if one's intent is to interpret, then words become a text to be broken down, so as to allow that other meaning hidden in them to emerge and become clearly visible; lastly,

> language may sometimes arise for its own sake in an art of writing that designates nothing other than itself.[12]

This discovery of Language in the period of Goethe's *Faust* Foucault also refers to as the "reappearance of language as a multiple profusion," saying of it that words "rediscovered their enigmatic density." The relationship he is tracing is the hidden nexus that links the Word of the sixteenth century with the new words of Language of the nineteenth century, and brings them together over the intervening centuries of Classical discourse. It is, of course, specifically the relation between the Renaissance Faustus and his Word and the modern Faust and his Deed. But even though these are both Fausts, and so carry one identity, they are by no means identical; in fact, a world and word of difference separate the two. Foucault is clear on that issue, and he indicates how the concept of language as a discovery of the quite new science of philology, for example, differs completely from any interpretation of the Word as practiced by the hermeneutical exegesis of the Renaissance.

Foucault goes on to add "that we are already, before the very least of our words, governed and paralyzed by language."[13] That phrase must even at this point elicit a murmur of critical demurral that will in time call for a review of Foucault's overdeterministic approach to language, which obviously derives from and is in sympathy with structuralist linguistics (though otherwise Foucault's thought is in no simple sense "structuralist"). As he puts it, "The grammatical arrangements of a language are the a priori of what can be expressed by it. The truth of discourse is caught in the trap of philology." That last reference shows that what he means by *grammar* is far removed from what Wittgenstein means by *grammar,* and only in Wittgenstein's sense of a logical-grammar of concepts, not an epistemē of discourses, could such a pronouncement possibly be true. Foucault's account of the origins of philology, the predecessor of linguistics, is also incomplete. He overlooks the ground out of which philology arose, and so he makes it seem an inexplicably sudden "coupure" or break; what made philology possible was the prior preparation of a whole new philosophy of language, which, as it happened, developed in the circle around Goethe. In particular, Goethe's friends Hamann, Herder, and Humboldt were responsible for initiating that philosophy and bringing it to maturity. Goethe's own hand in the matter was no less decisive. All this has been extremely well documented and interpreted in George Steiner's well-nigh exhaustive work on translation.[14]

It is clear that this new orientation to Language, so characteristic of Goethe and his circle, is bound up with the Faustian Deed. The Deed is here primary, so even for Language it is true that "Im Anfang war die Tat." Foucault reveals this quite clearly when he shows that the new sense of Language derived from a new sense of the relation of words to activity.

> Language is "rooted" not in the things perceived, but in an active subject. And perhaps, in that case, it is a product of will and energy, rather than of the memory that duplicates representation. We speak because we act, and not because recognition is a means of cognition. Like action, language expresses a profound will to something.[15]

Foucault's reference to the "active subject," which he elsewhere calls more imposingly the "Sovereign Subject," introduces another major thematic, that of Man. According to Foucault, the modern conception of Man arose only in the early nineteenth century out of the new epistemē that Foucault analyzes into Language, Life, and Labor, and which according to him brought about the epistemological break at the inauguration of the modern period, for out of it emerged philology as against classical discourse, biology as against natural history, and political economy as against the analysis of wealth. Man is for Foucault part of the "historical-transcendental structure which the philosophy of the nineteenth century has imposed" on our "discursive field" and from which he hopes "to liberate it."[16] That "structure" is made up of "the themes of Meaning, of Origin, of the constituent Subject, in short all the themes which guarantee history the inexhaustible presence of the Logos, the sovereignty of the pure subject, and the profound teleology of an original destination."[17] It is the destruction of this "structure" that Foucault has both predicted and devoted himself to furthering, nowhere with more zest and even glee than in his attempted "murder" of Man, the constituent Subject, whose imminent death Foucault has already declared as following on that of God.

Whatever one may think of the outcome Foucault has in mind for Man—or for the rest of his so-called "historical-transcendental structure" of the modern discursive field, questionable as that may be[18]—there is much that relates Foucault's pan-historical scheme, at least in its account of origins, to our own "Faustian translations" based on the Deed. Certainly, Man as constituent Subject cannot be said to have emerged out of the Faustian Deed, even in the way that the new concept of Language might be said to have done, and neither can Time as "the profound teleology of an original destination." Such notions of Man and Time are indeed age-old, or at least as old as the Logos, as Foucault himself seems implicitly to acknowledge. Humanisms of all modes and teleologies and eschatologies of Time all pre-date modern Faust; they are certainly already there in the original Faustus. If modern Meaning can be said to be a continuation of the Logos, then modern Subjectivity is also a continuation of older themes of Man as Subject going back at least as far as the subjectivity of the Cogito; and modern schemes of Time are equally continuations of much older time articulations arising from past teleologies and eschatologies. However, it is true that the Logos, the Cogito, and the old Actus underwent a fundamental Faustian translation, and out of that emerged the Faustian Deed that promoted a new notion of Language, allied with a new Subject as Faustian Man, and a new time of historical Progress with its peculiarly modern sense of a final End (all of which we shall consider in Act II).

Independently, other historians and philosophers have remarked on the change in the nature of Man and Time during this period of the Faustian "revolution." Werner Marx, one of the outstanding commentators on Heidegger, tells us in no uncertain terms that what irrevocably separates Heidegger's still tradition-oriented preoccupation with "essence" from the *ousia* of the whole metaphysical tradition is precisely the inescapable repercussion on his thinking of the notion of Man and History developed in modern philosophy. "Awakened, moreover, by the transcendental turning point, especially, however, by Hegel's insights in the *Phenomenology of Spirit,* philosophy has seen itself ever more strongly forced to think the essence of man as a *doer,* if not indeed as a creator or co-creator, who not only can alter his world but fashion the new."[19] This "transcendental turning point" is indeed a most decisive break in the history of philosophy, but, as we shall see, it is not identical with the Faustian revolution. It is still very much a turning within the history of philosophy alone; inaugurated by Kant, it did not come into full effect till the later Idealists. Werner Marx puts this another way, with an orientation toward Heidegger and his Dasein, which he contrasts to the Kantian and Idealist transcendental Subject.

> The producing of the *general* transcendental Subject was carried out categorially and to that extent remained bound to the tradition. This applies to Fichte's "deed-act" as well; the doctrine of science can derive only the traditional categories (substantiality, causality, reciprocity, etc.) from it. And yet it can be said that Fichte's conception of the "primacy of practical reason," together with Hegel's determination in the *Phenomenology of Spirit,* began to view man as a *doer* in a way which goes beyond the traditional limitations to his power. The post-Hegelians (Feuerbach, Marx, Stirner) already stand outside the history of thought which is customarily called "the tradition."[20]

As we shall eventually see (Act III), Fichte's "primacy of practical reason" is a first intimation of modern *praxis,* one of the fundamental consequences of the Deed, which eventually, drawing on all kinds of other sources as well, received its culmination as a theoretical notion in Marx. The so-called left-Hegelians, whose thinking was contemporary with the young Marx, spoke explicitly of "the praxis of the Idea" and of "the realization of philosophy." Starting with Cieszkowski, then Bruno Bauer and Moses Hess, the left-Hegelians developed Hegelianism into a "philosophy of the Deed,"[21] seemingly along Faustian lines. Marx himself, however, abandoned this Idealist Deed and developed a much more practical notion of productive labor or praxis by, in the first place, going behind the young Hegelians' backs to Hegel himself. In his early work Marx was much taken with the notion of self-realization through an activity of objectivation which he derived from the *Phenomenology of Spirit,* and he tried to link this to an economics of labor derived from Adam Smith. The *Phenomenology,* which appeared at the same time as the final version of *Faust* Part I, develops a notion of activity that is closely allied but at a tangent to that of the Faustian Deed. Activity (*das formierende Tun*) is for Hegel an objectivation of Subjectivity, and it is not productive work but a struggle for recognition out of which arises the master-slave dialectic. Self-realization comes before the creation of a joint human world in Hegel, whereas the Faustian Deed begins with the creation of a common world in the course of which the self also forms itself.

## III

We are still at the start of the philosophical passage of Faust. Fichte, Hegel, the "philosophers of the Deed" are certainly there constituting the necessary background, but they are not themselves part of the passage of Faust. Inother words, they are not decisively modern philosophers. The whole Idealist movement is double-faced: it is at the start of modernity but is also the continuation of the tradition. Hegel is the last of the great metaphysicians, but is also an important influence on the formation of modern philosophy. Hence, we must look to Goethe rather than to Hegel for some of the most decisive early traces of modern philosophy. From Goethe's *Faust* we trace a succession of widely dissimilar minds who, therefore, in no sense constitute a modern tradition—indeed that would be well-nigh a contradiction in terms—but who among them map out the field of modern philosophy, just as Brahms, Wagner, Stravinsky, and Schoenberg do for that of music after Beethoven.

Marx, Nietzsche, Wittgenstein, and Heidegger: they are the heirs of Faust and together they describe the passage of Faust. Each of them in his own way takes as his starting point Faust's first principle, "Im Anfang war die Tat," but each interprets and develops it differently.

Thus they have not only a commitment to the Deed but also to Language as following on the Deed, and that is not to be found in Hegel[22] or any of the Idealists. For that matter, it is not there in quite that Faustian way in most subsequent philosophers, including Schopenhauer and Husserl, or in any of the major schools of philosophy, such as Positivism or Psychologism or Historicism. It is this primary predisposition to Language that also determines, as we shall see, the sense of Man and Time of our Faustian thinkers.

The passage of Faust already begins and proceeds within Goethe's *Faust,* for the two parts of the drama contain quite different, and developing, conceptions of the Deed. In Part I the drama opens with an individualistic, subjective act; in Part II it closes, with the Deed as a collective, shared communal activity in which Faust has only the guiding leadership. (Goethe himself remarked on this fundamental difference between the two parts.)[23] Thus the Faustian Deed of Part I is not unlike the Fichtean deed-act that is capable of creating or destroying the world on its own. In Part II this Fichtean Act is subjected to a derisory criticism when all such Fichtean and Idealist views are put into the mouth of the returned, brash young Baccalaureus, whom even Mephistopheles now has trouble in handling. The Baccalaureus is partly also a parody of young Faust. At the end of the drama the very old Faust explicitly abjures all his youthful activist excesses, and, like Goethe himself, looks for freedom within limitation and necessity, but above all in the communal labor of building a human world out of and against the elements.

It is almost as if by some cunning of history that Marx takes up this communal vision of a society based on productive praxis. Engels was later to say explicitly that the first principle of Marx's dialectical materialism is "Im Anfang war die Tat."[24] Marx puts it as follows:

> The first premise of all human history, of course, is the existence of living human individuals. (The first historical *act* of these individuals, the act by which they distinguish themselves from animals, is not the fact that they *think* but the fact that they begin to produce their means of subsistence.)[25]

Production is thus the primary Deed, and the whole Marxist theory of economy does not begin, as do the classical economists, with human needs but with human deeds: consumption is consequent on production. In a similar way, in terms of the Deed, Marx distinguishes his own historical materialism from all previous materialisms.

> The chief defect of all previous materialism (including Feuerbach's) is that the object, actuality, sensuousness is conceived only in the form of the Object of perception [*Anschauung*], but not as sensuous human *activity,*

> practice [*Praxis*], not subjectively. Hence in opposition to materialism, the active side was developed by idealism—but only abstractly, since idealism naturally does not know actual, sensuous activity as such [the Deed].[26]

We have already seen the relevance of the last remark on Idealism.

It might be wondered how and where, in this Deed of Marx, Language belongs. And it must be admitted for a start that Language is not as central there as it is in our other three thinkers, nor is it as developed in Marx as it is in them. Nevertheless, it is there and necessarily so, for "from the start the 'spirit' is afflicted with the curse of being burdened with matter, which here makes its appearance in the form of agitated layers of air, sound, in short of language."[27] Human activity, consciousness and the very being of Man, is for Marx a matter of social relationship, and the basis of all social relationship is language. "Feuerbach resolves the religious essence into the human essence. But the essence of man is no abstraction inhering in each single individual. In its actuality it is the ensemble of social relationships."[28] It is from this need for social relationships that languages derive, but languages also mediate and make social relationships possible, for languages constitute the primary social consciousness.

> Language is as old as consciousness. It is practical consciousness which exists also for other men and hence exists for me personally as well. Language, like consciousness, only arises from the need and necessity of relationships with other men.[29]

Language is for Marx the primary paradigm of the social nature of Man and of productive labor. He refers to it repeatedly, whenever he wishes to reestablish the social character of anything human.

> Man is in the most literal sense of the word a zōon politikon, not only a social animal, but an animal which can develop into an individual only in society. Production by isolated individuals outside society—something which might happen as an exception to a civilized man who by accident got into the wilderness and already potentially possessed within himself the forces of society—is as great an absurdity as the idea of the development of language without individuals living together and talking to one another.[30]

Here Marx is using the paradigm of language to destroy the presuppositions of individualism in classical economics, to show the impossibility of the "Robinsonades" which hold a place in classical economics equivalent to that of the Cogito in classical philosophy. Marx's argument in refutation of the idea of "private production" by reference to common language is thus a distant premonition of Wittgenstein's refutation of "private-experience," also by reference to language. In both cases it is made clear that what is being refuted is not a nonsensical idea per se or something inherently meaningless, but something that was indeed meaningful in another mode of thought and is no longer so within modern thought. This gives us a simple instance and an early intimation of a subject we shall take up elsewhere:[31] how a philosophical argument functions, and how Wittgenstein's later reductio-ad-absurdum "private-language" argument against the Cogito does indeed reduce it to nothing but does not render it meaningless in itself, only in relation to another kind of meaning. Marx tries to put this point, as is his wont, with irascible impatience, almost contradicting himself in the process: "It would not be necessary to touch upon this point at all, had not this nonsense—which, however, was justified and made sense in the eighteenth century—been transplanted, in all seriousness, into the field of political economy by Bastiat, Carey and Proudhon and others."[32] So "this nonsense" did "make sense in the eighteenth century"—what could be a more striking indication of the impact that the arrival of the modern conception of Language would make on what from then on was considered sense and nonsense in economics or in any other sphere!

Despite all this, there is no fully autonomous philosophy of Language in Marx. Certainly, one could be developed on the basis of what Marx does say. It could be expanded to take in Marx's whole theory of consciousness as the superstructure on the material base, including his remarks on cultural production as well as his critique of ideology. One could thus say that Marx's critique of ideology is the first critical philosophy of Language in modern thought. One might even go further, with Althusser, and read *Capital* as presenting a theory of the theoretical production of itself—which, of course, would be a theory of theoretical language—but to go that far would be to enter into the treacherous tunnels of Marxian interpretation, which we are not as yet ready to explore.

With Nietzsche, by contrast, there is no need for lengthy exposition to establish his constant and fundamental preoccupation with language. He began his academic career as a philologist and lectured extensively on rhetoric, a subject from which he derived his early view of language as metaphor. Foucault goes so far as to say that he was "the first to connect the philosophical task with a radical reflection upon language";[33] though it is more likely that, as we have shown, the priority could be given to Humboldt or to Marx, Nietzsche was the first to do so explicitly. He declared that "we cease to think when we do not do so in the form of language."[34] It was Nietzsche, too, who first located the source of the concepts and categories of philosophy in the grammar of language. He went so far as to ask rhetorically how we could cease to believe in God as long as we believed in grammar and its substantives. His investigations into the metaphysical consequences of the personal pronoun *I* taken as a substantive also foreshadow much of Wittgenstein's later investigations into subjectivity. All this is, as it were, on the sober, philosophically Apollonian side of Nietzsche's language; on the other, Dionysian, ecstatic side of his language there is his preoccupation with the poetic word of symbol and myth. Here his language is related to Heidegger's "dichtendes Wort"; Zarathustra's language-play is on the way to Heidegger's fourfold play of the world that is also a play of words.

"He was a Faustian, after all, in his deep-rooted belief that in the beginning was the Deed"[35]—in Nietzsche, too, Language abounds with the Deed. In the first place, however, Nietzsche's Deed is a quasi-aesthetic activity of creation and destruction. In his early work this aesthetic dimension is most pronounced. In his later work the Deed becomes in turn more specific and more generalized. It is more specific in his theory of the making and breaking of values. All Nietzsche's preoccupations with "genealogy" and with "revaluation" turn on these two value-activities. Indeed, so strong is Nietzsche's sense of the making of values that he frequently refers to it as a fabrication, and to the values so created as fabricated fictions. This is why values are always made to be broken, and why he wields his Hammer on idols and ideals alike—that is, when he is not using it more subtly as a medical-psychologist's small mallet. Having been thus on the one side narrowed down to a human cultural activity, on the other it is generalized into the universal activity of the Will to Power: the dehumanized surging of the creative-destructive flux of the world as an exchange of energy and drive for increase. Here it is almost as if Nietzsche takes a step back in Faust's translation, from the *Tat* back to the *Kraft,* but really it is both at once. And in some respects it is so for Faust, too; he moves from the Power to the Deed in his translation only because of a powerful urging of the "creative spirit," and, as it were, actualizes the power of his inspiration in the deed of writing the "Deed." Power and act cannot be separated: here the Will to Power is the Deed in its potency, and the Deed is the Will to Power in its actuality.

Wittgenstein pronounced explicitly the Faustian principle: "In the beginning was the Deed; language, I should like to say, was a subsequent refinement."[36] Thus, he at first wished to give priority to the Deed over Language. Later, however, he realized that "words are deeds"[37] and that Language and the Deed belong together. Language is a human life-activity, a play of language-games: "Here the term 'language-*game*' is meant to bring into prominence the fact that the *speaking* of language is part of an activity, or of a form of life."[38] The Deed as life-activity is thus principial: "What has to be accepted, the given is—so one could say—*forms of life*."[39] This basic given, forms of life-activity, is at the same time that of language-activity, for "to imagine a language means to imagine a form of life."[40] The forms of life Wittgenstein is most intent on describing are the common forms, or the basic life-activities which are, as it were, most "natural" to Man and on the basis of which the most common of the meanings of the words of a language are founded. He insisted, "My life consists in being content to accept many things."[41] For Wittgenstein, as for Marx, a language is based on the fundamental but changeable social life-activities of men, which are in the first place also economic. Any change, real or imaginary, in these basic forms of life brings about a real or imaginary change in the basic meanings, that is, in the basic grammatical forms of concepts and thereby in the whole of human consciousness. For Wittgenstein, too, as for Marx, when the consciousness of a certain society or age is false, that is because its language habits are distorted or "sick." When it is plagued by contradictions, problems, and quandaries, then this is not a malaise that philosophy can cure by, as it were, resorting to a universal Reason to reveal the truth of things in the classical ways, for the roots of such a condition go down to changes and contradictions in the basic forms of life, which are beyond the reach of philosophy alone.

> The sickness of a time is cured by an alteration in the mode of life of human beings, and it is possible for the sickness of philosophical problems to get cured only through a changed mode of thought and of life, not through a medicine invented by an individual.[42]

To Wittgenstein these sicknesses appeared as "neuroses" of language. He did not believe he could cure them by himself, but he did not refuse them treatment, devising for that purpose linguistic-analytic methods that he likened to the psychoanalytic methods of Freud. The philosophic school known as Linguistic Analysis took as its point of departure Wittgenstein's treatment of language. However, it never appreciated the general conception of Language that Wittgenstein developed out of his treatment of particular language-problems but instead ended up uncovering linguistic trivialities in its effort to elucidate the classical problems of philosophy. At the start Wittgenstein had warned that "the essential thing, I believe, is that the work of clarifying must be pursued with courage: if that is wanting, then the work becomes just a clever game."[43]

Wittgenstein was never sanguine about the influence his work would have. He was even doubtful of its ultimate value.

> I believe there is something true when I tell myself that in my thinking I am really only reproductive. I believe I have never invented [erfunden] a movement of ideas, it always came to me from someone else. I eagerly snatched it up at once for my work of clarifying. In this way Boltzmann, Herz, Schopenhauer, Frege, Russell, Kraus, Loos, Weininger, Spengler, Sraffa exercised an influence on me. Can we cite Breuer and Freud as an example of Jewish reproductive talent? What I invent [*erfinde*] are new similes.[44]

The self-deprecation of the opening remark is characteristic; at the same time it is not, strictly speaking, solely personal, for it is bound up with his qualified judgment of "Jewish reproductive talent," a judgment which, since it embraces Freud (Einstein is not mentioned), must surely extend to much of modern culture and particularly to philosophy, to which those of Jewish extraction have made such a signal contribution. The influence of the self-hating thinking of Weininger is here unfortunately in evidence. The influences of most of the names Wittgenstein refers to before that of Weininger have already been extensively explored in the literature on Wittgenstein, but we know only a little of the importance for him of the two following, Sraffa and Spengler. His remarks on culture and civilization are redolent of Spengler. Only rarely does he make an original historical observation, as when he notes: "Our civilization is characterized by the word "progress"; progress is its form, it is not merely one of its properties that it progresses."[45]

There is almost no relationship at all between Wittgenstein and Heidegger. However, some writers have begun to discover fundamental common concerns; one maintains that "the pre-linguistic horizon of meaning or Being is for both philosophers human activity."[46] However, it would not be quite correct to speak of the Deed in Heidegger's philosophy solely as "human activity." The active nature of Dasein is apparent from the start by its basic orientation to the world as *Zu-handesein,* a compound term that encapsulates the hand as well as being; Dasein's active character is inherent, too, in its temporality. But it is not only Dasein that is active—so, too, is Being itself. As in the passage of the Deed from Goethe's *Faust* Part I to Part II, so there is an analogous passage or turning (*Kehre*) in Heidegger from the subjective Deed of Dasein to the more universal Deed of Being. One commentator puts it explicitly: "The individualization of man, which came out so strongly in *Sein und Zeit* and seemed to find its starkest experience in man's being-unto-death, is now complemented and balanced by the communal element of belonging to a historical people."[47] History for Heidegger is *Seinsgeschichte,* the eschatological activity of Being itself. Hence, what separates Heidegger's philosophy from the tradition is this active character of Being, which Heidegger explicitly distinguishes from human activity. For Heidegger, in the beginning is the Deed as the advent of Being. Time itself originates with the advent of Being "as the ever constant new beginning,"[48] "it is the ever-abiding, ever-present advent of the beginning."[49] History is the activity of Being in its self-revelation and self-concealment. History begins with the event (*Ereignis*) whereby Being deeds, gives, or sends (*Geschick*) itself to Man: "By revealing itself to Man historically, it is the determining ground and source of all history, it is itself 'history,' the ever continuing primordial 'event.'"[50] Man thinks and thanks this temporal present given to him by Being.[51] The historical locus of this sending of Being is the first speech of Being carried out by the thinkers whose few words (*physis, logos, aletheia*) originate all of Western philosophy, and that is also the originating act of the history of the West. Here to a confusing extent Heidegger conflates and ambiguously jumps from one such Deed of Being to another, making it appear that for him Time, History, and the History of the West originate in one and the same Event—as in this extract: "The existence of historical man begins at that moment when the first thinker to ask himself about the revealed nature of what-is, poses the question: What is what-is? . . . The initial revelation of what-is-in-totality, the quest for what-is-as-such, and the beginning of the history of the West are one and the same thing."[52]

Perhaps one way to understand this is to realize that the Deed is for Heidegger, too, a matter of Language. The Deed or event of Being takes place in and through language: "The event is considered the primordial speaking by which Being first expresses itself."[53] "In language Being itself speaks, but in such a way that it needs human speaking in order to make itself heard."[54] Without language nothing really is; "language alone brings what is, as something that is, into the open for the first time."[55] Heidegger puts it decisively that "only where there is language is there world." He also states that "we—mankind—are a conversation. . . . We have been a single conversation since the time when 'it is time.' Ever since time arose, we have existed historically."[56] Hence, for Heidegger, the speaking of Being is at the same time the establishing of Being: "poetry is the establishing of Being by means of the word."[57] And the same, of course, can be said of thinking, for the thinker thinks Being just as the poet names the gods such that "the essence of things receives a name, so that things for the first time shine out."[58] This partly explains, within Heidegger's conception, how it is that by speaking Being the early Greek thinkers brought about the advent of Being, or what could also be called the Deed of Being. And in so doing they brought time into being as well, not merely the time of Western history but of history as such, and in fact of all temporality in its essential being. For Heidegger all periods of subsequent history are merely phases of the articulation of Being in language, in the first place in the language of philosophy become metaphysics. In our own technological time of the metaphysics of Will, Being has concealed itself from language—except, perhaps, from the language of Heidegger himself. Heidegger never manages to account satisfactorily for his own role in the eschatology of Being or to explain how he alone has succeeded in recollecting Being. There are even indications in his very late work that Heidegger thinks that in and through the language of his own thought a new advent of Being is about to occur.[59]

Never before has a philosopher made such extensive claims for his own language or for language itself. Not surprisingly, Heidegger has to base his claims on the poetic intuitions about language of a poet, Hölderlin, who invokes the very words of the gods. Nothing could be in sharper contrast to this stance than Wittgenstein's modest and humble sense of words. Wittgenstein's plain words in all their simpleness and poverty stand out against Heidegger's grandiloquence of words in their profusion and confusion of multiple meanings and intentions. Yet despite this utmost contrast, the words of Heidegger and Wittgenstein belong together as against the words of Marx and Nietzsche, for the words of Heidegger and Wittgenstein are in retreat from the world, whereas those of Marx and Nietzsche are so engaged in the world as almost to be lost in it. The thought of Marx and Nietzsche is fully involved in the substantive issues of their, and still our own, time, whereas that of Heidegger and Wittgenstein seems remote and deliberately disengaged from worldly concerns. From the start, Heidegger removes his thought from real, substantive concerns through his fundamental separation of the ontic from the ontological and his preoccupation with the ontological alone. Thus, his much-vaunted concern for death is not an interest in real death at all, but merely in death ontologically conceived, that is, merely as a quasi-formal notion. It is this that at least partly justifies Adorno's gibe that Heidegger undertook to make of death "a professional secret for academics."[60] Even the Heidegger scholar Demske has to admit that though "death is the point of departure not only for a part, but in a certain sense for the whole analysis of

Dasein," yet "there is no such thing as a fully developed philosophy of death in Heidegger. Such a philosophy would consider death from both sides, the ontic and the ontological. It would investigate the ontic-existential phenomenon of death as it is ordinarily encountered in everyday life, i.e., in the dying of other men."[61] If Heidegger's philosophy has not as yet done that, what, one wonders, is the value of his purely ontological approach to death? Demske does not realize that what he is describing as the necessary task to complement Heidegger's ontology is precisely what a Wittgensteinian investigation of death would have been like, although Wittgenstein also never got around to carrying it out. Was it because for him death was not sufficiently interesting as a concept? He very rarely mentions death.

The analogous distinction to that of the ontic and ontological is in Wittgenstein that between the empirical and the conceptual or grammatical, and that distinction, too, comes to exercise a similar etherealizing and rarefying function in his philosophy. Wittgenstein makes it part of his philosophical method "not to advance any kind of theory,"[62] to "leave everything as it is,"[63] and he is so indifferent to substantive findings that he goes as far as to say that "one might also give the name 'philosophy' to what is possible *before* all new discoveries and invention."[64] In the same spirit, Heidegger remarks in his *Vom Wesen der Wahrheit* that the essence of truth could be better known when little was known. In giving an apologia for this concern with etymology, Werner Marx states that "if the word is that which 'nominates the topic', then the word seems to be more important than the topic. ... The words are the 'wellsprings' to which thinking must go again and again; they are the 'fountainheads' in which even the 'unspoken of the saying,' the 'mystery' prevails. These words are 'signs' which hint at what is 'to be thought over,' the 'essence of the topic' to those who think."[65] Thus Heidegger's search after the original, archaic, fundamental meanings of a "few Greek words," and some German ones as well, is strictly analogous to Wittgenstein's search after the basic, primitive meanings of some of the common words of our language. The style of exegesis is very different, but word exegesis it nevertheless is, for both seek to go down to the roots of words and uncover their truth there.

By contrast, to Marx or Nietzsche it is the topic, not the word or the concept, that is uppermost. The meanings of their words emerge out of the topic: in Marx the meaning of "value" emerges out of "das Kapital" or the economics of capitalism, and in Nietzsche the meaning of "value" emerges out of "the transvaluation of all Values" or the onset of European nihilism. However, being immersed in the topic they suffer the penalty of lacking a sensitivity for the specific, individual meanings of words; anything approaching Wittgenstein's concern for simple words and Heidegger's for the words of philosophy is rarely in evidence. In Marx and Nietzsche Language does not have the self-sufficient autonomy it has in Wittgenstein and Heidegger. But for that very reason, in the latter two, because they isolate Language words stand out of the silences surrounding them; they shine forth with a luminosity they had never possessed before in philosophy. This withdrawal of Language into itself is indicative of the withdrawal from the world of our contemporary thinkers. Their words, like those of our greatest artists, are often balanced on the edge of silence and madness, and sometimes slip over that edge. They are words uttered in solitude, silent words as far as the public world is concerned; and this silence of their words is their quietism in the face of the hostile, uncomprehending and disturbing world. This is why it would be pointless to try to synthesize the thinkers of the last century with those of this century to have, as it were, the best of both worlds, for their worlds are so different that to try to join them together would be like trying to have one's youth over again in one's old age. Only the Devil can perform such a feat for Faust. We, who do not command the Devil's help, can only relive the passage of Faust by reflection—as something that is already beyond recovery. Our world is different again; we can only try to find our own way of living and dying in it.

## SCENE II
### *Word, Thought, and Deed–once again*

The beginning of the Deed was a momentous event not merely for Western thought and history but for the first time for what we might now call planetary history. It marks the opening of the great thrust of Western activity, which from that point expanded to engulf the whole globe and which in its course transformed every other society. It is this activity that came to be known as Progress—the "form of our civilization," as Wittgenstein remarks.[1]

Considered more narrowly in relation to the passage of Faust, the Deed inaugurated a new and unprecedented relation among Man, Language, and Time that brought about a total reconception of the world, of common human being, and of individual existence. Whereas it had been hitherto a mere commonplace of popular lore, little regarded by philosophers, that Man distinguishes himself from the beasts by his capacity for speech, this simple observation took on unprecedented importance because of the new conception of speech as Language. Man could no longer be the rational animal (*zōon logon echon*) of Aristotle and the classical metaphysical tradition or the thinking reed of Pascal and the new subjective epistemology of science; Man had now become primarily both the creator and creature of his language. Whether Man was considered to be such right from the beginning of philosophy because, as Heidegger insists, the Logos meant language all along, is very doubtful, and is possibly simply Heidegger's way of reading back into the original beginning what only came with the beginning of the Deed.

It was only then that, through the discovery of Language in the modern sense, Man became the creator and destroyer of his worlds. For it is languages which speak, that is, open up, reveal and realize the world in relation to Man. And it is languages, too, which make silent, that is, obscure and render unknown the world to Man. The world of reality that each language reveals at any one time is thus necessarily partial, and even in a certain sense arbitrary, for it is but the reflection of one of indefinitely many possible human language-worlds. What other possibilities there are of uncovering the world cannot be known to those situated within their own language-world. To them, that is reality, and frequently they think of it as the only possible reality, calling it Being, God, or Nature. It is only when their language begins to crumble—when it is racked by insoluble antinomies or when it is confronted by an opposed language—only then can they begin to grasp that their own language-world is not the whole world.

What it is that a given language-world obscures and makes unknown of the world can only be discovered in the process of destroying that language-world. However, even that process is imprisoned within language, from which Man can therefore never escape, for even to destroy a language-world is to begin forming another in its place, no matter how incipient or purely negative that may be. So it is that Man only comes to know the world through this process of creation and destruction of language-worlds that takes place through a complex interaction of speech and silence. For every specific language-world contains its silences—both the things that are tacitly assumed and the things that are repressed without ever being admitted—and it is on these as much as on its consciously elaborated words and meanings that what it speaks depends. But when these silences are exposed—either when the tacit assumptions begin to be doubted or when its repressions begin to surface—then the truth of its speech is shown up as at best partial and at worst as a downright lie, and by this process the language-world is destroyed. Modes of knowledge, moralities, art-forms, even whole cultures and civilizations are placed in jeopardy when their languages are undermined, as we shall show further in proceeding to unfold the effects of the Deed on the tradition. And in the course of this creation and destruction of language-worlds Man also destroys and re-creates himself, for as old worlds perish and new ones emerge, so men redefine themselves and the nature of Man's being changes.

A change of this scope and historical magnitude was brought about by the translation of the Logos into the Deed. The world and Man as society and individual, that is, both as collective mankind and as individual existence, changed utterly. The whole metaphysical-theological language-world of the Logos was destroyed through the exposure of the hidden silence within it—the human all-too-human realities of Language it necessarily must deny and conceal. As a result, the Logos-world of Reason collapsed, that is, the world could no longer be taken as a rational whole suffused with an immanent order or "ratio" that men could discover because it harmonized with an innate rationality in themselves. The world of Reason could no longer be a "true" world. Even the world of scientific rationality became merely an abstraction, as Weber remarks: "The intellectual constructions of science constitute an unreal realm of artificial abstractions, which with their bony hands seek to grasp the blood-and-the-sap of true life without ever catching up with it."[2] And it was Nietzsche, more than anyone else, who exposed and undermined the notion of a "true" world, revealing it to have been the great Lie of our civilization. Similarly, the Cogito-world was destroyed when rational cogitation or universal thought could no longer be taken as the ground of Reality and when the world could no longer be deductively elaborated or even rationally thought through on the basis of a transcendental Subjectivity. Thought itself now tends to be mistrusted in its very attempt at revealing the truth of the world, as Nietzsche, with characteristic exaggeration, puts it: "Parmenides said, 'one cannot think of what is not'; we are at the other extreme, and say 'what can be thought of must certainly be a fiction.'"[3] With the destruction of the Logos and the Cogito, Man's own being and his relation to the world have become extremely problematical, for there is no longer any central reference point to act as a basis for securing truth. There is no Reason or Thought to serve as the center of Coherence, Reality, and Significance, the basic categories of language.[4]

For modern science, too, "in the beginning was the Deed" in that "nature is placed under the sign of active Man, of Man inscribing his technology in nature," as Bachelard puts it.[5] The operationalization of modern physics is part of that same translation of nature into activity: "In atomic physics, matter is defined by its possible reactions to human experiments . . . we are defining matter as a possible object of man's manipulation," as von Weizsäcker states.[6] The indeterminacy principle of quantum mechanics has analogous consequences in ruling out the possibility of signifying a true state of affairs on the subatomic level.

Thus in science, too, the Deed itself becomes the only possible criterion of truth; truth is judged by effectivity (*Wirklichkeit*). In its ultimate sense effectivity means the creation and destruction of language-worlds. One language-world is truer than another when it can comprehend the other within itself, as one of its own possibilities. But what is so comprehended is translated, and frequently it is even destroyed in the process, as is the case at present with traditional languages subject to scientific comprehension. Such a destruction is not a matter of annihilation, that is, of brute overpowering or any other such method of sheer liquidation; the question of which language is to win out as the truth is not decided by superior force or utility or the number of its adherents. Questions of power are, of course, at stake in any discussion of truth, but the power in question is not any extraneous external force but the inherent capacity of all languages: the power of devising and destroying concepts and arguments, erecting and demolishing experiences, experiments, or other testing procedures, and forming and unforming significances and values. It is the power of Coherence, Significance, and Reality, the basic categories, as these are affirmed in and through a particular language. Other modes of power have a predominantly causative role to play in relation to the power of a language, but they are not in themselves constitutive of truth, though it is important to stress that in the last resort even truth depends on some kind of power, not necessarily Nietzsche's will-to-power.

Prior to the nineteenth century it would have been barely possible to conceive of a language as a "world," an order of meaning that is all-encompassing for those who speak this language. This idea of Language arose in the course of the translation from the Logos through the Cogito to the Deed. However, as with the modern notion of Man, it is not to be denied that men have always had some awareness of language as not only their creation but their habitation and that at certain periods of history this has been explicitly conceptualized. There has always been thought about language because thought must take place in language; being self-referring language must be self-conscious: to whatever else words refer they must also refer to themselves. Nevertheless, no previous awareness or even conceptualization of language could ever be as aware of itself as is the modern, Faustian conception of Language. As we have shown, no matter how the word was previously conceived, either as sacred name, symbol, hieroglyph, or as logos, reason, thought, idea, representation, or sign, it was never understood as an element in a total system of meanings comprising an articulated structure of usage and expression; nor was any dialect or speech or discourse conceived of as the basis of cultural activity that touches on and embraces the whole of social life.

Innumerable differences distinguish the modern conception of Language from all previous ideas on speech and sign. Perhaps what is essential and decisive for the formation of a modern concept of Language is that it entails a certain way of theoretically relating the functions of word, thought, and deed such that these are not taken as separable from each other, but all three notions are seen as belonging within Language and shaping it. The deed has primacy only in the sense that under the instigation of the Faustian Deed both the word as Logos and the thought as Cogito are translated and transformed into Language. But this does not mean that deeds are somehow prior to words and thoughts.

The historical relation of Word, Thought, and Deed in philosophy is perhaps symbolically instructive of their actual relation in the analysis of language. Is it perhaps a symbolic irony of history that the Cogito is the middle term standing between the Logos and the Deed? Is it a further, not altogether fortuitous, fortunate coincidence that the Cogito emerges in the course of Descartes's *Meditations,* for *meditatio* is the Latin for the Greek *noesis,* which means thought, mind, intellect, and meaning—indeed, the same word as the German *Sinn*—and that in turn, as the cunning of history would have it, is the middle term of the passage from Faust? Taking that irony still further, we might say that this "thought" is the mediating term between word and deed, that it is the meaning-function which brings together words and deeds. Words without thought are separated from deeds, that is to say, from the life-activities in relation to which they can have a meaning, becoming at best nothing but sound systems such as communications signals. Similarly, deeds without thought are separated from words, that is to say, from speech and discourse, becoming nothing but blind gestures or the motions of sheer behavior. Thought itself is not anything separable from words and deeds, for it is the meaning-function in terms of which words and deeds relate to each other; or, in Wittgensteinian terms, it is the use-function that gives words a meaning in relation to deeds. Thought as meaning is not a disembodied sense; it is the connection between the body of discourse and the equally palpable body of life-activities. If thought is the "soul" of words, animating them and keeping their meaning alive, then it is not a "soul" that can survive the demise of its body, it is a "soul" only in the Aristotelian sense of being the form of the body of words and deeds; or, as Wittgenstein expresses it: "thinking is not an incorporeal process which lends life and sense to speaking, and which it would be possible to detach from speaking, rather as the Devil took the shadow of Schlemiehl from the ground."[7] The literary allusion is, of course, to Chamisso's folktale of Peter Schlemiehl, which brings us once more back to the passage of Faust, for this is a popular, comic Faust, deriving from Hasidic sources. We can interpret it to mean that though the Devil can steal the soul of Faust from his body he cannot remove the "soul" of thought from the body of Faustian Language.

Despite their inseparability, it is, nevertheless, deeds that have primacy in the Faustian conception of Language—so much so that the misconception has tended to arise that words and thoughts are themselves nothing but deeds. Thus, Foucault remarks that "modern thought, from its inception and in its very density, is a certain mode of action."[8] And this is certainly true of many extreme tendencies of modern philosophy: for example, in the Idealism of Croce and Gentile, where thinking is taken as a kind of creative activity; in pragmatism, where thinking is practical action and effectiveness; in the activist philosophy of Sorel, where thinking becomes passion and intuition; and in the numerous behaviorist psychologies that transform thinking into mere reflex and instrumental behavior. But these are not typical of true Faustian thought—there, the aim is always to strike and maintain a balance between word, thought, and deed. Perhaps nowhere is this more apparent than in Wittgenstein's philosophy of Language. There the Deed is given its primacy, for Language is primarily conceived of in terms of the "language-game" as life-activity or the "form of life." However, the language-game is taken only as the primitive basis of any language and not all there is to it, though even so this activist emphasis is often overplayed.

This poised balance of word, thought, and deed Wittgenstein only attained in the late sections of the *Philosophical Investigations*. And, paradoxically, that work was made possible by his earlier *Tractatus*, in which the word, the thought, and the deed are totally separated. In the *Tractatus* philosophy the Deed—as willed action, as "the ethical deed," as the work of art—lies outside language and the world of facts; or, better put, it is immanent inside language and the facts as something that only shows itself and cannot be said. It is in the realm of the unspeakable, in silence, and so even outside the *Tractatus* itself, though, as Wittgenstein shows—that is to say, makes implicitly clear within the work and explicitly so in the preface—this unsayable Deed is the most important thing for him both in the world and the work. It is that which shows itself in the world, which cannot be spoken but can be done, and seen, that the work sets itself to demonstrate, as it were, from the inside by delimiting what can be spoken. What can be spoken is determined by a pure rationalistic logic, for language is ultimately logic structuring the world of atomic facts with inexorable severity. It is the world-picture of a totalitarian Logos, a bounded totality dominated by pure logic, from which there is no exception or escape. It is at once a totally objective world of facts and a totally subjective world of thoughts: the world and the "I" are coextensive in a completely solipsistic Cogito that embraces the totality of things.[9] To paraphrase Hamlet, it is both bound in a nut-shell and counting itself king of infinite logical space.

It was from such a dangerous impasse, which led him to abandon philosophy for a time, that Wittgenstein saved himself by a return to the most humble word of all: spoken language, even as it comes from the mouths of babes. Just as Faust is brought back to life by mingling in the throng of humble townsfolk on Easter Sunday, so, too, it is likely that Wittgenstein was brought back to philosophy, and had his attention turned to living language, by his encounter with the children that he taught in an elementary school.[10] It is also likely that it was from the experience of teaching children that he derived his fruitful, though potentially misleading, idea of the language-game. Wittgenstein instances as examples of language-games such culturally and intellectually varied activities as the giving and obeying of orders, at one extreme, and the forming and testing of hypotheses, at the other.[11] Even from this it is apparent that he is not narrowing the idea of Language down to what came later to be known in Linguistic Philosophy as "common" or "ordinary" language. In fact, the German expression Wittgenstein employs, *allgemeine Sprache,* which is usually translated as "common language," also means universal, overall, and general—the very opposite of *common* in the sense of ordinary and conventional, though it does convey some of the implications of "vulgar speech." Any translation of the German expression can only be adequately carried out if it is also understood that by *common* Wittgenstein means, above all, mutual and shared. The translation of a single word is here of crucial importance for the whole of modern philosophy, for this is perhaps the most important word in Wittgenstein as well as in Linguistic Philosophy. Language is common language for Wittgenstein only in a very complex and ultimately philosophic sense, one that Wittgenstein himself never attempted to explicate fully or render theoretically. It needs to be so rendered, for this word *common* is itself no longer a common word; that is perhaps something Wittgenstein was himself unable fully to grasp, and so he opened the door to the kind of mistranslation and resultant miscomprehension that gave rise to Linguistic Philosophy. This whole philosophy is built on the foundations of that one equivocal word: for a church to be founded on the rock of a pun might be a mystery beyond human comprehension, but for a modern school of thought to be so founded must surely be a joke of history.

The language-game approach to language is thus a reaction against the extreme forms of the Logos and Cogito of the *Tractatus,* against the formal logic and solipsistic subjectivity that are severed from willing and the ethical deed and that relegate it to silence. Wittgenstein was himself only partly aware of how this is also a destruction of the Logos and Cogito of the metaphysical tradition, for he seems to have been relatively ignorant of the historical antecedents of the *Tractatus'* logic and subjectivity; nor was he fully aware of what kind of a metaphysical dream the *Tractatus* was, despite itself, fulfilling in its own annihilation of metaphysics. His most pressing personal concern was to wake from the logico-solipsistic nightmare in which he felt himself imprisoned, and so he made no serious efforts to locate it or himself within the great tradition of philosophy. Nevertheless, it is no mere accident that the *Investigations* opens with a long extract from the *Confessions* of Augustine expounding how a child learns to speak a language, for Augustine stands at the end of the civilization of antiquity, and so he has a central place in the great tradition: he looks back on the classical past and forward to the Christian future; he inherits the Logos and presages the Cogito, since his confessions lead into and are the model for the meditations of Descartes. Descartes is himself not mentioned in the *Investigations,* but his presence is strongly felt there, especially when the issue of "private-language" is in question. The vision of the child as a soul coming into the world like a solitary thinker and deducing the relation of words to things from the actions of its parents and teachers—an emblematic vision of the human condition in the world—is the one that Wittgenstein sought to dispel through the opposed vision of the collective, common play of men as children—the language-game.

The language-game view of language sees it as a play of word, thought, and deed. The word is the signifier, that which carries the burden of signification, either as speech, or as marks, or as any other material medium. The thought (German: *Sinn*) is the meaning or the signified; it is the meaning-function that may be referred to, depending on the context, as sense or idea or concept or notion. The deed is the activity of signifying, the language-game activity that surrounds the signifier and signified; it is the form of life in which they are both embedded. What is so distinctive about the language-game approach to a general theory of signification is that it treats the opposition of signifier to signified as no more than a formal distinction within the sign as language-game. It is useful to make this separation in any study of signs, because it permits each side of the distinction to be studied separately, but no real division into two separate elements is involved: the signifier only exists in relation to the signified, and both are merely functional parts of a totality that is a language-game—akin to two distinguishable roles within a play. The signified is not any detachable element or item of thought or meaning that is separable from this play. Thus, the Wittgenstein "theory" of signs would be fundamentally opposed to that of de Saussure, for whom "the linguistic sign unites, not a thing and a name, but a concept and a sound image."[12] For de Saussure, concept and sound image are separate psychological elements, so that the sign "is then a two-sided psychological entity" whose "two elements are intimately united, and each recalls the other."[13] It is almost expressly in opposition to such psychological theories of signification that Wittgenstein developed his language-game critique.

Thought as the meaning-function can, of course, be analytically identified as the concept or idea or sense, but it is not an item, as it were, lodged in the mind; for example, Wittgenstein shows that it can never be identified with the image or mental representation that might, as a matter of psychological fact, accompany the use of the word. The "thought" emerges as the meaning that is inherent in the complex social interaction of the word and the deed. The word as the body of the sign, the material meaning-bearer, can only be analytically separated from the deed seen as the whole context of human activities in which the word has a meaning. Words do not exist as acoustical facts in themselves, they are only analyzable portions of the total language-game activity; we even hear them differently when we hear them as words. Nor do words or sentences or any other units of language have any meaning in themselves, but only in the total act of signification which is the human praxis in which they have a function and play a part. As Wittgenstein put it, "a sentence only makes sense in the midst of the stream of life."[14] And, of course, a sentence can never on its own be a proposition, judgment, or even statement, but only in the context of a given discourse, and ultimately only in relation to the whole language in question together with its grammar, logic, and what Wittgenstein calls its logical-grammar. But in turn, a language and its structures only exist insofar as they can be studied in the language-games people enact. Hence de Saussure's other opposition of *Langue* and *Parole* is also not a difference of two entities but only a theoretically formal distinction useful in the science of linguistics. Both the Langue and the Parole are theoretic entities that grammarians, logicians, and linguists artificially elaborate on the basis of the heterogeneous mass of linguistic activities they observe in practice. Thus, one might speak of them as ideal-typical theoretical constructs; and, as with all ideal-types, they can be based on real ideas or rules, for those people who speak languages with formulated rules of logic and grammar—usually high-cultural and literary languages—consciously orient their speech to these formal rules, which thereby act as real determinants on their language.

A Wittgensteinian approach to signification can thus very easily be developed into a general theory of meaning, one which could be made to combine with Max Weber's *Verstehende* sociology. A bridge must be established between Wittgenstein's notion of the language-game and Weber's meaningful social action. This can be done by extending the language-game approach beyond language into other meaningful areas of human action, and by realizing that this approach itself is based on a general theory of "ideal types," which Wittgenstein fitfully glimpses when he remarks that "nothing is more crucial than the construction of fictive concepts which teach us to understand our own."[15] Thus, the meaning of non-linguistic modes of social actions could be examined and understood on the model of linguistic ones; hence, a general theory of meaningful action has to cover both linguistic and non-linguistic action.

Such a theory might be elaborated by developing an account of thought or meaning in terms of at least three fundamental notions: sense, significance, and explanation or ground (German: *Sinn, Bedeutung,* and *Erklärung*). The meaning of any linguistic or non-linguistic act can be examined in terms of either its sense or its significance or its explanation, or any conjunction of these. The sense is the kind of meaning that primarily linguistic entities have, though other signs also have sense, and it might even be ascribed to non-signifying entities. The sense of a word, sentence, or other language unit is its meaning-import—what it is saying—looked at in terms of the meanings of its constituent elements: the concepts involved, their logical-grammar, the conventional grammar if it is a sentence, its coherence as a statement, etc. It is the sort of meaning that lends itself to being analyzed, explicated, or translated in a formal manner. Sense is the basic notion behind all formal studies such as logic, grammar, syntax, formal semantics, and structuralist analyses of systems of signs or objects. Significance has more to do with importance, point, and value: it is what something—which need not necessarily be a linguistic unit—points to or refers to, what it is directed or oriented toward, its "value" implications, its emotional charge or mood, etc. Significance contains the notions of reference and import (which must be further distinguished). It is the basic notion underpinning all informal semantic studies of language as well as all critical studies of signs and objects in their cultural bearings. Finally, explanation concerns the more objectively conceived circumstantial "subjective" meaning, which is primarily directed at words, actions, or cultural objects independently of any sense or significance; it is "subjective" meaning in the sense of reason, motive, cause, and grounding such as must figure in any common-sense account, legal justification, or sociological explanation of the thing in question. Thus the explanation or ground of a sentence is why it was uttered by a given speaker on a certain occasion, what its utterance was intended to achieve, what its utterance reveals about the speaker's motives or reasons for acting—in other words, what is its cause and what it can cause, in all the senses of that complex word. Usually, of course, the sense and significance of a sentence will disclose its cause, or give a lead to it, but it can happen that these only hide the real cause. And, of course, acts that have no sense or significance only have an explanatory meaning, for example, the symptoms of a neurotic or the panic of a crowd.

We have deliberately used the term *significance* both in connection with the fundamental categories of logic and truth, Coherence, Significance, and Reality, and with the three kinds of meaning, sense, significance, and explanation. There is a reason for taking that as the unifying central term that relates truth and meaning. It is out of significance as meaning that Significance as truth and logic derives. Significance is the basic notion behind all signification, and signification is basic to meaning as a whole. Without signification in signs, and ultimately without language, there could be no human meaning. Hence, language is the basis of human action as such, even when that action is in no way linguistic or symbolic—which, of course, is not to say that language in any way pre-dates or is prior to such action. We need still to affirm the Faustian pronouncement that in the beginning was the Deed, not the Word or the Thought. However, a deed has significance only because it occurs in the context of language, outside of which there can be no deeds or meaningful social action as such. But language in turn depends on the significance of deeds; it arises out of the signifying activities or language-games in which significance is constituted through the interest, importance, utility, and general orientation of human beings toward words and things, as this is established in their acting together with and in relation to those words and things. In thus establishing the significance of things and words, human beings come to communicate, and so create language. And it is this primary sense of significance that underlies all signification and meaning, so that out of it through a long process of intellectual development and refinement derives Significance as our primary philosophical category and criterion of truth. Truth is thus grounded in human significance, in which power plays an indispensable part.

As we have indicated already, the power that is so crucial to the establishing of truth is ultimately the creative and destructive power of language. It is that notion of Power *(Kraft)* which is very closely attendant on Faust's Deed. All our Faustian philosophers have emphasized it, but invariably only in its creative forms; the destructive workings of this Power are only there, as it were, by implied contrast. It is the creation of language and its creative workings that they stress; destruction they can only accommodate as a necessary prelude to new creation. This is the "silence" within these philosophies, the absence formed from what they are intent on repressing. The exposure of this silence has a destructive effect on them. The inversion of this relationship of creation and destruction brings about a fundamental overturning of Faustian philosophy, provided that destruction is understood not simply as the inverse of creation. This brings on the nihilistic recursion of the passage of Faust. It is a repetition of the Deed, but this time as a deed of negation, which, of course, it secretly was from the beginning. But, as such, it can no longer be Faust's Deed; it must be the deed of someone symbolically quite other than Faust. The Faustian philosophers of the Deed are by the nature of their thought unable to see that other side of it, that which contradicts their conscious intent. This is perhaps most clearly apparent from their attitude to language, which they tend to perceive in its creative workings with destruction as merely an implied contrast. This perception of language is relatively obvious in Marx and Nietzsche, so we will illustrate it by reference to the less straightforward cases of Wittgenstein and Heidegger.

Wittgenstein places great stress on the creation of new concepts and little on their destruction, even though that was what his language analysis in fact achieved. Conceptual creativity, he insists, is an indispensable prerequisite even of logic and mathematics; repeatedly he speaks of "conceptual change" and "new concepts" even with respect to mathematical and logical necessity, as in this passage: "The mathematical Must is only another expression of the fact that mathematics forms concepts. And concepts help us to comprehend things. They correspond to a particular way of dealing with situations. Mathematics forms norms."[16] And again, "The introduction of a new rule of inference can be conceived as a transition to a new language-game."[17] Unfortunately, nowhere in Wittgenstein is there any proper theoretical explanation of the creation of concepts; he makes no attempt to set out the conditions and restrictions on this basic intellectual activity. Part of the reason for this failure is that there is no sense of dialectical development in Wittgenstein, and this precludes his studying the historical origin, alteration, and destruction of concepts, especially of the concepts of philosophy. Wittgenstein conceives of his own philosophical activity—which he speaks of as the dissolution of metaphysical puzzles, without being aware that it also involves a destruction of concepts—in a quite undialectical and unhistorical fashion, and that must surely be the main reason why he is so unaware that this is a mode of conceptual destruction. He sees it naively, as if it were no more than a clarification or purification of concepts, as if all that was involved was seeing through misconceptions, untangling muddles, and removing the cramps or the "neuroses" of understanding. He does not properly realize that there is a critical, destructive edge to all his conceptual clarifying activities, that they do not leave language untouched, and that considerable theoretical elaboration of how the destruction of concepts can take place is required before we can explain what it is that these dissolutions amount to, since his own explanations are no better than the rules-of-thumb of the practitioner. As they stand, Wittgenstein's notes on the practice of philosophy make it sound like a craft of language, a kind of practical criticism, rather than the historically decisive intellectual activity it really is. There is a touch of the *philosophe naïf*, to which we have already alluded, in this as well.

The main deficiency in Wittgenstein is the lack of any explicitly developed notions of time and history, and in particular of a history of philosophy in terms of which he could interpret his own work.[18] This lack is, however, an opening created by that work itself; for even though it leaves absent the dimension of time because of its own non-historic practice, yet at the same time it creates an absent presence of time as a gap in its own "problematic," in Althusser's sense, which once perceived demands to be filled. Such an absent presence of historical time is implied by Wittgenstein himself in his continual recourse to imaginary constructs of anthropology and natural history as surrogates for real history. Thus, for example, all his fictions of imaginary tribes playing fantastic language-games are really ways of historicizing the practices of language; like the *Ficciones* of Borges, they are miniature imaginary possibilities of real historical worlds. He explains the point of his fictitious natural history as follows: "But our interest does not fall back upon these possible causes of the formation of concepts: we are not doing natural science; nor yet natural history—since we can also invent fictitious natural history for our purposes."[19] Elsewhere he insists on real natural history: "What we are supplying are really remarks on the natural history of human beings; we are not contributing curiosities however, but observations which no one has doubted, but which have escaped remark only because they are always before our eyes."[20] This need not necessarily be inconsistent. However, the difficulty remains: how are we to know whether the real or fictitious "natural history" remarks are not mere curiosities? And if fictions are allowed just as well as facts, then in what sense can they not be doubted? And, in any case, how can facts or fictions that are so obvious as not to be doubted fail to be mere curiosities, since only that which is trivial gains immediate universal agreement, whereas any serious observation is bound to provoke dispute, if only in interpretation? The nub of the matter is that neither historical anthropology nor fictitious natural history is any substitute for real history, and the latter is missing in Wittgenstein, though a place stands waiting for it.

In this respect Wittgenstein is deficient as compared to all our other Faustian philosophers, in each of whom there is a strong sense of development and historical time attendant on the Deed. Historicity as stemming from the Deed is one of the hallmarks of all Faustian thought, as we shall go on to show. Even though each Faustian thinker has his own conception of time and history, there is a common preoccupation with active development or progressive movement.[21] Thus time in Marx, despite Althusser's admonitions, seems still quite close to the Hegelian dialectic of unfolding development from one stage to a higher one. Nietzsche's time is, by contrast, much more organicist; it moves in cyclical curves of genesis, maturation, decadence, and demise. Heidegger's time is, as we have seen, quasi-eschatological, directed toward a future end, whether that be death or new beginning.

In Heidegger, language assumes something of the role of God's creative Deed, for by its creative power it brings forth truth and time, human-being and beings themselves. Such a strain of thought occurs in most of his works, seemingly even becoming more pronounced in his late ones.

> Language is the precinct (*templum*), that is, the house of Being. The nature of language does not exhaust itself in signifying, nor is it merely something that has the character of sign or cipher.[22]

Heidegger's approach to language goes beyond signification and significance, entering into things themselves: "When we go to the well, when we go through the woods, we are always already going through the word 'well,' through the word 'woods.'"[23] Things themselves take on the character of words. Heidegger's unacknowledged Alexandrian orientation toward the word as Logos is evident. This Logos is itself the creative Deed giving rise to the world, which is, as he states, a mode of activity: "the perpetually altering circuit of decision and production, of action and responsibility." Language for Heidegger, since it is essentially creative, is preeminently poetic: "Language itself is poetry in the essential sense."[24] But "poetry" is to be taken here to mean creativity as such, and not merely the work of poets, though that is its highest form. It is the "projective saying" by which things are brought into being, "the saying of world and earth."

> Poetry is the establishing of being by means of the word. . . . But, because being and the essence of things can never be calculated and derived from what is present, they must be freely created, laid down and given.[25]

Language is this poetry, in that it is the free creation of the essence and being of things. It is not merely that "essence and being express themselves in language,"[26] a view quite compatible with Wittgenstein's dictum that "essence is grammar,"[27] but that language brings the things themselves into being and that without language they would not be.

In these approaches to language, poetry, and creativity, Heidegger is most evidently recollecting the early-Faustian German Idealist speculations on language deriving from Vico and harking back to the Renaissance "alchemy of the word"—those speculations of Herder, Hamann, and Humboldt which were to give rise to the modern notion of Language. But Heidegger goes far further in elevating language than any simple early Romantic appreciation of it, one that states merely that "poetry is the primitive language of an historical people."[28] Following on Hölderlin, he develops a kind of onto-theology of poetry as essential language. "Poetry is the saying of the unconcealedness of what is. Actual language at any given moment is the happening of this saying, in which a people's world historically arises for it and the earth is preserved as that which remains closed."[29] In Heidegger's elaboration, words such as *language, poetry, creativity, History, People* no longer have anything like their mundane meanings; they have been exalted in a kind of freely creative, quasi-poetic way.

Against this Heideggerian poetic evocation of language it is imperative to stress a Wittgensteinian practical materiality of the language-game. Language is itself something only in relation to things, and these it does not bring into being, for language as word is a material medium quite like things themselves, a medium by which human beings can act on things in a way not unlike the way they can act on them with their tools. As well as this instrumental function, language as deed is a human social praxis by which people interact with one another. And language as thought is a meaning-function which arises out of these relations brought about by words and deeds, relations that can themselves be reflected on and described by means of language. Though language does not bring things into being or create them, it does enable human beings to relate to each other and to things, and in so doing to realize creatively the nature of themselves and those things. To realize something is not to create it *ex nihilo* or to bring it fully into the open; it is merely to reveal or open up one aspect of it relative to the language at one's disposal, with its specific characteristics and deficiencies of word, thought, and deed. It is only in this sense that language can be spoken of as disclosing things. But here it must also be remembered that every such disclosure is also a concealment, for to reveal some aspects of anything is necessarily to conceal others equally capable of being disclosed. If a language may be said to "create" something, it must also be said to "destroy" it at the same time. This is why the destruction of one language by another can sometimes be a liberating act that reveals new truths, for what the one language by its very nature had to obscure, suppress, and render unknown or unknowable may be revealed and made known by the other. For that which is unsayable in one language can be said in another. The ineffable which is outside all language is for that reason outside all knowledge.

The language of the Deed is itself subject to all these limitations of language. And though we have no other language that is sufficiently "other" to expose its limits, yet we can trace them by registering the antinomies that arise within that language itself. To do so we must follow through the dialectics of the Deed.

# ACT II

---

## *MAN, TIME, AND NOTHING*

◆

## SCENE I
*Dialectics of the Deed (quasi una fantasia)*

### I

"And an eternal, living Activity works to create anew what has been created, lest it entrench itself in rigidity."[1] Out of the hand of Goethe issues the Deed as living activity (*lebendiges Tun*), in pristine purity. It is the Deed in-and-for-itself: activity that is both subject and object, perpetual movement without datable beginning or end, never staying still; it is always Becoming, never Being, since to be arrested in Being even for a single moment is to fall into Nothing. By this creative power of the Deed things emerge out of Nothing in their striving to become. Hence the Deed is a *creatio ex nihilo* analogous to God's original act of creation; it is that act itself understood as continuing forever, and so maintaining creation in constant Becoming.

Because Goethe could keep his Deed so close to God—to the theological, metaphysical, and hermetic sources from which it originated—he was never forced to face difficult questions about it. Analogous to God's creation, his Deed remained self-evident; and though it was no longer the traditional God that was being invoked, yet the Eternal could still be appealed to in a spirit close enough to the tradition for it not to make too great a demand on modern credulity. It was only when the Deed fell into godless hands that the difficulties began. It was no longer so easy to assign an Eternal as the original agent of the Deed; it was no longer so simple to speak of eternal activity in time that moves without cease; it was no longer possible to think of Nothing as the void prior to creation. The traditional conceptions of Agency, Time, and Nothing, on which Goethe had still implicitly relied, could no longer be invoked in a post-Idealist problematic in which God was already absent. And so, surreptitiously or openly, difficult questions began to be asked about the modern Deed, questions analogous to those that theologians once asked of the Deed of God:

Who did it?

When was it done?

What was there prior to it, and what will there be after it?

These questions sound as childish or as profound as the questions that theologians used to ask, such as "What was God doing before the creation of the World?" And just as this theological question could either be dismissed as beneath contempt (he was preparing a hell for such as ask foolish questions) or could be followed into the depths of the mystery of God's creation (theological speculations about time from Augustine onward), so, too, the modern questions can either be dismissed as too silly for words or pursued into those regions where the thought of modernity itself begins to quake and dissolve. For modern thought, which invites and simultaneously rejects such questioning, has no ready answers to them; that is to say, it has too many answers that are incompatible with each other. These opposed answers generate the antinomies of the modern world, which are in many respects like the antinomies Kant generated by the questions he posed to the "pure reason" of the post-theological world of the Enlightenment. And so, as Kant did, we too must conclude that though these questions demand to be asked, yet they cannot be conclusively answered within the ambit of the thought that provokes them.[2] They point to the limits of "modern reason," that is, to the inherent limitations of our intellectual world. We shall find that from its very beginning the modern world was racked by these antinomies of the Deed, as modern thought is stretched from one to the other of its contradictory sides.

But let us put our questions to the Deed and see what contradictions they provoke. "Who did it?" That question touches on the agency of the Deed. And the initial and most obvious answer to it is that it is Man who is the doer of the Deed. Man is the sovereign Subject, the supreme Actor, the cogitating consciousness through which the Deed is enacted and by which the human world is created. But no sooner is that answer given than it becomes obvious that Man himself is no more than a being within that world, merely an outcome of its creative activity. And so Man very quickly appears as the resultant of the Deed, its object rather than its subject, not the creator but the creature, not the producer but the product of his world. Does Man do the Deed, or does the Deed do Man? Both are equally possible within modern thought, as we shall presently discover, but both together are impossible, for one answer generates all the varieties of modern humanism, the other of modern anti-humanism, and these are locked in irreconcilable contradiction.

"When was it done?" The initial answer is that it was done in the very beginning, in other words, that the Deed is the beginning of Time itself. The Deed on this count is the primordial activity that gives rise to the movement of Time, which can either be the cosmic time of the world (Big-Bang) or the evolutionary time of nature, or the developmental time of history, or of Western civilization, or of modernity. It is a complex time of Progress which generates its own internal antinomies. The questions that can in turn be asked of it are these: does this time of

Progress have an end or is it endless? Did it have one specific beginning or has it always been re-beginning? Depending on the answers to these questions the whole meaning of Progress will alter: it can be seen as the progress of history leading to a preordained culminating end, or as the progress of human evolution with no end, or as somehow both together, one within the other, an end to history leading to further evolution. But no matter how one seeks to reconcile them, these answers insist on contradicting each other. Just so, the whole complex of the time of Progress, as being coextensive with the Deed, is itself contradicted by the opposed answer to the original question: that time does not begin with the Deed but, rather, that the Deed takes place in a time that is prior to it, that this other non-active time gives rise to activity, and that it is not a time of continuous movement in Progress but a quite different complex of times. On this view, progressive time is but the illusory outcome of other non-progressive times. Once again both answers to the problem of time and the Deed seem necessary; once again they cannot both be right.

The third and final question, "What was there prior to the Deed and what will there be after it?", introduces another of the basic modern dilemmas, that revolving around Nothing. The Nothing of modern thought is no longer the nothingness of theology; it is a nothingness that is to be given the new secular meaning of Nihilism. And so the question introduces a new problematic relation, that between the Deed and Nihilism. Is Nihilism something that is there prior to the Deed, or does the Deed itself bring Nihilism into being? Put historically, does the time of Progress originate out of a preexistent Nothing, or does it bring about that Nothing? Furthermore, does the time of Progress end in Nothing, or does it end that Nothing? To each question both answers are equally possible; hence, the whole relationship between the Deed and Nihilism is fraught with antinomies. The Deed as creative activity might be seen paradoxically as giving rise to the nothingness of Nihilism, and as destructive activity it might be seen, equally paradoxically, as destroying that Nothing. The Deed contains within itself all these contradictory possibilities; depending on which one chooses, one will answer the decisive question of modern times, "Can Nihilism be overcome?", quite differently.

The antinomies of the Deed and Man, of the Deed and Time, and of the Deed and Nothing mark out the limits of modern thought. They are the contradictions of humanism, of Progress, and of Nihilism. All modern thought is trapped within them and cannot get beyond them. No modern thought can have the answer to the problem of humanism, that of Progress, and that of Nihilism. We live inside these problems, and for us they have no solutions. The fact that proposed answers to them veer from one extreme to the other and back again shows them to be limit-problems—ones that establish the inner boundaries of thought from the inside, as it were. Hence, here we do not need to go beyond the boundaries to know them to be such. The inner limit is that extreme of thought which is by itself untenable but which cannot be overcome or gone beyond; from it one can only recoil into the thought again, eventually to end up at another, equally untenable, extreme of the same thought. Being thus tossed from pole to pole eventually forces one to recognize that these opposite extremes belong together as the inner boundaries of a single thought-field, and that the one demands the other.

So it is with the modern thought of the Deed. So it is with every mode of thought—with every theory, system, philosophy, science, logic.[3] Ultimately it is so, too, with every culture, society, and civilization. All human forms and constructs contain within themselves contradictions that reveal themselves as insoluble antinomies, for, ultimately, all human forms are based on language, and antinomies arise from the nature of language as a mode of signification or symbolic form. Every specific language and every symbolic totality can only signify by being partial: to say one thing it must deny, reject, or ignore another; it must exclude some things in order to include others; it must blank out even in the process of revealing; it can only notice one aspect by simultaneously denying itself the capacity to see another that conflicts with it; it can only see what it highlights by not seeing what it places in its own shadow. The exclusion may be more or less implicit in the inclusion itself; it may be more or less conscious to those who speak the language in question. Thus, if the language is a system of concepts propounding certain truths, then that which is said in the language to be a lie is itself self-consciously part of the language; similarly, where a moral language enjoins things it is at the same time aware of the things it is prohibiting that are contrary to itself. It is in this way that just as every morality forms its own immorality and every legal world forms its own underworld, so, too, every system of truth forms its own lies, for these lies are only such in relation to the truths. And just as the law forces some people into crime, and morality pushes them into being immoral, so a system of established truths will compel some into affirming its own lies, as, for example, every religion spawns its own heresies. These are the social contraries of every language form.

Beyond such explicit contraries, however, there are also deeper unconscious contradictions that arise from the nature of language as a mode of signification necessarily partial and incomplete. Beyond the more or less conscious denials, oppositions, and suppressions of every language there is an even darker unknowing, one of which the speakers of a language cannot in principle be aware, which forms, as it were, its repressed unconscious. This is the dark un-reality that a language necessarily obscures in realizing the Reality it illumines. And just as every light casts its own shadows, so every form of speech promotes its own silences. Thus, every language carries within itself its own counter-self, or alter-Reality, that which is made up of all the things the language must necessarily exclude from awareness, deny to consciousness, keep from being recognized in order to be able to make known the things it does. These are its inner silences, which act as the tacit background enabling its outward speech to be heard. Without them there could be no speech. And it is the exposure of these silences that, as we have indicated before, destroys a language. Such silences are not merely the things that one language does not speak about but which some other does, they are not simply the things a language neglects; rather, they are the specific things that a language does establish precisely in and by its necessary repressions and unconscious denials. Hence, they are not merely its omissions but are indeed the absences created by what is present.

In the language of every society, culture, civilization, or epoch of history there must always be such a concealed Silence, an obverse dark side like the hidden face of the moon, necessarily masked by the bright side of what is actually spoken about and open to view. This is why no language can ever fully know itself, for as soon as it begins to disclose itself to itself, it begins to destroy itself. Only with the hindsight of history is it possible to know what it is that a language conceals. A remark of Adorno and Horkheimer is illustrative of this:

> Europe has two histories: a well-known, written history and an underground history. The latter consists in the fate of the human instincts and passions which are displaced and distorted by civilization. The Fascist present in which the hidden side of things comes to light also shows the relationship between written history and the dark side which is overlooked in the official legend of the nationalist states, as well as in the critique of the latter.[4]

This comment stands at the head of a short discursus on what might be called the secret history of the body in European civilization. If developed further it would have to be a history of the languages of the body current at the various periods of Western culture, intended to reveal what it is of bodily reality that these languages conceal. Of course, it is not facts about the body that are denied or simple natural instincts that are suppressed, for what is concealed of the body is itself an alter-reality conditioned by language, one that requires for its disclosure a meaningful historical interpretation functioning as a language-analysis on the model of psychoanalysis.

However, there is one way in which the absences in a language do make themselves known within that language itself, and that is through the contradictions and antinomies that emerge as conflicts and insoluble problems within it—as it were, the neurotic symptoms of a culture. In every language, there must be that which it denies, rejects, and leaves unspoken, and also, at an unconscious level, that which it represses and renders utterly unspeakable, and, because of this, limits are formed which cause contradictions to develop. The partiality of language makes limitation and contradiction unavoidable; in formal terms, it is because in order to establish an inclusion, an exclusion is required, that a division or boundary line must also form between the inside and the outside of any language. Because every language form involves delimitations, it has its limits, as it were, its inner forms, marking off its distinctive shape and establishing its formal identity. And it is these limits that by exclusion and repression give rise to contradictions and irresolvable antinomies within the language.

It is in the nature of Language to be in contradiction: for, on the one hand, insofar as a language or symbolic form discloses a certain kind of Reality it represents itself as being the truth; but, on the other hand, insofar as it omits other potential realities, and, specifically, conceals its own alter-Reality, it is excluding other truths, so that it itself is merely partial, a half-truth at best, if not an outright lie. Every language is thus contradictory, both truth and lie at once. As Eliot said: "The knowledge imposes a pattern, and falsifies" ("East Coker"). This is an antinomy that is in principle irresolvable, since it is inherent in the paradoxical nature of language which cannot itself be overcome; hence, there is no synthesis, no sublation, no dialectical reconciliation of this contradiction. Dialectics itself derives ultimately from this basic antinomy in language. Or, as Adorno puts it: "The name dialectics says no more, to begin with, than that objects do not go into their concepts without leaving a remainder, that they come to contradict the traditional norm of adequacy."[5]

As well as this ultimate contradictoriness of Language as such, there are specific contradictions inherent in every particular language. These are the contradictions that arise when the language strikes against its own limits. As we have said, limits are the outcome of delimitations, and delimitations are necessary to establish identities, since nothing can be identified without being delimited. But as soon as a delimitation shows itself as also a restriction, then the thing so identified reveals itself as other than it is, that is, as other than its identity. It is, and is not, that same one thing, for "as the heterogeneous collides with its limit it exceeds itself."[6] Out of such collisions contradictions are bound to occur, both because within a language, as it were, different delimitations come sooner or later to conflict, and because externally, as a language changes under the impact of general changes of history, it will break through its restraining boundaries. This latter case is above all precipitated by the clash of opposed languages, which can occur as part of a general clash of cultures; in such a situation one language opens up and exposes the limitations of another and so serves to provoke contradictions within it. But even where there is no conflict of languages, contradictions are still bound to arise: where a multiplicity of delimitations operate they are bound to conflict, since there must be something one includes that another excludes; like non-parallel lines, they must meet and clash somewhere. The dream of complete consistency can only be bought in logic or mathematics at the expense of completeness, as Gödel's theorem demonstrates, and where there is completeness there can be no logical guarantee that paradoxes will not arise. It requires less rigorous proof, since life confirms it every day, that any moral system of prohibitions and injunctions would sooner or later entangle itself in contradictions if one tried to keep to the letter of the law and did not constantly exercise judicial discretion. It is at points of contradiction that the limits of a morality, system, or language reveal themselves. And it is because there must be such limits that the seemingly arbitrary and problematic nature of any language or symbolic form is exposed. Because of its antinomies one learns that every language lies in the same breath as it speaks the truth. Consequently, one knows that no one mode of it can be absolute or even very long-lasting.

As Adorno stresses, such antinomies are not dialectical contradictions in Hegel's sense; they are not inherent in the movement of Becoming, bringing it about through the initial contradiction of Being and Nothing, for contradictions as such are not the motor force of development from the simple and abstract to the concrete and completed. Of themselves, contradictions need not necessarily promote development, as dialecticians suppose; they can just as easily provoke degeneration. Faced with, to them, insoluble contradictions in their language, men can in sheer desperation of defeat keep on narrowing and restricting the scope of the language at their disposal, and in so doing constrict their lives to the point at which they choke in a cultural asphyxia. However, they can also, if they possess the required energies and powers, break through the limits of their language and destroy those limits in the process of changing that restricted language into one that is freer. Such are those most radical acts of translation in which a language is overcome and converted into another. And it can take a step as destructive as that to resolve a basic antinomy or overcome an inherent contradiction, for any such problem that is crucial to a given language can never be solved or overcome in that language itself but only in a newly formed language in which the limits of the former have been broken and surpassed. Only in the new language will the limits of the old no longer function as defining extremes. There they can be surveyed, as it were, from both sides, and the reasons why they gave rise to specific contradictions be understood—provided it is a language that is philosophically self-conscious.

Wittgenstein was wrong when he maintained that the "bumps that the understanding has got by running its head up against the limits of language" are no more than "the uncovering of one or another piece of plain nonsense" and that these are all one can expect from "the results of philosophy."[7] It is perhaps true that these may be some of the results of his philosophy, but the results of other philosophies have been to effect profound changes in the limits of particular languages. The limits of a language are not, as Wittgenstein seems to imagine, fixed once and for all in an unchangeable nature of language. They are, rather, shifting boundaries that alter as a language itself moves about in exploring different facets of the world, and thereby expanding reality or, as sometimes happens, narrowing it. The limits of a language are never fixed. And in the history of Western Man philosophy has possibly contributed most to altering those limits. It may be regrettably true that modern philosophy may no longer be capable of performing this task, that the best it can do is to uncover "nonsense." And calling it so should not prejudge its value, for what looks like nonsense to us may make profound sense in a later age and a new language.

Man is by nature impelled to bump his head against the limits of his Language, for he is constantly driven to excess by the antinomies of Language. Because Language is inherently problematic and paradoxical, Man can never rest content with it, or with himself. If he did, then he would cease to be Man, for if Man were able to define himself without self-contradiction he would define himself as something other than himself, and so by definition not as Man. This is why Man's being is itself paradoxical and contradictory. As long as Language is contradictory, Man cannot be defined within it, and so long will Man continue to be Man. Is, then, this saving perversity due to Man's own nature, or to the nature of Language? If we focus on Man as producing Language, then the contradictoriness of Language arises from the very nature of the contradictory being of Man. Thus, it might be argued that the inclusive-exclusive workings of Language are based on an analogous structuring of the human psyche. As Freud has shown, the psyche of every individual is founded on mechanisms of suppression and repression that give rise to the differentiations of the conscious, preconscious, and unconscious. And as Lacan has interpreted it, these mechanisms of the psyche are mediated through Language, and they therefore determine the basic nature of Language as the symbolic mode of realization and repression. Similarly, as many sociologists and anthropologists argue, all human societies are structured on principles of inclusion and exclusion, on rules of the allowed and forbidden, and it is these, perhaps, that determine the operations of a language. But in a contrary manner it might be argued that the repressions of the psyche that constitute the psychic economy and the exclusions of society that are responsible for social differentiation are themselves the resultants of the more fundamental workings of Language. On this view, society is Language writ large and the psyche is Language writ small—as it were, the macrocosm and microcosm of Language. Which of these contradictory views is right?

This whole antinomy of Man and Language is the outcome of the uniquely modern conception of Language that emerged with the Deed. Such a set of contradictions could not have arisen in the thought of Man or of Language prior to the thought of the Deed. Prior to the Deed, Man had an allotted place in the scheme of things, whether as the intermediate being in the great chain of Being or as the point of instantiation of universal Reason, or as the locus of Experience, and Man knew his place in the world, where he belonged and what he could and could not be. Thus even as late as the Enlightenment, on the very threshold of the Deed, Kant could still say the following: "If there is any science man really needs it is the one I teach of how to occupy properly that place in creation that is assigned to man, and how to learn from it what one must be in order to be a man."[8] Such an idea of Man could be in no difficulties with regard to language, for Man could know his place and being quite independently of language, by the light of Reason or the deliverance of Nature or the revelation of God. It required a completely new language of Man and of Language to produce an antinomy in which the limits of that language would reveal themselves. As we have shown before, the beginning of the Deed brought in its train a reconception of Language; this in its turn brought an end to metaphysics, and together with it a new idea of Man. Or is it, as Foucault tries to insist, really the end of metaphysics that enabled Man to appear? "But the end of metaphysics is only the negative side of a much more complex event in Western thought. This event is the appearance of Man."[9]

## II

Who is the doer of the Deed? At the heart of this, like any "whodunit" question, there is a mystery. However, it is not the mystery of discovering the culprit, who is already known, but, rather, that of establishing an unproblematic relation between the doer and his Deed. In modern thought there is only one possible candidate for the Deed. It is Man. Who or what else could have done it? However, there still remains the question, who is this Man who does the Deed? What kind of a Man is he? In other words, what is the modern conception of Man?

The Man who emerges as the doer of the Deed is a new kind of Subject. He is not a uniform Subject—he can vary as widely as from creative Man, for example, "the subject of production," as Marx envisages him, to destructive Man such as is the "subject of rebellion," as Bakunin sees him: "To revolt is a natural tendency of life."[10] In either case, Man is the supreme active agent, the doer of the Deed, and so founder and destroyer of his world, the only world available for modern thought. The Deed Man performs thus assumes many forms in modern thought, ranging from an Idealist act of consciousness to a Materialist activity of labor. In the latter case, the doer of the Deed is frequently the Man of the hand, literally so. He is either the Man of the open hand—the manipulative man, *homo faber,* the creative player and artist, the tool-maker, the maker of things whose being is thereby determined as readiness-to-hand (*Zuhandenheit*) or present-at-hand (*Vorhandenheit*).[11] Or he is the Man of the closed hand, the fist *(Faust)*—the violent Man, the rebel, breaker, killer, destroyer, or annihilator. Or, as Bakunin wants to have it, somehow both at once: "The passion for destruction is a creative passion too!"[12] And, as we shall see, Faust, too, is at once the fist and the working hand.

The hand has become the primary symbolic organ of modern Man; it is no longer the head, or the heart, or the belly, or the blood that determines Man's being. Hence, the modern doer is different from the man of reason (logos), or thought, or feeling (pathos), or appetite, or will, as he was once wont to be considered in different philosophical traditions. The hand need not be mere symbol—it can be literally the bodily hand; and from it derives a completely new sense of Man's bodily being as activated by the hand. The most literal expression of this manipulative being of Man originates from Darwin's evolutionary theories, which place such a heavy emphasis on the tool-making abilities of the species *homo sapiens,* due to their erect posture and capacity to oppose thumb and forefingers. These themes of manipulativity were given philosophic expression in Pragmatism and in modern psychology, where a new emphasis was placed on tactile perception and locomotive orientation. The senses are no longer conceived of as windows of the soul, modeled primarily on the eyes, as all traditional philosophies taught; rather, they are seen as active material agents modeled on the hands. As a result, the relationship of subject, object, and sense-organ has been altered; the gulf separating the perceiver and the perceived—which once was so unbridgeable as to bring into question the very existence of an external world—has now been reduced to the gapless contact of the material surfaces of the hand and the object held. A view of perception as involving the activity of the body does not entail problems of the materiality of what is perceived or of the external existence of its object. Its problematic is the very different one of how separate contacts can give rise to a coherent object, or, in general, how perception is structured. The issue of atomic sensation and Gestalt becomes the key preoccupation of modern experimental psychology.

The role of the hand in the self-awareness of modern Man can hardly be overestimated. It engenders a new awareness of the whole body. The sense of the body in modernity is no longer that of the carnal, corrupt vessel of the Christian dispensation; nor is it that, so characteristic of the Renaissance, of the Colossus, bestriding the world, whose form is the pattern of the universe; and neither is it the mechanical "homme-machine," the clockwork contrivance of the classical age of Reason. In discovering the hand modern Man regained a real sense of the body for the first time since the Renaissance, for in the intervening period there had occurred a veritable suppression of the body (might it have perhaps been at least partly due to the refusal by refined aristocratic and bourgeois culture to dirty its hands with manual work?). During this period the body was subjected to so much covering over, disciplining, ordering, and refining that it might be said to have temporarily disappeared from view; only the face as the image of either soul, spirit, or mind could be seen, and it attained that subtle expressivity attested to in the perfection of the art of portraiture at this time.

The reemergence of the body in the modern period at first seemed a veritable "resurrection of the flesh," as the early French Positivists preached it, and this romantic impulse was backed by the emergence of new positivistic sciences of the living body such as biology, embryology, physiology, and genetics, and the new vitalist philosophies of organicism, *Naturphilosophie* and the evolutionary *élan vital.* At the same time there was a new kind of interest in the dead body. The corpse was not simply analytically anatomized in the rational medical manner; a new science of pathology arose whose concern was to trace the process of dying through postmortems.[13] Romantic literature, too, was fascinated by the newly rediscovered sense of the dead body, and Goethe, so given only to the living body, satirizes it mercilessly: "The poets of Night and Charnel-house beg to be excused because they have just struck up an interesting conversation with a newly arisen Vampire, and this might lead to the development of a new genre of poetry" (*Faust* Part II, Act I). If Goethe could have foreseen some of the poems of Baudelaire he would have realized how right he was in jest, but how wrong in assessment. The dead and living bodies are now no longer as clearly distinguishable as they were in Goethe's time; the living body is itself now treated more as if it were a corpse, and the corpse is no longer so irrevocably dead—it can, after all, be medically resuscitated even after it has been dead by ordinary standards, so that the very distinction between life and death has come to be disturbed. Adorno and Horkheimer trace this disturbing phenomenon back to the revival of the body at the beginning of the modern period, which they interpret negatively from the very beginning:

> The romantic attempts to bring about a renaissance of the body in the nineteenth and twentieth centuries simply idealize a dead and maimed condition. . . . The body cannot be remade into a noble object: it remains the corpse however vigorously it is trained and kept fit. The metamorphosis into death was simply a part of that perennial process which turned nature into substance and matter.[14]

The fact that the myth of Frankenstein's monster, first conceived as a Romantic horror story, now so haunts the popular imagination is some indication that this early literary awareness of the new ambiguity of life and death has now become a universal fear.

The revival of the body, as either living or dead, could not have happened without the active participation of the hand. Modern man feels his body as something that an active hand discovers: he is made aware of its specific qualities by the sensitive hand of art, or the skilled hand of science, or the hard hand of labor, or the brutal hand of violence. His awareness is therefore an active and external one of what the body can do, what it outwardly feels like, how it responds, how it behaves, what moves it, what kind of an impediment it is, its dead weight, inertia and, so to speak, its corpse-quality. It is no longer an inner awareness of the passive contemplative, ecstatic, sensual, sensory, or serene state of one's inner being; or of the inner plasticity of the body's finer shades of mannered action, aesthetic nuances, beauty of appearance, rhythmic order and regularity of deportment or music of movement; or of the body as completely unself-conscious, blind to itself in a primitive immersion in its feelings, actions, and responses, like the body of a dancer in the midst of the dance. Modern man feels his body as an extension of his hand; it seems as if it were itself an organ of the hand. Hence, the body as a whole acquires the hand's suppleness, dexterity, and sensitivity, but at the same time it is manipulative, unfeeling, and unecstatic like the hand, and like the hand it finds it very difficult to be still; it must always move, fidget and stir when it cannot act. Any encounter between two bodies is like a meeting of hands, the bodies knowing each other as their hands do: this is surely part of the reason why the modern experience of sex is tending to become a manipulative game, why writing has the overwhelming predominance it has in our communications, and why all work is increasingly becoming a movement of fingers. The last is perhaps the most socially important point.

The substitution of the fingers for the whole hand is the latest outcome of the ever more skilled utilization of the hand. As Canetti points out, the skill of the hand is due to the dexterity of the fingers perfected through all the "finger exercises" that children are taught in being trained in skills. According to Canetti, there is "a separate destructiveness of the hand" that derives from the skill of the fingers: "It is of a purely mechanical nature and mechanical inventions are extensions of it"; "it is this mechanical destructiveness of the hands, now grown to a complex system of technology, which, whenever it is linked with a real intention to kill, supplies the automatic element of the resulting process, that empty mindlessness which is so particularly disquieting."[15] It is questionable whether the fingers alone are responsible for the destructiveness of technology or, more correctly put, for its annihilating capacity. But it is unquestionable that through the fingers technology can exercise its destructive and annihilating effect on the whole body. The more technical work becomes, a matter of watching dials and screens requiring only a finger-twiddling of knobs, the more the hand tends to atrophy; and insofar as the body derives its sense of itself from the hand, it too becomes numb. Through such inactive activity the body's being is localized predominantly in the eyes, as each man is tending to occupy his time increasingly as a silent spectator only, whose fingers react to the promptings of his eyes. The fingers themselves are thereby losing their dexterity, for the main use they receive is to depress buttons, guide wheels and levers, or make simple marks. To have a painter's or musician's fingers is no advantage. This transfer of activity from the hand to the eyes is a much greater threat to the body, and thereby to a person's sense of his bodily self, than was the suppression of the body's manual being in aristocratic and high-bourgeois culture prior to modernity. A passively visual life almost completely negates the body's being. If that were ever to happen it would be an extremely ironic outcome of the Deed of the hand.

At the beginning of modernity only Goethe realized the inherent incarnation of the Deed in the hand, and he conceived his Faust partly on this realization. This is all the more remarkable as it was not at all evident to the early Idealist philosophers of the Deed. For them the Deed was an ideal activity of consciousness whose subject is the bodiless Ego. Man as the impersonal Ego of consciousness is the subject of all Idealist philosophy, including Hegel's *Phenomenology* and also including most philosophies between that and Husserl's phenomenology, notwithstanding all Husserl's attempts to transcendentalize consciousness. The transition from the idealistic interpretation of the Ego and its Deed to a material one in which Man assumes a solid bodily being is first clearly apparent in the transition from the left-Hegelian activism of Moses Hess to the more Faustian productive activity of the humanistic Marx who could say: "To be radical is to seize things by the roots. For man the root is man himself."[16] To what extent and up to what point Marx was to remain a humanist is the quesion Althusser provokes; for late Marx, Althusser insists, "the true subjects are the relations of production," so Man is nothing but "the support of these relations."[17] In other words, for us the question at issue is this: Is Man the doer of the Deed, or does the Deed do Man?

It is on this question that Foucault's thought turns, too. For Foucault, all modern thought following eighteenth-century classical discourse is inherently humanist. But according to him this humanism, which he also calls Anthropology, is now to be overcome—or, better put, it is about to overcome itself by dissolving Man. For Foucault, Man as understood in modern thought is an impossible kind of being, one only temporarily constituted by what he calls the "anthropological quadrilateral" of modern knowledge. He sets himself to "destroy the anthropological 'quadrilateral' in its very foundations" and thereby to wake men from their "anthropological sleep."[18] However, he is not definite as to whether this destruction of Man is itself still within the ambit of modern knowledge or whether it is already outside that knowledge in a new field of thought. On the one hand, he writes, "It would be false to place it from the outset upon the horizon of some new thought or new knowledge"; but, on the other hand, he also writes that with the disappearance of Man there will be "the unfolding of a space in which it is once more possible to think," and he speaks of "an imminent new form of thought."[19] However, he is decisive on the point that the death of Man is the end of modern humanist thought. For him this event is an ending, located no sooner than the present moment, of that thought which first began in the nineteenth century; thus the origin of Man and the death of Man are to him the beginning and end of one form of knowledge.

Unfortunately, Foucault has failed fully to appreciate that they were also simultaneous; he did not notice that Man was first in doubt almost as soon as he arose, that the death of Man was being announced at the very moment of his presumed birth. It seems that no sooner was Man born than he was already dead. Foucault himself somewhat anachronistically on his own time-scheme locates the death of Man as early as Nietzsche: "The promise of the Superman signifies first and foremost the imminence of the death of Man."[20] What Foucault assigns to Nietzsche, Althusser claims with even greater certitude for Marx, whom he quotes as saying, "My analytical method does not start from Man, but from the economically given social period"[21]—and with this assessment of Marx Foucault himself seems to concur in later writings. George Steiner makes an even earlier claim on behalf of Humboldt, whom he quotes to this effect: "Albeit language is wholly inward, it nevertheless possesses at the same time an autonomous, external identity and being which does violence to Man himself."[22] It seems from this quotation that Man was already threatened with extinction the moment Language constituted him from the Deed. What are we to make of this tendency that seems to want to push back the death of Man to the very moment of his presumed birth?

In every major modern thinker from Hegel onward there is an indubitable prior tendency toward some form of modern humanism, and this is often followed by a countervailing reaction to an anti-humanism.[23] In each of them Man is first constituted as either Subjectivity or Consciousness, or as Creator or Producer, or the Ego of individualism or the "We" of humanity, or personal Existenz or impersonal Dasein. Thus each of these thinkers had first to constitute Man even if he was later at least partly to de-constitute him; this process of constitution-de-constitution seems to have gone on from the very beginning and seems interminable within modern thought. To shift from humanism to anti-humanism is in no way to leave the field of modern thought, since this step is present to a greater or lesser degree in every modern thinker: each one is both humanist and anti-humanist at some stage in his thinking career. And as Althusser's attempt to locate a break in Marx shows, at no given point of their work can one say with any assurance that *there* is the break where humanism leaves off and anti-humanism begins. Any forced distinction between the "young" and "old" thinker is always merely partial, for one can never be sure that one will not stumble upon something of the tender humanist in the seemingly hardened old anti-humanist, and vice versa.

This analysis, here outlined merely for modern thought, could be developed further into modern literature, culture, and social history. Thus, for example, the tendencies toward both subjectivity and extreme impersonality are there in the modern novel right from its beginning. The impersonality of the authorial presence by no means begins with Flaubert; it is already there in Kleist. Hence, the abrupt switch in post-war France from the existentialist novel of subjective consciousness to the neo-objectivity of the *nouveau roman* is by no means a radical new departure in writing but merely a late exemplification of a tendency toward such abrupt alterations that had already occurred many times before. The change-over from romanticism to classicism and back again which has kept on repeating itself in so many guises and disguises is itself an extended exemplification of the constant oscillation between subjectivity and impersonality, self-consciousness and objectivity, humanism and anti-humanism, Man and anti-Man. In our time it has only become more abrupt and bewildering, for the deification of Man and the debasement of Man had never before taken the extreme manifestations evident in our own time nor ever before oscillated with such rapidity. And the reason for this must be because these tendencies belong together, the extremity of the reaction being only the resultant of the extremity of the original action.

We seem to have stumbled here upon a fundamental antinomy of modernity, inherently there from the very beginning of the Deed. Man is the doer of the Deed, but the Deed also does Man. Man is the creator, the producer of all productions, but is also the product of production and so the creature. Man is the speaker of languages, but he is himself spoken by Language. Man is the sovereign Subject of History, but also the dependent object. Modern thought veers from one side to the other of these contradictory answers to the question: "Who did the Deed?" It shifts precipitously from humanism to anti-humanism, from Subjectivity to Subjectlessness, from a new Cogito to a new Incognito. The two contradictory sets of answers belong to the one question. There will always be those who will attempt to overcome this contradiction through some kind of forced dialectical synthesis—just as theologians once attempted to overcome the contradictions of the God-Man with the aid of Greek metaphysics. Thus it might be argued that Man is both the subject and object of production since what he produces is always only himself, that he is both the speaker and the spoken of language since he speaks himself, that he makes the History that determines him. But it is doubtful whether such theological subtleties can be maintained except under the threat of excommunication or worse.

It were best simply to acknowledge openly that the antinomy of Man and the Deed is irresolvable within our thought. Hence, it marks one of the limits of our thought. We can no more step outside those limits than we can jump out of our skins. To acknowledge this is no easy matter, for it means that our whole notion of Man is contradictory, ambivalent, and problematical. Man has become a highly unstable being uncertain of himself. He is both the ground of All and the basis of Nothing—good for Nothing and worse for All that. Man can no longer situate himself within his knowledge of things, for he no longer knows what kind of being he is. It is not merely that he has no fixed place in the world or that he is an amphibian between the elements, or a chameleon of substances but, much more seriously, that he can no longer know who or what he is without entangling himself in contradictions. The perennial questions such as "What is Man?" or "What is the end of Man?" no longer have an answer. Man can no longer know himself, for he has made himself unknowable to himself. He has made himself indefinable. So, too, Man in modern thought is forever beginning and ending without ever having really begun or come to any final end. He can no longer even know whether he does or does not come to any end, for his time is as problematical and doubt-ridden as he is himself.

## III

The antinomies of modern Time can be generated by simply asking the seemingly innocent question: "When did the Deed begin?" The initial simple answer is analogous to the theological answer to the parallel question about God's creation of the world: the Deed did not begin in time, because time began with the Deed. It is the activity of the Deed that originates time and through its continuity maintains it. What Goethe calls living Activity (*lebendiges Tun*) through its creative and re-creative action establishes and maintains the movement that is Time. Time is, therefore, forever in movement and never at rest, for even what seems like a still moment is only apparent. The Deed activates Time to arise out of Nothing, and by its continuing activity prevents it from sinking back to Nothing again. And for Goethe, at any rate, this movement is eternal—there is no end to it. As a result of this, as we shall see, time for Goethe is perpetual active development. For other modern thinkers it has a somewhat different shape and movement, but invariably it is linked to the Deed.

What emerges from the Deed is a time of Becoming of a peculiarly modern shape, because Becoming is no longer to be understood metaphysically as mutability, degeneration, corruption, or alteration but, rather, as a directed movement usually referred to as Progress. This new time has often been called Faustian; that is how Spengler names it, but unfortunately he then goes on to attribute it to the whole of Western European civilization. To avoid this misunderstanding we shall refer to it as the Faustian time of Progress, explicitly restricting its discovery to our modern period. In this sense the discovery of the time of Progress begins with Goethe's Deed.

Like Faustian Man, Faustian Time has from its inception been subject to questioning and put in doubt, and out of this have arisen the antinomies of the time of Progress. Its unquestioned assumption as an a-priori principle presupposed in all scientific explanation, making of all science a tracing out of evolutionary sequences, was rejected very early on in the natural sciences. In the human sciences it remained much more firmly entrenched—with some notable exceptions. Its arbitrary nature as a principle for ordering and relating human phenomena had been repeatedly exposed, perhaps nowhere more evidently than in Wittgenstein's comments on Frazer's anthropological explanations:

> Historical explanation, explanation as a hypothesis of development, is only one way of drawing the data together—of providing their synopsis. It is just as possible to see the data in their relation to one another and to draw them together in a general picture, without putting it in the form of a hypothesis about temporal development.[24]

In this remark Wittgenstein is almost prognosticating the methodological conclusions of the structural anthropology of Lévi-Strauss, partly from which, in turn, Foucault's criticisms of historicism originate. It seems, therefore, that these criticisms are themselves firmly within the scope of modern thought; they exemplify an aporia of the time of Progress which, like the aporia of Man, was there from the very beginning of the Deed. The relation between the time of Progress and the new temporalities that arise from its denial is, therefore, by no means a matter of simple succession, as Foucault assumes it to be, such that the current rejection of historicism signifies its overcoming and the inception of a new sense of time. Rather, it seems that such a dialectic of time has been playing itself out all along and that the latest altercation is merely one example of it. Even in the sciences "explanation as a hypothesis of development" cannot be completely abandoned, even here the time of Progress is not at an end. In this sense we are still trapped in progressive History and doomed to its time.

The time of Progress is itself by no means such a simple issue as it appeared to be when Goethe first presented it. It too, is fraught with contradictions and antinomies. For the opening question "When did the Deed begin?" in turn compels the closing question "When will the Deed end?" The time of Progress is racked between the poles of these two questions, in the problematic of its origin and end. As Foucault has noted:

> At the very moment when it became possible for it to denounce as fantasies the ideal geneses described in the eighteenth century, modern thought was establishing a problematic of the origin at once extremely complex and extremely tangled; this problematic has served as the foundation for our experience of time, and, since the nineteenth century, as the starting point of all our attempts to re-apprehend what beginning and re-beginning, the recession and presence of the beginning, the return and the end, could be in the human sphere.[25]

It is because of its inherent reference to the origin and end of the Deed that the time of Progress is so insistently eschatological. But it forms an eschatology that does not directly derive from or have any necessary connection with that of theology, despite the obvious formal analogies. The eschatologies of modern Time are made necessary by the need to posit an origin and end to the Deed, and by the unavoidable linkage between its origin and end, since the end is already predetermined by the origin. It only requires the postulation of a fault or Fall close to the origin to produce the full eschatological patterning. The eschatological patterning of the time of Progress is more or less pronounced depending on the extent to which Progress is historicized, that is, on the extent to which it is Man's progress in any of the multiple forms this can take: for example, as unfolding of the Spirit, development of consciousness, or creative activity. On the other hand, where the time of Progress is naturalized, conceived of organically as the progress of Nature, there it becomes flattened into one smooth continuous movement without interruption or break and without marked beginning or end. The Deed as an organic, quasi-natural mode of activity results in a time that is uniform, continuous, and homogeneous; the time that arises out of a temporalization of a naturalistic Deed is a kind of stretching out of activity in the space of Nature.

We can illustrate this latter time by reference to Darwin's evolutionary time, where the temporal space of Nature is the chronology of geological epochs against the backdrop of which takes place the quicker evolutionary activity of the development of species. This evolutionary striving is a will-to-life negatively conceived of as survival, whereby each individual and each species strives to maintain itself in being in competition against all others for limited space and scarce resources. The Deed of evolutionary activity is thus a kind of active *principium individuationis,* an active maintaining oneself in being and preserving one's identity, whereby to perpetuate itself each individual strives against every other, thereby promoting the improvement of its species and the evolution of higher species—and, ultimately, at the very apex of evolution, the triumphant march of human civilization. The formal analogues of this scientific time of Progress to the historical time of political liberalism and capitalism have often been taken simply as evidence of the workings of ideology in science. This is, of course, unjustified, for all that it shows is that there is a common time-sense in science and in politics deriving from similar predispositions, without one necessarily being the source of the other. As we shall see, the advances in the science of genetics culminating in the decoding of the DNA molecule have radically transformed evolutionary time; instead of a time that is the outcome of the Deed, as either struggle for survival, will-to-life, *élan vital,* or even, theologically, an upward reach to higher spheres (de Chardin), genetics shows any such apparent time to be no more than a purely phenomenal outcome of the atemporal, structural interplay of combinations of genes and molecules. The time of genetics is the outcome of a play of exact replication and spontaneous variation, that is, of repetition and chance, the contradictory principle to that of the Deed from which the time of Progress derives. However, neither of these opposed times can win permanently in science; the struggle between them, under different guises, is still continuing. Crude Darwinian time has now been replaced by a time of ecological equilibrium, but it, too, is at odds with the mere combinatorial analysis of information genetics. Analogous conflicts over time have taken place even in the most exact sciences, physics and cosmology. The anticipation of the principle of entropy by Carnot in 1824, its discovery by Clausius in

1865, and the consequent prediction of the heat-death of the universe brought for the first time an eschatological element to the scientific time of Nature itself. The resultant clash between the entropy principle and that of continuous universal development without any inherent end has still not been resolved, nor has the parallel problem of the Big-Bang beginning.

There are contradictions of this kind at all points within the time of Progress, for sometimes it is conceived of eschatologically with an origin and end, and at other times purely linearly as continuous, uniform succession that is endless and without beginning. The contradiction is at its most acute at the point at which Man's time as historical has to be fitted into Man's time as evolutionary, for the time of Man's historical human-being tends to be seen as tending toward an end, whereas the evolutionary time of Man's species-being is seen as endless. Man qua "natural" being progresses to no ultimate end, whereas Man qua "spiritual" being has an end in history. However, this historical end must not be confused with theological eschatology where Man as spiritual being has an end in the spiritual progress toward God that culminates in the end of the world, for secular Man as historical being is part of a natural order of things that can be endless. St. Augustine's double-time scheme of the "two cities" is thus the opposite of the modern one of evolution and history, but just as the traditional clash between pagan and Christian times had no reconciliation, so that ultimately, as in Augustine, they could only be set one above the other and allowed to go their separate ways, so, too, the modern conflict of the times of nature and history cannot be satisfactorily resolved.

Both Marx's transition from pre- to post-history and Nietzsche's goal of the Superman and the goallessness of eternal recurrence are unsuccessful attempts at such a resolution. Marx sought to postulate an end to pre-history in communist society, which when attained would commence the endless evolutionary development of mankind. In the Marxian vision of the future one time ends and the other begins; pre-history comes to a close and true history commences, and between them intervenes and mediates the cataclysmic Deed of the revolution—the point of intersection and transition from one time to another requiring a radical translation of Man. Analogously, Nietzsche's translation of Man into Superman, which is even more radical, is also designed to serve as a way of overcoming the fundamental problem of natural and historical time. Insofar as "Man is a thing to be surmounted,"[26] that amounts to an end of historical time, but insofar as "Man is a rope stretched betwixt beast and Superman—a rope over an abyss," that means that history is itself placed within a larger time-scheme of nature, which is itself embraced within the cosmic time of eternal recurrence. However, Nietzsche is well aware that his notion of the Superman is nothing better than a metaphor,[27] and that it can only at best poetically suggest a solution to the problem of Time's ends. Thus neither Marx's end of history nor Nietzsche's end of Man is a solution to the difficulties of the contradictory ends in Faustian time.

The problem of "ending" is endemic to all modern thought on time, for the original question "When did the Deed begin?" inevitably prompts the final one "And when will it end?" All modern eschatologies, just like the traditional ones, are premised on and directed to an end, all the more so as the promise of such an end has, since the cataclysms of the two world wars, seemed to come closer to being fulfilled. Especially among writers between the wars, the vision of an apocalyptic close has repeatedly arisen.[28] The Apocalypse oratorio Leverkühn composes in Thomas Mann's *Faustus* sums up many of these themes. However, it is essential to remember that this Apocalypse is not the End in the book: it is not Leverkühn's final work, which is a "Faustus," nor is it the sense of ending of the work itself, which invokes a much more complex end than any simple *Götterdämmerung* or Last Judgment following the wars of Gog and Magog: Mann's eschatological ending incorporates the endless end of Goethe's *Faust* as well as the endlessness of Nietzsche's Eternal Return. As we shall see, this ending is one that belongs firmly within the Faustian passage, for despite its complex elaboration of endings and cyclic repetitions it is still a variant of the time of Progress. But from the very beginning of the Deed repeated attempts have also been made to dispense with any progressive ending as well as with the whole tradition of eschatological ends. The refusal of such endings is invariably the rejection even of that marginal consolation offered by a formal close. The endings of Büchner's *Woyzeck,* of some of D. H. Lawrence's works, and of Schoenberg's compositions are all examples of counter-eschatological ends. Perhaps no such attempt has been more explicit than Beckett's aptly named *End Game.*

Thus within the modern Faustian time of Progress there ensues an extremely complex problematic of the end-endlessness, finitude-infinity of Man. For man, as the subject of evolutionary development, is both endless and finite (somewhat on analogy with Einstein's universe)—endless, because without any inherent end, but also finite both because bound by the limitations of Man's corporeal nature and because Man has now the capacity to finish himself irrevocably. But on the other hand, Man as the subject of history has an end but is infinite (somewhat on analogy with traditional eschatology)—Man's end is the End of history, but that End has no finitude, for nothing limits his further Progress beyond any end, so that in that respect and with that prospect Man is infinite. Both these variants have their analogies in traditional thought, where they would be exposed as follows: Man as natural being is endless and finite (finite, because bound to death and endless, because without any telos) whereas Man as spiritual being is infinite but has an end (infinite, because he is an immortal soul; having an end, because of the coming end of the world). However, traditional and modern formulations, though formally analogous, are opposite in meaning. As we have already seen, the modern eschatology of history is very different from the traditional one of Providence, and the traditional finitude of individual death is also nothing like the modern finitude of the death of mankind. Nevertheless, the formal analogies extend even further, for it is possible to propound other combinatorial variants of the end-endless, finite-infinite problematic within the modern time of Progress, just as it was possible to do so within traditional time. It is also possible to propound the endlessness and infinity of Man, as well as its opposite, the end and finitude of Man. The first is the position taken up by ideal exponents of Progress, like some of the early positivists, who held that there is no goal for Man's development and that it is infinite; the second is the position of those who now call for an end to Man. Foucault shares this latter view, for he seems to identify Man's finitude and his end, such that Man is doomed to perish since his end is the point where his finitude is attained, and his finitude drives him toward the end.

This problematic of the time of Progress—of its end-endlessness, finitude-infinity—is there from the start of the Deed. It originates from the temporality of the Deed, symbolically deriving from the possible answers to the original question: "When did the Deed begin?" The temporality of the Deed, as it first reveals itself in Goethe, gave rise to a time of Progress in its most ideal form as a time of Development. For Development is the original ideal mode of Progress; later notions of Progress became much more material and materialistic, and that is already evident in the neo-Darwinian conception that begins with Spencer, of Progress as evolution. However, Goethe was not the sole progenitor of a time of Development; equal place must be accorded to Hegel. Goethe in fact said, partly out of tact and partly out of ignorance of the philosopher's work, that Hegel in his abstract way was saying the same thing about time that he was himself saying in a concrete-poetic manner. Goethe was partly right, in that both derived from the temporality of activity a similar time of Development; but he was also wrong, because the Hegelian activity is nothing like the Faustian Deed. Hence, the Development deriving from these two different notions of the Act has two quite different forms. For Hegel, Development means a rational unfolding of the Idea in a teleological movement to an End that is a growth in Spirit or self-consciousness. For Goethe, by contrast, Development means metamorphosis as a change of Forms, proceeding from the simpler to the organically more complex, which is always individualized, particular, and incarnate, not merely spiritual or self-conscious, and not bound to any teleologically predetermined end. We shall try to spell out this difference more fully.

For Goethe, natural, organic Development is the original and fundamental Time; for Hegel it is merely the initial, primitive time of Nature. It is on this point that we can distinguish the two most sharply. For Hegel, the time of Nature is mere duration, to be contrasted with the time of historical development, which is time properly understood. Hegel calls natural duration "bad infinity" because it is an endless but finite reproduction of natural objects, a constant self-abandonment of Reason in nature. As opposed to this, true development is the activity of self-conscious reason, that is, of the concept making itself self-explicit. This activity is thought, which is subjectivity as productive action that is conscious of itself. The motor of this activity is the dialectic of negation, and it gives rise to becoming as a movement of time. It is a time which is in-finite, but it has an end, for it is a teleological movement whose end is inherent in itself. The end is always the concrete realization of the origin: "The result is the same as the beginning solely because the beginning is purpose ... realized purpose, or concrete actuality, is movement and development unfolded."[29] Thus, for Hegel, real time can only be historical time, and historical time is one of Ideal development, or the development of the Idea. The historical analysis of any development is always in Hegel an exposition of the "logical" stages of the Idea. Hegel, indeed, goes so far as to oppose History as temporal and Nature as spatial: "History in general is therefore the development of spirit in Time, as Nature is the development of the Idea in space."[30]

It is precisely on such a point that Goethe chides Hegel in the conversation between them recorded by Eckermann. Speaking of the "disease" of the dialectic, Goethe says: "I therefore congratulate myself upon the study of nature, which preserves me from such a disease."[31] Not history but Nature is the source of time for Goethe. What to Hegel is mere natural duration or perdurance is for Goethe the organic time of individual development. Everything that develops in time does so through natural stages, and that which undergoes this process is always a real, concrete individual. Hence, Goethe's development is organically metamorphic, rather than conceptually dialectic as in Hegel. Development goes through the natural stages of formation, maturation, and transformation—the image of the chrysalis becoming butterfly is one that he employs for all becoming. Hence, the two moments of becoming are those of creation or slow maturation and destruction or the upheaval that is a violent breaking-through of already outgrown forms, as contrasted to Hegel's dialectical moments of positing and negating. Goethean development is organic and not teleological; it is the nisus of potencies tending toward transformation rather than an unfolding of potentialities toward a preestablished actuality as its end. For Goethe every ending is but another transformation, a death and becoming (*Stirb und Werde*), so there can be no final end. Even death is no end, but another becoming—Goethe's refusal to countenance ending goes that far.

Goethe's notion of transformation leads him deliberately to blur the distinction between individual and species: the individual need not die, for it can transform itself as if it were a species, and the species goes through the stages of individual growth. Thus, for example, the evolution of plants can only be conceived of by Goethe as like an individual plant, which develops through the various species as if it were one individual form, from the seed, to the leaves, to the stalk, to the flower and fruit—"the whole, like each of its parts, a living thing."[32] This is why the *UrPflanze* was for Goethe like the seed of the whole kingdom of plants, a real originating organism from which the evolutionary Deed proceeds in an "impulse that seems limitless and endless,"[33] and he ever refused to accede to Schiller's more Kantian-inspired suggestion that it was an ideal prototype. This individualized view of Development contributed much to Goethe's own literary achievements and to the subsequent idealized historicist notion of time that was so predominant throughout the nineteenth century—indeed, Meinecke in his monumental study points to Goethe as the true originator of historicism as such, despite Goethe's own preference for Nature over history.

Meinecke is surely right, for it is an irony on Goethe that his principle of individualized development, which proved so fruitful in the study of history, should have had disastrous results in the study of nature. Goethe's own scientific accomplishments, on which he prided himself, were stultified by that principle. It was perhaps the main reason why he could not devise a more scientifically adequate theory of evolution. It also misled him in his theory of colors and was the main cause of his misplaced contentions against Newton. He sought to show that colors went through a process of individualized temporal development. Hence, as in his search for an *UrPflanze,* he tried to find an initial seed or simple form for color development. This primary color origin he identified in a struggle of Light and Dark, the symbols of the primeval universal moral conflict; and out of that nature-dialectic he tried to derive the primary colors, and then, from the interplay or mixture of those, the whole color-world. As Eckermann reports him as saying:

> I discovered light in its purity and truth, and I considered it my duty to fight for it. The opposite party, however, did their utmost to darken the light; for they maintained that shade is a part of light ... for they said that colours, which are shadow and the result of shade, are light itself ... are the beams of light, broken now in one way, now in another.[34]

The refraction of light had enormous symbolic significance for Goethe. Light transforms itself from its pure original state into its motley of colors through the interference of the dark: pure spirit is broken up by matter, or as Faust puts it: "Life is not light, but the refracted color."[35] The Newtonian interpretation of refraction as a procedure of analyzing complex white light by breaking it up into its color components—broken light—Goethe scorned because such mechanical analysis killed the wholeness and life of what it analyzed and only studied its dead remains. Misguided though he was in applying the principle of temporal development to a physical theory of colors, he inadvertently opened up the new field of color psychology in which the temporal individuation principle was not so misplaced, since the development of color vision is subject to temporal evolution. At the same time, as Wittgenstein shows, he contributed much to clarifying the logical-grammar of color concepts and set out a kind of conceptual phenomenology of the color-world.

Goethe's predisposition toward a time of individualized development was much more than a philosophical or methodological preconception; it also derived from, and was designed to satisfy, his moral and artistic requirements, but even beyond that it was the outcome of his deepest psychological needs. Above all, it was intended as the intellectual answer to his need to overcome death as an ending. If every development is itself like an individual, then the earlier stages in the development are akin to the earlier stages in the growth of an individual; all that is attained in those formative stages is passed on to the later ones and is a precondition of their formation. The child is father to the man, and as the child develops itself so will the man become; analogously, later species are the heirs to what the earlier ones have achieved, just as later nations are the heirs to what the earlier ones have accomplished. Goethe was insistent that acquired characteristics can be inherited; the idea of a purely mechanistic genetic inheritance, had he been aware of it, would have been repugnant to him because it would have gone counter to his whole belief in Nature as gathering and garnering her successful achievements rather than allowing them to go to waste. This husbandry of Nature was at the root of his so-called pantheism. Hence, no matter how radical the breaking of old forms to produce new ones, no matter how volcanic the eruptions of the earth and sea, no matter how turbulent the metamorphosis of change, it could never carry out complete destruction, for otherwise development would have to start from scratch each time. Each generation could not begin again from nothing, but must inherit the achievements of the activities of its predecessors. So, too, death cannot lay waste to everything that has been achieved by individuals in their lifetimes; it has to be passed on to their successors to comprise the one organic growth of the Individual writ large. Hence, Goethe felt that the individual himself continues to be in essence or spirit; in a sense he does not completely die at all but is metamorphosed, translated into another sphere. "To me, the eternal existence of my soul is proved from my idea of activity, if I work on incessantly till my death, nature is bound to give me another form of existence when the present one can no longer sustain my spirit."[36]

Goethe fondly imagined that the Deed can never be completely done with; thanks to it he felt assured of a kind of immortality. This is why Faust is never referred to as actually dead, even though Mephistopheles prepares for the burial of his body. As we shall see much later, there are complications in Goethe's conception of the end of the *Faust* drama deriving from Goethe's need to have Faust die and yet to continue on after death. These are the problems Goethe has in conceiving of ending and finitude in a time that is endless though not infinite.

Goethe's time of individual development must not be mistaken for the time-sense of the character Faust in Goethe's drama, a mistake that was encapsulated in the notion of Faustian time as this was given currency by Spengler. As we shall see eventually, Faust's time is but one of the partial time-forms that together with all the others opposed to it—the times of Mephistopheles, of Lynceus, of Philemon and Baucis—together comprise the overall time-shape of the drama. Spengler's Faustian time is not Goethe's, and neither is it the modern ideal time of literature and culture so influenced by Goethe. To speak of it as the time of European civilization as a whole, as Spengler does, is the kind of anachronistic extrapolation back into history of the historian's own predilections that makes of historical writing a species of aesthetic appreciation. Spengler's Faustian time represents the culmination of the debasement of the time of Goethe that had already been steadily proceeding in the art and thought of German late Romanticism.

Despite such ultimate perversions, it is undeniable that Goethe's time of individualized development was his most lasting legacy to the art and thought of modern times. As a principle of artistic form it was introduced by him in the form of the *Bildungsroman,* which became perhaps the most important novelistic convention of the nineteenth century. Its close analogy in music is the time of continuous development (*Durchführung*) introduced into composition by Beethoven. Localized at first only in the so-called development section of the sonata form, in Beethoven's later works it was to become the compositional principle embracing the total work. Continuous development was still very conservatively, but very subtly, utilized by Brahms without disturbing the traditionally inherited musical forms, but in the revolutionary Wagner it was applied with full self-consciousness so pervasively as to shatter nearly all the form-building structures of music. And this, by a paradoxical dialectic, led to a self-negation of development that gave rise to a static time in which the seeming continuous, never-ceasing movement produced the effect of a standstill, like the turmoil of currents in a whirlpool that is quite still. The logic of this dialectic was ultimately to complete itself in the music of Schoenberg, where the principle of continuous development was eventually formalized into the twelve-tone law, and musical time was not merely stilled but threatened to be completely suppressed. A very similar dialectic of time can be traced in the modern novel: the novel of character development (the Great Tradition, as Leavis presents it) with its continually moving time eventually ended in the static time of Joyce's "Bloomsday" and Proust's "remembered time," and ultimately in the no-time of Beckett's "dead-ends." What happened to Goethe's ideal time of individual development in art is symptomatic of what happened to the modern time of Development as an ideal Progress. The translations Progress underwent since Goethe, in word, thought, and deed, reveal a similar dialectic of time.

In the early period of modern Progress the time of individualized development was influential in all cultural and social endeavors—in education, morality, politics, and economics. Educational reforms were directed toward individual maturation, guiding the growth of the child and adolescent to self-fulfillment and self-realization (educational theories from Humboldt and Froebel onward), reforms still with us today in their degenerate stages as the educational catch-cries of uninhibited self-expression and permissiveness. Individual development in morality shifted the emphasis away from all the traditional moral virtues, away from the salvation of the soul, conscience, character, duty, the passions of the heart, toward moral self-development as a unique individual so as to achieve a self-conscious ideal subjectivity through self-fulfillment; what that has become today is too obvious to need enumerating. In politics, the growth of the individualized nation toward independence and the development of its national identity and cultural character became the form of historical time by which nationalism was promoted; and with it came the cult of the national hero-figure as founder, savior, Führer, or simply Father. In economics the individual entrepreneur—conceived of, like Faust, as both a captain of industry and a robber baron—became the heroic leader of industrial development all over the world. Enshrined in the notions of individual initiative, this emerged as the predominant ideology of capitalism that has survived to this day in the slogan of free enterprise. But, except as ideology, few of these notions were to last; now they mainly remain as survivals of a once-living past whose main use is to befuddle the populace.

As Progress proceeded apace during the course of the nineteenth century, its time-sense began to alter; the ideal time of individual development gave way to a time of cumulative growth directed increasingly to material and power expansion. In thought and science the time of Progress took on Darwinian evolutionary characteristics and lost its Goethean refinements of form. Progress began to be measured in mere accumulation or quantitative increase rather than in respect of any qualitative individualized identity; the individual's existence became increasingly lost, immersed in the mass, and as a result he tended to assume a mere species-being; even the identity of the nation became dissolved in that of the race—it was all a case of quality being reduced back into quantity. The faster the accumulation process proceeded, the more accelerated the movement of Progress became; and the faster that movement, the more every individual form was reduced to a quantum or statistical mass. Eventually, as in our own day, the movement of time has become a motion of mechanical repetition that can, therefore, be propelled at a rate faster than any before known. But a time that is mere motion is without any real temporal movement; so, paradoxically, from the ever-faster movement of the time of Progress there has ensued a tempo of accelerated time that is a mere motion whose real time is quite static. A static time of no change, in which nothing really happens, has the appearance of a furious onrush of events in which everything seems to be changing at every moment. For example, the ever-increased momentum of technological change, with which it seemingly is impossible to keep up, could actually be a situation of total standstill in which history does not change at all. It is such an onrush of Progress that threatens to bring historical time to a stop and signals the possibility of an end to history. Progress, which had once seemed endless, even though finite, now seems infinite and about to reach its end, for it can go nowhere and achieve nothing.

We can briefly illustrate this speeding-up in the rate of the time of Progress by the progress achieved in production. The early ideal of production current in the modern period was that of self-expression or self-objectivation, for which the work of art was the ideal model. The time of production was that of individualized development. This was the time of production of all romantic and utopian dreams: from the Gothic guild revivalists, to the communism of early Marx, to present-day handicraft nature-ecologists. Only on the sidelines, and as a mere sideline, could this productive movement stand up to the productive pace of abstract labor harnessed to the machine-power characteristic of industrial capitalism. This capitalist time was no longer individualized, though it pretended to be; it was, rather, an organized collective tempo of work-motion whose time was quantitative and cumulative. Yet, insofar as labor-power was measurably involved in it, it was still a visibly human time, and Marx in *Capital* could still analyze it as a process of exploitation of the time of countless individuals. This was the time of high Progress, measured by all the indicators of increase—expanding output, accumulation of capital and resources, the exponential growth of power, whether as energy, military might, or state authority. Today, in the name of this Time every non-European nation is abandoning its traditional times for the new tempo of moving ahead. However, it is now evident that the time of high Progress is undergoing another transformation in the most advanced industrial nations. The new industrial revolution is one in which the process of production becomes automated and has less and less to do with direct labor-power. The speed with which production can be increased is thus no longer limited by any natural time of human work, of effort and rest, and has no longer much to do with the exploitation of the labor-time of countless workers; in principle the new productive motion could be accelerated indefinitely. The time of production is thereby becoming a motion of the technological system itself that has little to do with any direct human time.

Thus by its inherent momentum the time of Progress has put itself in doubt. Who can now believe that this is the be-all and the end-all of all time? But this doubt, which is now apparent to everyone, was already there right at the start of the Deed of Progress. Thinkers such as Schopenhauer questioned the ideal time of Goethe's individualized development and Hegel's development of the Idea almost as soon as they originated. And there have always been those who have contested the succeeding times of Progress. All along there have been those who opposed Development on theological premises, in the name of Eternity. But it was not till Kierkegaard that this was given a modern philosophical form and explicitly directed to a refutation of Hegel and, implicitly, of Goethe as well. Kierkegaard's subjective-existentialist conception of the eternal moment was not fully taken up until much later, in the philosophy of Heidegger, quasi-nihilistically by reference to death,[37] and in a much more conventional theological spirit in the late poetry of T.S. Eliot. Another strand of opposition to the time of Progress was taken up by Nietzsche in his notion of eternal recurrence and was passed on by him to Thomas Mann and other exponents of a mythic and unchanging time of eternal variation. The rise of the new sciences of sociology and anthropology had important, and sometimes unintended, consequences in countering the Western-oriented times of Progress. Weber's comparative studies of religions and civilizations, though overtly still wedded to developmental sequences of rationality, actually serve to relativize them and to break up the unity of any linear progression of historical time into discrete series of differentiated modes of rationalization and of tradition whose continuity was punctured by unpredictable irruptions of charisma. Anthropologists, too, in a quite different way, because of their preoccupation with historically static societies eventually came to question the earlier presuppositions of a uniform development of evolution from primitive to civilized to advanced societies. At present this questioning has received a new impetus from the work of Lévi-Strauss, whose critique of the time of Progress based on a new structuralist problematic has been continued, though in a highly modified form, by Althusser and Foucault.

Lévi-Strauss develops his thoughts on time by way of a critique of Sartre's historicity, which is founded upon the Deed as a mode of historicist praxis. Instead he propounds a notion of history that is in principle no different from the ahistorical studies of anthropology, so that the temporal succession of the periods and epochs of a civilized society is treated just like the spatial spread of different kinds of primitive societies. Or, as in another version of this reduction, any unified and progressive history is broken up into a conjunction of numerous temporalities each of which is merely a certain kind of diachronic ordering of a selection of events in a chronological succession—an idea of history that had previously been put into practice by some of the "Annales" school of historians, for example, in Braudel. For Lévi-Strauss, historical thought is a form of rational or "domesticated" knowledge that is "a manifestation, in the temporal order, of knowledge which is interstitial and unifying rather than discontinuous and analogical,"[38] the latter being a characterization of mythical or "savage" thought. Hence, history—and its temporality—is in no way original or fundamental to human thought, and the timelessness of the savage mind is simply a different way of structuring knowledge from that of the temporality of the civilized mind. Lévi-Strauss criticizes all forms of historicism, and Sartre's in particular, for "making historicity the last refuge of a transcendental humanism," and instead insists that "history is tied neither to man nor to any particular object."[39]

Foucault takes up this criticism at that point and tries to show that the temporality of the Deed originates together with Man at the start of the modern order of knowledge. Foucault, too, attempts to break up any such primordial historicity based on the Deed by scattering it into numerous discontinuous temporalities:

> Since man posits himself in the field of positive knowledge, only in so far as he speaks, works and lives, can his history ever be anything but the inextricable nexus of different times, which are foreign to him and heterogeneous in respect of one another? Will the history of man ever be more than a sort of modulation common to changes in the conditions of life . . . to transformations in the economy . . . and to the succession of forms and usages in language?[40]

Althusser, like Foucault, attempts a destruction of the time of the Deed by scattering it into numerous temporalities, but he does not do so in his own name or in the name of a new order of post-modern knowledge but, rather, in the name of the late Marx. For Althusser, the decisive break in time had already occurred inside Marx himself as a "coupure" separating the young Marx of the humanist Deed from the old Marx of structures of production. This break in time is what distinguishes history and the dialectic as understood in Hegel from Marx's understanding of it as this emerges from *Capital.* Hegelian time, according to Althusser, possesses the two essential characteristics of "homogeneous continuity" and "contemporaneity."[41] The first feature refers to the successive unfolding of phases in accordance with the Idea; the second refers to the vertical unity of all the layers of a temporal whole, which permits the extraction at any one moment of what Althusser calls an "essential section"—a vertical cut through the layers of a time stratum revealing the contemporaneous presence of every item in it at exactly the same stage of development. This is because the Hegelian whole is a "spiritual whole" in which "each of the parts is a pars totalis."[42] By contrast, Althusser insists that the Marxian whole is a "structured whole containing what can be called levels or instances which are distinct and relatively autonomous, and coexist within this complex structural unity, articulated with one another according to specific determinations, fixed in the last instance by the level or instance of the economy."[43] Althusser distinguishes four main levels—economic, political, theoretical, and ideological. And it is on account of this structural articulation of levels that he credits Marx with the destruction of the organic unity of the time of humanism, and instead propounds a series of differential times:

> We can argue from the specific structure of the Marxist whole that it is no longer possible to think the process of the development of the different levels of the whole in the same historical time. Each of the different levels does not have the same type of historical existence. On the contrary, we can assign to each level a peculiar time, relatively autonomous and hence relatively independent, even in its dependence, of the times of other levels.[44]

Althusser's fragmentation of the unity of historicist time, like that of Lévi-Strauss and Foucault, in turn brings its own difficulties. If every level is to have its own relatively autonomous temporality with its own rhythm, development, break, and continuity, then why is it that the levels coincide where and when they do? Althusser attempts to overcome this problem with his notion of the "conjuncture" and to argue that "the presence of one level is, so to speak, the absence of another, and this coexistence of a 'presence' and absences is simply the effect of the structure of the whole in its articulated decentricity."[45]

The last phrase quoted is a very complex maneuver on Althusser's part designed not to have to admit that the economic level forms a kind of base time that determines all the other times, as a more conventional Marxist would hold, or to allow, as a more conventional structuralist would, that there is a superordinant structure governing the structures of the different levels, a structure of structures. If this sophistical move does not work, if the quoted phrase is no more than an escape mechanism, then Althusser is either forced back on a single basic time, and so is back where he started, or is forced to concede that the coincidence of levels comprising a conjuncture is simply due to chance, which in turn generates its own difficulties and is incompatible with his Marxism. Foucault has already partly embraced the last alternative in dealing with this problem; he states that "we must accept the introduction of chance as a category in the production of events."[46] Hence, no matter which way one turns there are bound to arise difficulties and anomalies in any theory of differential times that are no less easy to overcome than are the contradictions of the unified time of historicism.

But that is still not the end of the difficulties generated by the idea of differential times. Heraclitus said: "One cannot step into the same river twice," but Althusser seems to be saying that one cannot step into the same river even once. If any step that is taken in history takes place at quite different levels, each with its own time, then what is there to show that all these levels and times are in fact a single historical act performed in the present moment? What is this presentness of the act, or of the conjuncture, in which all the other times coincide, what kind of a time is it? Is it merely a subjective illusion of consciousness to suppose that there is such a present time of the Act? But to believe that would be to argue that all action and consciousness is nothing but illusion—a conclusion, indeed, to which Althusser seems to be drawn. However, if the temporal unity of the act in its present moment is illusory, then it becomes impossible to show what is real, or which are the real levels and real times out of which the conjuncture is compounded. A present act—so Althusser would maintain—has but four main levels or dimensions of time in which it takes place—economic, political, theoretical, and ideological. But by what right or theoretical sleight-of-hand has he distinguished these as real, as the levels of real time? Unless this is simply dogmatically insisted upon, there is no reason to affirm or deny the unreality of some of these levels: for example, why should theory have a time of its own—or why should it not? There is also no reason not to put forward innumerable other levels equally justified in demanding their own time: why not art, music, society, sexuality, the unconscious, and so forth as the real times? Are the requirements of Marxist politics to be the deciding criteria? In effect, there could be as many times as the levels one chose to institute. Althusser himself admits that his times are "constructed out of the reality of the different rhythms which punctuate the different operations of production, circulation, distribution";[47] but unless he were bound down by Marxist dogmatics, why should anyone else restrict himself to this one reality, why not as many others as he cares to construct? Why not have as many times as there are objects in history? Althusser himself grants Foucault the right to construct the "concept of the time of the unconscious," and he goes on to say that all that needs to be done is "to construct and identify the object itself, in order to construct from this the concept of its history."[48] But he does not seem to see the implication that if one bothered to construct an infinity of "objects" one would have an infinity of different times. Since every single historical act can in principle be infinitely conceptualized, in theory one could construct on the basis of each such act an infinity of historical "objects." Hence, the act itself can in principle take place in an infinity of different times. Ergo: not only can one not step into the same river twice, but one cannot step into it even one time, for new times are ever upon one.

Thus by this step into the river of time, which is also one step down the passage of Faust, we have passed from the unitary Time of the original Deed to the infinity of differential times that arise from the undoing of the Deed. We are caught between these extreme poles of time and can rest securely with neither. We are tossed from one to the other and back again. Of course, after all that has been thought it is impossible to return naively to the original four-square rhythms of the march of Progress as it first emerged out of Goethe's developing Deed or Hegel's unfolding of the Idea. Yet neither can we be content with the syncopated play of temporalities of decentered structures. Some measure of unity, continuity and presentness must be sought in time; the force of origination must be recognized in history, the principial must be placed in its beginning. The Deed with which everything began, and by which it continues to become, can no longer be understood as Goethe understood it. The goal of Progress to which it gave rise cannot be accepted as the promised deliverance of historical time itself. The end-endlessness, finitude-infinity of the time of Progress cannot be harmonized in such a way as to ensure the continued upward expansion of Man, for, as Faust discovered when approaching his end, time is now contracting and Man is in danger of his own approaching end. The time of Progress has revealed itself to be also other than it was thought to be at the start of the Deed; another time has now come to the fore by which the ideal unity and continuity of the time of Progress has been forever shattered.

This is the blow by which Progress has now been struck down. This deed is not, however, the blow of Faust's fist by which the "beautiful world" was destroyed; it is that other deed which "might be the be-all and the end-all here, but here, upon this bank and shoal of time" (*Macbeth* I.vii). As we stand here in the present we know that the high tide of Progress has left us stranded high and dry in this moment which is our be-all and end-all. Time no longer flows forward; it stands still, despite the swirling eddies it sets up by its ever-continuing onrush. The tide of Progress has turned back on itself and is now repeating itself round and round again in a dizzying maelstrom that sucks everything into its hollow core. It is this fatal turning of the time of Progress against itself that generates in the minds of men all the other times that are denials of the time of Progress. As Progress turns back on itself it also reveals itself for what it had really been all along; we now know it to have been quite other than what those who furthered it supposed. Its time can also now be seen to be other than what they imagined; it is an Other time. This Other time is our time, the time of our present moment. We now know that the time of Progress is not endless—or, really, it is endless, for it goes nowhere and achieves nothing, but that is also its end. Progress does indeed achieve Nothing, a Nothing achieved in Deed that could not have been achieved in any other way. Progress has become what it was always becoming: "And now one realizes that becoming aims at nothing and achieves nothing."[49] But this nothing is its greatest achievement; it is our greatest achievement.

What are we saying here? How can Nothing be an achievement? How can it be a great achievement? How can greatness and Nothing ever come together? How can the Deed achieve Nothing? These are the questions that lead us into our next and last antinomy: that of Progress and Nihilism. We can move into this potentially fatal antinomy by once more asking the simplest, most naive of questions.

## SCENE II
## *The Language of Nihilism*

### I

What was there prior to the Deed, and what will be there after it? Once again there are two diametrically opposed answers to this simple question. Neither is independently tenable, but together they form a contradiction giving rise to the antinomy of the Deed and Nothing. In its very naïveté this antinomy lies at the heart of the whole relationship between Progress and Nihilism. Hence, the question we are here asking is perhaps the most decisive one for modern thought.

The first answer to the question parallels closely the theological answer to the question of God's creation—that prior to it there was nothing; so, analogously, prior to the Deed there was Nothing. This is the original Nothing out of which everything comes and back to which it threatens to fall if the ceaseless activity of the Deed stops even for a moment. Inherent in this answer is the notion of the Deed as a *creatio ex nihilo,* though, as we have already seen, this creative Act is rendered human; it is anthropomorphized and humanized at least insofar as the creation of the human world is concerned—for Man, not God, is now the creator of himself and his own world. He creates it out of Nothing by means of his Word, though that is no longer the Logos but the Deed of Language. By means of Language Man gives meaning to the world, and so enacts a meaningful world. Prior to Man's creation of his meaningful world there was the original Nothing of senseless Nature: matter without form, timelessness without history, sensation without self-consciousness, things without words, world-chaos without world-order, human nature without human culture, bestiality without law; but also conversely: innocence without crime, spontaneity without self-consciousness, time without corruption, life without death. The Nothing prior to the Deed is conceived of variously, depending on the specific cultural context and the philosophy in which it appears, but in different forms and formulations from Goethe to Heidegger this is the basic answer of Faustian thought to the original question, whether explicitly given or to be found there only by implication.

Perhaps the simplest and clearest formulation of this original answer invoking the original Nothing is to be found in the philosophy of the Deed of Moses Hess: "The beginning of a new creation does not emerge according to the so-called developmental sequence out of an old creation. Every new creation is a jump that arises from Nothing, from the negation of the old creation."[1] According to this conception, every creative act is a *creatio ex nihilo,* so all creative activity is an instance of the original creation out of Nothing. In particular, the creative Deed brings forth time as history out of the non-temporal Nothing at every moment of historical development. Stirner, following Hess, saw self-formation in these terms, thus "grounding the individual upon creative nothingness," or, as he himself put it in the English words of the Bible: "I have placed my case upon Nothing."[2] We find here the beginnings of an existentialist Nothing that was to persist at least till Sartre's early philosophy.

But there is also another answer to the question, one which does not, strictly speaking, any longer belong to Faustian thought, though it is inherent in modern thought as such and reveals the hidden side of Faustian philosophy. Negative indications of it are to be found scattered among the Faustian philosophers, in the tendencies in themselves against which they struggle, the ones they are rarely willing to acknowledge. To find analogues to this answer we shall have to hark back to the Renaissance, that is, prior to the Deed of Faust, prior also to the Classical order of representation, and specifically we shall have to reach back to Shakespeare, to his most terrible play, the one in which he approaches closest to our modern preoccupations with Nothing—the murderous drama of *Macbeth.* It is in this play that the deed is presented as a "deed without a name" (IV.i). This is the inverse of the original creative Deed; it is the act of reduction whose most concrete human manifestation is murder, and which in the present world takes on the monstrous dimensions of total annihilation—the last act. Also in its deeper philosophic meaning every act of destruction is that by which Nothing is done: it is the destructive production of Nothing out of Something. Once more, of course, we shall have to conceive of it not theologically, as if what was being invoked were some kind of peculiar Gnostic heresy, nor metaphysically as if it were some kind of modern pessimism à la Schopenhauer, but in terms of Language; for Nothing, as we shall show, can only be produced in and by Language.

The idea of Nothing is invoked in both answers to the original simple question, but, as it were, from opposite directions, for one kind of Nothing precedes the Deed, whereas the other kind follows it; they are two quite different "qualities of Nothing" (*Lear* I.ii). The first is the original Nothing—it might be called an Idealistic or Faustian Nothing; the second is the Macbethan final Nothing and it is by contrast reductive, that is, either destructive or annihilatory. Out of these there follow two quite different conceptions of and approaches to modern Nihilism. Once again it must be firmly stressed that this is no idle theological or metaphysical speculation; at stake are very specific and concrete issues touching on all facets of modern life and history. These issues bear on the whole problem of Nihilism: its nature, manifestations, causes, and likely consequences. The further question as to whether and how Nihilism might be overcome can only be answered in the context of one or the other of these answers. All this can easily be made evident by reference to the modern conception of Language, for it is only through Language in this sense that all talk of creation out of Nothing and the "creation" of Nothing can be given a specific meaning and a concrete sociological and historical import.

Goethe himself had not succeeded in defining the Deed or its Nothing in terms of Language: "In all that lives the Eternal Force works on; for everything would dissolve into Nothing if it were to remain in Being" ("One and All"). The language here is still quite naively theological and metaphysical, though the thought struggling to be expressed is on the threshold of modernity. In the play *Faust* that expression succeeds much better, for when Faust declares, "Out of thy Nothing, I shall win my All" (*Faust* Part II, I.vi) the Nothing is concretely embodied in the figure of Mephistopheles, and so it can be given much greater specificity. However, the Nothing of Mephistopheles has many qualities throughout the play. To begin with it is the Nothing of negating activity, involving an identity of Nothing and Negation that is the hallmark of Idealist philosophy. Because of this identification the Nothing is conceived of as the negative moment in the dialectic that is the process of Becoming. Thus Hegel opens the dialectic of his Logic with the contradiction of Being and Nothing out of which emerges Becoming. Analogously, Goethe begins his *Faust* by having the Lord define Mephistopheles as one of the "spirits that deny." But the Lord makes it quite clear that this negative activity of the Devil can only help create insofar as it is directed to provoking the actions of men, which is why he assigns him as Faust's companion. The Devil is himself aware of this irony of creation which will in the end make him lose his bet and deprive him of his prize, the soul of Faust. He explains himself as the "spirit that negates," who represents evil and destruction, but who, far from being able to bring the world to Nothing, only succeeds in promoting its further creation. Though Mephistopheles changes his role in Part II, Goethe's basic optimism remains unimpaired, for in the end even Mephistopheles is momentarily overcome by love (though in his case it is the lusts of pederasty, the crudest stages of Love's ascent, that are provoked in him by the bare behinds of the heavenly boys). What subserves and promotes this optimism, apart from the belief in Love as ultimate Reality, is the belief in the inherent identity of negation and Nothing as a destructive activity that is but the negative moment in the dialectic of creation—which is itself the intellectual aspect of the belief in creation as Love.

If that identity were to be denied, if Nothing were to be seen as other than the negativity of the dialectic, then a different view would emerge of destruction as well. It would be possible to reverse the accepted relation of creation to destruction and see creation itself, insofar as it is humanly promoted, as part of the total process that is inherently destructive. Man would emerge from this as the destroyer in the creative world of Nature, the bearer of death in Nature's plentitude of life. Man's uniqueness in knowing death is precisely what compels him to evil and destruction; at its crudest and most basic the knowledge that he will die prompts him to kill others. It is this vision that leads us to see Man also as Macbeth and not simply as Faust. It is Macbeth who in the end "signifies Nothing," for it is Man himself, and not a Devil external to himself, who introduces Nothing into the world. He does so by means of his Language and its power of signification. It is in terms of Language that Man most fully exercises his destructive function. He destroys everything in Language, for no sooner is something signified than it is broken and divided against itself, for by what is known of it something else is made unknowable; it is no longer the thing wholly itself, but only as it has been differentiated through the medium of Language. Metaphorically speaking, Language kills.[3]

In the Faustian view of it, Language is solely creative; its creative function is not merely its own self-formation and transformation, but, as in the course of its own constitution it constitutes the meaningful world, it is the creation of the world. Through its capacity for negation, which gives it its power of forming what is taken as Reality, it creates the world out of Nothing. Language can do this through its inherent capacity to signify and so endow or deny significance. As we have already shown, the significative function of Language arises out of human interrelatedness, for men's interactions are oriented around things and they thereby establish significative relations to those things. In pursuit of their common human life men interact with each other and together they act on things, and in doing so they set up networks of significances; these are indicated by the signifying meanings of the words that are employed in the course of those interactions. Putting it in Wittgenstein's terms: what we are given are forms of common human life, and the meanings words have they acquire by playing a part in the gamelike language-activities that comprise these common forms of life. But in so giving rise to Language, men create their human world, and that entails the simultaneous constitution of the Reality of the world of things. Reality is thus dependent on Significance. And it is also bound up with Coherence, for all relations in turn relate to each other and need to be made coherent and to be unified. Hence, the ultimate Faustian dream of Language, and it is the dream of all Idealism, is that of a completely coherent world filled with significance comprising one Reality. The ideal wish-fulfillment is continually frustrated by the unyielding character of things, which will not allow themselves to be completely realized, and by the opaque character of Language, which conceals as much as it reveals and obscures as it enlightens. Language is not a medium for perspicuous representation, as Wittgenstein termed it. The transcendental frustration of every attempt to impose an absolute Coherence, Reality, and Significance on the world gives rise to intellectual Nihilism, as Nietzsche points out.[4] And with Nihilism there emerges another Nothing, one that can no longer be accommodated in Faustian thought, for it is the Nothing that emerges out of Language itself.

The Faustian Nothing is, by contrast, the Nothing prior to Language. In its earliest manifestation it is the metaphysical expression of Kant's thing-in-itself, the thing prior to all apprehension and conceptualization. But first in Schopenhauer and then in Nietzsche the thing-in-itself takes on the more irrationalist, quasi-metaphysical form of Will. In the

Faustian tradition proper, Nothing is the chaos of unformed Nature prior to Spirit or Culture, or matter prior to its formation or realization—symbolized by that thick materiality in which Mephistopheles seeks to ensnare the Light and to which he seeks to reduce all spirit. For Marx, this matter is the raw stuff to which productive labor is applied and so objectified, and Nature is the site of this formative activity. The Nothing that is prior to the Deed takes as many forms as there are versions of the Deed in modern thought: whatever it is that the Deed realizes, that was Nothing prior to its realization. And consequently, it is also Nothing as soon as the Deed's active power gives out, for what the Deed creates out of Nothing would fall back into that Nothing were the Deed to cease.

The threat of Nihilism, on this Faustian view of Nothing, is thus no more than the danger of Mephistopheles: it is the threat of falling back into the original chaos of uncreation. It is analogous to the classical fear of the recursion back into primordial chaos were Order to be destroyed. However, there is this difference, that in modern thought the fear of universal anomie is not simply one arising out of the disruption of a preestablished universal Order but, rather, of the cessation of the ordering activity itself. Hence, it is no longer an active attacking onslaught against Order that is required to bring it on, but much less than that: it is merely the passive inability any longer to create new forms or maintain the permanence of old ones. Modern Faustian Nihilism, unlike classical chaos, is liable to recur at every moment; nothing extraordinary needs to be done to bring it about, no crime against Being, or God, or the law of the cosmos, no transgression of any limits set for mortals. Goethe's Faust is in danger of falling into the Mephistophelean Nothing not because he has damned himself in selling his soul, but merely when he ceases his active striving and utters the annihilating formula: "If to the fleeting hour I say 'Remain, so fair thou art, remain!'" (Part I, "Faust's Study"). This formula is precisely the unsaying of the Deed, for it seeks to arrest the movement of developing time and hold it still in the one enduring moment, which would therefore make everything revert back to Nothing again. It would be like the moment prior to the Deed.

On this view, the Deed itself is the only answer to Nihilism, for so long as it continues there cannot be any fall back into Nothing. The Progress that the Deed unfolds is the only counter to the stagnation that is Nihilism. More Progress seems the solution to any temporary faltering, or if not simply more Progress, then at least better Progress or one of a different kind. One Faustian writer after another has presented the solution to the problems of modernity, which we would call Nihilism, in this way. Thus, for example, in the Marxist tradition the reifications attendant on capitalism are overcome by progressing from it to true socialism; the remythification resulting from the fatal dialectic of Enlightenment or rationality is overcome by an appeal to a higher form of dialectical Reason; the one-dimensionality of post-industrial society is overcome by introducing in opposition to it a countervailing negative dimension. In other approaches the activity propounded is quite different, but it invariably involves a continuation of that very Progress which provoked the problems of modernity. Nihilism is to be overcome by the very Deed that brings it about. But "there's the rub." For to continue the activity of Progress must surely mean to further the Nihilism that is attendant on it, and yet it would seem that it is not possible to stop Progress, for, on the premises of Faustian thought, as soon as Progress threatens to halt at any level attained it freezes at that moment and comes back to Nothing again. Like Faust, it can never say to the moment: "Remain, so fair thou art." Faustian thought is caught in this dilemma: it can neither stop the activity of its Deed, for to do that would be to fall into Nothing, nor can it keep on continuing it, for that obviously leads to Nothing. This, in a nutshell, is the dilemma of modern Progress and of every mode of thought wedded to it.

The realization of this dilemma leads to an opposite answer to the original question "What was there prior to the Deed?" and consequently to an anti-Faustian view of the relation of Progress to Nihilism. On this view it is the Deed itself that produces Nothing. Spelled out fully in historical terms, this means that it is Progress itself that gives rise to Nihilism, and nothing but Progress could have done so. The consequence of this thought is that Progress can never in principle lead to any overcoming of Nihilism; on the contrary, as long as Progress lasts so long will Nihilism be there. But before this relationship of the Deed and Nothing or Progress and Nihilism can be properly stated or even explained there are some very difficult questions to be answered. How is it possible to produce Nothing? What sense does it make to speak of it like that? What has it to do with Nihilism?

Once again the issue is not to be left up in the air or speculated about in a metaphysical vacuum; it has to be settled on the solid ground of Language. Nothing only has its being in Language and through Language. "Nothing is but what is not" (*Macbeth* I.iii) in Language alone. To say this, as *Macbeth* reveals, is not merely to make the commonsense and otiose, logical observation that falsehood, negativity, denial, absence, the counter-factual, and the hypothetical all have their being in Language because only through a language can they be signified. It is, rather, that through its signification of Nothing, Language gives rise to negative phenomena of non-being—"nothings"—usually associated with Nihilism, such as meaninglessness, absurdity, estrangement, alienation, anxiety, dread (the fear of Nothing), privacy (being a nobody), dying (approaching to Nothing), and finally death itself (being Nothing). Death is the decisive instance of the Nothing that takes its meaning and being from Language, for outside Language death is nothing at all. In a sense, therefore, death only exists in life, even though it is the very thing that is the denial of life as it brings life to Nothing. Hence, in the very process of being given a meaning in Language, death in turn threatens to deprive Language of its meaning, to render it mere "sound and fury, signifying nothing." But in that very act of self-destruction—and here the paradox is raised to an even higher power—Language is enabled to signify nothing, literally to give Nothing its significance; and it is this that gives Language its supremely destructive power of reducing everything to Nothing. The reductive power of Language derives from the nexus between Language and death by which Nothing is signified. In this knot intrinsicate lies also the being of the Nothing that is Nihilism. (The reductive language of science shows this. See page 172.)

To understand the "production of Nothing" is simply to understand the reductive power of Language. There, too, lies the key to Nihilism, which is an historical process of the production of Nothing by the Language of modern civilization. Ultimately, all the specific phenomena of modern Nihilism must be referred back to the reductive manifestations of this Language, for in the process of its own self-reduction Language reduces the whole of the human world. Man thus appears as the prisoner and victim of his own Language, which both made him and now threatens to unmake him.

We can tentatively make this a little clearer at this point by explaining that meaninglessness, or any other negative phenomenon, is not simply given as such of its own accord. Something might be encountered which has as yet no specific meaning and in that sense is nonsensical or senseless, but it need not be meaningless; for example, the utterance of nonsense syllables or random words can be a highly meaningful act. The meaningless understood as that which is absurd is made, not given or found, in contradistinction to the nonsensical, which is simply given and there—a distinction which will be elaborated in what follows. The absurd is made by means of an act of language-reduction, since it can only arise through a withdrawal of meaningfulness—literally, through a voiding of meaning. Something is rendered meaningless in the sense of being made absurd only when its meaning has been withdrawn from it or when its significance has been made insignificant. There are innumerable ways whereby a meaning is rendered meaningless or unsignified: sheer repetition, or boredom, or traditionalistic habitualness can accomplish this. Clearly, though, that would not be the way it occurs in modern Nihilism; there it is, rather, acts of annihilation or destruction that are required. We might recall here the reductive process of modern science whereby metaphysics was finally made meaningless. The present meaninglessness of metaphysics is a supreme testimony to the reductive voiding power of the discovery of Language that arose out of the Faustian Deed. However, in the process of unmaking metaphysical meaning this same modern Language threatens to fragment—partly by breaking up into specialized sciences—and so make itself meaningless. And here we encounter what is perhaps the supreme paradox of Language. In reducing something to meaninglessness Language renders it a "nothing," that is, it signifies it as Nothing; but in the process Language signifies itself as Nothing as well—Language, that is, signifies itself as "sound and fury, signifying Nothing." But, of course, the supreme act of signification is that whereby Language signifies Nothing. Hence, Language in the very act by which it realizes its utmost powers of signification deprives itself of any significance. Language is everything and Nothing at once: in declaring itself to be Nothing it makes itself everything, and in declaring itself to be everything it makes itself Nothing. We shall be returning to this paradox of signification in what is to follow, but some explanations are required beforehand.

First, we must distinguish better the two forms of meaninglessness which we have called the nonsensical and the absurd. Nonsense is that which has no meaning because it never had any; it is a failure to attain to meaning. Absurdity, by contrast, is that which once had a meaning but has somehow been deprived of it. The absurd in this sense is the meaningless that has been rendered such, whereas the nonsensical is the meaningless that has never had a meaning.[5] The difference is analogous to and closely bound up with that between the strange and the estranged. The strange is that which has never before been encountered, whereas the estranged is the long-familiar which has become estranged precisely because of its over-familiarity. The strange is that which is unexpected, new, unknown, and unnamed; the estranged is totally known, predictable, and designated. Once something has become estranged it can rarely, or only under exceptional conditions, be made familiar or close again, and it can almost never be made strange and new. For the strange is such precisely because it has not as yet been acted upon, whereas the estranged is made to be such by the kinds of negative activities that have an alienating effect. For example, when at the climactic moment following the resurrection of Banquo's corpse, Macbeth exclaims: "You make me strange even to the disposition that I own," he is referring to estrangement in our sense, specifically to self-estrangement: a condition of existential Nihilism. It is a state of existing as a Nothing: in a void, devoid of relationship, reduced to one's single self, suspended in empty time, unspeakably "there"—yet in closest proximity to death. But, paradoxically, it is in such a state of estrangement that one can also be intensely existing, but only in loneliness and silence or in the secrecy of one's own language of privacy, aware of one's very own death. A condition of estrangement is in that sense made, and cannot be had except for this making, which is accomplished through the negative activities of severing, alienating, voiding, self-destruction, and annihilation, or all of the existentially reductive activities.

This making of estrangement is strictly analogous to the making of that mode of meaninglessness we call absurdity, in contradistinction to nonsense. The absurd has to be made in one or another of the modes of language-reduction, the most important of which we have already encountered as destruction and annihilation. These modes of reduction are literally a reductio ad absurdum or reduction to Nothing. The mode of argument classically so called is the logical analogue of language procedures that go far beyond mere logical reasoning, though, taken in a broader sense, reductio ad absurdum can be interpreted as a mode of language-destruction by argument, the converse of deduction, the mode of language-construction by argument. In fact, de-construction is a mode of language-destruction that Derrida has made his own—though he does not seem fully to realize that this is a mode of destruction and that what it does is to reduce that which was meaningful to meaninglessness. Thus the de-construction of metaphysics has indeed the effect of what he calls a "reduction of sense,"[6] but that is the effect of rendering it meaningless—not, of course, in the positivistic sense of showing it up to have been nonsensical all along, but in the opposite sense of making that which was once supremely meaningful lose its meaning or, better put, to retain it as only an historical meaning that is dead and void as far as our present anti-metaphysical language is concerned. Through being placed, as it were, in a museum of dead languages, metaphysics is preserved embalmed as the corpse of former meaning. Its continued existence is as something that is at present absurd; only if at some future time it were to be resurrected and to take on meaning again would it emerge from its limbo of absurdity, but that is as unlikely as making the estranged familiar again. The specifically rational way of rendering metaphysics absurd is often by means of arguments that have the outward logical form of a reductio ad absurdum. But, as we have already hinted, what is really involved in such an argument is an exposure of "silences": the revelation of all that metaphysics makes invisible, all that it represses and is unable to own up to, all that cannot be said in its language.

The production of the meaningless as the absurd takes place in all provinces of modern language and life; it is the process of reduction that is the historical formation of that Nothing we call modern Nihilism. Language-reduction in both of its opposed forms, as destruction and as annihilation, is there behind the "progress" of modern art, culture, science, politics, and society in general. The future course of the modern world depends crucially on which of these will prevail, for the distinction between destruction and annihilation is our modern ontological difference on which the whole of our being rests.

The term *destruction* has been employed in art criticism quite unselfconsciously ever since the beginning of the "modern" art movement. For example, one critic seeking to specify the difference between French and German modern painting puts it quite spontaneously as follows:

> While the French destroyed form in a deep desire to analyze its properties as form, the Germans destroyed form and colour emotionally, to find the universal significance of what lay behind the reality they had just negated. The disparity between the logical fragmentation of Cubism and the decorative distortion of Fauvism in France and the strong emotive and mystical distortions of Expressionism in Germany would indicate more qualifying background difference than similarities.[7]

With perhaps more philosophic awareness, Adorno utilizes the term *destruction* or a cognate word like *dissolution* or fragmentation to describe the musical language of Schoenberg: "Musical language dissociates into fragments."[8]

> Musical language is polarized according to its extremes ... towards a crystalline standstill of a human being whom anxiety causes to freeze in her tracks. ... In the intensification of musical "communication"—not even suspected by this school in the beginning—the difference between theme and development, the constancy of harmonic flow, and the unbroken melodic line are *destroyed* by this polarization.[9]

The same term *destruction* occurs in a different context in the literary criticism of Barthes, where it is significantly linked to *murder* along the lines already established by Mallarmé, Camus, Blanchot, and Robbe-Grillet. *Destruction* in Barthes is a process of objectification and solidification whereby the world is reduced to objects whose Form literature reveals. Unfortunately, none of the above critics distinguishes between the two modes of reduction, destruction and annihilation; frequently what they call destruction is annihilation in our sense.

Thus the whole history of modern art can be seen in its most general aspect as a passage of reduction in the two dimensions of destruction and annihilation, figuratively as indeed the Deed of Faust through time contracted to his end. But that would no longer be a Faustian view of it. It is possible to see each outstanding "modern" art movement as effecting a new kind of destruction both of the sanctioned tradition of classical art and of its own predecessors in modernism. Each such movement is like the invention of a unique way of destroying; it is the creation of new practices and concepts of destruction. These successive movements by which the passage of destruction has been propelled have not, of course, followed each other haphazardly, even though there has been the greatest imaginable discontinuity in their succession. But neither is there any simple dialectical law governing their relationship. Rather, there occurred a passage of reduction in which each movement was based on a destruction of the previous ones. In painting, for example, the sequence of Impressionism, post-Impressionism, Cubism, and Abstract Art is one such passage. The dissolution of the static forms of classical and Romantic art through the sensationalist and phenomenal vision of the Impressionists is followed by Cézanne's attempt to consolidate and dislocate his "petites sensations" into temporary solidified geometric shapes arising out of the flux of sensations; these shapes then become the abstract forms which Cubism was to de-structure, thereby disordering the whole of object-space; finally, out of the fragments of Cubistic forms came the collage technique dis-assembling all objects into a patchwork carrying only furtive reminiscences of reality, and this could be handled quite abstractly. One could study in great detail any one aspect of this destructive passage, such as the dissolution of objects, and explain how and why it took place—in terms of painterly technique and style, in terms of the alteration of perception and world-view that it signified, and finally, how it was significant for European culture as a whole. (See page 172 on the reduction of the object in science.)

European culture underwent numerous such passages of destruction; it was literally an historical passage of reductio ad absurdum, the process whereby the Absurd was produced by successive reductions. This production by reduction is the making of Nothing, which in our time takes on the specific quality of Nihilism.

At this point we begin to glimpse another startling paradox: it is precisely the making of this Nothing that seems our accomplishment as modern men, and one of the "greatest" achievements that we have performed on behalf of mankind, for, as Nietzsche said, "Something might be true even though it is harmful and dangerous in the greatest degree; it might in fact belong to the basic make-up of things that one should perish from its recognition."[10] But can we say this now, when it is Man who might perish from the recognition of this truth? Is the death of Man worth such an achievement? Leonardo da Vinci said, "Among the great things which are to be found among us the being of nothingness is the greatest." These words of the loneliest and most enigmatic of men no longer have the meaning they would have had for him, for the being of nothingness was to this greatest of painters the boundary between two visible surfaces, which was nothing because it had no breadth, being the line by which the surfaces could be delineated and so seen. For us the being of nothingness is our Nihilism; is it, too, the greatest thing to be found among us?

We can realize something of the truth of this paradox if we once more reflect on the paradoxical achievement that is our destruction of metaphysics, or, even better, if we reflect on the undoubted greatness of modern art. It is an achievement of an unparalleled kind, quite incommensurate with any of the canons of artistic perfection as laid down in classical art or in any other artistic tradition. In relation to the rationality of classicism the meaning of modern art is absurd, its order is truly a chaos, and its reality is unreal. But this, despite the fulminations of the conservatives among us, is not a judgment on ourselves that we must accept as the verdict of history. From our own perspective we can now judge the past and perceive in it achievements that are like our own, those that go against the standards of tradition and thus had not been appreciated or properly understood in their own time but had to await discovery in ours. For example, in Greek tragedy, the very locus of classicism, Nietzsche was able to discover qualities constituting an achievement quite different from any ascribed to it in traditional criticism from Aristotle onward. In Rembrandt we see a vision of the anatomy of death that had been imperceptible before.[11] In Shakespeare we read a foretaste of our own Nihilism. In this way we can now rewrite the judgment of tradition on itself and make it yield a different verdict on ourselves as well. The book of the past is like a palimpsest to us; beneath the sacred text we detect lurking an effaced sacrilegious writing that is the precise "other" of what the text seeks to convey. In that invisible writing, as in an invisible mirror, we see a past reflection of ourselves. Thus we can see ourselves precisely in that which the tradition seeks to suppress of itself; we hear our own speech in its silences. But in giving words to these silences which tradition forbade itself to speak we succeed in destroying tradition. By breaking open the silences in the heart of the discourses of tradition we destroy these discourses and take upon ourselves the guilt of murder—like Macbeth thrusting his dagger into the heart of Duncan, his sacred king. And that, too, is part of our terrible greatness.

These destructive achievements of our time are at one with the annihilating failures that bring us to the brink of total ruin; they have the same provenance. Both the destruction and the annihilation are reflected almost indistinguishably in the reduction of our arts, as well as in that of the sciences. The forces of annihilation that devastate speculative thought and threaten to bring it to an end are also threatening to bring art itself, Man's most delicate register of self-consciousness, steadily but surely to its end. In the music of our time Adorno has already heard the difference between the great destructive achievement of the School of Schoenberg and the annihilating propensities of their present-day followers: "The sounds are still the same. But the expression of *Angst,* which made their originals great, has vanished."[12] Something similar is taking place in all the arts, and, as it proceeds further, there remain fewer critics able to distinguish what is destructive from that which is merely annihilatory; the art that strives to give meaning to the meaninglessness of the world is all too often confused with that which is mere meaninglessness incarnate. The expression of absurdity is not separated from sheer nonsense, and so the nonsense prevails.

As it is reflected in art, so it happens in language in general and, ultimately, in all of life. For the quality of many activities of life and language is bound up with that of art: the finer perceptions of time are inherent in music and those of space are localized in painting, and the finer feelings of life are realized in literature. Hence, if these arts were to disappear then our whole language and life would be most seriously impoverished. For example, what would be left of our moral language if everything that is sustained by literature were to be removed from it? That is to say, what would be left of moral life if there were no lyric expressions, no didactic influence of parables and stories, no cultivation of feelings and manners in novels, no patterning of life and the formation of character through drama? Surely all that would remain would be rules and regulations, conformist dicta, purely self-willed approvals and disapprovals, subjective effusions of sentiment, and unbridled emotionalism—in effect, precisely that which the positivistic philosophy of the language of morals still admits of discussion, and to which a bureaucratically administered state apparatus gives legal credence. It makes for a life pared down to the lowest particulars, those which can figure as statistical indices.

This phenomenon of demoralization is but one of the facets of modern Nihilism, and a proper understanding of it would have to distinguish it sharply from all other moral negativities such as immorality and amorality. Demoralization takes place as much in language as in conduct. In fact, to all outward appearances conduct can remain basically unaltered—men may act in a law-abiding manner and do each other no legal hurt—while the language which is to give their acts their moral meaning is totally absent. For it is through and by means of Language that Nihilism exercises its reductive power. We could go so far as to say that Nihilism is the reductive power of Language itself become visible for the first time in human history. It is certainly true that it is because of the historical onset of Nihilism that we can apprehend—for example, in science—in its full momentousness that reductive power of Language which Wordsworth feared at the very start of the Deed.[13]

Reduction is the language-power opposite to that of language-creation. If through its creative power Language can form the world *ex nihilo,* then through its reductive power it can bring that world back to Nothing again. But it is not merely, as Faust and all modern Idealists would have it, that only that which has previously been created can be destroyed, if only so as to be re-created; rather, this destruction is the process by which the world is formed. On this anti-Faustian approach, Language is inherently reductive; it is such primarily because it destroys or even annihilates that which is prior to itself (Nature, Life, the thing-in-itself, basic sensation, etc.) and only out of that reduction does it create its own world of Reality. Abstraction, conceptualization, reasoning: the highest language attainments are on this view nothing but activities of reduction of things as they are prior to Language. Language thus appears as the primary and ultimate destructive weapon in the hand of Man, who is himself the inherent destroyer of the world. The traditional view of Man as creator, who works hand-in-hand with the creative powers of a benign God or Nature, is here reversed and cancelled. Man is not in harmony with his surroundings. Thus we encounter in the course of a discussion of modern Nihilism a theme that has hitherto had little exemplification outside the imagination of the very greatest of tragic writers.

They have taught us that Man destroys because he alone is aware of himself as mortal. But if Man were not to destroy, his death would have no reality, as it is through his own destructive acts that Man creates his death. Destruction makes for death, and death it is that drives to destruction. This is the fatal knot intrinsicate tying Man's awareness of his mortality with his propensity for death-dealing, which if put into effect makes him all the more aware of his own death and all the more prone to act on it. In modern times, given the ultimate weapons of technology, this has become a potentially fatal nexus not merely for the individual destroyer but possibly for the human race as a whole.

What accompanies this new and unprecedented possibility of total annihilation is a novel awareness of death, an unprecedented translation in the meaning of death, for it now embraces humanity as a whole. Man is mortal in a collective way never dreamt of before. All the historical phenomena that we identify as modern Nihilism are at least partly the symptoms of the unconscious awareness and dread of this new death. Nihilism is the secret, insidious presence of a new horrendous death sitting like Banquo as the uninvited guest in the midst of the modern feast of productive and creative life. The Faustian Deed, which was a translation of the Word, has now eventuated as the inconceivable "deed without a name," the undoing doing of a death beyond our imagination—the death of All. The presence of this death even prior to its eventuation is the new Nothing of Nihilism; it is the void in the heart of Progress, the heart of darkness within its Enlightenment. Even such a simple fact as that the main occupational activity of most modern men is governed by the constant repetition of machine production, which controls their whole social existence, points to the inroads of a repetition-compulsion that is also unconsciously an historical will to death, as Freud has shown. Progress as sheer repetitive accumulation of goods, services, machines, and men, whether for peace or war, is like a repetition-compulsion of history—a kind of karma of time itself. The need to introduce chance and accident into this totally determinate system in order to give men some illusion of freedom and free-play only confirms the compulsion. The hazards of chance that give an unpredictable momentary surprise and provide a fillip of excitement in the wheel of repetition are the only permitted accidents in the whole human lot. It is possible that through such an accident Man might annihilate himself, but it is also possible that he might accidentally free himself, too. The outcome is unknown.

To sum up: the manifestations of Nihilism in the modern world have to be understood in terms of this radical translation in the meaning of death that has occurred in modern times. Death has been voided of meaning, and so reduced to absurdity. Out of this absurd death has come the new "quality of Nothing" that we experience as Nihilism. It is, therefore, a Nothing that is produced—in the first place, by means of the reductive powers of modern Language. These powers of Language—which are themselves, in turn, perhaps ultimately manifestations of an unprecedented power of death—render death meaningless in the two previously specified modes of a death of annihilation or a death of destruction. The workings of modern Language, that is, constitute our sense of the meaninglessness of death in two contrasting forms: either as the Nothing of annihilation or the Nothing of destruction, either as the death of sheer oblivion that is the outcome of annihilation or as the violated death that is the outcome of destruction. The former is the meaninglessness of death that arises from its sheer ignoring and denial, as is to be found among those given over to an unlived life of unending Progress: it is the death of an utter unawareness of death. The latter is the absurdity of death that arises from the awareness that the meaning of death has been destroyed and that death is all the more present as the Nothing that makes nothing of the whole of life.

So it is that through a language of destruction death acquires a negative meaning in modern life as, paradoxically, the very thing that has been made meaningless. This is the unavoidable contradiction of every attempt to realize death in modern Language, namely, that it can only be a realization of the meaning of its meaninglessness. We know our death only as that which has been deprived of meaning. We are no longer in a position, given the language-powers at our disposal, to give death a positive meaning. The meanings of death as sustained in the languages of the great axial religions or in the language of classical tragedy or in metaphysical philosophy are the meanings that have suffered a reductio ad absurdum under the impact of the modern language of the Deed. The same language cannot, therefore, give death a meaning. However, in its nihilistic function of destruction it can be aware of itself as that language which has deprived death of all its traditional meanings. "Death" is now the word that signifies nothing—its present significance is precisely as a very peculiar signification of Nothing.

We return here to the paradox of signification that is at the heart of the being of Language, Death, and Nothing. The thought of signifying that which is in every way nothing seems to go against the notion of signification itself, since it is well-nigh grammatically determined that to signify is to signify something. How, then, can Nothing be signified? If the very being of language is to signify something, how can it go counter to its own nature in signifying Nothing? The problem is compounded when it is remembered that Language is a kind of nothingness, being mere "sound and fury, signifying nothing." But if Language is nothing, how can it signify itself? The question is one of how that which itself signifies nothing can at the same time be a signification of Nothing. It is the root question of signification itself, for it poses the problem of Language signifying itself. Language is thus a paradox to itself, for it would seem to be able to signify everything except itself. It would seem to be at once the signification of everything that signifies nothing, at once full of all possible meaning and empty of meaning.

The issue of the signification of Nothing arises with equal force and urgency in relation to life and death itself, for if death is the final nothingness then how can Language signify it? Put another way, what can give significance to death and, by extension, to life as well? Language, which it would seem can signify all in life, seems unable to signify death, on which the significance of life as a whole depends. If that were indeed so then death would be a nothing without significance, one that could not be spoken of in life but must be consigned to inarticulate silence. Speech would be totally given over to life and be quite unable to touch on the deeper reality of death, the reality of its silence. That silence would remain forever speechless. There would, thus, together emerge and merge a parallel incapacity of Language—that of signifying itself, and of signifying death. Both of these as nothings bring up the problem of how Nothing can be signified. The being of Language is as problematical as the being of death. Both are at once everything and nothing, and they threaten to make of everything a nothing and of nothing everything. Perhaps the most profound statement of this ultimate paradox is enunciated in Macbeth's last soliloquy: "Tomorrow and tomorrow and tomorrow . . ." (V.v), where the ultimate questions of death and life, of time, reality, and existence are grounded in that most paradoxical capacity of Language to signify Nothing—"a tale . . . signifying Nothing."

This paradoxical capacity of Language is central to any definition of Nihilism, for Nihilism is a kind of nothingness, being a kind of "death" within historical time and existence, and so it provokes similar paradoxical questions. How can Nihilism, which is a denial of meaning, be given a meaning? And if it cannot be given a meaning then how can it be spoken about? How can it be defined or even indicated? Is it even possible to be silent about it? The problems of signifying Nihilism are thus analogous to those of signifying death and Language itself.

If that is so, then what are we to make of the achievement of thinkers such as Nietzsche in speaking of Nihilism, and even in defining it? Is it a self-cancelling accomplishment? Is it beyond all language, in the sphere of deeds alone? Is Nietzsche's writing nothing but one speechless act of destruction—a deed of the hand that undoes the Deed? For it would seem that a language could only undo itself in speaking of that which destroys it. All these are problems in the signification of Nihilism which Nietzsche himself was quite unable to take up. If meaning is conceived of in Nietzsche as "value," then the loss, withdrawal, and destruction of values present no dilemmas. Values, like any other immaterial "objects," can be created and destroyed without, it seems, giving rise to antinomies. For example, there seems to be no difficulty involved in conceiving of the creation and destruction of art-objects, or any other such "values," so what difficulty could there be in so conceiving of meaningful values? However, if meaning is not a matter of value but of signification, this does raise paradoxes in speaking of Nihilism. If one significance could only be denied by means of another, just as one diamond can only be cut by another, then it would be impossible to deny all significances, but Nihilism is precisely such a denial. Putting it another way, if to assert that something is meaningless is itself to say something meaningful, then it would be self-contradictory to say that everything is meaningless. So it would seem that either Nihilism is impossible, or, if it is possible, that it cannot be said. But of course we know that it can be said, so how is that possible?

All our attempts to signify the Nothing that is Nihilism are fraught with such paradoxes. These paradoxes entangle the very language in which the attempt to signify Nihilism is being made, and put it at risk. By this we can know it is at the utmost limits of our language. But it also indicates that we are at the limits of Language as such, for it brings out the paradoxicality in every attempt to signify Nothing. As we have previously mentioned, it is the same kind of paradox of Language encountered in *Macbeth*[14] in the attempt to signify Nothing as death. The realization is slowly forced on Macbeth through the course of the play that death is the "Nothing-is-but-what-is-not," that is to say, that its being is that of non-being. In realizing this peculiar presence of death in himself not only is Macbeth's own existence put at risk and eventually forfeited, so, too, is the very language of the play in which this realization is attained. In endowing a significance on death, the play's language signifies a Nothing that threatens to unsignify everything else, render everything meaningless, and so make of the whole of life "a tale told by an idiot"—the tale that is the play itself. Death, that is, makes of Life a mere tale, nothing but language or words which are themselves mere breath, and so nothing. Hence, insofar as any language signifies the Nothing of death, it is itself made by death to signify nothing, to be nothing but "sound and fury, signifying nothing." Language is, thus, the ultimately paradoxical being that is a nothing signifying Nothing which it is itself. The Word which began by being All, the agent of the creation of the world, ends by undoing that world and reducing itself to a mere word which is Nothing.

This status of Language as everything and as Nothing is also the subject of our modern dialectic of the Deed. If Language began with the Word as Deed as the means of the creation of the world *ex nihilo,* it now ends with the speechless "deed without a name" as the means for the reduction of that world back to Nothing. The Faustian beginning to end has now come to its Macbethan end to end. And if it is Man who in the beginning does the Deed that creates the world, then it is Language which in the end undoes both Man and his world. The reductive power of Language seems to be, therefore, inherent in itself. It could, perhaps, derive ultimately from the nature of Language as a nothing that signifies Nothing. In our historical time it would manifest itself as the reductive power of a Language which brings about the Nothing of Nihilism, and which is itself given over to that Nothing. It would follow from this that the present annihilating and destructive potential of Man ultimately comes from Language itself. This is a potential that Language has always possessed because of its inherent capacity to reduce everything to Nothing; never before, however, has this potential been realized in historical practice to the extent that it has in science and technology.

## II

As we have already indicated, it is likely that the most fundamental cause of this historical development is the changed significance of death. Language and death are both "nothings" in the closest proximity to each other, and together they govern the being of Man. As we have shown, death has no being apart from Language, for Language endows its significance as a mode of non-being: of absence, of silence, of timelessness. But Language can never succeed in completely signifying death once and for all, it cannot ever make it fully meaningful or comprehend it completely, for the attempt to signify and comprehend death is contradictory since it attempts to signify the insignificant, comprehend the incomprehensible, and give meaning to that which is the source of meaninglessness. Death is, thus, the ultimate contradiction that drives Language to its overcoming and breaks it in its failure—but in the process forces Language to make and unmake itelf over and over again and so to transform the whole of human life and time. Death is the supreme instigator of Language but is also its supreme denigrator. In seeking to signify the Nothing of death, Language only signifies in the end its own nothingness; in seeking to realize death Language reveals its own unreality and the unreality of everything that it realizes. Ultimately, that is the unreality of the world. In our time, through the historical workings of Nihilism, this self-realization of Language has been pushed to an extreme perhaps never attained before, taking Language to its ultimate limits—which we are here seeking to explore.

This exploration of Language and its limits must also lead to a total reconception of modern Nihilism. Once again it appears that Nihilism cannot be the Nothing that is prior to the Deed such that it is the Deed alone that prevents everything from falling back into that Nothing. Man's Deed as Progress is not the constant counter to Nihilism but, instead, the visible manifestation of it. What appears to Faust as his creative Deed of Progress extracting All from Nothing is viewed from the other side as nothing but the invisible workings of Language reducing his All to Nothing. Modern Nihilism exemplifies on the level of world history the fatal propensity of Language toward its own reduction. In reducing itself, Language at once destroys or annihilates All that is bound up with it. If this were to become a total self-annihilation of Language it would also entail the total annihilation of Man and his world. In such a condition Language would cancel itself completely; it would no longer merely signify Nothing but would become nothing. That Nothing would be the nothingness of an annihilatory death of total oblivion, the death without significance. Man, too, as subject to that kind of a death would lose all significance and so cease to be human. We have already shown that such a possibility is not unthinkable and indeed, that the practical means for carrying it through are available even now. If one entertained the thought that this was inevitable, one would finally have to conclude that Man is nothing but a creature of his Language; and that Language, which gave birth to Man, finally brings him to his death because of the ineluctable working-out of its own annihilatory dynamic.

Fortunately, this thought is as yet not conclusive. Insofar as Nihilism also manifests the destructive workings of Language, in opposition to its annihilatory ones, the conclusion of modern Nihilism presages a fate that is infinitely more hopeful for Man. Terrible as they may be, the destructive workings of Language are the ones that testify to the greatest achievements of modern Man. Through these achievements, and not through mere Enlightenment, Man has for the first time historically attained his adulthood in the knowledge that he is mortal—that he has both the capacity to effect his own demise and that he is capable of doing so. For the first time all the long-cherished illusions and cultural "lies" that humanity has lived by ever since it attained to consciousness have been exposed and destroyed. What previous achievement can equal that? Leonardo da Vinci's dictum "among the great things to be found among us the being of nothingness is the greatest" surely applies to us as well. If Man is the destroyer in Nature par excellence, then surely he has attained a highly dangerous but nevertheless distinctive stage of his self-realization in modern times, one that could be fatal. Man has never been in greater danger. Is it possible that this danger might be averted precisely by the power of that greatness? It is possible that destructive Nihilism is our only counter to the Nihilism of annihilation.

If so, then destructive Nihilism would constitute a counter-movement to the passage of Faust, or not so much a movement as the end-moment of that passage, the moment of the end of Faust. There is as yet little in modern thought to realize that moment, for it is explicitly still firmly bound to the movement of the Faustian passage. Perhaps in the one outstanding thinker of Nihilism, Nietzsche, this moment comes closest to being attained, though even Nietzsche conceives of Nothing in the explicit Faustian way. He is, however, an important stage in the conception of modern Nihilism, and is therefore, as it were, the fulcrum on which the whole passage of Faust pivots. Prior to Nietzsche, nihilism was still largely a speculative and purely literary concept, with some political overtones; only after Nietzsche did it become the key concept in terms of which to conceive of the whole history of the West since its origins, hence the decisive concept for an understanding of world history. But even in Nietzsche the concept still shows its largely theological and metaphysical roots; it has not as yet attained a sociological specificity. And this is partly because Nietzsche could not conceive of it in relation to a fully developed philosophy of Language.

The first historic record of the word *nihilism* dates from Jacobi's famous letter to Fichte (from which we have already quoted). Jacobi castigates Fichte's philosophy of pure Reason as nihilist because it denies the thing-in-itself, and is "consequently only possible if everything except reason is changed into nothing."[15] He adds: "In order to comprehend completely, it must dissolve into thought and destroy the object and its being as existing for itself in order to make it become completely subjective."[16] According to Jacobi, this entails that "the human spirit, therefore, must become 'world-creator'—and its own creator,"[17] and consequently that is must reduce first the world and then itself to nothing. For if the object as an independent thing-in-itself is abandoned, then the Ego also loses its being, becoming a nothing whose "mere weaving of Meaning" gives it "the illusion of pseudo-infinity."[18] Though this is the first time Jacobi used the word *nihilism,* the thought of it had already occurred to him in his very first work, "Eduard Allwills Papiere"—the name All-will is, of course, highly significant—dating from his first encounter with young Goethe, who was then working on the first version of *Faust.* It is also highly significant that the thought of nihilism occurs to Jacobi together with a recollection of *Macbeth;* he expressly speaks of "the work without a name."[19] This "work without a name" is to be found also in the identical vision at the end of *Faust* Part I, in the fragment of a scene entitled "Night, Open Field."

As yet, all this is nothing more than fleeting allusions; the editor of Jacobi's early work is surely being too precipitous when he comments: "The abyss of Nihilism opens up."[20] Yet it was from this starting point that the notion of nihilism developed in the artistic and philosophic circles at Weimar and Jena surrounding Goethe, where simultaneously Romanticism in literature and Idealism in philosophy arose. There was a constant and continuing preoccupation with the thought of Nothing in the circles around Goethe, a thought-event that was soon to spread out from its narrow epicenter of Weimar in concentric waves all over Europe and beyond, eventually to reach us now on the broadest of fronts after it has encircled the whole earth. Here merely a few references and quotations will have to suffice to indicate this preoccupation. Tieck in his novel *William Lovell* writes in character as follows: "I feel ashamed of myself in front of myself, I wake up in myself, and everything turns to nothing that was already in itself so empty."[21] Hölderlin writes in the same vein in his "Hyperion," and Novalis declares categorically: "No act is more usual in us than the act of annihilation."[22] Statements of this kind incurred the accusation of "nihilism" levelled at these new Romantics, especially at Schlegel by the more traditionalist Jean Paul Richter.

The term *nihilism* thus began to circulate outside the sphere of Goethe mainly in reactionary circles as a word of opprobrium, but at some indeterminate point during the nineteenth century it was picked up as a badge of distinction by the very atheists and anarchists against whom it had been directed. Even to begin to name all the major figures involved in this translation of the word would be like inserting a catalogue of ships into our epic, but to name a few: first there were the authoritarian theological dogmatists like von Baader, Görres, and Juan Donoso Cortes, and following them, but in a theologically much more profound sense, came Kierkegaard and Dostoevsky; the former coined the cognate word *acosmism* and the latter uses the word *nihilism* itself, for by then it had become public property in Russia, translated from theology into politics. Stirner and the left-Hegelians had already given the word a decidedly political connotation. Bielinski and Bakunin were the first Russians to follow this political lead, and they, too, redirected the Hegelian concept of "negation" to "the political negation of existing circumstances."[23] It was from these that Turgenev took over the term *nihilist* and on the basis of it created the character Bazarov, who was the first to proudly dub himself such. Bazarov became the prototype of a new radical intelligentsia. Dostoevsky in his first great novels depicts them sympathetically, though highly critically, and with his literary instincts he begins to differentiate the destroyers from the mere annihilators; thus, in *The Devils* he sets up the opposition of Stavrogin to the young Verchovensky, and in *The Brothers Karamazov* of Ivan to Smerdyakov.

Nietzsche derives his concept of Nihilism from all the sources referred to above, not least from the then contemporary newspaper headlines recounting the latest outrages of the Russian nihilist propagandists of the deed. He was also inspired by the sense of nothingness he found in the ahistorical pessimistic pathos of Schopenhauer, and the converse historically somber stoicism of Burckhardt. With Nietzsche the concept of Nihilism is translated into a new constellation. Arendt, whose account of the origins of the concept stops before Nietzsche, fails to realize this. The very nature of his polemical undertaking ensures it, for it is designed to unmask the concept and make it unfit for present use by reminding us of its *pudenda origo,* its unworthy antecedents in Idealism and reactionary theology. For Arendt, nihilism originated in and has ever since remained "the reverse side of idealism."

As a first step against such a too-easy overcoming of Nihilism we may consider the words of a no less distinguished exponent of "ideology-critical reason" than Adorno:

> The true nihilists are the ones who oppose nihilism with their more and more faded positivities, the ones who are thus conspiring with all extant malice, and eventually with the [annihilating] principle itself. Thought honours itself by defending what is damned as nihilism.[24]

That counter-asseveration does not, however, expose Arendt's basic error, which is to believe that the exposition of the history of the origins of the concept nihilism enables us to overcome Nihilism as a contemporary cultural problem. The basis of this erroneous critique is grounded in the principle that the origin of the concept of something reveals that thing's roots, and so its true identity forever after. Arendt is mistaken in believing that the Sphinx disappears into its abyss when its origins are revealed to it; it only does so when its riddle is truly answered. The riddle of Nihilism is not in the derivation of the word, but in the nature of the present baffling problems to which the word refers—just as the problem of Capitalism is not the origins of the word *capital*. The only way to refute the notion of Nihilism is to give a different account of the cultural and social phenomena said to be nihilistic: for a start, the reductive workings in science and art, the devaluation of values, the demoralization of men. It goes almost without saying that a notion of Nihilism that wishes to grapple with these contemporary manifestations will no longer have much in common with its origins in theological or Idealist or Romantic notions of the original Nothing prior to the Deed. This original Nothing has already numerous times been, as Nietzsche puts it, "reinterpreted in terms of fresh intentions,"[25] never more decisively so than by Nietzsche himself, and most of its earlier speculative metaphysical and theological meanings have been "obscured or lost."

Nevertheless, what is, perhaps, Arendt's primary intention can be vindicated, and that is to draw a parallel between contemporary ontological thinking on Nihilism, mainly that of Heidegger, and the early Idealist origins of that thought. As Arendt puts it: "Between the subjective-idealistic and the individualist-ontological thinking, between the philosophical speculation of Idealism and the philosophic belief of existentialism, which are both a thinking above the abyss of nothing, there appears to exist despite the existential-ontological difference a striking relationship."[26] But this relationship exists only because Heidegger has deliberately returned to the original thinking on Nothing, back to Schelling and Jacobi, in developing his own thought on Nihilism. Heidegger's understanding of Nihilism is still fully within the Faustian passage, and in many respects it is a regression to the early stages of the Deed. The reactionary character of that understanding is sometimes so pronounced that Adorno goes so far as to charge him with experiencing Nihilism as no more than traditional religious accidie: "There are reports of taedium vitae even during periods of unchallenged state religion; it was as common among the Fathers of the church as among those who carry over into the jargon Nietzsche's judgement about modern nihilism, and who imagine in that way that they have gone beyond both Nietzsche and nihilism—Nietzsche's concept of which they have simply turned upside down."[27] The reference is doubtless to Heidegger, who speaks of himself as having already carried out an "overcoming of

Nihilism" and who also maintains that Nietzsche's concept of nihilism is already to be relegated as "classical" and therefore superseded, because it is a misconception of the problem of "Nothing" which is only to be correctly understood in terms of his own Being.

In the celebrated letter criticizing the post-Nietzschean Nihilism of his friend Jünger, Heidegger distinguishes sharply the nihilistic Nothing (*nichtiges Nichts*) from the essential Nothing (*Wesen des Nichts*), the latter being the Other aspect of Being. Both modes of Nothing thus belong to Being, for in both Being is present through its absence, since this absence is only a self-concealing of Being. Nihilism is for Heidegger this self-concealing of Being that conceals itself, which is what we in our nihilistic state experience as the "oblivion" of Being. This reassuring presence of Being, which can never be threatened by the Nothing of Nihilism, since that belongs to it as one of its own possibilities, is constantly there simply waiting to be discovered. A philosopher like Heidegger himself, who has seemingly found it, has thus already overcome Nihilism. Our fall into the abyss of Nihilism is simply our failure to understand the essential Nothing that is so close to Being. Nihilism "unfolds itself between Being and essential Nothing,"[28] and to emerge out of this intermediate state of non-being it is only necessary to effect a recovery of essential Nothing. Thus for Heidegger to enter into the essence of Nihilism is "the first step by which we leave nihilism behind us. The path of this entry has the direction and manner of a going back."[29] It is a going back to the origin, to that time when the oblivion of Being began, the time of the fall of thought into metaphysics. The recovery of thought requires an effort of recalling the simple original words of Being, "to reflect on old, venerable words the language of which gives us promise of the realm-of-the-essence of Nihilism and its overcoming."[30]

Heidegger's understanding of Nihilism, bound up as it is with his thought of Being and essential Nothing, seems indeed, as Adorno accused, of being within the ambit of early-modern Idealism. His Nothing of Nihilism is no greater a danger than was Mephistopheles', it is ultimately in the service of Man, since it is enclosed within a larger Being that is proof against the assaults of any Nothing. Heidegger has not caught up with the fact—which Nietzsche proclaimed as having already happened—that Being itself has been reduced to Nothing in the course of modern Nihilism. There can be no meaning of Being any longer; Being is what has been forever destroyed; Being is now absurd, it is meaningless—though that is itself a withdrawal of meaning that has its own historical meaning. Hence, Heidegger's attempt to recover, or recall, the meaning of Being leads him into an anachronism that takes him all the way back to pre-metaphysical archaic philosophy. His efforts at "back-tracking" to the *archē* only promote the archaism of his original thought. He seems to think that he can somehow establish a direct link to the original sources from which spring the healing waters of a remembrance of Being that can wash away the Lethe of forgetful metaphysics. Having thus recalled Being, he seems to believe that he has already overcome all the sicknesses of the age, of which he presents himself as always the physician and rarely the patient. But can anyone today procure such a diplomatic immunity?

It is true, however, that Nietzschean Nihilism is now over, for the great heroic phase of destructive Nihilism has almost run its course. We are now in its aftermath, beset all the more by the gradual creeping encroachment of annihilating Nihilism. That insidious, hitherto secret presence is now coming into the open. Nihilism is now revealing itself; it has entered into a virulent pathological phase at least since the Second World War. The great issue now is no longer that of the recovery of the West, or even of civilization and barbarism; what is now at stake is the survival of mankind. The situation of the still surviving individual seems hopeless. The last generation of great individuals, the heroic destroyers, has almost completely died out and no one has appeared to replace them. The cultural institutions at least of affluent countries continue functioning seemingly unimpaired, but the personnel is no longer the same though the matériel has remained unchanged. It is part of their ideological function to keep on inculcating the comforting belief that basically nothing has changed, for only thus can they preserve their belief in themselves. Through this they attempt to prevent everyone else from realizing what has happened. As for those who do realize it, they prevent them from saying it aloud. And even where this wall of silence is broken, the old institutions ensure that the sound is dampened and absorbed within their four walls and carries no echo outside.

Thus the situation of the present moment of Nihilism is one in which nothing much can be done. The deed is beyond our power, but the thought and the word can still be exercised, at least in private. What kind of thought and word can it be? It must be recollective thought, in all the multiple senses of that word: in the first sense, it aims to remember and recall what indeed has come to pass, and so to try to dispel some of our collective amnesia; thereby, in the second sense, it can strive to effect a recollection of oneself, a momentary dispelling of the confusion and fear that prevents one from coming back to oneself. During this present moment of recollection the words we should seek for are the ones that will speak Nihilism, those that will afford us a signification of our Nothing. This attempt to speak Nihilism is the effort to give voice to the silences in the heart of Progress that are by their very nature suppressed, for only if these silences are spoken can the hidden Nihilism within Progress be exposed, and thereby Progress be destroyed. This destruction of Progress is a precondition for any end to Nihilism, for so long as Progress lasts so long will Nihilism be there.

Is it possible, then, that there can be an overcoming of Nihilism after all, or is such a thing unthinkable to us now? Once again we return to the basic antinomy of all our thought on Nothing. Can the Deed overcome the Nothing that is prior to and outside of itself, or is this Nothing inherent in the Deed itself and so not to be overcome by it? This question brings us back to our two opposed approaches to Nihilism, neither of which is a proper answer to it. Hanging on the question, we remain suspended between hope and hopelessness. For us there can be no final resolution: we are trapped within the question, for it is the problematic of our existence. All the great discoverers of Nihilism have been driven to speak of its overcoming, for invariably they saw it as a problem that they felt must have a solution; they heard it as the great question to which they felt impelled to give an answer. We shall go on to examine why it is that the answers so far given are unsatisfactory, but that does not mean that the impulse to give an answer is in itself wrong. There must always be those searching for an answer. But there will also be those who will insist that no answer is possible for us. They will maintain with equal justification that to give an answer to Nihilism is to speak a language that is outside Nihilism, and that it is in principle impossible within Nihilism, for when a language beyond Nihilism is available then Nihilism will no longer be a problem requiring any answer. Such a language, they will say, need not ever arrive; it is not guaranteed, for there is nothing inherent in Nihilism that must ensure its overcoming. Nihilism need not be an ending that must itself have an end. It could be a permanent state. It is possible that the future of mankind, were it to have a future, lies from now on within Nihilism, not beyond it. Is it our ineradicable or inalienable humanism that considers such a thought an expression of despair? Or is it the humanist hope that is itself hopeless?

# ACT III

---

## *THE DEED IN DEED*

◆

## SCENE I
### *The Origins of the Deed*

I

*Im Anfang war die Tat.* Before we ask what is the Deed, we must ask what is a beginning. What is it to make a beginning, to initiate or bring something about? There are parallel questions to be asked about ending. The question of genesis has always been linked to that of telos and eschaton. The original beginning was in orthodox thought always linked to the Final End: "As it was in the beginning, so it shall be in the End." This linking, however, presupposes some overall Order or design: whether it be that of Providence, or some organic relation between beginning and end such that the beginning is the seed and the end is the mature fruit or that the beginning is the abstract form and the end the realized concrete particular, or some other such theological or philosophical way of linking beginnings and endings. In the absence of such presuppositions we can no longer be sure whether the beginning and ending have anything to do with one another. Perhaps there is no direct relation between them at all. However, the question "What is a beginning?" is analogous to the question "What is an ending?" which we shall tackle at the end.

One can question the possibility of a real beginning just as one questions the possibility of a complete end, for just as nothing can end without consequences and hence without continuing to be, so nothing can begin without predecessors, that is, without prior beginnings. If, then, every beginning is already there before it began, there can be no real beginning at all. There would then be a total continuity of beginnings and endings only arbitrarily distinguished, for everything would run indistinguishably into everything else, without break or pause, caesura or full stop; or, as the Earth Spirit tells Faust, Nature is God's living, seamless garment. But no matter what may be Nature's truth, it is clear that this cannot be the truth for men, since men do begin and end. And it is precisely by their deeds that men begin and end. Action, as Hannah Arendt insists, is like a second birth for men, a way of initiating something, and thus the way men uniquely have of being able to insert themselves into the world anew.[1] Hence, if in the beginning was the Deed, that is because only a deed can begin.

Birth as a metaphor for action goes some way toward explaining how a beginning is possible, but, of course, it only explains it metaphorically.

The problem at issue is not merely that of action itself; ultimately it is that of the continuity and discontinuity of historical time. History, too, seems like a seamless garment, but it also resembles a patchwork quilt. Clearly, it is both and neither. Insofar as it is made up of deeds, history is full of new beginnings, but insofar as it is made up of developments nothing seems ever really to begin. It is largely a question of perspectives. Choosing a perspective with reference points focused on actions and events and alterations, one can locate breaks in history; choosing another one with overarching terms of reference one will find nothing but continuities. The historian's task is to choose the proper perspective for the object he is studying, to change it when the object changes, and to be able to relate and explain these changes to each other. From the perspective of the Deed, then, there are new beginnings; they are the revolutionary changes that bring to birth a new historical configuration. As Goethe declared on hearing the cannonade at Valmy: "A new epoch of world history begins at this place; and you can say you were there." Whether epochs begin quite like that, with a few shots in the dark, is a moot point, and it is even more questionable whether history can be neatly divided into epochs. Nevertheless, Goethe was right that something new had begun.

Faust's Deed is itself such a new beginning. It is new even though it is a translation of the old Word, for the translation is no mere transcription but a transformation impelled by the "guiding spirit." Faust is inspired to translate the Word into the Deed, having first passed through the Thought and the Power, and then to make it his new beginning. In the passage of this act the continuity and change of history are manifested, for a translation must both conserve the original meaning and at the same time transform it. A translation is at once faithful to its original and a betrayal of it. A translation in history is no simple rendering of any one word, but it, too, might be read as a change in meaning that is yet a preservation of older meanings. It, too, both betrays and is faithful to its past. Of course, there is no question of intentions here, for it is not a matter of knowing what history wants to do but only what it may be read as doing. To read the passage of time is to follow its changes of meaning from one sense to another as if one were a translator without an original text.

Let us consider Faust's passage as an historical translation. What does it achieve? It declares the Deed to be the beginning, and takes it as its own beginning. Insofar as it is a declaration it is no more than a word, and a mere literary word at that—nothing but a metaphor, someone might say. Has it any practical meaning? Put another way: what does it mean in practice? By practice we mean here the social and historical practices of the time in question, Faust's time. Hence, to answer these questions we shall have to undertake an historical sociology of the Deed.

The meaning of the Deed in practice was precisely to constitute Practice. It was the Deed that effected a translation of Theoria into Praxis—theoretically and practically this occurred when the Logos and the Cogito were translated in terms of the Deed. By this move every type of theory became itself a mode of practice—specifically, theoretical practice, as Althusser calls it. Strictly speaking, *theoria* is itself neither the Logos nor the Cogito but the way in which these are contemplated and apprehended. It is the "essential vision" of the Logos as the order of word and world, and the "intuition" of the Cogito as a self-subsistent thought. As Habermas has argued, *theoria* in its basic sense of "vision" remained fundamental to all traditional philosophy, up to and including Husserl.[2] The Faustian declaration "In the beginning was the Deed" effected this most radical translation whereby, as Cotta puts it without necessarily having Faust in mind, "the primacy of Praxis over theory is thus enunciated." And he goes on to say that "in this way, at the start of the nineteenth century, we are given the definitive formula, which contains in itself the overall meaning of the main line of development of the last two centuries (last in a literal sense? It is a legitimate question)."[3] The question is certainly legitimate and once more puts us in mind of a possible relationship between beginning and end. Will that which began early in the nineteenth century with the Deed of Faust end with another deed? Will the creative deed of the beginning have as its counterpart a destructive deed of the end? Such questions spring readily to mind, but till we do get to the end there is no answer to them. However, one needs to beware of simple symmetries that link beginning and end in neat oppositions. The one "good" Deed does not necessarily deserve another.

Cotta refers himself to a contemporary of Goethe's who in his own way asserted the originality of the Deed.

> Henri de Saint-Simon is the philosopher who better than any other had seen and indicated the new way to follow. This is the task that he assigned to the Man of the future, the new Man: "To concern himself solely with acting on Nature in such a way as to modify it as far as possible to the benefit of humankind. The desire to dominate men is transforming itself gradually into the desire to make and remake Nature according to our

> will." With these words of momentous import all essential features of our time are presented to us as the key to the drama that we are in the course of living out.[4]

The drama here left nameless has for us a distinct identity and shape, it is our *Faust.* Faust's fist shattered the old "beautiful world" and inaugurated "the century of Will and of unleashed Power,"[5] and we now carry fragments of that world into the Void (Chorus of Spirits, "Faust's Study").

The Deed as Praxis is only one side of the Faustian revolutionary transformation. The other is the Deed as Progress. The two sides go together, for modern Praxis would not be what it is without Progress, and vice versa. Praxis and Progress, as we shall see, are old ideas; it was only when they came together in a unique way that the modern Deed was constituted. Praxis is a world-transforming practice which can only be that in relation to a developing historical time called Progress, and, inversely, there can only be a time of Progress where there is a practical, cumulative transformation of the world. The Praxis-Progress coupling is the Deed bifurcated into its two major aspects: it is practical progress and progress of practice in the same act. The one could not be without the other. Hence, we can refer to this doublet by the more common name of Progress.

The Deed is thus the revolutionary transformation that inaugurated modern Progress. But how can that be, since Faust's Deed is a mere symbolic act at best, whereas the Deed of Progress is an historical occurrence of momentous proportions? What, if anything, relates the passage in the text with the passage in its historical context? Surely, between the Deed as idea and the Deed as reality there is an historical world of difference. One might say here that Faust's Deed is the ideal form of the Deed of Progress, that the passage of Faust is a sublimated reflection of the real passage in the historical world. But that might be taken to mean that Faust's ideal is no more than an ideology, a sheer reflection, and this would be to underrate it since, as Max Weber insists: "Very frequently the 'world images' that have been created by 'ideas' have, like switchmen, determined the tracks along which action has been pushed by the dynamic of interest."[6] The passage of Faust was one of those world images that marked out the historical passage along which Progress was to travel, propelled by all the interests of European Man.

Thus specifically modern Progress dates only from the Deed, even though, as we shall see, ideas of "progress" can be found in many preceding periods. Prior to the Deed, European Man had not begun to progress in earnest; the expansionary drive of power and practical transformation had not yet commenced on a world scale, though the preconditions for it had been established and many things had been achieved in Europe that separated it from the tradition-bound mankind of the rest of the world, as well as from its own traditional past. Progress in that practical sense is, therefore, something relatively new—though Faustian thinkers, taking their Deed to be the genesis, pre-dated Progress to the origin of things. They saw their own Progress as simply the accelerated final stage of an historical process going back to Man's beginnings and, even prior to that, to the evolution of animals and plants. "In the beginning was the Deed" was taken as literally that: everything begins through a creative activity—an *élan vital* or will to life, as it came to be called—and it drives everything in an upward direction from start to finish. Man is the winner in this race of time, for he stands at the apex, having reached furthest into the future, leaving all other beings behind him, immobilized in the past, where they now remain as fossilized monuments to his own advance. The Deed is for Faustian thought the very dynamic of time; nothing can escape it and wish to survive, nothing can stand still; in order to stay in being it must move on. Everything must be becoming as long as it is, for what is not becoming must perish. And if European Man is the highest to which mankind has attained, then he is justified in acting as the scourge and executioner of time before whom all the less-advanced rest of humanity stand condemned. European colonial expansion, an important element in its Progress, thereby received its rationale and could be pursued in good conscience. From the conquest of the people of the earth it was but a short step to the conquest of the earth itself.

The idea of modern Progress, molded as it is by the idea of the Deed, is thus fundamentally different from every prior idea of "progress." It emerges out of a new conjunction of thought and reality. No combination of prior ideas would on their own have been capable of constituting this modern idea of Progress. Hence, no conventional history of ideas can account for it in terms of prior ideas. There was no normal developmental continuity operating; a radical conceptual break was required. The landscape of European thought had to change catastrophically under the pressure of the Deed before the elements making up the idea of "modern progress" could have fused together. Nevertheless, these elements had been lying about inert for a long time. In particular, there were older ideas of progress at a remove from older ideas of praxis, and so in no danger of entering into an explosive fusion. The fatal Progress-Praxis conjunction shapes itself first in an ideal form in Goethe's *Faust,* and simultaneously, as it were, in a utopian form in Saint-Simon and his successors. However, it was not till Marx that it realized itself self-consciously in revolutionary action. In the hands of Marx, that great theorist of the Deed as productive labor, Progress becomes a world-transforming activity, a revolutionary act both in theory and practice. The unique fusion of Progress-Praxis in Marx's thought is the basis for the materialist interpretation of the history of the past and for a revolutionary program for transforming the history of the future. Simply put, Praxis is the material transformation of Nature by means of human productive labor, and Progress is the dialectic of History as the class struggle leading to the expanding domain of human freedom. The nexus between these ideas is inextricable in Marx, and it had never before appeared in quite that form.

The revolutionary character of the modern idea of Progress can be gauged by contrasting its unique configuration in Marx with all previous ideas of progress and praxis. Hence, even though Marx did have predecessors in every particular of his thinking, he did not merely put together a combination of older ideas; he accomplished a mutation of these ideas into a completely new thought. Fundamental differences distinguish that thought even from the very influential one of Saint-Simon, for the latter is still very close to the Enlightenment thinking of the French philosophes. In the *Encyclopédie* there is an extremely progressive sense both of progress and of praxis, based largely on artisanal production, which Diderot wanted to improve by the application of systematic philosophic thought.[7] Saint-Simon made the vital step forward of rethinking this project in terms of industrial production. However, for both the enlightened philosophes and the utopian positivist socialists, progress still presented itself as the ideal of the perfectibility of Man and praxis as the growth of material civilization through mechanical invention. It was thought that gradually, through rational reform, human needs would be satisfied and a society of comfort and civility established in which men would become happier and slowly begin to make themselves better. A vision of historical progress leading to this kind of result was promulgated at the very moment of the catastrophe of the Enlightenment, during the Revolution, by the incarcerated and condemned Condorcet. Thus, even when these earlier ideas of progress and praxis are given an historical underpinning they still differ from the Marxist sense. This is obvious when one compares Marx's thought with the contemporary utilitarian-liberal ideals of progress current in England, for example, in J. S. Mill; and that is the reason why the latter seem only tangentially to touch on modern thought and why they often sound as if they were a throwback to the Enlightenment.

Prior to the Enlightenment, ideas of progress and of praxis had only occasionally and rarely come into contact. The philosopher, the historian, and the mechanic were quite separate identities. It is remarkable, therefore, that already in the period of the first Faust, Bacon—the father of experimental philosophy, as Voltaire called him, or the first rationalist magus, as we might call him now through hindsight—should have propounded a clear program of mechanical invention for the gradual historic betterment of the material conditions of human life. For Bacon, knowledge was practical power over things. Hence, knowledge could take the relatively new form of inductive reasoning on the basis of experimental trials, which was a total change in the idea of practical knowledge as it had been inherited via the Middle Ages from Aristotle. The Renaissance revival of humanist and naturalist philosophies of the ancients, such as that of Lucretius, played an important part in reviving ideas of natural development and the free invention of arts and crafts. During the long interlude of Platonic and Aristotelian scholasticism all such notions had been excluded and repressed. Aristotle "placed dianoia and episteme praktike, practical insight and political science, at the lowest rank of his order, and puts above them the science of fabrication, episteme poietike, which immediately precedes and leads to theoria, the contemplation of truth."[8] Most subsequent philosophers took their cue from Aristotle, so that despite the Aristotelian emphasis on organic development in teleological terms there is nothing in this classical tradition of metaphysics to place natural development on an historical basis.

History and Nature were two separate spheres of being for all classical thinkers: the one the realm of chance and fate, of Tychē, Fata, or Fortuna, the other the realm of necessity and law, of *physis, nomos,* and *logos*; history was a matter of accidents, nature one of essences. This is why, despite all his foresight, the idea of history as a dynamic fulfillment of time, so essential to the idea of Progress, could not have entered into Bacon's thought. Because he was still so much the natural philosopher, he excluded from his consideration all such notions of history, which in his own time would have belonged, in their eschatological setting, to some of the more extreme Protestant sects. It is in that un-classical tradition that the time sense of modern Progress is to be found. Behind all the schemes of ages and stages of progressive development lies the early medieval eschatology of Joachim of Flora with its three ages of the Father, the Son, and the Holy Ghost, and the hermetic and cabbalistic grades of creation, descents, and ascensions. Behind that again are all the providential schemes going back to the Apocalypse of John of Patmos and the Prophets, as well as the neo-Platonic Alexandrian conceptions of a scale of Being from the One to the Many. It is in Augustine that for the first time the biblical providential schemes are set side by side with the classical view of the natural state of things, but placed together only so as to be better separated, for the one is the heavenly path to salvation, whereas the other is the fallen state of nature. And so it was to remain almost throughout Christian thinking. In their Reformation Protestant guise all these ideas reappear in the basic premises of Spiess's chapbook *Faust.* To seek illicit power over nature is to forfeit grace and incur most certain damnation, but it is also to peer into Creation itself. Humanistically conceived, it is what incites and tempts the first heretical revision in Marlowe. Would it be too farfetched to consider that to be the first Faustian transgression on the way to Progress?

However, it is a long way from Marlowe to Marx, and it is only in Marx that the two Western traditions—the classical philosophical and the Judeo-Christian religious—come almost unrecognizably together to forge the revolutionary notion of Progress-Praxis. But this does not mean that Marx's revolutionary idea can be explained away by reference to its constituent beginnings. Marx's theory is neither a communistic prophetic eschatology nor simply philosophical enlightenment utilizing violent revolutionary means. It is a completely new interpretation of the world and how to change it.

II

But what is Progress? What does it involve? To understand something of the meaning of Progress we must return once more to Faust's original translation, for just as he translated the Word and the Thought in terms of the Deed—which also had its older originals—so, analogously, Progress is a translation of the Logos, the Cogito, and the precursors of the modern Deed. The metaphysical Logos becomes translated into the modern logic of Techno-logy, the classical Cogito becomes translated into the modern one of Subjectivity, and finally, the older versions of the Deed or Actus become the modern Activism. The meaning of Progress is thus to be found in the changed meanings of these three fundamental notions.

The new Logos of Techno-logy, the new Cogito of Subjectivity, and the new Actus of Activism carry within themselves the signs of their translation; they are suffused through and through with Progress and Praxis. Techno-logy, Subjectivity, and Activism are all practical and progressive: they move as a practice, are practices of movement and so, in turn, are practical movements. In Techno-logy the praxis element is clearly visible in the stem *technē*. The element of progress is less overt but is also inherent, since the technē must be a developing and accumulative one: the simple application of unchanging techniques to practical activities (as, for example, all ancient empires carried out on a vast scale) is not technology, for technology demands the principle of continual obsolescence, which is one of the features of progress. In Subjectivity it is the element of development that is apparent, since the subject must form itself and undergo continuous self-transformation (*Bildung*); the element of praxis must be there, too, since modern subjectivity is a productive practical life to be realized in the world and not simply a mode of contemplation or of theorizing; thus it does not oppose itself to an active life as did all previous modes of inwardness. Subjectivity in one of its main theoretical *cum* practical applications is the new science known as psychology. Similarly, in Activism the element of praxis is visible in the "act"; the element of progress is hidden but also there, for every Activism is a movement tending to an end, and moving historically in stages already accomplished toward it; all its actions are thus developmental (modern action is never conceived of as an end-in-itself).

Techno-logy, Subjectivity, and Activism are the Word, Thought, and Deed of our time. The Word is a highly rationalized system or formalized "logic," the Thought is a self-reflecting self-consciousness, and the Deed is a pure activism. Hence, there is no longer a unity of Word, Thought, and Deed, no intrinsic coherence between them, as there was in previous traditional culture, where to speak, to think and to act were in close proximity. By contrast, enormous distances separate Technology, Subjectivity, and Activism; it is as if the Word, Thought, and Deed have been scattered and fragmented under the shattering blow of Faust's fist. This fragmentation is apparent in all the divisions and dichotomies separating areas of modern life, such as those between object and subject, rationality and emotion, thought and action, necessity and freedom, fact and value—all of which seem to us utterly irreconcilable. The opposition and separation apply to the smallest particular; every object, feeling, idea, and relationship is categorized, compartmentalized, and departmentalized. Our world is continually being divided and subdivided; this obviously has much to do with the continual division of functions and their segregation from each other, and ultimately it goes back to the intricate division of labor that is the sine qua non of all our productive activities and of the industrial process itself. Thus, on the surface of society Techno-logy, Subjectivity, and

Activism are very widely spaced and have nothing to do with one another, but, as we shall discover, underneath the gulfs separating them, they are very closely connected, for they depend on each other.

Historically they originate in great temporal proximity but at a spatial remove from each other. Their origin corresponds approximately one by one to the three great bourgeois revolutions which, as every schoolboy knows, inaugurated our modern age: the English industrial, the German cultural, and the French political. The first carried out the decisive shift of the Logos of natural philosophy into technological science and machine power; the second transformed universal, rational thought into ideal, inward subjectivity; and the third concentrated activities and modes of acting into social and political activisms. Together they constituted the one event that is the advent of modern Progress. It was an upheaval that shook the whole of Europe, and steadily since then the rest of the world; the years of Goethe's maturity (1790–1815) were the epicenter of this historical earthquake, and the years of his active life (1775–1830) encompassed its eruption. By the time Goethe died the modern world was firmly set on its course, as he himself came sadly to realize. (This location of his lifetime partly explains why Goethe is no longer a great classic poet or dramatist, but the first modern writer and littérateur.)

The English industrial revolution was perhaps the earliest to begin, and it brought about unparalleled social changes with almost no violent political repercussions except for a gradual trend toward liberalization. But it transformed every mode of production and carried through all the technical and organizational inventions needed to make modern industry possible. At the same time it introduced new modes of technological science: political economy, symbolic logic, atomic chemistry, electrical physics, as well as all the sciences of engineering. At almost exactly the same time, in total dissociation from English developments, there took place a no less radical transformation in German thought and letters. The philosophy, literature, and music then created is still unquestionably the greatest achievement of modern culture. *Sturm und Drang*, modern classicism and Romanticism, established the models that all the arts were to follow; Idealist philosophies starting from Kant and culminating in Hegel and Schopenhauer are the basis of most modern philosophy; the cultural and historical sciences also took their origin from the newly uncovered fields of philology, folklore, anthropology, psychology, art-scholarship, and the new historiographies. It was largely through these cultural formations that the modern subjective individual was constituted. But perhaps Camus is ultimately right when he insists that "modern times begin with the crash of falling ramparts";[9] perhaps the fall of the Bastille is the first single act of modern Progress. In any case, the political revolution was the most visible one and gave its modern meaning to the old word *revolution.* The French revolution remains the prototype of all the recurrent political turmoils we call revolutions, and it is the one that established the new ways of acting politically. Out of it emerged the modern state in its first clear formation under Napoleon, an example that was quickly followed all over Europe, beginning with Prussia; it gave rise to new systems of rational law-making, new modes of administration and bureaucratization, new institutions of public welfare, and, most ominously, a new conception and practice of *army* and *armaments.* All our political ideologies stem from this period of revolution and counter-revolution; the words *socialist, liberal,* and *conservative* were then given their primary meanings.

The three revolutions of modern Progress, though occurring independently of each other, are no mere accidental conjunction of events. It is tempting to regard them as really a single event. Marx, who was the theoretical heir of all three—of English economy, German philosophy, and French socialism—was inclined to regard them as a single great bourgeois revolution. Thus, for Marx the modern age begins with the great Deed of the bourgeoisie and will end with the even greater Deed of the overthrow of the bourgeoisie at the hands of the proletariat. In Marx's thinking modernity is coextensive with bourgeois capitalism, and its three aspects of Techno-logy, Activism, and Subjectivity are but the three levels of the capitalist socioeconomic formation: its material forces of production, its relations of production, and its ideological superstructure. That these should have arisen in three different societies can be explained on Marxian premises as having to do with the uneven rates of development of the bourgeois class in relation to other classes in the three countries.

Undeniably the diverse roles of the bourgeoisie had much to do with the respective revolutions in England, France, and Germany. The bourgeoisie in each of these countries found itself toward the end of the eighteenth century in a quite different position in relation to the other classes and in a different stage of development. It was due to its own strength that the English bourgeoisie evolved an unwritten compact with the aristocracy whereby it was given a free hand in economic spheres provided it made few political demands; by contrast, the German bourgeoisie, never having properly recovered from the religious wars, was too weak to engage in anything but spiritual pursuits and to cultivate its "soul," which it did to perfection; the French bourgeoisie, growing ever stronger economically but suppressed by the absolutist state and the privileges of an idle aristocracy, could do nothing without first throwing off its political shackles, which it did at the first major opportunity. So far, then, we are fully in accord with Marx. However, the role of the bourgeoisie was not the sole factor in question, nor was it in some respects even the decisive one. Other pressures which had little to do with class relations were building to catastrophic proportions at this time. The whole impetus of European rationalism was pressing for a decisive change, all the modes of scientific knowledge had reached a stage where they could be given practical application, critical philosophical inroads had been made into traditional thought by the Enlightenment, and the churches had everywhere become almost totally ineffectual. Events outside Europe had reached the decisive stage at which the world was ripe for conquest and could be exploited on a vast scale as never before. Parallel with these developments and backing and supporting them, the state had become a relatively autonomous institution, and it could set the social classes against each other and play them off to its advantage. Thus even if the bourgeoisie had done nothing in Europe something decisive would still have ensued—though, of course, it would not have been what did happen; for that the bourgeoisie had to play its part.

Is, then, the onset of modern Progress one event, or was it the conjunction of three or more separate developments that chanced to come together? Once again it is a question of historical perspectives. If one takes an overall view at least from the Renaissance onward, if not from even further back, then all the seemingly separate events are inextricably tied together. Rationalization is a Western movement going back to antiquity. Capitalism, science, and the state, the basic historical forms of rationalization, began in their modern modes during the Renaissance, backed also in all kinds of ways by the Reformation and the counter-Reformation, and these can be shown to have moved together and determined the critical juncture out of which modern Progress arose. On that account it is one event, though it is not a simple essence, a spirit of the time, or even a coherent socioeconomic formation; it is more like a ground tone in which sound many separately vibrating partial notes. On the other hand, if we focus our attention on the partials, on Techno-logy, Subjectivity, and Activism, then they are clearly heard as separate notes; they originated in three quite distinct movements which only much later came together into the complex we call Progress. However, the mere fact that the bourgeoisie was involved in all three does not make them the one great bourgeois Deed. Nor are they necessarily bourgeois forms, or forever after tied to and dependent on the bourgeoisie as a class. As history has shown since then, the basic forms of modern Progress have become universal forms of modern life. They have been taken up by non-European societies with class structures where no such thing as a bourgeoisie exists. Those societies now calling themselves "socialist," where the bourgeoisie was completely eradicated, have faithfully retained or reproduced the forms of Techno-logy, Subjectivity, and Activism. These forms will persist even when the last vestige of a bourgeois class has disappeared into history. The impersonal "classless" world of modern technocracy is itself the great expropriator of the bourgeoisie, and when all the expropriators have been expropriated there will be but one sole appropriator: Progress.

## III

What we can now call, without misunderstanding, the three bourgeois revolutions only roughly approximate to the three basic forms of Progress; there is no exact correspondence between the historical events and the partial meanings of Progress. Clearly, Techno-logy means much more than merely the economic transformation that took place during the industrial revolution, Subjectivity is more than merely German culture or *Geist*, and Activism is revolutionary *élan* only at its most naive and direct. Conversely, the industrial revolution also had side-effects on Subjectivity and Activism, the political revolution on Techno-logy, and the cultural one on Activism in the first place but ultimately on Techno-logy as well. It would require detailed historical investigations to ascertain how and to what extent each of the major historical events contributed to each of the major terms of Progress.

But what do these basic terms really mean? What, in other words, was the change of meaning in the Faustian translation? By now we know a little about the terms from which the translation occurred, but as yet nothing of the terms into which it moved. Without attempting anything like a rigorous or exhaustive definition, we can simply describe them.

Techno-logy is the logos of technē. It is Progress as modern rationality become practical and cumulative, directed at the transformation of the world at an ever-accelerating rate due to its principle of obsolescence. Techno-logy is, therefore, a continuation of the Logos as logic and of the Ratio as rationality, but both the logic and the rationality have become techniques: the former as a mathematical-deductive technique of formalization, the latter as the socio-empirical technique of rationalization. These are the "logics" employed in all the forms of rational domination: the industrialized capitalist-socialist economies, the bureaucratized state and all its institutional dependencies, the intellectualized modes of scientific and scholarly knowledge. Techno-logy is the complex of ways of organizing the world by imposing on it purely logical-technical meanings that make it subject to calculation and thereby make it possible for it to be controlled and disposed of in accordance with a dominating will. That will ultimately becomes the impersonal demand of the technical system itself, for the end state toward which Techno-logy appears to be aiming is to transform itself and its world into a self-regulating mechanism—which is why cybernetics is now the ultimate symbol of technological Progress. Human society would be incorporated into such a self-adjusting system as merely one of its functions among others. If this can be called the "ideal" aim of pure Techno-logy, then it is an aim still far from being realized, for Subjectivity and Activism cut across it in various ways; sometimes they further it, but more often they deflect it into other directions, which is one reason why the world is not yet the "iron cage" Weber warned us against.

Subjectivity is the being of the single man become a private subject. Hence, in our time all modes of individual existence are modes of a subjectivized private life, modes of an "inner" being. All the old "natural" relations of individuals to each other have become subjectivized: the family is a self-chosen, purely personal and impermanent attachment, religion is a private practice, the "natural" norms of law, morals, and manners as codes of adherence are a matter of self-selected, consciously decided upon, and fungible values and styles of life, at best a matter of individual commitment, at worst mere conformist habit; so, too, the arts depend purely on personal predilections, if not on mere impulsive choices. Thus, what used to be called human nature, individual identity, and character have all been subjectivized—they are the isolated inner modes of being which some individuals create within themselves in the face of an invariably hostile external world. Hence, the world of subjects who are still individuals must be a private world. Those pseudo-subjects who have been completely subjected to the technological world of impersonal relations and the activist world of collectivities are no longer individuals in any meaningful sense. The ultimate choice for the subject is between subjectivization and subjection. The workings of Techno-logy and Activism on Subjectivity are in some respects ambiguous, for though, on the one hand, they exclude individuality and compel a withdrawal into subjectivity, yet, on the other, they make it possible for individuals to survive and sustain themselves in isolation; they satisfy basic needs and provide the means of education and culture without which no private life would be possible. In particular, the technological "machine," in order to operate efficiently, has to allow a degree of tolerance or free movement which can become a measure of subjective freedom—as even the rigidly controlled "socialist" state economies have discovered—though all societies constantly strive to nullify that subjectivity through activist mobilization or prescribed intrusions into privacy through the media.

Activism is the common life of men become a public world of organized collectivities. At present it is the world of mass phenomena—of controlled crowds, regimented groups, organized mass movements, and public manifestations. Politics is largely a matter of party machines with a mass following, and history is becoming increasingly the chance "events" resulting from the clash of wills when such activist movements or their leaders collide. People are impelled toward Activisms of one kind or another as an escape from technological impersonality and subjective isolation; in the close density of the mass, in proximity to their fellows, they can recapture a feeling of human togetherness. When in danger they seek protection in a united body, and when attacking together they can feel themselves invincible. Largely through revolutionary upheavals, activist bodies in action have effected an almost total change in the public life of societies. By contrast to this, Activism can be a very conservative force for conformity insofar as people seek to be alike, and that produces many of the uniform herd phenomena of modern daily life—patterns of life, habits, tastes, fashions, the mass spectacles of sport and the media, and so forth. Techno-logy and Subjectivity in reaction push people into crowds, even though those very crowds are often in rebellion against both. The effect of such rebellions is to make it all the easier for Techno-logy and Subjectivity to enter on their heels, and that in turn promotes another outburst of Activism of perhaps a different kind. And so the cycle goes on.

Much of the history of modern times is the complex interplay of Techno-logy, Subjectivity, and Activism. It is the modern mode of the interplay of the basic forms of being: the objective world or Nature, individual existence or single being, and common human being or society. Each of these spheres of being is more or less dominated by one or another of the forms of Progress: the natural world has become a technically processed assemblage of objects; the single man exists in a private world of subjects; and common human being takes place in a public world of activists. Our total modern world is thus one in which each man as more or less a single subject lives within an environment of organized, manufactured objects, and frequently throws himself or is thrown into some kind of crowd activity. It is a highly diversified or fragmented world in which the main spheres are segregated and sequestered from each other.

This is why the philosophies expressive of this world are in a state of mutual incomprehension. The Positivist philosophies of Techno-logy speak a formal language of their own in which the issues of Subjectivity cannot even be stated; analogously, the various Psychologisms or Existentialisms of Subjectivity can in no way relate to the various Historicisms or ideologies of Activism, and these in turn cannot comprehend Positivism—a situation that is analogous to Babel on the level of thought and higher language. And the further Progress has gone the more has this mutual incomprehension increased. For example, Positivism in its first Comtean phase was still closely in touch with philosophies of consciousness and with historicisms of utopian reform, but later logical positivism can have nothing to do with either subjectivist existentialism or historicist ideologies. The last vain effort to provide a unifying focus, that of Phenomenology, seems to have failed. It sought to establish itself as a "scientific" metaphysics and to perform something of the metaphysical function of unification, but obviously the whole tenor of the modern world is against that; the forms of Progress are too separate for there ever to be any integration among them. Every effort in that direction must prove futile.

The fragmentation resulting from the Faustian Deed is irrevocable; after this initial blow, like the expanding universe, the world scatters into the Void, rolling away from its lost center toward what Nietzsche called the unknown "X."

> This prodigious event is still on its way, and is travelling—it has not yet reached men's ears. Lightning and thunder need time, the light of the stars needs time, deeds need time, even after they are done, to be seen and heard. This deed is as yet further from them than the furthest star—and yet they have done it![10]

Whether he knows it or not, under the impact of the Deed each man becomes a fragmented being; and the languages he speaks are also fragments of the Word. Technological man is a technician or, more generally, a worker, submitting himself to an objectified work-process; and the languages he speaks are those of technical symbolism, in which the word is a logical tool. Subjective man is a private individual, alienated, alone and without external significance; his languages are those of privacy, in which the word is an expressive means. Activist man is an actor who plays assigned roles in public performances; his languages are public speeches, in which the word is an affective act. Each man is at present to some degree, and at some time, technical worker, private subject, and public activist. Each man's life is thus divided among these roles he has to play; most men's being is so split it is almost as if they had different personalities—which is why modern men are schizophrenic precisely when they are most normal. Some men unable to bear their divided selves take on almost exclusively one or another of these main roles—they become nothing but worker, subject, or activist. For the vast majority the work role is the only available one apart from family life. They tire themselves out in work, and so extirpate any lingering longings for subjective satisfaction and suppress the always dangerous propensity to act together.

Men relate to each other in basically these three ways: as workers or outer functioning beings, as subjects or inner beings, and as activists or outer acting beings. As workers men relate to each other only indirectly, through the medium of the work-process, into which they enter by exercising a function within it. The work dominates them, for they are completely fungible in relation to it. They communicate only in terms of the technical languages the work makes available to them, and these are instrumental languages of information and calculation. The word is very frequently a sign or formula. Outside the work-process men can relate to each other as subjects only if they are conscious of themselves as such. Most are so alienated as to have lost that sense of themselves; those who do have it feel alone and isolated. The private relations of subjects are purely personal, with no social or institutional supports; hence, they are always very fragile, tenuous, impermanent. The languages they speak are private modes of expression that can range from pure effusions of feeling to intricate private languages of "secret" intercourse, such as those perfected in modern literature. Such private relations are always in opposition to public relations. Public men relate as official performers. The dynamic of the "movement" or of "affairs" brings them together. They share a goal or value and are imbued with the same feelings. They feel themselves to be the public, or the people, or some chosen elite. Their languages are those that move, that have a force in compelling action or at least enticing behavior. The public word frequently functions as an image, slogan, label, flag, or trademark. These languages are mostly incomprehensible to each other, not because there are no people who can speak them all, but because what can be said in one can scarcely be said in another; this is why for most people who only speak one of these languages the other spheres do not exist.

It is precisely because of its fragmentation that the total modern world depends on each of these sub-worlds for its continued existence. Much of human hope is still invested in each of them, for what would men become if they had no private world to which to retreat? From where would the hope for changing public life be drawn if not from activist activities? Finally, what will solve the almost insurmountable material problems of the world if not technologic work? Our fears and our hopes reside in the very same places. If any one of these spheres were lost, human life would scarcely be conceivable; but if all of the world reduced itself to one sphere then that would surely be the end.

## SCENE II
*The Equivocations of Progress*

> For it is by no means a one-sided decadence (curable through organization—in itself a rational approach) that is being lamented, but rather only the shadow of progress. The negative aspect of progress is so visibly dominant in the current phase of development that art is summoned against it, even though they both stand under the same sign.[1]

The shadow cast by the light of Progress—what is that but the negative image of Nihilism? Nihilism is only the philosophic name for what Adorno calls "the negative aspect of Progress." To call this by the old name of nihilism is by no means merely tautologous, since to see Nihilism as the dark Other of Enlightenment reveals what Progress and Nihilism are to each other as well as what they are in themselves. One might also put it negatively, that Progress is the positive afterglow of Nihilism—the shine on the shadow, as it were—and that way of putting it is a more daunting challenge to the prevailing view of both Progress and Nihilism. Nihilism is not a decadence in the midst of Progress; if it were, then, as Adorno comments parenthetically, it would be curable through organization, through the determined effort to summon up and energize the resolution and order that would overcome any prevailing tendencies to weaken and degenerate. And this, as Adorno insists, would itself be a rational approach, based on and contributing to that very Progress which is at the root of the condition. Dealing with Nihilism as if it were decadence only serves to aggravate it. Modern Nihilism is not the decline of Western civilization, it is not, in Spengler's words, the "Untergang des Abendlandes"; on the contrary, Western civilization is in most respects at its peak and has already become a global civilization. Western civilization has transformed itself from a regional entity into what is now the fate of the whole human species. There is no possibility that it might now suffer the mischances of previous, regionally localized civilizations. It is not subject to the slow, drawn-out agony of a decline that is the natural organic demise of a culture past its bloom, nor can it disintegrate in one fell swoop, in a violent death through internal irruption or external eruption—there are no charismatic fanatics lurking inside or barbarians battering at its gates. He who knocks is a quite different visitor, the stranger in our midst, "that strangest of all guests."[2]

We ourselves are that Nihilism we so readily identify in others: "We are nihilistic thoughts in God's mind," Kafka said of a God who is now dead and nothing. Nihilism is no unknown stranger but the strangeness in ourselves. It is our Doppelgänger, the silent companion by our side, the shade that follows us as we look forward and stride ahead, which we can no more evade or surmount than we can run away from or jump over our own shadows. Nihilism is as old as our modernity; one will last as long as the other does, and will only end when the Other ends. When and how that will be nobody can as yet pretend to know. As long as there is Progress there will be Nihilism, and what is beyond both awaits future uncovering. There are those who see all kinds of augurs and signs of an imminent end to Nihilism, and those who try to prognosticate this from the fulfillment of original predeterminations, much as people once tried to foretell the Second Coming—and with about as much certitude. For there is no eschatology of Nihilism, no preordained pattern it must describe, no natural term set for it, no bounds to how far it can stretch, no limit-point of its contraction which it must attain—hence, no foreseeable end.

Nihilism itself is no end, and it cannot be conceived of as an End. It cannot even be taken as the natural passing of something that had to die. It is more like the onset of a peculiar madness, more painful even than death, a highly paradoxical passage without a passing. For the passing of something long familiar that eventually had to pay its "mortal due" to "custom and to age" would be all too readily understandable, and could be grieved for with a full and anguished heart. But the heart cannot grieve for something that seems so utterly incomprehensible, registered in a rising tide of horror beyond fear, a paralyzing dread that eventually renders itself insensible and yet is all the more there. "O horror, horror, horror! Tongue nor heart cannot conceive nor name thee!" (*Macbeth* II.iii). In the sense of conception and naming or speech as we think of it in ordinary discourse, it cannot be spoken about; it is the nameless dread of waiting on the "deed without a name"—the final annihilation, the deed that finishes All, the nameless horror beyond the conception of heart or tongue. Nihilism, which began with the spoken Deed, ends with the unspeakable "deed." It is a silence within the speech of Progress, a silence which, once broken, breaks the speech of Progress that contains it. But in what kind of a language can that silence be spoken?

Tragedy is no longer adequate to convey this new unreality; all the traditional arts known to us tend to give out in the face of it. To seek now for tragic experience is only to pretend that the individual has a power in relation to his world that the world now denies by simply denying him. "The liquidation of tragedy confirms the abolition of the individual."[3] Of course, the individual refuses to be abolished, but he cannot speak his refusal in a tragic voice raised against the world. As Adorno maintains, art cannot really be summoned against it, for it stands under the same sign; it, too, partakes of the "negative aspects of progress." Modern art is not an answer to Nihilism. How could it be if it is itself an attempt to realize the reality of its time? Precisely when it is at its greatest and most profound, it is closest to the negative realities which otherwise would remain invisible to those who most suffer them. If it can be said to bring brightness, it is only to make the darkness visible. Art holds up the "configurations of obscurity" in "opposition to the prevailing neon-light style of the times" by which "the all-powerful culture industry appropriates the enlightening principle and, in its relationships with human beings, defaces it for the benefit of prevailing obscurity. . . . Art is able to aid enlightenment only by relating the clarity of the world consciously to its own darkness."[4] And even in that function the power of art is circumscribed, as it itself is highly vulnerable, so much so that Adorno allows himself to speak of "its demise today, which appears imminent." Modern art remains only as the dark image that one retains after having been blinded by the sun of enlightenment.

And what Adorno notes of art goes also for thought. Modern thought is not above what it thinks about. If its subject is the negative aspect of progress, which is the dominant reality, then, being part of that reality, it is subjected to the same domination. Only when it is truest to its subject is it true. Modern thought, too, precisely at its best, cannot bring any consolation, and it cannot give any more comprehension of the incomprehensible than that permits of itself, cannot speak more than lets itself be spoken. And so, in honesty, thought must frequently confess its own bafflement. It can offer no farsighted previsions of the future or provisions for it; hence, it offers no sure visions of the present, either. Even the past becomes less and less visible against this backdrop of a dimmed present and dark future. But this does not mean that the effort to think is to be abandoned; on the contrary, the less that can be known with certainty, the greater must be the effort to win something from uncertainty.

It will be said by some that this way of putting it is art, not thought—mere "poetry." In reply, we can turn to the scientific sociology of Max Weber to elucidate what might at first appear as merely poetic, opaque phrases. Under the heading of Rationalization, Weber made extensive studies of modern Progress. In his first major work, *The Protestant Ethic and the Spirit of Capitalism,* he located the hidden religious sources of modern rationality; later he went on to distinguish it from all other modes of rationality, precisely in terms of its practicality: "Confucian rationalism meant rational adjustment to the world, Puritan rationalism meant rational mastery of the world."[5] Weber has much to tell us about the origins, course, and consequences of the present state of Rationalization, of that aspect of it which is Intellectualization, and of what results from them: the Disenchantment of the world. Disenchantment, the key term of Weber's sociology of religion and referred to the Judaic and Puritan abolition of magic, is, of course, a word derived from Schiller, where it refers specifically to the Deed that "destroys the beautiful world."

How, then, is the meaning of Progress tied to the meaninglessness of Nihilism? According to Weber, what relates them is the question of the meaning and meaninglessness of death. Weber finds this issue discussed in the late work of Tolstoy. With the help of a remarkably apt paraphrase of Tolstoy, Weber sets out his own sense of the inescapable Nihilism attendant on Progress: "Because death is meaningless, civilized life as such is meaningless; by its very 'progressiveness' it gives death the imprint of meaninglessness."[6] There is here a paradoxical and fatal entanglement whereby the rational, disenchanted meanings of Progress render death meaningless, and the meaninglessness of death, in turn, makes Progress meaningless.

Why this must be so is explained by reference to the change in the meaning of time that took place under the pressure of Progress. Time for pre-modern and even more so for pre-civilized man was an "organic cycle of life." Death then took its natural place as the consummation of a lifetime: "Abraham, or some peasant of the past, died 'old and satiated with life' because he stood in the organic cycle of life."[7] By contrast,

> Civilized man, placed in the midst of the continuous enrichment of culture by ideas, knowledge and problems, may become "tired of life" but not "satiated with life." He catches only the most minute part of what the life of the spirit brings forth ever anew, and what he seizes is always something provisional and not definitive, and therefore death for him is a meaningless occurrence.[8]

The time of Progress does not allow for any other kind of existential ending than the mere accident of death, whereby one single subject passes away and is promptly replaced by another one who carries on the passage in exactly the same way. Each life, being a replaceable link in a chain, ceases to have any integrity or wholeness in itself, and so it ceases to require an ending for itself: "The individual life of civilized man, placed in an infinite 'progress,' according to its own immanent meaning should never come to an end; for there is always a further step ahead of one who stands in the march of progress."[9] Without the possibility of an end, the fact of death becomes bereft of any significance, for as a mere fact death is no different from any other meaningless biological occurrence. Time, too, becomes repetitive and empty. If Progress is the disenchantment of the world and its subjection to planned, rational calculation, then the time of Progress becomes a time of calculated succession, the mechanical time of schedules and watches. Those who first believed in Progress thought of its time as development, as the successive unfolding and actualization of ever higher potentialities or as the metamorphosis to ever more perfect forms; but since then development has revealed its negative aspect as sheer growth and accumulation without inherent ends, for as Walter Benjamin realized: "The concept of historical progress of mankind cannot be sundered from the concept of its progression through a homogeneous empty time."[10]

However, the way in which Weber presents it makes the argument a little too easy: the opposition between "Abraham" and "civilized man" is extreme, and both terms are too ambiguous to act as poles of contrast. Again, the "organic cycle of life" that it opposes against "progress" is far too weak a notion to bear such a weight of argument; what emerges from it is a simple opposition of organic versus mechanical time that cannot account for the problematic of modern time. Taken literally, the argument leads to a Tolstoyan condemnation of all civilization and a return to "peasant life." Weber himself does not go along with any such conclusions; his whole effort is, in fact, directed to defending civilization and science "in spite of all." Tolstoy's course toward "primitive Christianity" is impossible for Weber, the agnostic intellectual committed to science, and by implication, at least, he judges it impossible for modern Western man committed to his scientific civilization as well. But to Weber this is no more than a "choice" of values or a "commitment" to meaning that he is in all integrity compelled to make, even though he is sympathetic to those who decide to commit themselves otherwise. Nevertheless, he judges those others as the ones who "cannot bear the fate of the times like a man."[11] For Weber, it is a matter of accepting what this fate imposes outwardly, but inwardly meeting it resolutely and decisively in one's chosen vocation, thereby winning inner freedom out of outer necessity and meaning out of meaninglessness. We recognize here the time-honored tragic stance of the stoic puritan individual making his stand for autonomy against the forces that must eventually crush him.

But regardless of how one may be critical of Weber's own response, the link Weber has established between Progress, time, and death, in the precise meaning of that complex relationship, is the key to Nihilism. Nihilism as the negative aspect of Progress calls, therefore, for an analysis of the notion of Progress. Weber emphasizes the rational side of Progress, that which "means that principally there are no mysterious incalculable forces that come into play, but rather that one can, in principle, master all things by calculation."[12] His sense of modernity is thus directed primarily to what we have called Techno-logy, for by that term we meant not merely the technical means of scientific production but all the means whereby a rational order imposes itself in all the dimensions of social life. The other two aspects of modernity—Subjectivity and Activism, to which Weber devotes far less attention—are also needed to complete our analysis of Progress. If, then, Nihilism is the obverse of Progress, it is the shadow cast respectively by Techno-logy, Subjectivity, and Activism. But how do these highlights of Progress produce its dark counter-image?

We have already examined at length how Techno-logy is the new logos of technē, a logos translated through praxis and Progress. Techno-logy has embarked on a process of de-constructing the traditional world and re-constructing a modern one as a structure of production. It has carried through to a considerable extent the technologization of science, the formalization of logic, the mathematization of language, the operationalism of organization, the impersonalization of social relations, the legalization of all morality, the institutionalization of culture—in short, the rationalization of life. In so doing, it undoes itself. The logos of technē generates its own antithesis, which we can call Technocracy; it is the nihilistic aspect of Techno-logy.

Technocracy in this context does not simply mean the rule of functionaries, who are at present called technocrats, over society in general. Rather, it is the power of technology over those technocrats themselves.

Technocracy is the logic of domination, the domination of technē in and for itself, which imposes itself as a system of structures for its own sake; technocrats are merely its agents. Where technocracy prevails in its most insidious forms, there the norms of technical rationality are imposed without regard to their effects or effectiveness—though usually a pretense of utility or efficiency tends to be maintained. All the norms of technical rationality are ultimately governed by a principle of exact repeatability: only that is allowed, only that is recognized as true and real which is capable of being exactly repeated at will through mechanical processes. Rationality here really means repetition and repeatability. It is this principle that gives rise to the uniformity and standardization of our technocratic society. Men are likewise treated as uniform and repeatable components of the larger functioning social machine. They lose their freedom in this process of determination, and in reaction resort to blind chance. Pure chance gives them the illusion of freedom in a determined world. Exact repetition and pure chance are complementary limit principles toward which Techno-logy tends. They reveal it as a mode of Nihilism, for they exemplify a reduction of meaning as the production of meaninglessness.

Techno-logy as a mode of knowledge is inherently a drive for power. It aims for technical mastery. As modern scientific knowledge, it works by means of repeatable experimental control—a manipulative method that aims to reduce the object to be known to calculable dimensions which can then be reapplied to it in operational techniques. Objects are known in order to be controlled, so the knowledge itself is the means of control. As Habermas puts it: "Theories of the empirical sciences disclose reality subject to the constitutive interest in the possible securing and expansion, through information, of feed-back-monitored action. This is the cognitive interest in technical control over objectified processes."[13] Habermas is mistaken in believing this to be the constitutive interest of the empirical sciences per se, though he would be correct if he were to define this as the tendency of the modern technological sciences. As technical control, Techno-logy is already Technocracy. It becomes manifestly so when the objects to be controlled are human beings and when the control is exercised for its own sake, for then it becomes impersonal domination. This objectified "will to dominate" reveals itself when Techno-logy becomes a self-regulating system, or Technocracy, not merely in the literal sense of an impersonal rule of technocrats and bureaucrats but in that of the imposition of a technical structure for its own sake and its expansion into an imperialism of techniques. Ellul has demonstrated the tendency of technology to become a system that spreads itself and expands throughout the body of the social organism: "There takes place a total technification as each aspect of human life is subjected to control and manipulation, to experimentation and surveillance in such a manner as to produce everywhere a demonstrable efficiency."[14] Technocracy, far from being merely an undesirable side-effect of something otherwise wholly desirable—which somehow or other might be counteracted when we know more about it—shows itself as in fact the hidden reality of Techno-logy: the will to dominate is at the root of this urge to know. Thus one might in effect view Technology as the positive and enlightened expression of what was really Technocracy all along.

This is but one, though a key, instance of the revelation of the hidden Nihilism in the phenomena of Progress. This relation between Progress and Nihilism appears as if it were a dialectical inversion of positive and negative, but actually it is more like an exchange of the manifest for the latent, conscious for unconscious, visible for invisible, spoken for silent. Along these lines one could show how the visible order of formal rationality is subverted and finally overtaken by the invisible modes of unreason in ethics, law, economy, and even logic itself—Wittgenstein has noted how formal logic debilitates rational thought. Weber has commented on many of these reversals: how formally rational administration can become the irrationality of leaderless bureaucracy, how formally free labor can be wage-slavery, how both the formal rationality of a capitalist economic system and the purported substantive rationality of a socialist one contribute to the erection of an "iron cage" of administrative unfreedom. Marx's utopian dictum that in a future communist society the domination of men will give way to the administration of things might be fulfilled to the letter when men, too, become things. The *Dialectics of Enlightenment* is a sourcebook of such paradoxical quasi-dialectical reversals; it depicts how rational dreams turn to irrational nightmares. Already at the start of modernity the emblem of it all was etched with corrosive humor in one of Goya's *Desastros,* entitled "The sleep of Reason breeds monsters." And Goya is the closest we can approach to a Faustian painter; he holds a place in painting analogous to that of Beethoven in music and Goethe in literature.

All these are the revelations of Nihilism within Progress. Within the expansive drive of Progress there is also a contraction: in the process of the development by which Progress governs everything is also the inverse process of a reduction to Nothing. A reductio ad absurdum is clearly evident in the technocracy of modern epistemology. The "object" of scientific knowledge has been reduced to a species of nothing, having become no more than a set of technological determinants—position, velocity, energy quanta, etc.—or what in an earlier epistemology were misleadingly known as primary qualities. The object has been bereft of quality, nature, essence, particularity, even individual identity, and has become disenchanted. As an object of scientific operation it is no more than the set of calculations necessary for dealing with it, and as such it has effectively been annihilated. The subject, too, defined as standing over against such an object, is equally nothing. And this is not only the case when the subject is treated as an object, but more particularly when the subject is most firmly distinguished from the object. For it is then that the subject loses its specificity and identity; it becomes the standard observer or actor without other characteristics, one readily interchangeable with another, for there is no longer anything to specify who it is that is observing or acting. Complete impersonality is complete depersonalization. Such a subject is an Ego that shrinks to a dimensionless point in relation to the "extension" of the object—as Descartes had foreseen, though from that Archimedean point he had hoped to shift the whole world. He could not have foreseen that such an Ego becomes nothing at that limit-point, for this only eventuated when Descartes's universal subject had become modern subjectivity, and when his Cogito had also become an "incognito." The reductio ad absurdum of both object and subject are in this instance bound up with one another; they are together an expression of the will to domination through technical control. This will to power over the object is an expression of a will to Nothing of the subject: the more the subject senses itself to be a nothing the more it seeks to reduce the object to that which it is itself. The objectified and shrivelled self that takes itself for a rational subject posits itself as a model for the object and tries to make it, too, reduced and objectified. This, the secret spite of the subject toward the object, is the *ressentiment* behind scientific technological rationality.

As we have seen, modern subjectivity is no longer Descartes's Cogito; it is not the first premise in a deductive method of universal thought; it is a mode of existing, a *modus vivere* rather than merely a *modus cognoscere*—the earlier cognoscenti having in the meantime become private individuals. Already Kierkegaard had realized the negative implication of the Cogito, that behind the thinking, rational Ego there is a more fundamental Sum, an existence that remains in a dark "unknowing." "According to Kierkegaard, the individual exists within an opaque, impenetrable 'incognito,'"[15] says Lukács, and proceeds to develop on this basis an account of what he critically conceives of as "the ideology of modernism." It is not necessary to accept Lukács's ideological reading of the incognito—after all, what he has to offer instead is only Hegelian wishful thinking that "the inner and outer world form an objective dialectical unity"[16]—to agree with him that this incognito is the basic mode of existence as presented in much of modern literature, criticism, and philosophy. To Lukács it represents a "dissolution of personality" attendant on late-bourgeois capitalism. Without entering fully into debate with Lukács, is it possible to qualify the point he is making: the incognito is not merely a "bourgeois" self but the modern self as such; it is not a "degeneration of personality" but a way of maintaining individual integrity within modern society, for how otherwise except in incognito can the individual survive? The classic Hegelian distinctions that Lukács invokes of inner and outer reality, of abstract possibility and concrete potentiality, are no more than anachronistic idealisms; "real personality" in his sense cannot exist any longer.

The Incognito has its earlier pre-modern forms, some of them going back to Calvinist theology. But it only began to emerge visibly when the counter-Romantic trends in opposition to the cults of personality of Romanticism emerged in the latter part of the nineteenth century. The art of "masks" was the negative riposte to the excessive, uninhibited expression of romantic Ego. Benjamin says of Baudelaire: "Behind the masks which he used up, the poet in Baudelaire preserved his incognito. . . . The incognito was the law of his poetry."[17] Nietzsche had openly declared: "Always disguised: the higher the type, the more a man requires an incognito."[18] "What is noble?—That one constantly has to play a part. That one seeks situations in which one has constant need of poses."[19] For the artist, the need for an incognito was partly prompted by his changed relation to his audience; for whereas the romantic artist still had a public—albeit of bourgeois Philistines who were admiringly hostile—which he could openly address as himself, the post-Romantic artists were forced to hide themselves in all kinds of disguises, for they no longer dared show themselves openly to a world that had become totally indifferent to them. "Let me also wear such deliberate disguises, rat's coat, crowskin, crossed staves in a field," says Eliot, the expounder of impersonality in poetry.

In time the poseurs took over from the men of poses, acting out part-time roles of bohemian-aestheticist or ascetic, pseudo-artistocrat or pseudo-proletarian, and many other such. Now this has become the accepted weekend way of relaxing from one's weekday full-time roles. Role-playing is our mode of living, and the life-styles that we pick up and drop at will provide the costumes for the parts we wish to play.

Social life has something of the appearance of a masked ball, but behind the masks the faces are missing, so the masks can never be taken off, only overlaid on one another. The roles, too, become second nature. The borrowed incognito is the actual, the only identity. The total evacuation of subjectivity, leaving only an emptiness behind, is overlaid by the painted veneer of an incognito that is no longer a mask for an invisible self but an outward show that hides nothing, for it has nothing to hide.

This incognito reveals itself as the negative truth behind the modern Cogito all the more readily as the "I think" becomes an "I see": a process characteristic of an age of images, of images of reality and world-views. In an age of visual media it is the "I see" of unreflective absorption that typifies the mental activity of the Ego, itself become an image projected in public. Thus the "I" becomes a mere "eye," though in some cases one must add—as Cézanne said admiringly of Monet—"but what an eye!" An eye for impressions is, however, only an eye for surfaces, for phenomena that lie exposed to view. At its best the gathering of impressions is Impressionism in painting and phenomenalism in philosophy, but what results is always a culture of surfaces. Thus the "I" as an "eye" is a mere surface recorder which glides attentively or distractedly over surfaces and is itself reduced to a surface film. Whenever this Ego does not become totally coextensive with its "eye," beneath its surface self there forms the invisible "I" of an incognito. A philosophic instance of this formation is to be found in Wittgenstein's *Tractatus,* where the world as a "visible" world of facts is seen as coextensive with the "I" become an "eye"—as Wittgenstein's little diagram so clearly indicates; this is the quasi-noumenal self of ethical action, which shows itself but cannot be spoken about, the perfect incognito. On a more mundane level the media provide some seemingly trivial yet momentous confirmations: they permit the world to be viewed as projected on a screen by an observer who is doubly distanced from what he observes and who is himself an invisible presence in what is presented before him, a powerless witness who risks nothing in seeing what he sees. In consequence, this viewing self conceals itself in an unreachable and untouchable isolation, as one perceptive critic of the cinema has realized: "In viewing films, the sense of invisibility is an expression of modern privacy or anonymity. It is as though the world's projection explains our forms of unknowness and our inability to know."[20] The incognito is in this case also an ignotus—not a dark unknown but a perspicuous anonymity where there is nothing to be known. If one were to partially agree with Macluhan on the importance and far-reaching effects of the visual media in our culture, then one would begin to realize how far this kind of incognito can extend—depersonalization is too simple a word for it. However, fortunately it is not as yet necessary to concur with Macluhan's welcome to this brave new electronic world; viewed from another perspective, his theories can themselves be seen as symptomatic appearances of that world.

Anonymity is the most general mass manifestation of the incognito. The anonymous subject becomes subjectless. The mass of subjects, each an atom of society pursuing its own ends at the expense of every other, driven by its own interest, each a private, isolated self: this mass is an anoymous diffuse crowd, a dispersed crowd without a real crowd's volatility. If someone were to remain an individual, he could only do so in privacy, forced to retreat into one or another mode of social solipsism and prey to all the psychological ailments of solitude. All those who cannot stand being pushed so far into themselves have only to accept the easy solution of identifying themselves with their public selves. Thus instead of a culture of privacy there emerges its opposite, one of publicity—that is, a situation in which the distinction of public and private is no more than formal, where everything is open to view because there is nothing left that can be hidden. Where subjective man is deprived of his last refuge in privacy, he becomes totally exposed to view. He is only that which can be given public acknowledgment within the accepted norms of publicity, otherwise he is a nobody; hence, the desperate urgency of everyone almost without exception to "get on," to "get ahead," for only in this public acknowledgment do men have any being.

Activism, the third element of Progress, is the complement to and direct outcome of the subjectlessness of the masses. It is the resort to the collective act as a way of affirming oneself and being someone. However, by a paradoxical reversal Activism transforms itself into Inactivity: all the progressive movements of mass action eventually become the passive motions of mass inaction. Thus Activism generates its own nihilistic counterpart. This becomes apparent when one examines how Activism transforms action. By elevating the Deed above word and thought, it in effect reduces it below word and thought, for it then becomes separated from its meaning-giving functions. Action reduces itself to motion, for all that remains of the act is the outward gesture without its content of inner signification. Such a blind gesturing is already a species of Inactivity. And when even the motions cease, as they must from sheer exhaustion, then total inactivity ensues. This pattern of negative reversal is particularly evident in social and communal actions. Under the impact of Activism these take the form of mass movements, and when such movements collide—as they must, for they are formed in opposition to each other—there ensues the commotion of battle, which is itself a kind of frenzied inactivity. Eventually, one or another movement collapses from defeat or the exhaustion of victory, and those that remain sink into the stupor of organization and discipline. Hence, no matter what the eventual outcome, for the participating members there can only be the acceptance of the status quo in a more or less resigned spirit of fatalistic apathy. History has shown that such a fatalism of the masses follows every extreme burst of Activism. The Russian Bolshevik revolution and the German Nazi counter-revolution are almost perfect historical instances of such an outcome, and every other totalitarian movement has analogous consequences. Mass democracy is prey to a similarly inactive apathy.

In situations in which political movements do not provoke or invoke mass participation, participatory action tends to take the negative form of spectatorism. The potential actor deprived of every possibility of acting becomes an onlooker. The action itself is more and more staged for public entertainment; it becomes a sham activity performed in a public arena in which the individual is powerless to intervene. All such actions are spectacles in which the spectators participate only by watching, and in which the actors literally stage-act. This is as much the case with political events as with sporting ones, with religious spectacles as with pop concerts—the illusion is all that comes to matter, for these are mere shows. Only by the quiet desperation and fatalism of their utter powerlessness do people reveal their malaise of Inactivity.

Inactivity even comes to pervade all the dimensions of everyday life, changing the activities of living into routine motions. Work becomes the routine of production; and the life cycle of work and rest becomes a purely appetitive rhythm of productive effort followed by leisure for consumption, maintained by artificially induced needs. These features of modern living are well known and do not need expatiation; they do, however, reveal another factor not so well understood, that of automatism. In practical life and work automatism is well-drilled regularity and functional discipline. By contrast, in art automatism is totally uninhibited volition, mere impulsions of the unconscious, the opposite of spontaneity. In both extreme cases automatism is the reduction of action to gesture; it is going through the motions of what might have once been an act. The "action" painter goes through the fragmented brush-stroke movements of what was once painting, the musician elicits the sounds of what was once music, just as the factory worker repeats the fragmentary parts of what was once an integral working act. In all spheres of action automatism is promoted through the invention of automatic mechanical means of production and reproduction, of products as well as of works of art. Automation only concludes this process by completely excluding men.

As a general historical phenomenon the negativity of Activism evinces itself as widespread re-barbarization. This is, of course, no genuine regression to barbaric or savage modes characteristic of tribalism; on the contrary, it is the rationalized and intellectually prompted and controllable imposition of features derived from archaic institutions. The effect of this is to lead to modern modes of Inactivity. Thus, the rebarbarized is the opposite of the really barbaric. (We shall eventually see why this must be so.) Re-barbarization is, however, an inescapable feature of Activism. Weber had already realized this even before its most obvious manifestations were there: "Today the routines of everyday life challenge religion. Many old gods ascend from their graves; they are disenchanted and hence take the form of impersonal forces."[21] Weber was careful to remind us that the resurrected gods are not revered and feared as the ancient gods were, for "the bearing of man has been disenchanted and denuded of its mystical but inwardly genuine plasticity."[22] This new "polytheism" is not an index of a renewed contact with Nature or a recovery of natural energies; on the contrary, it is the necessary consequence of the scientific denaturation of Nature. Positivist philosophy and its scientific methodology destroy the unity of Nature, separate human nature from moral nature, and transform the latter into an arena for the struggle of gods and demons: "If one proceeds from pure experience, one arrives at polytheism."[23] In that scientifically induced polytheism of values the possibility is opened for a re-barbarization of culture.

Re-barbarization transforms action into pseudo-ritual performance and so renders it inactive. The mass acts of political re-barbarism, the meetings, demonstrations, commemorations, strikes, struggles, and battles that are increasingly ritualized, all these tend to make any other action impossible. Such mass modes of Inactivity are invested with the trappings of symbolization derived from archaic sources, but that is only a way of depriving them of real symbolic meaning. As long as their significance is ideological in the political sense, they are still socially significant, but when this ideology is displaced by concocted mythology then even that meaning is lost. Mythologies derived from old cults, from archaic survivals and primitive folk residues, from romantic historicisms and literary traditions and eventually synthetically concocted myths—all these are reused and reinvoked to serve as symbolic disguises. At their most dangerous they provide the sanctions for violation and violence: everything previously held sacred, everything still believed in, everything individual or even vulnerable, everything that resists submission can be ritually violated before it is physically eliminated. The act that violates everything is the last possible act; it is the act that destroys every other, for after it there can only be sheer violence, and that is sheer inactivity.

These negative tendencies of Activism manifest as Inactivity—such as mythology, ritualism, archaism, primitivism, cult and occult, fatalism and fatality—are in evidence in all cultural forms of modernity. It would be wrong to look on them merely disparagingly, for they have also been sources of vitality and strength. The modern arts have drawn inspiration from them. Modern religion has derived a new lease on life by becoming primitive and fundamentalist. Morality has temporarily been revitalized by basing itself on simpler group activities. The atrophied faculties of individuals have temporarily regained feeling through a release of "primitive" drives and desires long suppressed by civilization. Their bodies have begun to dance uninhibitedly to quasi-tribal rhythms—not without a neurotic twitching that betrays much. Even thought has returned to lost "origins," to myth and symbol, to the original words of philosophy. From Nietzsche to Heidegger, modern philosophy has sought to recover its lost *archē* and in the process found much else. Hence, it is apparent that the re-barbarizations of modern Activism in all their myriad modes are by no means merely a willful irrationality that can be critically expunged. They are an inherent tendency of modern Progress that is not to be avoided.

However, out of them derive some of the deadliest manifestations of that Progress. These occur when Activism gives way to an annihilatory Inactivity. This threatens to make of the movement of historical time a motion of sheer repetition in which the only novelty is pure chance. The nihilistic meaning of Activism will then have fully revealed itself. The revolutionary time of the Deed, of a violent new beginning breaking through to a new opening in history, will have become the time of permanent revolution perpetually revolving about the same fixed point, fixated for all time—as Adorno puts it: "Thus history seems to have been extinguished. . . . Events are the private affair of the oligarchs and their assassins; they do not arise from the dynamic of society but rather subordinate society to an administration intensified to the point of annihilation."[24] Such a point of annihilation has not as yet been reached, but the tendencies of negative Progress are steadily moving in that direction. As modes of annihilation, the negative aspects of Progress sustain and intensify each other: the fatalism of spectatorism is furthered by the impersonality of publicity, and that is maintained by the technocracy of administration. These further each other and spin round like a system of ever-deepening spirals of annihilation, which like a whirlpool sucks everything down into nothingness.

How otherwise could one account for the extraordinary rapidity of the process of annihilation in modern history? What prevent it from irresistibly sweeping ahead and carrying everything before it are counter-tendencies deriving from that same negativity of Progress. One mode of Nihilism counters another; the force of destruction prevents annihilation from consuming everything. As long as there still remains an interplay among Techno-logy, Subjectivity, and Activism—precisely in their negative forms—so long does history remain in play. But if ever Techno-logy were to dominate completely in its negative mode of Technocracy, absorbing within itself both Subjectivity and Activism, then the play of history would be over. Then Progress as Nihilism would be everywhere present in its most annihilatory mode, and that would literally mean the death of Man. What prevents it from coming about is the still-unpacified human rage at the inhuman conditions. Men still fret in frustration at the potentialities denied them, they still make collective demands that are unsatisfied, they refuse to enter tamely the "iron cage." But intransigence and refusal are no solutions. What is the solution, it will be asked, for surely there must be one?

Invariably, those who spoke of Nihilism heard it as a great unasked question to which they felt impelled to give an answer. They thought of it as the great problem to which a solution must be forthcoming, as the great Despair against which some even greater Hope must be mustered. This is so in Goethe's *Faust* where Faust's great curse on life and everything life has to offer is followed straight away by the deed with Mephistopheles. It is as if Nihilism were only to be entertained, not persisted in, as if the mere mention of its vacuum of nothingness were sufficient to make heaven and hell come rushing in to fill it. Every *Faust* is a counter to its own sense of Nihilism, even when it ends in damnation. So, too, it has been with every writer on Nihilism. Invariably, each has provided some answer, some way out or way through, some escape clause. In fact, one suspects that the problem of Nihilism was only stated so that its solution could be given. It was the question for a predetermined answer.

Now we must learn to live with a question mark hanging over our heads like a sword of Damocles. Our whole existence has become questionable. We have no more answers to our own Nihilism, which has become a permanent condition. The drama of Faust, now played out, gives way to a much grimmer play. In our passage through the Deed we have passed on to the horror of the "deed without a name" which there is no surpassing.

# ACT IV

---

## *THE END OF FAUST*

◆

## SCENE I
### *Beginning and End*

In the beginning was the Deed; in the end is . . . what? And is it the same Deed at the end that it was at the beginning? If the Deed is the beginning of Faust then what is the end of Faust? Is the end of Faust in fact also Faust's end? And if it is, then what kind of an end is it?

There is a close relationship, inherent in Faustian thought, between the beginning and the end, and it is the Deed that brings the two together. The Faustian conception of the end takes its bearing from its conception of the beginning. It is this that gives Faustian thought its eschatological cast. The beginning determines the end, so that if the beginning is a creative act of initiation, then the end is the inverse, concluding act of completion. Whether this end-culmination is itself creative or destructive depends on whether it is viewed as a fulfillment or as an emptying; both views are possible within Faustian thought. On the first account, time as history is the progressive movement toward the end as the high point wherein it is fulfilled; on the second, it is the slow decline toward its zero degree—either time attains to All or time recedes to Nothing. The thought of an end that is neither completion nor depletion, neither All nor Nothing, is unthinkable within Faustian thought. Such an end would be no end; it would be like a beginning that did not begin. That there might be no such beginnings or ends is something that Faustian thought cannot entertain. The Faustian turning to the Deed compels it to become preoccupied with beginnings and ends, origins and conclusions. The involvement of Faustian thought with History is expressive of that preoccupation, one that can become an obsession, temporalizing everything.

Faustian thought is inherently temporal, time is of the essence for Faust. Faust is a creature of time: his time is the life-day of 24 years which he can fill in any way he wills—for it begins with the Deed by whose terms the Devil is on hand to do his bidding—but which must come to its appointed end. Death must ensue to Faust as to any man, but not just any kind of death. Faust's is the specific death that is stipulated in his Deed; that Deed determines when and how Faust must die, but it decides, too, what is to be the meaning of death for Faust. In deciding that, it establishes the meaning of death for every man, since Faust is a man of the highest potential: he is Man writ small, the microcosm of all humanity. And in this way it also establishes the meaning of life for every man, since the significance of the end in turn reacts back to signify, and give its meaning to, the whole that preceded it. In Faustian thought as in Christian theology, the whole of life takes its meaning from the end even more than from its origin, though, of course, origin and end are linked—Faust's death is inscribed in his Deed, his last will is written into his first will.

Thus, the meaning of death as an end is already decided for Faust by the meaning of the Deed as a beginning. The beginning demands that there shall be a certain kind of end, and in turn the end refers back to the beginning, revealing it retrospectively for what it was. Each of the several Fausts has a somewhat altered beginning and end, but invariably, for that is part of the Faust thematic, beginning and end are brought together: death and the Deed are at one. In describing the progression of changing meanings of the end from one Faust to another, we are tracing also the passage of the Faust theme itself, that is, of the universal Faust who passes on through history. Inevitably, therefore, the question must arise of whether that Faust, too, has his end, and whether that end is the same as the end of the last Faust or whether it is a different kind of end altogether. Does the story of Faust itself conclude with a Faustian ending? And if we see the story of Faust as symbolizing a whole history, that naive question assumes larger dimensions. What kind of an ending might we expect Faustian history to have? All kinds of endings have already been written, rehearsed, and even tried out many times now. Has any of these actually succeeded in making an end?

To find an answer we had at the start begun to question the Deed. We had asked of it: Whose is it? When was it? And what was prior to it? And we had received our contradictory answers, those which begin by telling us that it is Man's Deed, that it occurred before time itself, and that there was Nothing prior to it; and then end by taking back and inverting these initial replies, telling us that on the contrary it cannot be Man's Deed since it is the Deed that does and undoes Man, that it takes place within an historical time, and that Nothing only has emerged out of it. We discovered that within those contradictions lie the limits of modern thought.

Now we need to ask whether within those limits there is also the end of that thought. But before we come to the end we need to begin once again at the beginning and pose the same question once more, this time reflecting back on the entire passage of Faust. Reading the Deed back into that passage we see that it is really Faust's Deed, that it is not the first Man or any other original Man who does the Deed, but Faustian Man. The Deed that creates the modern world is the first act of modern

Man as Faust. It follows from this, too, that the Deed inaugurates not time itself but a specifically Faustian time, and that the Nothing that precedes it is not universal chaos before the creation of the world but a new Faustian Nothing. The latter is that peculiar Nothing called modern Nihilism, seemingly unlike any Nothing ever known before. And that Nothing determines the end of Faust—for from the start Faust has had his appointed end. He is a creature of finitude. The end is inherent in the very terms of the Devil's Deed: in the day of life, the 24 years Faust is given as his own, there is the unavoidable moment when time runs out, there is the last moment before the clock must stop. His whole active life as Faust leads up to that end; and at the last moment the question is most agonizingly posed of whether that life had been worth living, whether it amounted to anything at all in the face of the nothingness of death. It is this that is always behind the simpler question of Faust's damnation or salvation.

The initial and basic orthodox answer, the one that says Faust is damned, is premised on the supposition that even the best things of this world are worthless compared to the state of one's soul at the moment of death, that the Devil's 24-year life term is a cheat whose illusory nothingness is revealed as such by the annihilating but testing touchstone of death, the only thing that counts, for its last timeless moment is the one that persists for all eternity. Are we, then, to pass this last judgment on the whole passage of Faust, too? Must the Devil's Deed signify a fall from grace, and must Faust's ending reveal him as damned? Has he been a dupe of the Devil all along? Has his time been nothing but a brief, fitful day of history? Is he doomed to disappear without trace, swallowed up in the hell of Nihilism? As we know, this is even now the orthodox answer to the question of the end of modernity.

Yet, even in the delivery of the orthodox judgment, sly heretical whispers subtly insinuate themselves. At first these are merely natural human stirrings which question the religious verities. If all Faust's attainments in this life are as nothing when weighed against his last moment, then what of the attainments of any life? Does not the judgment of death render all life worthless, all vanity and illusion? And what, then, is any time when matched against eternity? Is there not a hatred of time and life and all human striving behind the verdict of the priests? And if that is so, what can it mean to have all that life can offer and yet lose one's soul at the last moment? And even if it is lost, what can that soul be worth that is given over to the Devil only when life is complete? What can the soul be after life, if not a shadowy nothing, and what can any last moment of damnation be when weighed against the achieved years of this life? What is death itself as against the certitude of life? Is it not a nothing about which we need not think when we are still alive, and will not think if we are fully alive—and when we are dead, then that is past the time for thinking? So we come to the full humanist rejoinder which dared not speak itself openly until much later, when the new enlightened faith of human progress had ousted the old obscurantist faith. But the humanist blasphemy is there implicitly in the theme of the Faust myth, setting up within it all kinds of deep-seated ambiguities. What else is the fascination of Faust? From the start the apprehension and horror at his damnable Deed is mixed with amazed appreciation of his daring. Then, as the action unfolds, there is envy for the power and satisfaction he can command and enjoy which must invoke a certain degree of self-identification with him. It is only at the end that there is a distancing from Faust, but this can never become a complete rejection, since together with the horror there is also the pity for his fate; Faust becomes the scapegoat for all our illicit longings, including the very viewing of his play. Thus even at this most naive level there are complexities of feeling and divided emotion evoked by the thematic of the myth. These multiply themselves in subsequent Fausts.

### SCENE II
### *Dr. John Faustus–the first Faust*

In Marlowe's rendering there are already much more dangerous ambiguities at work which indicate intricacies of feeling that here become perverse. The interplay of religious orthodoxy and humanist atheism is merely the foreground and background to the body of the play. The former serves as the formal structural framework into which the action of the play is set—in places, chopping it up as upon a Procrustean bed; the latter appears openly as the point of departure for the action but is later retracted into the implicit background. Faustus begins as a freethinking, libertine humanist—at a time, of course, when the magician was the precursor of the scientist. Knowledge for Faustus is both scientific truth and the ability to conjure; his universe is the Renaissance one of the book of Nature which the books of magic can read and so command. "Knowledge is power" for the magician in a much more direct sense than for the sober empiricist Bacon, and the book of Nature is writ in numbers and figures that are much simpler to control than the mathematics and geometry of a rationalist like Galileo. Yet, there is a continuity of purpose there; Faustus, at the inauguration of the scientific quest, also wants to command "All things that move between the quiet poles. His dominion that exceeds in this stretches as far as doth the mind of man" (I.i). All the old learning—the logic and physics of scholastic Aristotelianism, the medicine of Galen, the jurisprudence of Justinian, even the divine theology itself of a Jerome—all pale into vapid futility before this new knowledge. We seem to be uplifted on the grandiose sweep of Renaissance Man, to be about to share in his aspirations. The Logos in all its orthodox forms is here for the first time explicitly and openly rejected in disgust. A new Logos is to take its place: the Word that has the power of command over things, though it, too, harks back to some of the forms of the so-called Alexandrian *logos spermatikos*. However, as a scientific Logos, it appears here in its earliest, most naive guise as the conjuration or magical formula with seemingly little relation to the mathematical function which, much later, would emerge as the power of technological control. Yet, in both cases knowledge is power, and both desire to read the "infinite book of Nature's secrets." It is a short, though decisive, step from Bruno, the last of the magicians, to Galileo, the first of the scientists—Kepler was both at once.

Already here—as always in the utilization of knowledge for power—there is a catch, and it is much more subtle than the simple theological one that such knowledge is impious and damnable. If knowledge is for power, then what is power for? The answer that is thrust at us over and over again both in the speeches and action of this play—as well as later in the history of technology—is that power is for glut of appetite: "The God thou servest is thine own appetite." This holds not only for Faustus but for any man in the play. Faustus himself desires all possible satisfactions that man can savor: base and noble, crude and refined, egotistic and altruistic, mercenary and just; he craves for recognition, fame, and deference, as well as all the delights of love, art, scholarship, and fellowship. At its most sublimated and sublime, as one perceptive critic has remarked, Faustus modifies his desire for "'sweet pleasure' in a way that transcends mere 'voluptuousness' and becomes a passionate love of beauty."[1]

> Have I not made blind Homer sing to me
> Of Alexander's love and Oenon's death?
> And hath not he, that built the walls of Thebes
> With ravishing sound of his melodious harp,
> Made music with my Mephostophilis?
> Why should I die, then, or basely despair?
> (*Faustus,* II.i)

The recourse to music as the antidote to despair is touched on here for the first time in the play. It will become the concluding note when despair threatens to overwhelm us all at Faustus' end. Already, in the first Faust, the fundamental Faustian thematic of music and time is firmly and explicitly established. In time, at the very end of Faust, it will grow into the complex composition of time and music that is the last Faust. There Mephostophilis will once again reappear as musician and timekeeper, and Faustus will once more sell his soul for music.

The pleasures of music are the most sublime that can be experienced in the world of Marlowe's play, yet as pleasures they enter into the fatal entanglement of appetites that turns pleasure into pain and become part of the torment that is Faustus' and all men's being in the world. This is a dialectic of appetite or will whereby a striving for pleasure must end as a desire for pain. All men are will-driven, so all men are driven to torment. Nietzsche remarked that "men would rather will Nothing, than nothing will," but for Marlowe there is no suggestion of choice in the matter—men are condemned to will, and in willing will what is Nothing. That, for Marlowe, is the hell that is human life. Here hell is not others, hell is oneself, as Mephostophilis testifies to the incredulous Faustus. Or, as Baudelaire was later to say, "Man, be damned and live!" This dialectic of will unfolds in the dramatic case-study of the character Faustus himself. Will in all its senses dominates him: his will to knowledge is itself a kind of desire, and his will to power is lust. In this he is like all men, as his servant Wagner says: "For is he not *corpus naturale*? And is not that *mobile*?" Wagner is himself just such another natural being—"That I am by nature phlegmatic, slow to wrath and prone to lechery (to love, I would say)" (I.ii). Wagner well knows that any man driven by appetite "would give his soul to the devil for a shoulder of mutton though it were blood-raw." The clown comically demurs, only to reinforce the point: "Not so neither. I had need to have it well roasted, and good sauce to it, if I pay so dear, I can tell you" (I.iv). In any case, in his lice the clown already has his bloodsucking familiars. Later in the play, in a comic commentary on the main plot, the goings-on of the apprentices Robin, Dick, Rafe, and company reinforce this theme of knowledge, power, and will: "Here I ha' stol'n one of Doctor Faustus' conjuring books, and i'faith, I mean to search some circles for my own use. Now will I make all the maidens in our parish dance at my pleasure stark naked before me" (III.iv). It is no different in learned or high society; the motives may appear different but the psychological drive is the same. Faustus looks on and experiences it all both at the pope's palace and the emperor's court: "While I am here on earth let me be cloyed with all things that delight the heart of man" (III.ii).

And cloyed he is, for that is the logic of the working of appetite. Each hunger gluts itself with its own satisfying, so if the level of satisfaction is to be sustained then a keener hunger must be aroused. This rhythm of arousal and satiation is the basic sexual rhythm of life as sensuality. As the action of the play moves from adventure to adventure, Marlowe dramatically exhausts each of the things "that delight the heart of man." A bored, corrosive cynicism is evident in the writing in those middle parts of the play. The playwright despises the audience to whom these spectacles appeal as much as he does the characters who enact them; in fact, he detests humanity in its common run. Only Faustus in relation to Mephostophilis holds his interest, and ours too. But why so?

Only in Faustus is satisfaction fraught with torment. Each of Faustus' gratifications is bought with the pangs of a guilty conscience aware of its damnation. Faustus, who had at first made light of soul and judgment and scoffed at hell—"This word 'damnation' terrifies not me, for I confound hell in elysium" (I.iii)—is led step by step to the conviction of his own damnation. It is Mephostophilis who is the agent of faith. Mephostophilis insists, by the mere force of his presence, that there is a hell, for he is in it, and that hell's torments are as real as the pains of life. In this Mephostophilis is a staunch empiricist; he insists on the sensual reality even of the supernatural: "Come, I think hell's a fable. Ay, think so still, till experience change thy mind" (I.v). Far from seeking to minimize what by the terms of the contract awaits Faust he insists on stressing it with absolute literalness: "Why, have you any pain, that tortures others? As great as have the human souls of men" (I.v). The basic relationship of tormentor to tormented is here set up between Mephostophilis and Faustus. Faustus seems fascinated by the very prospect of these torments, and hell is the first thing about which he questions him. Before long the anticipated pains of the flesh become the ever-present anguish of conscience. Suicide, total extinction in death, seems the only escape, but that escape is precluded by the very fear of eternal damnation from which it seeks to escape, as Faustus is to find out at the very end, when he prays for dissolution. During the course of the action it is repeatedly postponed because, as Faustus admits, "And long ere this I should have done the deed had not sweet pleasure conquered deep despair" (II.i).

For the playwright Marlowe it works the other way: deep despair conquers sweet pleasure. His cynical interest in the pleasures of life becomes a perverse involvement in its pains and despairs. The logic of that transformation in Marlowe is not fully explicit in this play, but it can be filled in from his other plays; one only need recall the death scene in *Edward II*. It works somewhat as follows. The pursuit of pleasures that cloy, as life's motive, ends in the savoring of pain both because all pleasure intensified turns to pain, and because—as pain never cloys—it is a self-sustaining motive for continuing to live. The sensualist's ultimate desire is to give and receive pain, as we have since learned from de Sade. But mere sensual, physical pains of the de Sadean kind have a limit; prolonged to excess, they result in loss of consciousness and oblivion. The ultimate in pain is that which cannot be stopped and so need never have an end. Mental torments, being self-inflicted against one's will, are those which one cannot stop; they continue as long as the mind lasts. The anguish of conscience has this property. Where this conscience is one that cannot be appeased, then we reach the ultimate in anguish. The certitude of damnation on the part of the reprobate is such an anguish of conscience.

Such a man is Faustus, whose present "store of pleasures must be sauced with pain" (V.ii) of thinking on the future. Mephostophilis is there both devilishly to provide the pleasures and sanctimoniously to affirm the pains, for Mephostophilis, like every orthodox Devil, is the best upholder of orthodox religion. The Calvinist God is far away; one senses only his "heavy wrath" in the nearness of his avenging instrument, the Devil, whose existence is affirmed on-stage, as in fundamentalist theology, with explicit literalness. Faustus needs to believe in him literally if he is to experience his anguish, for nothing but a bodily hell with real pains could provoke that kind of fear in him.

But where does Marlowe himself stand in this respect? Marlowe is both the tormentor and tormented of the play, and at the same time he is also the author, outside the terms of the play. As author Marlowe is above any belief in the reality of a stage devil and of a hell conceived in accordance with popular lore, but as author he needs such a devil in order to torture Faustus, in the action of which he himself sadistically participates. At the same time, Marlowe is imaginatively participating in the torments of Faustus: he enters imaginatively into Faustus' most agonizing moments, above all in the silent, anguished despair of Faustus' "last supper" with his disciples and in the bitter writhing of his last moment of abandonment. In these scenes Faustus is conceived with anguished sympathy and quiet compassion as a man who takes upon himself the damnation of the world, bidding other men to "Talk not of me, but save yourself and depart" (IV.ii). Yet in order to participate in these pains of Faustus Marlowe has to share imaginatively in Faustus' belief in irrevocable damnation, and so has to suspend his initial disbelief in the theology he needs to give himself the frissons of torment he desires. He must disbelieve and believe at once. Really it is thus: intellectually he cannot believe, but psychically he so desires to believe in the very worst that there is to be believed that, in effect, he also believes it.

These ambiguities of thought and feeling are not unknown to us from other cases since; in Marlowe's day they were very likely unprecedented in literature, with the possible earlier exception of Villon. We know of poets and authors—Baudelaire and Dostoevsky come readily to mind—in whom the desire to believe springs precisely from the need for the worst fears that theology has to offer. Such men need to believe in damnation so that they can give themselves to evil, for without evil nothing in life has any savor or sense: "La volupté unique et suprême de l'amour gît dans la certitude de faire mal" (Baudelaire). It is with a similar intention that Dostoevsky has his Faust, Ivan Karamazov, invoke a material devil to appear to him in his nightmare. This devil, in whom he cannot believe, is also the real guarantee of the possibility of damnation, without which life would cease to have any meaning. It is above all sensualists, for whom reality is carnal and close to the senses, who are most driven in this direction, for only the possibility of sin and damnation can give meaning to a life that threatens to become a mere flux of sensations. Yet, when at the same time such sensualists are also intellectuals they feel themselves unable and unwilling to accept the crude fundamentalisms of the beliefs they desire. This incredulity becomes a further source of guilt demanding to be expiated by even firmer adherence, and so the pressure mounts to believe precisely that which is most repugnant to the intellect. "Credo quia absurdum est": Tertullian, perhaps the first such intellectual-sensualist believer, long ago expressed the paradoxical nature of such a state of mind. Such inner turmoils and contortions of mind as well as of body can in a great artist produce the complexities of a *Brothers Karamazov*; in a lesser being it can equally well result in nothing but morbidity, or cheap perversity, or a criminal sado-masochism, of which propensities even the great artists are never completely free.

It is among such writers that Marlowe belongs, without being quite capable of composing his contradictions in a work that fully contains them. The closest he came to this is the Faustus of the last act. Let us look at him there, starting with the very end, at the very last instant of his life.

(*The clock strikes twelve*)

Oh, it strikes it strikes, now body form to air,
Or Lucifer will bear thee quick to hell.

(*Thunder and lightning*)

> Oh soul, be changed into little water drops
> And fall into the ocean, ne'er be found
>
> (*Thunder, Enter the Devils*)
>
> My God, my God, look not so fierce on me.
> Adders and serpents, let me breathe awhile.
> Ugly hell, gape not, come not, Lucifer!
> I'll burn my books. Ah Mephostophilis!

"That cry of erotic self-surrender and horrified revulsion"[2] at the very end has already been well-prepared-for in the preceding action of the play. It is there in his attraction-repulsion to "sweet Mephostophilis"; it is there in the passion for Helen—"Her lips suck forth my soul"—who is, therefore, at once the longed-for beauty of antiquity and a paramour succubus; it is there, too, in the last speech's irony of the quotation from Ovid's *Amores*: "O lente, lente, currite noctis equi." The prayer of the Roman lover that night might never end so that he could remain with his mistress interminably is placed in the mouth of a Christian sinner who begs that it might "make perpetual day" so that his demon-lover should not come. But here "The stars move still, time runs, the clock will strike, the Devil will come."

Time has at the end assumed an insistent relentlessness that is the opposite of the classical even gait of the "noctis equi." Time is now measured by the clock whose insistent ticking and regular striking on the hour and half-hour produce here for the first time in literature a new awareness of the dread of time. Fear of time is here not something metaphysical or theological, not a general knowledge of time's flux or time's corrupting power; here it is the physical sensation, conveyed through the ear, of time's abstract, relentless motion that nothing can hold back. The ticking of the mechanical clock makes possible an existential *Angst* of time, the sense of the emptiness of a time that is the background to every event and occurrence, drawing it into its reiterated rhythm and bringing it down to its own pointless repetition. This is the vertigo of time that men since have not ceased to feel. The life of a man, his day of 24 years, becomes nothing but such and such a number of minutes and seconds, the last of which is no different from the first. In accepting the Devil's bargain Faustus sets his own clock going; he has a life-day of years before him which must as surely end, and end as meaninglessly, as the day of minutes on a clock. The action of the play gradually contracts, winds itself down to the last day, in its last hour of its last minute.

The years move swiftly and imperceptibly after the Devil's deed; one exciting adventure gives way to another. Time jumps over years and distances. It is only toward the end of Act IV that Faust sees for the first time the approaching end: "the restless course that Time doth run with calm and deadly foot . . . calls for the payment of my latest years" (IV.v). For the last act the scene changes once more to Wittenberg and the collegial setting of scholarly fellowship. The time of the play telescopes and closes in; it is now the days of ordinary living that are presented on stage with their meal-times and bedtimes. The act opens on the last feast of the last day. The feast ends, Faustus completes his last will and bids farewell to his scholar-friends on his last night. Then the time of the action contracts once again, to the last hour, but as such it has also expanded to be nearly coextensive with the time of playing; we as audience are almost living out the same minutes and seconds that Faustus is living on stage. The striking of the clock enforces that on us, so that Faustus' time-anxiety becomes also our own. Hence, with what exquisite irony against himself does Faustus open his last soliloquy with the lover's classical tag invoking time that runs slowly and smoothly, for we and he know what "demon lover" he is awaiting and what tormenting delights are about to approach him.

For Faustus the fear is the traditional one that even with death time will not stop, that it will go on into hell with years on years of torment, going on for aeons without end, for a just but wrathful God has ordained it so. So he begs "that time might cease," that for him there might be an extinction of time and so a limit set to pain. For Marlowe it is in some respects the reverse; what fascinates him is the thought of a never-ending time of physical torment, of sensation without end, of precisely that which fills Faustus with horror. The thought of damnation in perpetual pain is somehow perversely preferable to him to the thought of total extinction—that time might end in nothingness, that the end of a lifetime might be no different from the last tick of a clock.

Thus, there is in this last speech an inverse and perverse relationship between Faustus and his creator Marlowe. What Faustus dreads fascinates Marlowe, and what Marlowe dreads Faustus longs for. To the reprobate Faustus the skepticism of atheism seems like salvation: if only his body were drawn up "into the entrails of yon labouring cloud" to be "vomited forth into the air"; if only his soul were that of a beast, who is happy "for when they die their souls are soon dissolved into elements"; if only he were "a creature wanting soul"; if only his body could turn to air and his soul "into little water drops." For Marlowe it works the other way: to be ingested and vomited in Nature, in that disgusted vision of the natural processes as digestive cycles of a universal will or appetite, to be oneself sunk in hebetude like any other beast, to sink into the elements and be dissolved to air and water and forever lost—all these prospects of atheism are just as appalling as damnation. Marlowe has conceived of a Faustus facing damnation in his last moment in order that he can himself experience imaginatively the alternative to his own sense of futility. But at the same time Marlowe is also with Faustus. The separation of creator and creature is not one that can be made neatly, for the art in this play is not one of aesthetic objectivity and ironic distancing but a dramatic art of imaginative participation. Marlowe is with Faustus; he also is horrified by damnation and envious of natural extinction.

How is this peculiar, paradoxical, perverse contradiction, in which lies the greatness of the play, to be understood? There is another peculiarity that subtly asserts itself throughout the play which might explain it. Faustus is conceived as a kind of counter-Christ. This is unmistakably so in the deeding scene. Faustus has to write his deed to the Devil in his own blood, just as Christ gave his blood for mankind; Faustus' blood refuses to "stream"—"Why streams it not that I may write afresh?" (I.v)—while by contrast, "See, see where Christ's blood streams in the firmament" (V.ii); finally, when the deed of blood is completed, Faustus "makes an end" with the last words of Christ on the cross, "Consummatum est." It is also at that moment that he reads on his arm the words addressed to Judas—who, as we know, also sold his soul—"homo fuge." The contrasting parallels with Christ do not end there; they are once more taken up in the last act. Faustus' carousing with his disciples at his "last supper" is the inverse of Christ's; he also dismisses them so that he may suffer his own Gethsemane alone while they sleep untroubled nearby; yet, Faustus does not ask them to "abide with me," but the opposite—"Talk not of me, but save yourself and depart" (V.ii). Faustus' calm, tragically accepting demeanor is like that of Christ, but his despairing sense of hopelessness and his inner agony are like Judas'. He is, as it were, Christ and Judas at once, an identity of opposites that is the very ultimate in heresy but which has been just beneath the surface of Christianity since medieval times. It is the identity of the irrevocably damned and the Savior, of utmost hopelessness and hope, of despair and faith. In *Faustus* Marlowe has brought that identity to the surface and revealed it. He has dramatized himself in it, and it is this self-dramatization that produces the most moving tragic dignity of the last act.

Marlowe conceives of Faustus as a Judas who takes upon himself the damnation of the world. He damns himself for the sake of the world. He is torn limb from limb in his torments so that we other men can sleep in peace. As such, he is also a Christ who sacrifices himself for us. Damnation and salvation here become identified. Through his damnation we are saved, but in effecting our salvation he, too, is saved. He is the martyr of damnation. But the paradox is even more twisted than that, for to be a Judas he must cease to believe in God, since only that can be the ultimate disloyalty. So it is as an atheist that he becomes the Judas, who is thereby also a Christ. Strictly logically, as always with such contortions of disbelief and faith, none of this makes sense, but psychologically it is understandable. As we know from psychoanalysis, denial when it is strong enough is itself a mode of affirmation, and affirmation can also be denial: faith and doubt are bound up with each other, as are also disbelief and belief. Need we once more mention Baudelaire and Dostoevsky?

Though Marlowe only fitfully presents such an interesting case, what separates these two modern authors from him is much more than a matter of individual talent or insight; it is the modern experience of Nihilism which both Baudelaire and Dostoevsky have felt with their senses, even though neither could think about it adequately, and of which Marlowe had no premonition—unlike his contemporary, Shakespeare, whose awareness of Nothing was so profound that it partially encompasses our own. The Renaissance ambience of orthodox religiosity and naive humanism within which Marlowe created his popular art is one that does not permit any approach to Nihilism, just as Nihilism in turn excludes it. It is not just a matter of historical distance, for a modern humanist or believer is equally unable to sense the Nihilism of his time, no matter how much he may know about it. We see this clearly revealed in the very interesting case of Eliot, whose initial sense of Nihilism, incipient as it is in his early poetry, disappears completely as his religious commitment deepens. By the time of the *Four Quartets*, the negativities of modern life that Eliot invokes have become universalized into the traditional religious despairs of life which are the obverse of faith: emptiness, vanity, futility, accidie, taedium vitae, loss of hope—that which the mystics have always known in their dark moments. Similarly, a humanism no matter how pessimistic is unable to approach Nihilism, for example, in such great writers as Ibsen or Henry James. The modern thought of Nihilism dates from the time of the next *Faust,* Goethe's, and it is to that we must turn to see how it begins to shape itself in literature.

## SCENE III
## *Heinrich Faust—the middle Faust*

### I

It is a long jump from Marlowe's *Faustus* to Goethe's *Faust,* one that overleaps two centuries: the centuries of Baroque Classicism, of Absolutism and Enlightenment, of civilization as civility, culture as cultivation—of the pursuit of refinement. Goethe's complete reworking of the meaning of the myth is premised on that historical fact. The Marlovian original meanings figure merely as an archaic residue in Goethe's rendering. Those original tragic conflicts having in the meantime become comic buffetings to be looked on with undisguised irony, a quite different dramatic problematic informs the myth, now already at a second remove from the original. It is no longer an issue of damnation in the theological sense, for this has been transformed into the question of Man's end. It is true that the Christian world is there in Part I, but it is there as the presupposed background; in Part II it seems to have completely disappeared except, toward the end, as a source of symbols. In Part I it figures as part of folk life, where Easter and spring are intermixed and identified, and it is woven into the memories of childhood. Only as such is it valued. In its naïveté it informs the purity of Gretchen and makes for the pathos of her fate, condemned by that sterner Christianity of the church and society which she is unwilling to escape. Her pathetic tragedy is indeed that of the Christian folk-world itself. In destroying Gretchen through her innocence, Faust is also destroying the whole Christian small-town life by which she lives and dies and which was also the world of his own childhood and youth. And Goethe as dramatist concurs and participates in that act of destruction of innocence for the sake of experience; he leaves the pathos of the Christian world behind him for the sake of the higher comedy of Faust's progress into the larger world of Nature and Art.

Right from the start we are made aware that the original Faustian psychomachia of damnation and salvation, of curiosity and piety, of magic and grace is no longer to be the substance of this drama. Faust himself with savage irony explodes such pretensions in the Devil. Though Gretchen still instinctively dreads him, Mephistopheles is no longer the traditional Christian tempter, he is more like Job's accuser-adversary *cum* Voltairean cynic-sensualist, who is dared by Faust to satisfy him or make him self-satisfied. This is why the old Devil's deed as a contract of exchange has now become a wager—indeed, a double one, between God and the Devil and then between the Devil and Man. The wager issues in a contest between Mephistopheles and Faust that for most of the play does not cease and that is much more dramatic than the staged show of inner repentance and despair in Faustus. Above all it is the Faustian striving which has been so radically altered: Faustus' searching for magic power through the power of the Word has become Faust's turning to the power of the Deed. Everything that had made it possible for a Renaissance man to conceive of the power of the word over things—correspondences and signatures of the world, essences and virtues slumbering in things, intrinsic properties of words themselves—all this had almost completely disappeared in the rationalist-classical interregnum. At first the young Goethe sought to reinvoke something of this earlier aura of the Renaissance by playfully toying with it as he has Faust conjure with the signs from Nostradamus' own book, but the mature Goethe quickly put paid to such youthful literary escapades and only allowed them to remain in the finished work as the vestiges of its birth and derivation.

It is this evolutionary inner development of writing that gives this Faust work its peculiar literary structure. It contains within itself all its stages of composition. Hence, Goethe's *Faust* is itself a series of reflections on the passage of his character Faust—and also indirectly on his own passage in life, for throughout his life it was a work in progress, ever transforming itself in the constantly changing totality of its meaning. The various stages of the work are there encapsulated in its final form, contained within it as so many levels of its own self-awareness. Thus, it constitutes not a single, perfectly unified work of art but an artistic document whose various stages of composition must be read into it in order to be able to read its meaning. It is a developing form comparable to the variations on one theme that a painter might record on separate canvasses that must be seen as a series, like the series of self-portraits recording Rembrandt's preoccupation with his own face from youth to old age. But, possibly for the first time in literature, in *Faust* the changing states of a work are part of that work, the total work thus constituting a record of an exploration that covers a whole life, in the first place that of the character, but indirectly also that of the author, and ultimately that of Everyman.

Thus, in the structure of Part I it is easy to read how the dramatic kernel, the lyrical, beautiful play of his earliest youth—the so-called *UrFaust*—is absorbed into a more mature work that is the present Part I. The mature work provides not only a framework that gives a deeper meaning to the early action but is also a reflective commentary on it at every major turning. For example, the Walpurgisnacht scene, which interrupts the course of the Gretchen romance, is a comment on the sexuality there right from the start in that "innocent" affair and which could not be otherwise exposed on stage. Thus, structurally Part I is in many respects like a play within a play, and is so presented dramatically in terms of the device of Faust's rejuvenation. But that is much more than a mere dramatic device; it is part of the play's integral meaning.

Faust, who had already lived his life once and rejected it, is taken over that same life again so as to reexperience it in different terms and find a different meaning in it. It is as if the playwright Goethe were to seek to answer Job's ancient complaint against his Maker by taking him through life again and making him feel what it has to offer, for the proof of life can only be had in the living of it. Like Milton in his epic, Goethe in his drama strives to justify God's ways to man, but not as an argument in theological terms—rather, as a dramatic enactment that is itself to be experienced just as life is experienced. Life is drama just as drama is life. Hence, structurally the whole play is also a play within a play, explaining the device of the Prologue in Heaven, which in turn is preceded by the play of staging the play, the Prelude in the Theater, to reinforce the dramatic convention. The whole work is concluded with a play in heaven presented strictly as a pièce de théâtre. Within this overall structural schema the relationship between Part I and Part II is dramatically articulated: the end of Part II is a return to the beginning of Part I, and the action in Part I following Faust's rejuvenation is but the opening act of Faust's life's progress, which continues with a marked break, but no interruption, into Part II. The dramatic action of Part II is, however, very different from that of Part I; the quality of immediate experience has disappeared, giving way to the play of symbolic allegory and poetic intellectualization. Part II is a kind of odyssey of the universal mind, not unlike Hegel's *Phenomenology of Spirit*; it is also a dialectical progression in which Dasein or human "being" moves from one abstract sphere of the spirit to another, finally to descend to the concrete realm of its earthly Ithaca and feel itself for the first time at home in the very place from which the journey began.

"In the beginning was the Deed": the creative-destructive ambiguity is inherent in that pronouncement in the opening passage. As we noted at the start, it is through it that entrance is afforded to the active spirit of negation, for "Deed" is the one word powerful enough to "destroy the beautiful world" and to bring the Devil to Faust's side, the word the Devil has been angling for. That the word was pronounced in the course of an attempted New Testament translation is one of the ironies of the Devil's ways. The spirit that guides Faust and compels his pen with urgency to arrive at the word we all along suspect is not only the Holy Spirit, as Faust thinks, but also one of those intermediate spirits "between earth and sky" whom Faust had invoked in the previous scene on his walk with Wagner.

The Devil himself is only in the service of a higher Power, and is the means to lead Man, straying, onto the right road: as he bitterly confesses, he is "part of a power that would alone work evil, but engenders good" ("Faust's Study"). In guiding Faust to the Deed, the Devil is responsible for the whole course of his upward progress. Out of the translation passage comes the passage of Faust from beginning to end. And it is at the end, in the moment of Faust's passing, that the ambiguity of the Deed fully justifies itself, for only then is the Deed realized as world-building activity. Only when he has finally realized this does Faust learn that to be free and to be man is to accept the natural and human limitation of the Deed. It is only at that point that Faust banishes witchcraft, takes back his great curse on life and regrets having invoked the hovering shades of night. But, having reentered mortal life, it is at that moment that Care enters to beset him, that same Care that once brought him to his curse on life. This is the Care that eventually Heidegger was to develop into his basic existentiale. For Goethe, too, it holds sway in life beyond Need, Want, or Guilt. Nevertheless, he has Faust refuse to recognize its sway and has him re-dedicate himself to the work at hand. Thus it is that Goethe's answer to the besetting despair of human life is still the Deed, finally transformed into men's mutual and common activity in Nature.

To what extent, then, is the ambiguity of Faust's Deed expressive of the ambivalence of the Idealism-Nihilism and Romanticism-Nihilism that Jacobi had first exposed in Fichte's philosophy, and which had subsequently prevailed in the Jena circles? As a character in the play, Faust is an Idealist-Romantic who is looked on ironically and critically—though ever lovingly—by Goethe. Mephistopheles is always there to prick Faust's ego-bubble whenever it swells too much. Besides that, the new Fichtean philosophy and Romantic poetry are parodistically put down whenever they enter the play, for example, in Part II, when Fichte's ideas appear in the mouth of the returned Baccalaureus. Nevertheless, Goethe's play from beginning to end is pervaded by a dialectic of All and Nothing that is akin to similar thoughts current among the poets and philosophers who were his contemporaries. The abysses and voids that they had felt threatening to swallow them were the same ones against which Faust contended. Faust's descent into the Void and Night on his way to reach the Mothers and recover the form of Helen is very like the wandering in emptiness of many a Romantic figure such as Tieck's William Lovell, or Hölderlin's Hyperion, or Novalis's own journey into Night. There is, of course, a difference here, for the solemn self-consciousness of the Romantics is evoked but at the same time ironically undercut in Goethe. The dread and chill of the Mothers, which the very word evokes, is also a mock-mystifying leg-pull—but not without its serious point. For whereas with the Romantics it is the either/or of All or Nothing, the disjunction taken with full passionate pathos, as when Hölderlin declares: "What is not all and eternally all to me, is nothing to me," for Goethe there is the paradoxical "In your Nothing may the All be found" (Part II, Act I), which suggests a reconciliation that underlies the comic spirit of the work. The basic joke of the work—played by God on Mephistopheles and overseen by Goethe—is that Faust does finally find his limited All through Mephistopheles' unlimited Nothing.

It is precisely this feature of Goethe's Nothing that distinguishes it from any conception of modern Nihilism as we have known it at least since Nietzsche. Goethe's Nothing is an Idealist notion, despite his efforts to separate himself from the more romantic idealisms of his time. Its Idealist nature is incarnate in the figure of Mephistopheles and reveals itself as such as soon as we interrogate his complex and paradoxical character. When he first introduces himself he identifies himself as "the spirit that negates" and brings everything to Nothing. Negativity and Nothingness are unified in Mephistopheles. Hence, all his efforts at bringing everything down to nothing only result in his carrying out a dialectic of negation that creates something higher. He can only work against himself, so it is impossible that he should ever succeed more than temporarily and locally. He is in principle a failure. It seems that with such a devil Faust could not fail. Goethe's cosmic optimism—producing the comedy of the play of creation—goes into the conceiving of this devil. That evil should subserve good and destruction subserve creation, that nothingness itself should be a mere moment of negativity in the dialectic of progress—that in God's own words, the Devil "must as Devil help create" ("Prologue")—all this is an idealistic assurance that became increasingly difficult to maintain after Goethe. The thought of Nothing could no longer be reconciled with that of a dialectic of negation; the former issued in the philosophies of nihilism, the latter in the various successors to the Hegelian dialectic.

Even in the play itself there is prefigured something of this severance, for though Mephistopheles is the personified Nothing, it is Faust himself who is the nihilist. It is his Deed that shatters the world to nothing, and it is his despair that brings him to it, and his disillusionment that provokes despair. It is the Devil who pulls him out of this state and provokes him to begin again—Mephistopheles, as the ideal Nothing, saves Faust from his nihilistic nothingness. One might have thought that if he had only had the sense to leave him to his own devices then he would have won his bet with God. Is this an illogicality in the play, or is it one of its higher ironies?

Once again the ideal nature of the Deed accounts for it. Faust's deeding himself to the Devil is the same thing as his turning to the Deed. It is this double Deed that puts in league the nothingness of Faust with the Nothing of the Devil. Since it is the Devil who pushes Faust to the Deed, it is, therefore, also the Devil who provokes in him the supremely destructive act of the great curse that shatters the world, but with the alternative possibility of building it anew. For in this act of bringing the world to Nothing lies the hope of bringing it out of Nothing again. Before the Devil's arrival Faust's nihilism was of a purely passive kind, more akin to the traditional taedium vitae, its only active expression having been the attempted suicide foiled by the Easter bells. In making Faust live up to the literal meaning of his name (*Faust:* "the fist"), the Devil, who is also a fist, makes of Faust one of his own kind. From that moment on Faust never ceases, not only to be active, but to be violent. In Part I he is legally a murderer—there is even a hint of his kinship with Macbeth in the brief glimpse of brewing witches in the penultimate scene, "Night, Open Field." In Part II his violence is present in act after act: he snatches at the ghost of Helen, he is the robber baron of the Peleponnese, the mainstay of the emperor's wars, and finally the soldier-settler, trader-pirate of the marginal seashore lands won by force from the ocean. Only at the very end does he explicitly abjure violence.

Violence is barren, Devil's activity, as Act IV of Part II makes clear, but it does express dissatisfaction and striving that require active involvement in the world, not escape from it, and so is a means to salvation. Or, in the terms of Goethe's meaning, Man is human so long as he is striving and would cease to be such if he became essentially complacent—only that would constitute damnation in Goethe's humanistic theology, not for Faust to be the over-reacher but to become an under-reacher. This is why Faust is necessarily saved as long as he is Faust. This is no mere optimistic tautology; it is the cardinal article of Goethe's faith in Man. It is no longer the Christian sense of salvation or damnation that is in question, however, for even if Man were to destroy himself it would still not be sufficient to damn him. This is why for Faust to commit suicide would not suit the Devil's purpose at all—it is the Devil who stages the diversionary interruption of "Chime of bells and choral song" just when Faust is about to drain the poisoned cup.

This move from attempted self-destruction to world-destruction is the decisive step that the Devil effects in Faust through the medium of the Deed. The succession of scenes in which it is dramatically enacted is perhaps the greatest artistic triumph of the work. We must follow them closely to read the structural logic of meaning through which the move unfolds. The move culminates in Faust's great curse that follows on his realization that it was the Devil's trick that saved him from suicide, and leads him, therefore, to engage in the bet and deed himself in desperation to the Devil, since he has nothing to lose anymore.

The great curse on life that is provoked by the Devil is thus the consequence of and also the answer to the speech of life-weariness that Faust had uttered prior to it, in which Faust's total disillusionment, his bitterness and restless anxiety and his confession of utter impotence find expression. But this time he no longer even has the illusions about death that he had had in the great second monologue that preceded the attempt on his own life. In that a Romanticism of death—not unlike that of Keats's "Ode to a Nightingale"—had made it appear as a better counterpart to life, the release through which one might escape to freedom. The poisoned draught of death and the brimful cup of life are seen as one by Faust—in lines reminiscent of Keats's "Ode to a Grecian Urn"—such that death appears as a transfiguration of life and an eternalization of its living activity in stillness. It is from this Romantic "half in love with easeful death" that Faust is saved by the illusions of his childhood Christian feeling, and then sent out on his Easter walk with Wagner to mix with the folk in the festivities of a folk-Christian religion of nature. But this folk life has no power to hold him; he passes through it as a distant observer.

When he lives in it as an active participant, of course, it will seem very different to him. Eventually, what we observe in the introductory scene at the city gate as only the carryings-on of wenches and louts and an attempted student pick-up will become a Gretchen episode; eventually, too, the mindless business of the folk will become a joint communal undertaking under Faust's leadership. But all that will only reveal itself much later in the drama, when Faust has begun his life anew. That new beginning is made possible precisely by the destructive life-hatred that makes Faust launch into his great curse. Death, too, holds nothing for Faust anymore at that point, even though he says in the speech prior to the curse that "death is desirable." The death he desires is merely the cessation of a life that he thinks is nothing but error, futility, and the Devil's dream-pleasures. It is at this nadir of disillusion that the Devil provokes Faust into cursing life, and so he transforms his weary, passive sense of nothingness into the active Nothing of destruction. With that the dramatic move completes itself, Faust's passage begins, and the rest of the play unfolds.

## II

The notion of destruction in the rest of the play is—on the level of character presentation—bound up with the characterization of Faust as a violent man. However, violence is only the visible working of destruction on the level of human action and of natural occurrence. On a deeper level it is one of the determining moments in the Goethean dialectic of development. The destructive-creative ambiguity of the Deed unfolds itself in time as an evolutionary development proceeding through stages that are transformations or metamorphoses. In each of these steps there is the moment of continual, gradual growth and the moment of violent, abrupt breakthrough—the gradual maturation of the chrysalis in the shell and the sudden bursting of its old shell to release the butterfly, to use a favorite Goethean image. Destruction is thus the negative principle, the Mephistophelean moment, in the work of creation. We have already examined how markedly this view of development differs from Hegel's rational unfolding of the Idea; hence, here we shall be concerned with it merely as a dramatic principle.

In the structure of the play the development takes place through a series of catastrophic endings. Faust's life unfolds through his failures, which impel him anew to other attempts, each time somewhat better grounded than the preceding one. Thus Part I ends with the pathetic-tragic death of Gretchen, which is a kind of Fall and expulsion from Eden: it dramatizes loss of ease, the assumption of guilt, the bursting out from the small-town security of a still untroubled world—this valedictory to youth is firmly placed in the play as a necessary transition from innocence to experience. Part II transcends it and begins with mature life, which is also therefore the life of ideas: the intellect as science, culture, philosophic thought, and the imagination as consciously wrought poetic forms, culled and adapted from all of world literature, are its predominant modes. It is no longer a dramatic enactment but a play of forms and ideas whose very playfulness prevents it from degenerating into mere intellectual allegory (though it has its bad moments where it is that). In effect, Part II is not a coherent dramatic unity at all but, rather, five separate poetic conceptions unified only by a dialectical development of theme, idea, and symbol. A well-thought-out conceptual schema operating as its underpinning alone propels the movement from one act to the other through a series of breaks or metamorphic transformations. Each of the acts of Part II ends in a catastrophe, but each breakdown initiates a new beginning in another sphere of poetic-intellectual abstraction until finally the dialectic is complete and reality is attained. (For an overview of Acts I–IV see Appendix II.)

Faust's wanderings in the first four acts are like an odyssey of the human mind through all the magic isles of experience, in search of reality. But it is only in the last act that the mind attains its Ithaca, and it is only then that Faust finally finds himself at home on earth as a man among men. In his last speech, at his last moment of existence, he in effect returns in imagination to the common life that he so impatiently spurned at the start in Part I. It is then that he utters the fatal formula: "Linger you now, you are so fair"—but only in the subjunctive conditional mode. His vision is of a future human condition freely accepting itself, not tempted by the errors that he himself had lived through. However, without these errings he would not have arrived at the truth of his final vision; hence, dramatically the whole of the preceding play is necessary to establish the authority of the last act. And, conversely, it is by the authority of the last act that all the previous ones are ordered and placed, for only in the end is the fundamental basis of human existence realized, and it is only on that basis that all the other spheres have their being. The volcanic political order of Act IV, the developing poetic-cultural forms of Act III, the evolutionary achievements through Strife and Love of Form and Intelligence of Act II, the illusory frivolities of society of Act I, and even the tragedy of innocence of Part I—all these are, as it were, the superstructures erected on the base of the material and existential realities of common and individual being. It is on that basis that life is justified and the great curse of Part I is at last withdrawn.

The final act begins with a mysterious wanderer's returning—"after a pilgrimage"—to the place where he was saved from the sea in his youth. Who is he? We suspect that he is the presence of the poet himself returning after a long detour to his own as yet unfinished work. In the meantime, Faust too has been at work. The two ancients, Philemon and Baucis, give the wanderer a report of how that work began and proceeded. Each gives his own version, one emphasizing the visible toil of human hands by day, the other intimating Satanic industry by night—a metaphor for the two aspects of the rise of technologic capitalism. Mephistopheles is, thus, still very much involved in Faust's project. Yet, the character of that project has changed: it is now a human effort to limit the sea and to win from its shore land for human habitation. Through the act Mephistopheles strives to keep Faust to his old ambitions pursued in the previous acts, to make him want treasures, empire, power—the supreme power of waging war on the elements, hoping thus to keep him ensnared in the old futilities and finally to make him expend himself in a losing struggle with the sea. Faust's moral progress can be measured by the fact that he now comes to reject these superhuman endeavors and devotes himself to that which is humanly worthwhile: productive labor in nature. Faust has at last realized that proper activity is human praxis.

In the last act, Faust's work is practical. It contrasts, therefore, with Goethe's own work, which is artistic. This opposition—but, ultimately, reconciliation—of the two modes of work forms the internal dialectic of the act. As Goethe expressed it in a poem on the reconciliation of "Nature and Art": "In me the antagonism has disappeared . . . honest toil . . . is the whole secret."[1] For both works—the builder's and the artist's—the problem is the same: how to make an end to an undertaking long since begun and grown already to mighty proportions. And for both author-creator and character-creature the end of the work is the end of life. So the problem for both becomes this: how to conclude the work and thereby to bring life itself to completion. However, Faust cannot bring his work to an end, so it seems his life cannot be complete, either, but that death only interrupts it, for, as "Nature and Art" has it: "Unfettered spirits will aspire in vain to the pure heights of perfection." Faust is one such unrestrained spirit. But Goethe himself in his art does know limitation, and so he can complete his work; and with its conclusion Goethe's life too can come to a fulfilled end. However, Goethe's work contains Faust's life, so if that work is complete then Faust's life, too, must somehow, somewhere be complete. Indeed, that is what the angels proclaim and rejoice over at the end: Love, sinful love, "helped the lofty work conclude and this precious soul to save."[2] So Faust's work, too, is completed—but not on earth, only in the higher sphere. That is the paradox of one "who ever strives with all his power": it is precisely because he cannot make an end but must ever go on that he gains "release" and thereby the relative conclusion of going on to a higher stage to continue his work. Put another way, Faust's work somehow completes itself in and through Goethe's work: what could not be finished in life finds its completion in art. And art in turn attains its consummation through the loving, sinful, and penitent "rose" of life, Love, the feminine principle that in drawing us onward helps us to conclude.

What makes it possible for Goethe, thus, in the same breath to speak of his own and Faust's work, to compare his own ending with that of his character, to refer to his play in his play, is the basic ground-metaphor of the "play of the world" that is invoked from the beginning. The play is both a play of and about the world, and it can be one only because it is the other. Faust has a vision of this in his first monologue, but he rejects it: "What a play! Yet but a play, however vast! Where, boundless nature, can I hold you fast?" However, Faust's attempt at an unmediated view of nature is repulsed by the Earth-Spirit. The only world he can look on is the world of the play: that of symbol and image, of light and shade, since everything that is, that which is passing, is itself mere play. The final Chorus Mysticus comprehends and vindicates the play-vision as a vision of the play.

The structure of the drama is itself a series of mirroring plays: the play of Faust's life takes place within the framework of the play in God's heaven, which is itself framed by the play of staging the play. The two framing plays are structurally analogous: the Producer's effort to bring the production into being with the aid of Poet and Fool is like God's setting up of the play of Man utilizing Faust and Mephistopheles. As we shall show, for Goethe both art and nature have the form of play, so that life and drama are of the same form and one can reflect on the other. This is how, at the end of the play, the question of the completion of Faust's work and of Goethe's work can be raised at once. The whole play can reflect on itself in itself, for it is a mirror of self-reflection.

The question of completing the work arises as soon as Faust enters in the last act. He sees in the midst of his newly built estate the surviving blemish of the old property: the dark lindens, the old cottage, and the chapel with its ringing bell which gives him no rest. His grand design cannot be complete without incorporating this remainder that is an obstruction to his unimpeded view and grand scheme of art. Goethe's problem in writing the ending to his work is exactly analogous; he, too, has somehow to incorporate the traditional material of Faust's end as it has been handed down to him. And that spells out Faust's death and damnation, which is so intractable to his own grand design. The traditional past Faust rages against is not merely a neglected remainder, it is also a reminder of the traditional end that Faust has so deliberately, and for so long, chosen to forget. The bell that he cannot bear to hear, for it reminds him of the incompleteness of his possession, is—as Mephistopheles is well aware and as he sardonically hints in his speech in reply—the knell of death. The outstanding property that Faust seeks to possess is every man's final patrimony, his last resting-place: "this sandy hill" before which his otherwise "all-powerful will breaks down" is one that he already feels "confines me as in aisle or tomb."

Mephistopheles pursues his irony on life throughout the last act: Man thinks he works to live, whereas really he works for death. The irony reaches its bitter conclusion in the two scenes of Faust's death and burial. The land that the Lemures survey is but his own resting-plot, the channel they excavate is but a ditch to bury him in, his palace has become his "little house": all his lifelong work and effort have been but to build himself a grave. Faust is completely deluded as to the activities surrounding him in his blindness; following his rejection of Care, he does not see what is happening when he calls his servants to complete the work according to his plan. His "great work" will not be completed. Death will overtake it, for the ocean will only temporarily be bounded; it will inevitably set itself free again, since the elements cannot be overcome. All human effort can accomplish is but a temporary respite. In the nature of things, human praxis in practical labor can have no cease, its work can never be completed. Mephistopheles is right about this; he is wrong only when, in asking rhetorically the question "What matters our creative endless toil?" he answers, "As good as if things never had begun. . . . I'd rather have Eternal Emptiness" (V, "The Great Outer-Court"). He is wrong insofar as this is all he is permitted to see; the meaningless round of material flux is his element and he cannot conceive of anything beyond it.

Faust can see something else: in his blind vision he looks into the future and in anticipation perceives the completed work, an earthly paradise conquered through free human activity in the struggle against natural obstacles. It is with that vision that he pronounces himself satisfied, to this future moment he sees that he may say: "Linger you now, you are so fair." Mephistopheles, however, seizes on this as an admission of satisfaction and promptly claims his stake by the terms of the original deed. The linguistic ambiguity permits him to do so, for a future conditional statement is still said in the present, and a vision of the future is not a future vision but a present one. Especially because the Devil does not distinguish among past, present, and future tenses—counting all time as nothing—it is possible for him to take Faust's pronouncement as timeless, and so as damning. However, the ambiguity also works against the Devil, for if the temporal distinctions are allowed then the statement refers to something that is yet to come, and possibly may never come, so Faust may never be satisfied. The Devil, in being right about the impermanence of human work, proves Faust wrong in his vision of an earthly paradise when his work will be completed, but in so doing he proves himself wrong in supposing that Faust will ever be satisfied. The Devil in Goethe's play, as we might expect, is wrong by being right, at least from our human point of view, granting time its reality. Thus Faust is saved from the Devil precisely because his earthly work can never be complete. His final vision is an ideal hope that is also in part a wished-for illusion.

A truer vision is that of the watcher Lynceus, who was "born only for sight." His is a present, contemplative vision of the now, here and near. His—not Faust's—is the eternal moment of the present, in which, again unlike Faust, he can take delight in himself and in all that his eyes reveal to him. For him everything can be momentarily perfect and complete, everything can shine with grace everlasting, so that he can say of it, in words echoing the fatal formula, yet without fear of damnation: "So fair has it been!" Yet in saying it he has to use the past tense, for the speaking follows the seeing, and that succession in itself introduces a fearful note of impermanence. Things cannot sustain themselves in the eternal present of contemplative vision, for the very next look has changed everything: Lynceus is forced to see the changing workings of destruction—indirectly Faust's work; being bound to the tower he cannot help viewing the fire spreading and the ensuing carnage of all he had extolled a moment ago. He is powerless and thus helpless to do anything about it; being a seer, not a doer, he can only bewail it. His manner of being is, thus, the direct opposite of that of Faust.

Being different, their manner of seeing is also opposed. In fact, there is altogether a fourfold opposition among the four fundamentally different beings, Faust, Lynceus, Philemon and Baucis, and Mephistopheles, each of whom has a different mode of vision. This is particularly evident in their perceptions of time and space. For Philemon and Baucis time is of the past, their lives are memories of what had been; space is of the tried and trusty "here." That is the same "accursed here" that Faust berates so viciously, for it is this "here" which he cannot stand for or stand on. His is the space of "there," just as his is the time of "then"—his last speech is the vision of a "then" and "there" that is out of sight, as yet nonexistent. Lynceus' time is the "now," and his space is the near and the far that is still within sight. His vision is bounded within the strict limits of the horizon, just as he himself is bound to his tower. By contrast, Faust seeks a boundless view and an endless scope. To Faust Man moves ever onward and "is never satisfied." "Care" sees the obverse to the optimism of this vision: she taunts Faust with the realization that his future hope and vision are only the outcome of his present anxiety, which makes him thrall to her and robs him of the "here" and "now": "Always on the future waiting/Nothing ever consummating." For "Care," therefore, this future vision is a present blindness, which is why she blinds Faust on stage. Mephistopheles, too, can work against Faust his future-directed vision because of its obliviousness to the past; seemingly at Faust's behest, he can eliminate the old couple and everything they stand for; he can carry through the destruction of the past on behalf of Faust because he can play on the ambiguity of Faust's command to replace the past—that is, to put it in its proper place—as meaning to displace it. And there is indeed this ambiguous attitude to the past in Faust's vision enabling him to do so. For Mephistopheles himself neither time nor space is real, the whole of infinity is as a point without extension that is nowhere, and all of eternity is endlessly the same and so is nothing. Mephistopheles' corrosive nihilism dissolves for him time and space, the medium in which he works, and thus he trips himself up once again.

Goethe's artistic vision, of course, comprehends all these dimensions of time and space. It is his vision in art that is circumscribed and firmly placed, and because of that open and free. This is why Goethe's work can be finished. In the poem "Legacy" Goethe sets out the conditions under which this consummation can be attained in life as well as in art: "where life takes delight in life. At such times the past lives on, and the future lives in advance, and the moment is eternity."[3] In the last act of *Faust* Goethe's art seeks to attain to this state. His vision can be characterized by all of those that he is dramatizing; it incorporates all of them into itself and places them in relation to each other. His is a vision of the past that does succeed in preserving it and keeping it alive: the drama does re-create the Faustian ending as it has been passed down by tradition. It is also a contemplative present vision of the eternal "now": the last act is one such present moment that sees in one dramatic glance the end of life. At the same time, it strives to look into the future, beyond this present life, to glimpse something of the meaning of it all—and this, too, the drama enacts through allegory and symbol. In so doing the artistic vision must comprehend and do justice to that which is most inimical to its own being in time, to the sense of futility and nullity of a Mephistopheles. Mephistopheles does not get everything in the end, but neither is everything taken from him; he is left with his "noble parts" intact, and that embraces those lower parts of the drama in which he moves.

To understand the deeper meaning of Goethe's awareness of his own art it is necessary to look beyond its being as artistic vision and take into account its being as artistic work. For Goethe, an artistic vision is not merely a dispassionate contemplation of things from the point of view of a god-like artist; it is also a work, which is, therefore, coextensive with the practical work that men do in life. Art and life are not dissociated; both are unified in Nature. Hence, according to Goethe, to work for a fulfilled end in art is also to work for one in life. But, why is it, then, that Faust in life cannot end, whereas Goethe in art can? And what can it mean to say that Goethe ends, as it were on behalf of Faust? To answer this let us briefly consider what is the end.

The end for Goethe is not merely finis, it is telos and eschaton as well. Faust does not merely die and so make an end of it, he also attains his end and ends in surpassing himself. Death is not a final closure, a permanent severance, an ultimate loss. There is no room for a tragic ending in Goethe's world; that is why his drama must be comic, though on a cosmic scale. Death is only another becoming, a radical transformation, a final, most radical, metamorphosis. The blessed boys who receive Faust's soul mark the first stage of his change of state: "Him as soul's chrysalis / Joyful receive we." In the poem "Ecstasy and Desire" Goethe employs the same classical image of the psyche as butterfly yearning for the light of the flame that is its consummation, to express the same thought that love consumes itself in death but through death it leads to a transformation into a higher stage: "Die and become!"

The two final scenes in the last act are, respectively, two successive visions of death and becoming. The working of Love in those scenes is more explicitly—if not also more crudely—explained by the last verse of the poem "Metamorphosis of Plants." Once again there recurs the image of the butterfly, since for Goethe as naturalist and poet the whole of evolution involves an organic change of forms that is no different from the growth of an individual organism: "The whole is like each of its parts, a living thing." The kingdom of plants or of animals is conceived of as going through stages of growth and maturation parallel to those of a single plant or animal. Conversely, therefore, the individual may be conceived of as transforming itself from stage to stage as the whole does from species to species. At the furthest extension of this organic thought, even the union of individuals in love can be conceived of by Goethe as a mutual growth and development, the note on which the poem ends. In its rather quaint—from a modern viewpoint—poetic-scientific guise we already have in anticipation the reunion of Faust and Margaret, which comes at the closing glimpse of the heaven of *Faust* II so unexpectedly, without adequate local preparation—even though it can be rationalized as the culmination of the earlier visions of Galatea and Helen, and as a return to the original love now transformed to a cosmic scale.

Given this kind of belief in transformation, Goethe can write his ending as a death and transfiguration that is teleo-eschatological: Faust dies in body, but his spirit rises higher. Given, too, his belief in the duality of Matter and Spirit or Form, it is possible for him to end the play on the unresolved ambiguity that Mephistopheles both wins and loses his bet—for he gets what belongs to him, Faust's body, but he cannot keep what does not belong to him, which must rise higher beyond him, "Faust's immortal part." Goethe is, of course, not simply invoking the orthodox Christian duality of body and soul; even though in the play he uses that imagery, he has artistically transformed its content and meaning in accordance with his philosophical thinking. In 1828, when he was writing the ending, Goethe conceived of this duality of matter and spirit as one of polarity (*Polarität*) and upward striving (*Steigerung*), each of which involved the other.[4] Spirit could not be without matter nor matter without spirit. This reveals the primary meaning for Goethe of the original Deed: it is the necessary working of spirit in matter without which it could not be effective and there could be no progress. In Goethe's philosophy it figures as an analogue of the traditional Fall without which there could be no salvation. The eschatological structure of the drama is thereby established: it is the world-drama of Man's fall into Darkness, the necessary prelude to and condition of his rise into Light. This schema of creation is already there in the opening "Prologue in Heaven"; in its closing counterpart, the "Epilogue in Heaven" as it were, it is finally confirmed and concluded.

Since this is the meaning of what is involved in ending, it is readily explicable why Faust cannot accomplish it in his own life. For Faust cannot fulfill and realize the Form of his earthly activities, immersed as he is in them and unable as he is to finish them. To realize that Form—which, as spirit, is also his soul—requires a higher vision, a more comprehensive vision, that only the Muse can give. It is, thus, the artistic vision that can grasp the Form of life and the artistic work that can make it real. In the other poem on evolution, "Metamorphosis of Animals," Goethe ends on a similar thought; once more he refers to the "sacred Muse" as granting the vision of Nature's wholeness and perfection and ensuring its certainty. Nature's Form is something art realizes, for it is itself form. Nature and art thus come together. This is why Faust's work in nature can be completed in Goethe's work in art, and its form there be realized; and also why Faust's earthbound future vision finds its culmination in Goethe's heavenly vision of the eternal present.

In the heaven of Goethe's art the form that is Faust's soul is revealed and released, and so saved. Life itself gets a mystic intimation of its own salvation through art. That is the import of the closing Chorus Mysticus: "Here the ineffable wins life through love." In the first place, the "here" obviously refers to the drama on-stage; that which has just passed is a parable, it has revealed as dramatic event and act what is unattainable and unspeakable otherwise in life. The passage of Faust as art gives an intimation into the meaning of the life that is Faust's passage. Art, that is, has the power to reveal in its symbolic forms the mystic truth of life, because only in art can the "passing" become surpassed, the insufficient be completed, the act become symbol, and the ineffable be shown. In the second place, the "here" refers also to the higher realm of that mystic truth. It is here that the meaning of life is revealed as indescribable event and deed. However, from that higher standpoint the passage of life appears as a parable, the transitory as symbol of something higher. Life as a whole, that is, takes on the form of art, revealing in its passing events and deeds become symbols a surpassing truth. In the third place, then, the "here" refers to life itself, where through art the symbols can be presented and the events and deeds shown that reveal the mystic truth. Art plays a triple role; it figures in all three realms of the "here." Art as the dramatic presentation is a symbol of life, which is a symbol of the mystery of things, which is itself a symbolic form of art as Creation. Hence, every "here" is a symbol of another "here" which in turn is itself symbolic. If all is symbol, then all is art, so everything is but a symbol of itself, just as art is, and the "here" of what we see on stage is the same as the "here" of life, the same as the "here" of the mystic truth—it is all one co-presence.

Goethe's final mystic chorus makes of All an ever-present "here" whose supreme symbol is the art of the drama itself. The passage of Faust is a symbolic passing that is at the same time a sur-passing, completing itself in the art—the symbolic act that is enacted—which is the real and ultimate Faustian Deed. The Faustian end is, thus, the end to which everything has aspired, the end of Life and Art as One—and that is its mystic truth. In that Faustian end, as we shall eventually see, lies the end of Faust. Faust is finished as soon as his end is realized, since it is an end that ends itself for us as soon as we know it for what it is, a Nature Idealism.

In "Metamorphosis of Animals" Goethe speaks of the work of Nature as "her supreme thought, the highest to which, in her creativeness she has risen"; and of Man as re-thinking this thought: "May your mind dwell with delight upon this noble concept of power and constraint, of caprice and law, freedom and moderation, movement within order, pre-eminence and deficiency."[5] These dualities which we think of as specific to the work of art are for Goethe definitive of Nature's work as well. Late in life, Goethe placed everything within the duality of Nature's two fundamental principles of *Polarität und Steigerung,* and out of these two he developed a dialectic of dualities in opposition—of which Goethe gives a long list, starting with subject-object, light-dark, soul-body, spirit-matter—such that the fundamental opposition of the basic principles (*Polarität*) leads to a sublimation (*Steigerung*) and the emergence of the more elevated ones. All of this is dramatically worked out in the end of *Faust*—the terms are certainly all there. Goethe's dialectic closely resembles Hegel's, though with the important difference that whereas Hegel's is a rational dialectic of concepts, Goethe's is a creative-dramatic dialectic of sensible symbols. Goethe's is the dialectic of the symbolic Deed, and it is in terms of it that the End is to be understood; the Deed's striving to complete itself in its need to reach the End is both telos and eschaton. Thus the End is already there in the Deed at its beginning.

It is apparent from this account that the Faustian end is the End of an Idealist nature-philosophy that identifies nature and art. As such it is a purely ideal end, and consequently for us it has only the reality of a beautiful idea. As a real idea of nature it has long since lost its reality; after Darwinian evolution, after Mendelian genetics, the idea of nature unfolding itself to a perfect end is about as tenable as the *UrPflanze* is in comparison with the DNA molecule. Even as a mere article of faith, it would be next to impossible to believe in that kind of an End, given the modern scientific rationalization of all natural phenomena. The accompanying notion of nature as an aesthetic whole is equally untenable. For us nature can no longer be complete, nor can it be a perfect form: the expanding universe, the proliferation of subatomic particles, the probabilities of quanta of energy, all these have broken the unity and beauty of Nature. It is the same with Goethe's Idealist dialectic, which together with Hegel's dialectic has been subjected to all the critiques of Idealism. The ideal Ends of both these philosophies are particularly susceptible to such critiques. As we have shown, the telo-eschatological ends of Man have been repeatedly called into question. At its most severe this criticism would maintain that this wished-for end is nothing but a wish-fulfillment and that it belongs to the collective, age-old dream of mankind—which has by now turned into a modern nightmare from which we must awake.

The end of Goethe's *Faust* is, from one aspect, such a dream-vision formed of archetypal symbolism. But that does not mean that it is mere wish-fulfillment or self-indulgent dreaming. It has indeed the appearance of a beautiful dream-work—like a vision emerging with perfect clarity from the furthest recesses of the unconscious. It echoes in the recesses of one's mind in long-forgotten visions, mingling childhood memories with the longings of old age. It reconciles one to and consoles one for death itself—but only momentarily. The reality of death, if it is acknowledged fully, will always shatter the harmony within which a literary artist seeks to contain it. A musician like Beethoven can create a harmonious world in which, while the musical moment lasts, death is both acknowledged and reconciled, but in literature such a moment must inevitably be broken, for ultimately it falsifies the tragic reality of death. This is what the greatest tragic writer knows he must do if he is to grant death its due.

Shakespeare composes in words one of the most touching musical moments in all literature, only the better to destroy it—a destruction that almost cannot be contemplated, and certainly cannot be accepted.

> CORDELIA: O you kind gods!
> Cure this great breach in his abused nature,
> Th' untuned and jarring senses, O, wind up
> Of this child-changed father!
> ...
> (*Enter Lear in a chair carried by Servants.*
> *Gentleman in attendance. Soft music.*)
> DOCTOR: Please you, draw near—louder the music there!
> (*Lear* IV.vii)

Lear has been through much more than Faust, for he has been down to hell itself, to the "sulphurous pit" to which Goethe at the end of the "Prologue" promises he will take his Faust, though he somehow fails to do so. At this point in the play, it seems as though Cordelia's music is about to wake Lear to sanity, bring him back to his senses and restore him to what he was. And momentarily, while the music lasts, it almost seems as if this is indeed happening. But we know it is not to be. The failure of the musical attempt at consolation and restoration is here registered as the failure of music itself, of its very truth as art. Cordelia, whose being is musical—"her voice was ever soft, gentle and low"—must die. Lear cannot, as he wishfully imagines, live with her in prison where they may "sing like birds in the cage." The harmony of her being and her power to harmonize all the conflicts of nature must be destroyed, just as her breath must be strangled in her throat and her melodious speech lost in the general cacophony of clashing voices, for only thus can death be known and acknowledged in words. That is the meaning of tragedy.

Goethe's art is, of course, by contrast deliberately comic. It makes no claims to tragedy, nor need it. But unlike most comedy which deals with life alone, it also at the end addresses itself to death. And that is where the problem arises. Goethe hopes to present death as an end in such a way as to make it adequate to life as a whole. Indeed, he strives to conceive of an End that will make of life a perfect whole, harmonious and complete. Inside the drama it is Faust's end that is in question, the end of Faust that will bear the meaning of the whole of his previous life.

For Goethe the dramatist it is a matter of finding an ending that will complete the work of art on which he had labored all his life, the work that contained more of his life than any other, whose completion would also be the conclusion of his life's work and by which he would himself become reconciled to his approaching death. It is as a solution to this complex problem—both dramatic and personal, both artistic and intellectual—that he conceived of the Faustian End, whereby Faust's inability to complete his work was Goethe's completion of his own. This is the End whose artistic and intellectual meaning we have spelled out at length in the preceding pages.

Now, if the meaning of this End is merely comic and ideal then it cannot accomplish any of the things that Goethe hopes to do with it. It cannot contain the reality of death or be a real way of facing up to it. All it can accomplish is to provide "musical" consolation by giving death an ideal meaning in the form of an art of visionary beauty. It is a way of ideally beautifying death. If this is not real death, it follows that the wholeness and completeness endowed to life by this End is not a real wholeness and completeness. It, too, is purely ideal. It is an ideal whose truth we can no longer maintain, for, as Heller says, it is based on a philosophy where "self and world are at one," whereas "now the relationship between soul and world, between self and reality, is not one of fundamental harmony but of total absurdity."[6] But what is at issue is not merely that the philosophy behind the art is out of date, for that is the case with most masterpieces of the past, including Shakespeare's. The issue, rather, is of an inability of the art to satisfy the demands it makes on itself.

The End of Faust is supposed to be the answer to Faust's Deed. The character Faust, in the end, takes back his great curse on life and accepts his human lot within the bounded terms and on the conditions available to every human being. He has not remained with the destructive impact of the Deed that "shattered the beautiful world"; he has accepted and realized the challenge to "rebuild it anew." The end Faust sets himself to is, thus, supposed to be capable of embracing his Deed and giving meaning to it; the productive work he undertakes, though endless, is yet meaningful as the End of Man. And Goethe as dramatist, in conceiving of this end, is able to complete his work. Thereby, in his art he can have a symbol of the completion and wholeness of the world itself, since work and world are harmonized. Furthermore, as man he can experience this completion in his own lifetime, crowned as it is with the conclusion of his life's task. Thus, the Deed as destructive action that threatens to break up life at every moment can be embraced within it. And the ultimate destruction of death itself can be taken up into the End.

However, if this ideal End is no answer to the reality of the Deed, then the tragic potential of Faust's Deed has not been realized in Goethe's work. The conclusion, therefore, does not fully meet the demands of the opening. In that sense it does not properly complete the work. In its ultimate consequences the power of Faust's Deed is such that it shatters the End that is supposed to comprehend it. It is in this sense that Goethe's *Faust* ceases to have a real end for us. Under the impact of its own Deed it begins to break up into separate acts and moments of varying degrees of reality. Its various strata of composition, the early and middle and late, begin to separate, and we read them separately as well as together.

The work has lost its intended perfection of form, but it has gained for us the incompleteness of an unfinished and unfinishable work, of a continuous work in progress, of a unique document of the stages of the development of a work. *Faust* thus ceases to be a masterpiece or a classic and becomes instead a modern work, as problematic, as incoherent, as fragmented as are most of the great works of our own time. Goethe's life, too, is no longer a living work fulfilled and complete; it too begins to decompose into its pieces. The mask of Goethe the consummate artist and Olympian sage falls away and we see the man beneath, as riven and torn, as self-deceiving, as is any modern man. The Deed that Goethe launched has finally caught up with him and has turned against him. The life that he so desperately sought to found on his greatest work and to conclude with its completion is destroyed by its own Deed. Is, then, this Deed any less than a kind of murder?

## SCENE IV
## *Adrian Leverkühn–the last Faust*

### I

At first sight it appears that with the Faust of Thomas Mann we have arrived at last at a quite different kind of end, both more modern and more traditional. This end harks back to the damnable end of the first Faust, but at the same time it is the up-to-date end projected by our modern anxieties of reductio ad absurdum. The ideal End of a Goethe seems to have been explicitly forsworn. Mann's Faust, his German composer Leverkühn, is sufficiently self-aware for that, and knows what his end is in relation to the great previous Faust. He knows, too, that he has come to the end of the passage of Faust, that there is no further for him to go. The novel is aware of itself as an end, is aware that it, too, cannot go on. But what kind of an end is it?

How does this Faust end? He ends with another Faust. Mann's own work completes itself with the work of his Faust, whose own last work is "The Lamentation of Dr. Faustus." That work is itself, therefore, a return to the original Faust. So it seems as if the passage of Faust, having come full circle, is about to turn in on itself and end with a return to its origins. Certainly the passage reflects on itself as it is about to come to an end, for that very moment of ending is self-reflexive: the work of Mann reflects itself in the work of Leverkühn. What is it saying about itself?

It tells us that the impulse for Leverkühn to return to origins in his Faust is his embittered reaction against and revocation of the great intermediate Faust. The reaction must occur because Progress has failed, the Ideal is not to be:

> "What human beings have fought for and stormed citadels, what the ecstatics exultantly announced—that is not to be. It will be taken back. I will take it back."
>
> "I don't quite understand, dear man. What will you take back?"
>
> "The Ninth Symphony," he replied.[1]

In the analogical structure of the book the Ninth Symphony is to Leverkühn's "The Lamentation of Dr. Faustus" as Goethe's *Faust* is to Mann's *Doctor Faustus,* and the figure of Beethoven has in the musical context an analogous role to Goethe in the literary one. It follows from this that the ending of *Doctor Faustus* is a revocation of the ending of *Faust.* And on one level that is certainly so: Leverkühn seems damned as was the original Faust, his damnable end recapitulates in detail the events of the original; as in his own composition of the chapbook text, so in the text of his ending there takes place a "Last Supper" during which to his friends and acquaintances he confesses his dealings with the Devil and reveals himself to them as a Faust—much to the astonished incomprehension of this modern, sophisticated, but unfeeling audience. But on another level, as we shall eventually see, this revocation is also its opposite, a fulfillment. The ending of Goethe's *Faust* is confirmed, for the Devil can once more take the body of this latter-day Faust, but not have his soul—though not in quite as clear-cut a sense as in Goethe. Leverkühn's life is indeed consigned to perdition—he sinks into the stupor of madness just as the life of Germany is about to sink into the terror of Nazism; but in his art his soul lives on, and in that art there is hope of salvation. In his last composition, the "Lamentation,"

Leverkühn attains to the grace elsewhere denied him; in it he achieves release, freedom, expression, and completion. That work is the heaven which draws him upward. Leverkühn does not have to wait for his author to complete his work, as it were, after his death; he can himself complete his work by remaining true to himself and his Devil, and so, paradoxically, be vouchsafed a glimpse of hope. It is almost as if the Devil himself were his Savior—and that is just one of the ambivalences of this peculiar ending.

It is an odd ending that contains both damnation and salvation, both a return to the original past and a move into the future, both a summation of all that Faust has been and a rejection of it, both the conclusion and the continuity of Faust, for it both affirms the death of Faust and promises his resurrection. It is the first and last Faust, so it is Faust everlasting; its end is the endlessness of the Eternal Return of perpetual recurrence, together with the finality of the Last Judgment. Is this, then, the "promised end" of Faust? Or but an "image of that horror" (*Lear* V.iii)? Is there another end yet to come? Is it a true or a false end of the passage of Faust? Is it the conclusion demanded by the premises set forth in Mann's work?

The ending duplicates the book as a whole. But, as we have just noted, it itself is a doublet; there is the ending of art, of the composition the "Lamentation," and the ending of life, of Leverkühn's "Last Supper." Each of these endings reflects on the other. Like two mirrors mirroring each other, we have the book reflecting on itself within itself; for as art it bears a relation to life analogous to the relation of Leverkühn's composition to his confession. The opposition of Art and Life thus becomes mutually reflective: life mirrors itself in art, which in turn mirrors itself in life, which then mirrors itself in art again, and so on. . . . The reflections recede like waves into the distance without end. So, for example, the life of modern German culture is reflected in the art of *Doctor Faustus,* which is reflected in the life of composer Leverkühn, which is reflected in the art of his "Lamentation," which reflects the life of an original Faust of the Reformation, etc., etc. But because the opposition of life and art is seen to be self-reflexive, it is no longer an absolute opposition and becomes instead a difference within a unity. In that sense the opposition is reconciled; each of the opposing poles inheres in the other, they are brought together. In Mann's thought, as in Goethe's, polarity is a principle of reconciliation, and as such it calls forth that other principle of ascension or forward progression (*Steigerung*). As Mann himself would have appreciated, this thought is in its basic form perennial; the *coincidentia oppositorum* is an old topos, and the idea that it leads to higher issue goes back at least to Boehme, if not back to the alchemists.

Out of the marriage of opposites issues the child of higher synthesis. In *Doctor Faustus* the issue is the twin one of double curse and blessing: the life and the art, and the marriage or bond that produces them are, of course, in the most literal sense those of Faust and the Devil. The opposition of Man and Devil is one of the basic polarities in the work. It contains within itself many of the other contraries and oppositions that we have already encountered in Goethe, viz., light-dark, spirit-matter, soul-body, life-death, upper-lower, inner-outer, heaven-hell, truth-falsehood, subject-object, ego and alter ego, expression-intellect, reason-irrationality, freedom-bondage, conscious-unconscious, speech-silence, word-tone, literature-music, civilization-culture, world-outside and world-inside, the Nations-Germany, bourgeois versus anti-bourgeois, liberal-democrat versus conservative-revolutionary, and, finally, the identity in opposition of Zeitblom and Leverkühn.

The Devil is himself the symbol of all duplicity, of all doubleness, doubling, repetition, variation, echoing, and reflecting. The Devil is, thus, ultimately the basic principle of polarity, and the marriage of opposites is symbolized by the Devil's bond, which is the Faustian deed. The Deed as the bond figures throughout the work as its dominant motive or motif, for out of it by variation and transition emerge most of the other leitmotifs. The unity of opposites as mutually reflexive has, however, a more implicit symbol in the book: it is that of the sphere, which figured so explicitly in Mann's previous major novel, the *Joseph* tetralogy: "The mystery is in the sphere. But the sphere consists in correspondence and reintegration: it is a doubled half that becomes one."[2]

*Doctor Faustus* is itself just such a sphere. However, its two hemispheres are not the earthly and the heavenly, as in the previous novel, but the earthly and the hellish, and its men do not change into gods but into devils; yet its structure of meaning is also spherical. As the narrator comments on one of his friend's compositions, the "Apocalypse": "It rests, I might say, on the curvature of the world, which makes the last return unto the first" (p. 376). That comment applies equally to Mann's work itself; it, too, combines the old and the new, the first and the last, and moves apocalyptically from one to the other by the "curvature of the world" that is the "revolution of the sphere." The very time-structure of the novel, as we shall soon discover, is spherical: time curves in on itself at the halfway point, and begins to move, as it were, backward, returning to the origin and coming to an end just where it began. Thus in the last chapter, the Epilogue (actually chapter 48), Zeitblom the narrator has reached the point in the narrative just prior to that at which he began his narration in chapter 1; so from the end of the book we move once again back to the beginning, as in a circle or ring. We already begin to feel the ending forming itself as a perfect completion, a return back to the origin, the point on the sphere where the upper and lower hemispheres reunite.

The work is itself a sphere; hence, the two hemispheres of the book are precisely its two halves counted by chapters, so that the point of the first revolution from upper to lower occurs at the change-over from chapter 24 to chapter 25. On the level of literary allusions, the first half corresponds to Goethe's *Faust* Part I and the second to Part II: thus, e.g., analogues to Faust's reminiscences of his father, of Auerbach's cellar, of the Gretchen episode occur in the first half, whereas analogues to the Emperor's court, the classical Walpurgisnacht, the marriage with Helen, the death of Euphorion occur in the second. As we might expect from the logic of the sphere, the two halves themselves reflect each other exactly, but as mirror images, back to front. This occurs not only on the surface plane of incidents and structural form but more deeply, inside the workings of the inner meaning. The first half is the positive upper-world, and the second half is its converse, the exactly reversed counter lower-world. The second is the first arsy-versy in more senses than meets the eye—the Devil has seen to that. We can analyze some of the themes of inversion that this logic involves. For example, the farm in the second half, in which Leverkühn spends the whole of his later life, is the exact mirror image of the farm of his birth; it is managed by the chattering woman Frau Schweigestill, the silent keeper of mysteries, who corresponds inversely to his father, old Leverkühn of the opening chapters, man of the Word and prober of mysteries.

In making the Schweigestill farm his second home Leverkühn retreats into seclusion and wraps himself in silence and solitude, remaining in a solipsistic state which he will only break through at the end. There he is in the under-world or Hades, into which he descends like Orpheus in search of his love to win her by the power of his song, but there he is also in hell, into which he is drawn to be delivered of the musical conceptions fathered on him by the Devil. Being himself "the son of hell," he has the Devil as his substitute father, so that all his conceived creations are a mode of self-begotten incest—a theme developed at some length in the Freudian terms of the Oedipus complex.[3]

Hence, the under-world is also the unconscious, that perverse region where all transformations can take place, where strange monsters are born, monsters as unnatural as those Leverkühn encounters in his imaginary voyage to the bottom of the sea. Inside the ocean of his unconscious he himself becomes a sea-wife, a nixie lusting for a mortal prince—the inverse of himself and his beloved butterfly Hetaera Esmeralda of the upper-world—in order thereby to become human and acquire an immortal soul. In the under-world region of the second half inverts and perverts have a field day; in fact, there occurs a general change of sex, or, better put, the male and female characteristics of androgynous beings become inverted: thus Adrian himself figures in a female role in his implied homosexual relationship with the violinist Rudolf Schwerdtfeger, who in turn plays the "woman" to the real woman Inez Institoris' "man." In the revolution from the upper- to the lower-world there takes place a general reversal and inversion of all dualities. The Devil's topsy-turvy logic takes over.

This is made explicit in the opening chapter of the second half, the crucial chapter 25. At that point the Devil reveals himself to Leverkühn and informs him of the changed state of things, thereby ratifying in word the bond that had already previously been entered into unknowingly in deed, in the fatal traumatic contact with the flesh of Hetaera Esmeralda, the poisoned butterfly. In other words, Leverkühn becomes conscious of his role as a Faust avatar. It is here that Jung joins hands with Freud (a reconciliation that is, surely, possible only in art, not in life) for the disease Leverkühn had contracted, which physically is syphilis, is psychologically a neurosis, developing itself into a complex in the Freudian unconscious and surfacing as a Jungian mythical, racial archetype—as, in fact, the Germanic myth of Faust. Hence, conscious and unconscious are also reversed as Leverkühn deliberately and knowingly acts out in his life what is actually an unconscious pattern. He is true to his archetype as well as his Devil, and, despite some futile attempts to escape it, completes his "life-task" by playing it out to the bitter end; at the end, in that lies his Jungian "cure" as against his Freudian collapse. Thus at the end the sphere revolves once again: it is only by being true to his bond that Leverkühn can become free; his last composition is bound both in word and in tone, but thereby it can attain to free expression. The first overturning of the sphere in the middle makes possible the second returning at the end; just so, the first reversal of all polarities enables their ultimate return to themselves. The re-turning of the end is determined by the over-turning of the middle, hence the mid-point turning is the crucial move in the structure of the book, the axis on which the sphere revolves.

At that mid-point, Leverkühn is found discoursing with the Devil in himself in an ambiguous mono-dialogue of ego and alter ego, as Ivan Karamazov once did in another novel. The Devil, as the radical principle of reversal, calls explicitly and implicitly on all the great inverters of modern times. In the first place he implicitly invokes Nietzsche—admittedly, in a somewhat misconstrued fashion—for the Nietzschean revaluation of all values is the model of all modern reversals. All the signs are reversed, all that was positive becomes negative and vice versa; all the values affirmed by Zeitblom in the first half of the book are here violently and savagely overturned, the whole bourgeois world has been placed on its head. We are now in the Devil's world of modern Nihilism. After this critique of civilization comes a critique of art, and the Devil takes on another mock guise, this time reminiscent of Adorno—"a theoretician and critic, who himself composes, so far as thinking allows him" (p. 238)—again as something of a parody. Mann's defense would presumably be that it is the Devil speaking, and he does twist things for his own ends, but one suspects that too many of the shortcomings of the book may thus be laid at the Devil's door. What follows in the text is actually a summary of Adorno's essay on Schoenberg, which has since appeared as the first part of *The Philosophy of Modern Music.* However, the main interest resides not in what is said about music but in what the work is saying about itself. It seems that here the premises on which Goethe's Faust was saved are firmly revoked. The Deed is not to be a time-expansion but a time-contraction, a contract in time for a limited end. The work will no longer unfold as a free development of progressive movement; it is to be reduced and retracted to an empty moment. The work cannot be completed, cannot be brought to perfection; the "beautiful work" is no longer possible. It seems that the work has ceased to believe in itself, that it has come to view itself as mere art, as illusion, play, pretense, and sheer form, and that these have lost their reality, for life negates them. It seems, too, that time cannot come to an end, for it cannot even begin to move since all movement is absorbed into the moment, so that there can be no development, no progression, no reaching of a goal, neither telos nor eschaton. All these are, of course, difficulties Adorno had perceived in the arts of modernity, above all with respect to music in its incapacity any longer to reconcile and achieve harmonious unity.

Yet all this, which is declared no longer possible, is precisely what Mann seeks to achieve in the end! Because he puts these difficulties into the mouth of the Devil, it is doubtful whether he really believes in them himself with full seriousness, except as problems to be overcome—as he himself proceeds undaunted to overcome them in his own work. The Devil, too, believes they can be overcome, though not without his help. And, as we know, Leverkühn then proceeds to attempt to break out of his situation (paralleling in this respect the political course of Germany), only to fail in his varied attempts—till in the very end he does break through and simultaneously break down (again like Germany) in that inherent ambiguity of the end. Unfortunately, besides this worked-for ambivalence there arises another which does not seem to have been foreseen: in his last confession Leverkühn speaks as if the difficulties of all that he encountered were mere temptations of the Devil, thereby implying they might have been overcome without the Devil's help after all.

> Yea verily, dear mates, that art is stuck and grown too heavy and scorneth itself and God's poor man knoweth no longer where to turn in his sore plight, that is belike the fault of the times. But an one invite the divel as guest, to pass beyond all this and get to the break-through, he chargeth his soul and taketh the guilt of the time upon his own shoulders, so that he is damned. For it hath been said 'Be sober, and watch!' But that is not the affair of some; rather, instead of shrewdly concerning themselves with what is needful upon earth that it may be better there, and discreetly doing it, that among men such order shall be stablished that again for the beautiful work living soil and true harmony be prepared, man playeth the truant and breaketh out in hellish drunkenness. (Pp. 499–500)

"Beautiful work"? "True harmony"? Can Leverkühn really believe in that after all he has been through, after having accomplished the break-through in his own last composition? Or is it that Mann is deliberately making him rave or be foolishly contrite at the end? But if that were so, it would constitute a serious failure in the conception of the character, Leverkühn being made to speak as if he were Zeitblom—and Zeitblom himself does insist that what Leverkühn is saying is "dead sober earnest . . . the truth" (p. 498). Perhaps that is the intention, perhaps Leverkühn is meant to be like Zeitblom in the end, perhaps that is the final affirmation of their joint identity as the two halves of the one sphere? If that were so, then it would appear that Mann really does believe in "the beautiful work" and in "true harmony." So it would seem as if the difficulties Leverkühn could only overcome with the Devil's help at the cost of his soul, Mann can overcome without the slightest risk of damnation to himself. But does not Mann need the Devil's help as much as his imaginary composer, for do they not both face the same predicament of modern art? And if Mann does not need the Devil to write his work, then how does the case of Leverkühn that he dramatizes bear on the ineluctable problems of modern art?

To account for these difficulties in the conception of the work—and they are ones that call into question the nature of Mann's art and the truth of his ending—let us consider the part played by the Devil in the structure of Mann's own work. The Devil's principle in the work is the

Deed or bond, which figures as a fundamental structural principle of the form and meaning of the work. The bond has much the same significance as the sphere, so much so that it is practically absorbed into the sphere; and the doubt arises whether it is a Devil's principle at all or whether it is really part of some higher unity that embraces the Devil and makes him impotent as a real threat. In other words, does Mann in his own art face up to the powers of Nihilism surrounding modern art and modern man, or does he merely mythologize them away into a comforting theology of his own making that promises him the harmony of the sphere? If the bond were completely absorbed into the sphere then this would seem to be the case.

As a motif the bond is of such musical plasticity that it can generate almost all the other motifs of the book. That in itself indicates the omnipresence of the Devil in the work. In the first place, in the most literal sense the bond is the Faustian Deed, the pact that is written in blood. So it is in a literal sense inscribed in the blood: it is the contracted venereal disease slowly working itself out in Leverkühn's body, as well as, of course, the virus of hate in the body politic of Germany. As the infection that provokes that disease, the bond is also the poisoned draught, the Devil's act of seduction and his constant action as seducer—it is the love-potion by which the seduction is effected. This love-potion delivers Leverkühn up to his fatal fame, as it once did Tristan to his femme fatale; it is also the intoxicating "half a bottle of champagne" that Bismarck is supposed to have said the Germans need "to arrive at their normal height" (p. 228). But in exact parallel to its infection in the blood is its inscription in the psyche. The bond is also the "complex"—in a psychoanalytic sense—activated by the fatal traumatic touch of the flesh of Psyche, the poisoned butterfly, to which the pure spirit of Leverkühn is drawn. This has also its theological meaning in that Spirit, being in love with Soul, is dragged down in search of it into base matter—and so suffers its Fall. However, as a complex it works itself out as a "normal" neurosis in Leverkühn's psychic life, just as, in the thematic of his musical life, it unfolds itself as the complex or constellation of notes made up of the tones *h, e, a, e, e-flat,* the serial musical chord derived from the fatal name Hetaera Esmeralda. Hence, the bond is the musical deed or conjunction of notes that a composition is fated to unfold and repeat over and over and by which it is bound and determined. It is, thus, the series or serial principle of composition, "the intellectual property" of Schoenberg—as Mann so ironically acknowledges—that Leverkühn presents as his own discovery in the chapter celebrating his perverse "marriage" with the Devil.

The series as constellation is fate—in this case the Faustian fate, the determining myth of Leverkühn's life-composition and of the composition of this book itself. The series as compositional principle is also the Law, the authoritarian pronouncement of a Moses or Beissel or Schoenberg—or even of the coming Führer of Germany, for this is the Devil's Law. The bond as series is ambivalently both the symbol of determination and eventually also of freedom, for it is also the Goethean law of bounds, of necessary self-limitation by which one becomes free. As a complex, it is equally something inherited and something contracted, it is both fate and chance; similarly, as draught it is both inborn viciousness and seduction of innocence, both compelled and willed. And the ambivalence of this symbolism once again makes it very difficult to judge whether Leverkühn's predicament as artist is necessary or contingent, and what relation, therefore, he bears to his creator. It also makes it difficult to judge whether Germany's fate is the inevitable consequence of the course of "bourgeois" history or whether it is an aberration of its own, and thus to tell to what extent Germany is representative of Europe and the world as a whole. For the Deed as bond is also the Faustian passage of historical time: it is the fatal course of events leading to the Nazi rise to power and, equally, the 24 years of "Devil's time" that Leverkühn is granted, as well as the principle of the time-structure of his compositions, especially of the "Lamentation of Dr. Faustus." But being that, as we might expect, it is also the time-structure of the book itself.

It is at this most fundamental level that the Deed as bond and the Work as Sphere combine. According to the Schoenbergian compositional law, there are four basic forms of the series or row of twelve tones: the original row, the inverted row, the retrograde of the inversion, and the inversion of the retrograde of the inversion, the last of which also happens to be the retrograde of the original. Hence, if one were to start with the original and go through the inversion and the two retrogrades, one would return once more back to the original, completing a perfect cycle or sphere. The structure of the book is just such a sphere: its forty-eight chapters divided into four groups of twelve correspond exactly to the four basic forms of the series. It is as if one were to travel along the circumference of the sphere—the book's time-course—starting with chapter 1, moving upward through the first twelve chapters, reaching the zenith with chapter 13 (that of the "theologian" Schleppfuss), which is the start of the row-inversion, then moving downward through the next twelve chapters—all this while still being in the upper hemisphere of the sphere and still moving forward in time or progressing. With the key chapter, 25, which we examined before, the book begins its retrograde movement; there we enter the lower hemisphere—the Devil's world of the under-world—and time is now moving backward, for it is Devil's time. In respect of formal structure, the retrograde working of the series is signalled very obviously by Mann in the turning from chapter 24 to chapter 25 by the mirror-image relationship of the Manardi farm and family to the Schweigestill farm and family, who in turn relate to the original Leverkühn farm and family: in first locating the Schweigestill household in chapter 23, then leaving it for its obverse in the Manardi pension-ménage in chapters 24 and 25, and then returning to it again in chapter 26, Leverkühn is literally in his movements describing the retrograde turning. Going on from there, the nadir of the sphere is reached in the next twelve chapters, but from that point, from the first chapter of the retrograde of the original, that of the "impresario" Fitelberg (chapter 37), the movement once more proceeds hopefully upward; it is now a forward movement to the end, as well as a backward movement back to the origin, the whole book charged with a nisus to reach that final goal of end-origin, telos-eschaton. With that attained, the book consummates itself in a perfect closure, the sphere is complete and everything within it has been contained and reconciled.

And it is the Devil himself who is responsible for this completion. His is the driving impetus that keeps up the movement along the sphere. This movement is time itself, which belongs to the Devil, for it is the Fall from eternity. He is indeed once more Goethe's Devil of the Deed who keeps Man moving and prevents his sinking down in lethargy, but this time the movement is not solely upward but circular: the path of natural myth and mythical nature as opposed to that of the myth of upward progress. It is the Devil's bond that is the driving impetus, for as series it determines the changes of direction in the time-structure. Every time the book takes a new direction, the Devil appears in yet another apotheosis to give it the decisive turn. The nature of each of these devils gives precisely the meaning of each turn. The three devils are, respectively, Schleppfuss (chapter 13, the unlucky one of which Zeitblom is glad to be rid), the apparition Devil (chapter 25), and finally Fitelberg the comic Jew-Devil (chapter 37). It is typical of the symmetry of the structure that each appearance of a devil is preceded by that of its opposite, a guardian spirit or Egeria; of these there is Kumpf (chapter 12), one of the three Mothers, Signora Manardi (chapter 24), and Madame de Tolna (chapter 36).

Schleppfuss is the devil who oversees the first change from the series to its inversion; he it is who, as it were, negates the first twelve chapters of positive origin, presiding over the next twelve, which are the antithesis to its thesis. And, in fact, he is the devil of traditional Christian theology, of temptation, possession, bad will, evil, and original sin: himself a lecturer of theology, he expounds his Devil's Law of traditional negativity in the midst of a faith grown slack and ridiculous in its Romantic-historical parodies (Kumpf). He is, therefore, a devil of the past, who holds under his aegis the whole of the past. The succeeding twelve chapters that work themselves out under his influence are all turned toward the past; the years they take in are the period of fin-de-siècle decadence that was wedded to the negativities of the past: Satanism, succubi, fleurs du mal, and other such aestheticist cultivations of evil.

It is only with the next epiphany of the Devil that the modern present is reached, for the uninvited guest who disturbs Leverkühn in Italy is very much a devil of modernity. It is he who combines the reactionary-revolutionary, regressive-progressive impulses of the present era. Through his regression time itself becomes retrograde, history moves backward toward the primitive and barbaric while seeming to be launched on a path of unparalleled progress. His twelve chapters cover the apocalyptic events of the First World War and the irruptions of "modern art," as in Leverkühn's composition "The Apocalypse" with its paradoxical conjunction of intellectualism and barbarism. This is the Devil of reversal, which is not mere orthodox negativity but nihilist destruction.

The third and last devil, Fitelberg the Jew, looks comically and hopefully to the future, poking fun at the self-seriousness of German gloom and apocalyptic tragedy. He looks forward to the coming end and beyond it. With the native genius of the Jewish people he is on the scent of coming things, he "can't help perceiving the role of Germany and Judaism on earth. Une analogie frappante!" (p. 407). Prophetically he foresees the conjoined tragedy of them both. But he also hints at the irony of history, which will transform the Germans themselves, bereft of their fatherland, into the future Jews of the world. He is implicitly aware of the secret of the sphere, of the tragic divisions of what belong together: "In my opinion the unhappiness of the world rests on the disunity of the intellect, the stupidity, the lack of comprehension, which separates its spheres from each other" (p. 405). But he also seems to be aware of the circularity of the sphere, of its comic unity, that every unparalleled tragedy is in the larger scheme of things but another repetition, another revolution of the sphere.

These three devils appearing inside the work divide the sphere of the book into four quarters: like the circle of the sun, or the four phases of the moon, or the four directions of the compass, and even the four seasons, which are also the four ages of man, of Faust, as well as the four stages of the Faustian culture, the periods of the Faustian "Soul" in Spengler's sense. Each of the quarters is also a whole epoch in the story of creation. The first quarter—the original of the series—is the Origin in a classical-Hebraic paradise, the childhood of the race and the life of childhood or the birth of the ego; it is the age of innocence. The second quarter—the inversion—is the Fall and expulsion, bringing knowledge of good and evil, awakening to guilt and the acquisition of conscience or the workings of the superego; it is the age of fiery-blooded youth. The third quarter—the first retrograde—is the Apocalypse preceding the end of things, the overturning of everything, the cataclysmic upheavals of the war of Gog and Magog when the world is plunged into the dark depths of the unconscious; it is the Middle Ages of turbulent regression. The last quarter—the retrograde of the original—is the End and Return, the completion and reconciliation, the coming to full consciousness of mortality, of confession and judgment; it is the old age and second childhood of death and rebirth.

In his schematization of the four ages of man, Mann is also very likely following the "whole ecstatic literature from the pre-Christian and early Christian eschatologies" (p. 356), which he has Leverkühn read; the four ages are, respectively, the ages of the Father, the Son, the Holy Ghost, and the End of the world with the Son's return for the Last Judgment. And indeed, that fits closely with the content of the four sections of the book. The first section deals almost exclusively with the Fathers: with the actual father, old Leverkühn, the eponymous German progenitor, and with all the other fathers and teachers, for example, the characters Herr Michelson, Uncle Nikolaus—or is it also Santa Klaus, the giver of gifts?—Kretschmar (Adorno), Director Stoientin, Kumpf, etc., and with the cultural fathers Beethoven, Wagner, Beissel (Schoenberg), and many of the other spiritual fathers of the German bourgeoisie. The second section is analogously devoted to Sons, the third to the workings of the Holy Ghost (speaking with tongues of fire), and the last to the Days of Judgment. Supporting this fourfold theological schema are literary parallels to other attempts at encompassing the whole of creation in four volumes. The most important of these are the constant allusions made to Wagner's Ring Cycle and to Mann's own "ring" of the four Joseph novels.

The book is also an autobiography of Thomas Mann as a representative figure of the bourgeoisie. The four ages of Thomas Mann's life are seen as four decisive epochs of bourgeois world-history. The first sets forth the origins of bourgeois art and thought, and thereby also the formative background of Mann himself: it is the old background-world of Kaisersaschern, of Reformation Catholic and Protestant theology, of Enlightenment, of classical and Romantic, of the "work," and of individualist bourgeois masters. The second is the period of bourgeois decadence, the early years of Mann's career as a writer (*Buddenbrooks* is echoed in Leverkühn's first major work, the opera *Love's Labour's Lost*): its art is the art of mockery and parody expressive of the decay of bourgeois subjectivity, of "the work of art as a travesty of innocence," of Strauss's *Salome* and Freud's psychoanalysis. The third is the period of the collapse of the bourgeois world before and after the First World War, and covers the same years in Mann's life (once again Leverkühn's compositions correspond to Mann's own works at this time; above all there is the close analogy between "The Apocalypse" and *The Magic Mountain*). This is the nihilistic time of revolution and approaching Nazism, not without its false hopes, as in the Weimar Republic, and its equally futile artistic endeavors at humanization, such as Leverkühn's Violin Concerto. And finally, the time of that world comes to an end, which in the end sinks into the catatonic stupor of the Nazi regime and then into the final extinction of the Second World War; it is the time leading up to Mann's exile and moving into it (the final correspondence of works is here the identity of Mann's and Leverkühn's *Dr. Faustus*); this is the period directed to and straining for the End—the defeat in war, the total breakdown, but also the promise of the breakthrough, the hope of resurrection and a new start.

This last period also incorporates Zeitblom's time, that during which the book itself is being written—which explains how it is that the time-circle of Leverkühn's life of the recent past can meet up with and flow into the time circle of Zeitblom's time of the present of the book, which is also the time of Mann's composition, and then be absorbed into the time-circle of the reading of the book, which is the book's future. But time can also move in the reverse direction, such that any present reading of the book flows backward into the past times of the book, back to Mann's time of composition and Zeitblom's time of writing, into the time-circles of Leverkühn's life, eventually into the history of the bourgeoisie, going back to the origin of civilization itself, and so ultimately coming to reflect on the future of that civilization.

This circular handling of time is made possible by Mann's identification of history and myth such that every cultural product appears as but an infinitely varied repetition of a mythical archetype that it echoes and re-echoes into the future. The myth of eternal recurrence makes possible the basic fictional convention of the book, wherein a modern composer and a modern nation are represented as enacting their own mythical stereotypes, namely, as being Faust. To question this assumption would certainly not mean denying the importance of myth in history, and in particular the importance of the Faust myth in German and indeed modern European literature and thought, as this book itself has demonstrated. But this importance has to be seen in historical terms, not in mythical ones. Historical time does not repeat mythical time; the circular recurrences of myth are not to be found in the time of history.

The novel itself is aware of such a criticism, as expressed in the naive question "How can a modern composer be a Faust?" It makes that awareness one of its own functional principles. The true identity of the main character is, as it were, the horrible secret that the narrator reveals only clue by clue right up to the very end. At the same time, what these clues reveal is that the main character, Leverkühn, is already conscious of who he is from the halfway point onward. The appearance of the Devil in the climactic middle chapter, as Leverkühn's alter ego, to ratify the bond can be interpreted psychologically as Leverkühn self-consciously identifying himself with Faust and then acting out that role for the duration of the book. There need be no psychoanalytic implausibility about that, as we have already seen. The main character's coming to a horrified self-consciousness of who he really is indeed becomes one of the most intensely absorbing dramatic struggles of the book. Leverkühn proceeds to act on the basis of this awareness; he knows that Germany is in an analogous danger, and by means of his music, his programmatic compositions, he proceeds to warn of the Faustian fate likely to befall the nation. Finally, with his last composition and confession he makes it all musically and verbally explicit, but, unfortunately, few take him seriously. That is perhaps the most moving moment, the one toward which the book has been working. The utilization of the Faust myth in this way by Mann is certainly artistically justified and fulfilled, but, as we shall see, it does not overcome the difficulties of the relation between mythical and historical time that the ending in particular raises.

The secret identity of Leverkühn, and the way it is unknowingly and knowingly disclosed by the narrator Zeitblom, reveals another secret identity which the reader gradually begins to suspect, that of Zeitblom and Leverkühn. We have, of course, Mann's own word for this outside the book in his *Story of a Novel.* Zeitblom's and Leverkühn's lives are the outer and inner facets of one life. The serial structure of the novel reflects this, for the last chapter, in which Zeitblom concludes the narrative and takes into his own life Leverkühn's memory and work for safekeeping, flows back into the first chapter, where the time of narration begins and where the main motifs of Leverkühn's life and work are first evoked; similarly, the second-to-last chapter, which exposes Leverkühn's secret of his daemonic existence, is the inner content of the outer form revealed in the second chapter of Zeitblom's uneventful, stolid career. Apart from these structural considerations, the inner meaning of the book makes for the identity. Zeitblom and Leverkühn are the two halves of one sphere; they are in all respects complementary opposites. Together they represent the positive and negative facets of the German bourgeois, and, even more generally, of the European cultural identity as such.

It would seem that what Mann is saying is that the modern tragedy of culture lies precisely in the division and separation of its unity into two such opposed hemispheres. In the continuing relationship between Zeitblom and Leverkühn is represented the historic course leading to the final breakdown. In the first half of the novel we are shown very clearly why Leverkühn must separate himself and distance himself from Zeitblom, why he habitually treats him with an irony bordering on contempt, and why despite this Zeitblom returns smothering love and friendship. Zeitblom's whole outlook and life embody the sterility, banality, conventionality, and emptiness of bourgeois culture; in him much of the European cultural tradition becomes reduced to sentimental clichés. One begins to understand why, to escape this impasse, Leverkühn deeds himself to the Devil and launches himself on his innovative but destructive career. In the second half there is something of a reversal in the novel's attitude. The consequences of Leverkühn's course of action become apparent in the course of history, dramatically enacted by the minor characters: Germany and bourgeois culture in their reaction against their own traditions and in their attempt to break out are taking the nihilistic path to final disaster. Zeitblom in these scenes often becomes the voice of moderation and sanity, but he is too weak to do anything. The sympathies of the novel are increasingly with him, so much so that at the very end his voice merges with that of Mann himself: "A lonely man [Mann] folds his hands and speaks: 'God be merciful to thy poor soul, my friend, my Fatherland!'"

In this complex relationship and multiple identity of Zeitblom, Leverkühn, and Mann himself lie much of the interest and strength of the novel. It is no mean feat for a novelist to have conceived of a dramatic rendering of the two complementary facets of modernity: the progressive, humanistic, and idealist, and the nihilistic, anti-humanist, revolutionary, and regressive. To have understood how the former demands and provokes the latter as its inner, secret self and how the latter will eventually reveal itself in its true identity is an imaginative accomplishment indeed. However, there are difficulties and ambiguities in its presentation to which the novel provides no definite answers. Are we to understand that Zeitblom and Leverkühn come together and are united in Mann himself? Is he at once the normal living bourgeois pater familias and daemon-driven artist-genius? If so, then in Mann himself or his art the bourgeois culture of modernity would find its fatal divisions reconciled, would overcome its separation of spheres and would have been able to avoid its tragic fate. But this is clearly an impossible conclusion, since Mann does not offer himself or his art as any kind of an answer, even if such a thing were possible in that kind of a book. Mann is far too modest to carry himself as a Goethe might, and anyway such a stance would be absurd in the present context. Hence, it follows that the Zeitblom-Leverkühn division must be as much inherent in Mann himself as it is in the world of his novel and in the real world as well. But if this is an unavoidable division in our culture, what are we to make of the suggestions at the end that Leverkühn's fate might have been avoided if only he had not gone too far? And if no compromise between Zeitblom and Leverkühn is possible, then there ought to be a much more dramatic conflict between them than the novel presents. The trouble seems to lie in their identification—Mann's conception of this seems to preclude a full dramatic working-out of their relationship. The simple unity of opposites is not a sufficiently dialectical principle for a meaningful confrontation—and it is this principle that in the end Mann insists on and invokes. It also causes difficulties with the ending that are in many ways parallel to the ones we have just broached.

## II

The ending of the work is rigorously determined by the overall schema. It is as through-composed (*durchkomponiert*) as is Leverkühn's last serial composition; every detail has its rigidly allotted place, every theme undergoes a meticulously planned development, every idea is unfolded through the cyclic dialectic. It is in this way, through an absolute determinism of structure, that Mann, like Leverkühn in his "Lamentation," hopes to have attained to freedom of expression. The Law makes free. But can a serial law do that? That remains the question. Unfortunately, there is much in the book that shows the flaws of sheer constructive constraint rather than any freedom of expressive ease. Nevertheless—granting many patent faults in local places—the book should be viewed as a whole. Does it, in the end, carry conviction? But first, how is the end attained?

The way to the Father is through the Son—as in theology, so in this book: the reconciliation with all the progenitors, with God the Father and with the Fatherland, is achieved through the sacrifice of the Son on behalf of Man. The paradox of the ending lies, however, in this: that the Father is also the Devil. Thus the Son who sacrifices himself on behalf of his brothers and takes their guilt upon his own shoulders is also the "Son of Hell," the scion of the Devil. Leverkühn is the son both of God and of the Devil. In fact, as might be expected from the logic of the sphere, God and the Devil are one Father. Hence, Leverkühn is ambivalently damned and saved: he is both Judas the anti-Christ and Christ. Like Dr. Faustus in the original text of the "Lamentation," Leverkühn celebrates his own "Last Supper" with his disciples and friends, whom he addresses as "beloved brethren and sisters" (p. 496), and in farewell enjoins them to "hold me in kindly remembrance" (p. 503). This Eucharist is, however, also inverted, "a deliberate reversal of the 'Watch with me' of Gethsemane" (p. 490), becoming thereby a Satanic Mass, for in it the Devil's doings are recounted; it is the inverse, too, of Beethoven's comic-heroic "late supper" after he engaged in the struggle with the demons of counterpoint in composing his "Mass," as described in Kretschmar's lecture. In Leverkühn's "Last Supper" the "brothers and sisters" are initially not brought together, but separated, as they flee in haste from what is at first to them merely the ravings of a madman—contrasting in this respect with the solicitude with which his visitors ministered to Beethoven, in the tales of the great bourgeois father, and thus casting aspersions on the present state of the bourgeoisie. Despite themselves, however, since what Leverkühn tells them is prophetic of their own Faustian fate, they will come to recognize it as such when its destined workings have revealed themselves to them, that is to say, after the war, when the book is to be read. It is then that they will recognize Leverkühn for what he was—the Son who in anticipation acts as the scapegoat for his brothers' coming sins in murdering the Father-land. This Eucharist is, thus, like a totemic meal of reconciliation for the murder of the Father in which the Son's body is consumed in expiation.

At this point Christian theology joins hands with Freudian psychoanalysis. What is being invoked is the Freudian account of the Eucharist as a development of the totem meal, explained as a reconciliation rite commemorating the original patricide—the main difference being that in the Christian Eucharist it is the Son's body that is consumed in place of the Father's. Hence, Leverkühn's "Last Supper" is a kind of German

Mass whose symbolic import is like that of the Eucharist and totem meal taken together—for just as, according to Freud, out of the original patricide and totem came law, morality, and civilization, and out of Christ's cross the gospel of love and Christianity, so, according to Mann, out of the sacrifice of Germany and its sons' expiation there promises to come a new dispensation. That is the extent to which the ending of the book is prepared to reach out in its hope for grace.

It is in this way that the ending can be read psychoanalytically as well as theologically. The way to the Father is through the Son: that can also be rendered in a strictly psychological sense. God and the Devil are, according to Freud, both substitute symbols for the father. Indeed, "God and the Devil were originally identical—were a single figure which was later split into two figures with opposite attributes."[4] The father, it seems, is the individual prototype of both God and the Devil. Thus, Leverkühn's sonship to both God and Devil has to be located in his relation to his own father. It is because of this oedipal bond that his Faustian psychic fate can be read simply as a neurotic compulsion—for Faust is also Oedipus. In fact, as we have seen already, it seems extremely likely that Mann was following Freud's own interpretation of the myth of Faust. Freud's Faust, like Leverkühn, suffers from "a little Dürer melancholia"; like him, to gain relief from his depression he enters into a bond with the Devil and takes himself to be "the devil's bounden son."[5] Freud interprets this to mean that the Devil acts as a father-substitute. Again like Leverkühn, he becomes "wedded to Satan" (p. 497), and "culminates in a phantasy of bearing him a child."[6] Leverkühn, too, conceives of the Devil and brings to birth the works that are the "sinful issue" of this incestuous intercourse. That is why he can come to identify himself with Anderson's nixie, the sea-wife who lusts for an immortal soul.

It is through the child of sinful issue, his own evil creation, that Leverkühn will be reconciled with the Father and find release from his bondage. As he himself hopes in his final words: "Perhaps through Grace good can come of what was create in evil" (p. 502). The harbinger of that grace is his own "son"; just so is he himself, as the "son" of Germany, the hope of grace to its sinful issue. In the book it is his sister's child Echo, whom he thinks of as his own son born of incest, who is the child of grace, the Christ-child. Echo is the totally unmerited and unexpected "envoy and message-bearer" sent to rescue him when he was at the nadir of despair, when the Devil held him tighter than ever in thrall after his "murder" of Schwerdtfeger. And this follows on the moral and artistic defeat of his attempt to come into contact with humanity in this perverse "marriage" of composer and performer and the abortive artistic "child" they had in common: the salon-music Violin Concerto. Echo brings with him the long-lost atmosphere of a German region outside the Reich and an age before the time of Faust; his speech echoes the German of an era before the Reformation.

But that graciousness is by itself not decisive. What is decisive is the unmerited suffering and death of Echo. Holding himself responsible, Leverkühn for the first time abjures the Devil, curses him in a somewhat melodramatic manner—the scene is not well done—and embarks on his final work of revenge, which is to be the retraction of the Ninth Symphony. Echo's sacrifice provides him with the impetus for and example of his own ending, the inspiration of the echo-effect in its deepest meaning and, besides, the general formula for the ending of the book: "Take his body, you have power over that. But you'll have to put up with leaving me his soul" (p. 477). This Echo-episode is fraught with difficulties; perhaps the only way of taking it is as a lead-up to the end; one must suspend the disbelief which even Mann himself has difficulty in holding in check, embarrassing questions must not be asked. But can one help asking how and from where is such an "echo" to come? If, as the book says, it is from "the sphere of the mythical and timeless, the simultaneous and abiding" (p. 467), then one would want to know how it is that the "sphere" decides to intervene just when it is needed? Is that kindly Providence any more than the writer's wishful interference in his creation?

In spite of the dubious logic of how it is reached, the book's ending, when it comes, is an impressive double-ending of music and literature, or tone and word, of the "Lamentation of Dr. Faustus" and the "Confession" of Leverkühn. It is a perfect end, not only in that it attains a rounded completion but also in that in it word and tone complement each other perfectly and together they reflect on the book itself, which is both literature and "music," written prose structured on the level of musical composition. Word and tone are formally united, for the literary "Confession" is verbal music and the musical "Lamentation" is tonal literature. The "Lamentation" is literature not only because it is the setting of the *Dr. Faustus* text, nor even because it itself only exists in words, but also because as music itself it finally attains to expression: it makes "a statement, a 'Thus it is'" (p. 489) and "'Alas, it is not to be!'" (p. 490), and finally, "speaking unspokenness given to music alone . . . the final despair achieves a voice . . . like the Creator's rueful 'I have not willed it'" (pp. 490–91). What the music says is what the book as a whole is expressing; it, too, is music in words. And the inverse can be said of Leverkühn's verbal "Confession."

Zeitblom wishes that "he would soon begin to play and give us notes instead of words" (p. 497), but in fact Leverkühn is both "praying and playing," as he lets us know in his Freudian slip. His words are the resumé of the "musical" themes of the book, of all the Devil's motifs that comprise his inner life. Zeitblom does not fully realize the truth of what he is saying when he speaks of "the advantage that music, which says nothing and everything, has over the unequivocal word; yes, the saving irresponsibility of all art, compared with the bareness and baldness of unmediated revelation" (p. 498). Mann is, of course, here being ironic at Zeitblom's expense, for he has already told us that music does say something, and, furthermore, that no word is unequivocal, and that the speech of art is no less responsible to the truth than is the speech of life. But does the irony perhaps finally rebound on him as well, for can his own art, this book, stand up to these requirements of truth-telling? Or is it merely musical, with "the saving irresponsibility of all art" in Zeitblom's sense? To decide that question requires determining what kind of art the book is, and that partly depends on what kind of "music" it is. Does the musical achievement claimed for the "Lamentation" fit the "musical" achievement of the book itself? Does the book achieve the breakthrough that it claims for the composition? That is the decisive question.

Even at first sight an odd discrepancy is visible in the meaning of the "breakthrough," as claimed for the composition and as achieved by the book. The breakthrough of the composition is achieved atonally and serially, whereas the breakthrough of the book is distinctly harmonic. It is as if the "music" of the book answered not to the music of a Schoenberg, on which it is modelled, but to that of a Mahler—as if it were the literary counterpart of Mahler's Faust, his Eighth Symphony. The truth of Schoenberg's music or, for that matter, of any contemporary music, could hardly lie in the *expressivo* of lamentation, no matter how frightful the wailing and gnashing of teeth. Adorno writes of Schoenberg:

> His last pieces give a fragmentary impression, not merely in their brevity but in their shrivelled diction. The dignity of the great works devolves on splinters. Oratorio and Biblical opera are outweighed by the tale of the "Survivor from Warsaw," which lasts only a few minutes; in this piece Schoenberg, acting on his own, suspends the aesthetic sphere through the recollection of experiences which are inaccessible to art.[7]

All the challenging questions one would want to ask of *Doctor Faustus* are implicit in that extract. The breakthrough Mann claims for Leverkühn's serial composition has nothing in common with the kind of breakdown Adorno claims for Schoenberg himself in his late work. In fact, they are opposites. Leverkühn's breakthrough—it seems—can be appropriated by Mann himself without risk of the breakdown it cost his character. The novel's end is offered as the perfect reconciliation of all the polarities of the sphere, as harmonic completion.

It describes a perfect cadence, a dying fall that is a full harmonic close. As in myth, all differences are resolved when the magic ring completes itself. The End is the conclusion of the forward movement of eschatology culminating in its return to the circular movement of eternal recurrence. In this "dialectic of enlightenment" the Western stream of Reason cycles back to its originating ocean of myth. The solar half-parabola of Spengler's *Untergang* has been transformed into a full circle that comes back to itself. In the end innumerable echoing circles of time and history fulfil and complete themselves "in the same way that concentric rings made by a stone thrown into water spread ever farther, without drama and always the same" (p. 487). These are the rings of mythical repetition, and they are the echo-effect of time and history, "in which every transformation is itself already the echo of the previous one" (p. 488). Circle on circle the time-spheres complete their revolutions. The life of one man, who is also Mann himself, comes to an end; the Faustian history of modern Germany concludes, as does one phase in the history of Europe; Christianity consummates itself, and the whole civilization of the West going back to Abraham's bond with God has its inverse concluding echo in Faust's bond with the Devil. The time-circles of the book itself also complete themselves. The end returns to the origin as the last chapters are unified with the first; the themes exposed as mere motifs in the early chapters receive their full realization in the end. In its comprehensiveness the ending of the book is a recapitulation of all that took place within it, finally comprehended and grasped together, made fully conscious in the Hegelian sense—the Ring is closed. Not only does the work recapitulate the life and work of this Faust but also the works and deeds of the whole Faustian cultural "soul." Just as Leverkühn lives through all the stages of the organic unfolding of the German people, so in the end the book echoes and recapitulates all the earlier stages in the history of the West as a whole—as if in its dying moment the West were being granted a synoptic glimpse of the whole of its previous existence.

In the end, all the mythic identities of Faust recapitulate themselves in Leverkühn. He is not merely the modern artist identical with Zeitblom the bourgeois, but he carries in himself all other possible identities of opposites: he is Faust and Orpheus, "brothers as invokers of the world of shades" (p. 488), he is Oedipus (Freud) and Philoctetes (Jung), he is Christ and Judas, and beyond that he is Joseph the Brother, son of Jacob the Father, grandson of the UrFather Abraham. Altogether he is the Son of Man in whose mythic fate the whole of mankind can recognize itself. His final work is of cosmic proportions, "the *Lamentation* of the son of hell, the lament of men and God, issuing from the subjective, but always broadening out and as it were laying hold on the Cosmos" (p. 485). The breakthrough of the work is, therefore, this ultimate reconciliation. In its all-embracing conclusion it is the fusion of the Deed as bond with the Sphere, the final identity whereby the Devil's duplicity is the same as the echo of grace—"oh, marvel, oh, deep diabolic jest!" (p. 488). The miraculous marvel is the deep diabolic jest—and does not that mean that somehow, ultimately, the jester Devil, Fitelberg, is also Echo the child of grace? Variation, repetition, doubling, duplicity, imitation, and echo are all one principle of the eternal repetition of the same in which everything is reconciled with everything else. And reconciliation is also consolation. Despite the gloom and lamentation of the ending it is a deeply soothing close. The "lament of men and God," we are told, has "a jubilant, a highly triumphant bearing upon this awe-inspiring faculty of compensation and redress" (p. 485). Yet we are also told that the work "permits up to the very end no consolation, appeasement, transfiguration," and in the end it is only "a hope beyond hopelessness" (p. 491). Are we ready to believe that—seeing that the whole book has been working up to all its restitutions?

Once again, is this end true or false? Is it the realization of a profound truth of modernity, or mere "music" with "the saving irresponsibility of all art"? In the end it is a question of whether one is prepared to accept myth as the truth of history. Can one accept a "dialectic of enlightenment" that offers a positive consoling significance? Mann's positive "dialectic of enlightenment" differs from Adorno's negative in this crucial respect, that whereas the negative dialectic postulates that enlightenment is despite itself becoming submerged in myth, that the mythical figures return in a de-mythified fashion as fetishized commodities and reified nature, the positive dialectic, by contrast, maintains that enlightenment was never removed from myth, for myth has always been the truth of history as all history is mythic repetition. The fundamental difference between history and myth is here obliterated. Yet, whatever the repetitions to which history is subject, these are not the recurrences of mythical archetypes; whatever cycles history describes, these are not the perfect rings of completion; in whatever ways history may give rise to endings, these are not the ends that return back to themselves. The fate of history is not the fatality of what must be fulfilled; the despairs and hopes of history cannot be the apocalyptic ones of last things. To mythologize history is to subject it to the very fate about which one despairs and from which one can only derive false hopes.

Mann's work is, therefore, directed to a wrong end. Obviously, he did not take seriously enough the understanding of the problematic status of art in modern times, which he put into the Devil's mouth, letting him speak Adorno's words: "Whether the work as such, the construction, self-sufficing, harmonically complete in itself, still stands in any legitimate relation to the complete insecurity, problematic conditions, and lack of harmony of our social situation" (p. 180). Mann's work is precisely that: a construction that is self-sufficing and harmonically complete in itself. Its "music" is the opposite of Schoenberg's. It does not seek to "suspend the aesthetic sphere through the recollection of experiences which are inaccessible to art";[8] on the contrary, it comprehends all experiences within the aesthetic sphere, thereby transforming them into art. Within this sphere there can be no such thing as an experience inaccessible to art, for the sphere is all being and becoming as an aesthetic universe. The "terror of men in the agonies of death, under total domination" is for Mann merely an analogy of a traditional hell—"Germany had become a thick-walled underground torture-chamber" (p. 481)—conceived in the traditional art-words of, say, Dante and the images of Bosch.

Can such an art tell the truth of our time? In the end it cannot, but on the way to the end there is much that it can say. It addresses itself above all to the intellectual, and speaks to him of the intellectualization of existence. In Mann's hands the novel has become art allied to knowledge. In it the intellect has become its own subject, for life has become the life of the intellect. Zeitblom's life, not being intellectual, is nonexistent, and Leverkühn has no life apart from the artistic and cultural problems of his works. These works themselves attest to the truth of the intellectualization of art. It is art become a play of ideas with the highest order of artistry and cleverness, with consummate irony, refinement, and tact. But in this way art is reaffirmed as aesthetic intellect. By contrast, in Schoenberg's late work "artistic maturity and intellectualization abolish not only sensuous appearance, but with it art itself . . . artistic intellectualization moves emphatically towards the dissolution of art."[9] The "synthesis of freedom and determinism" does not in this case lead to any breakthrough, because "the latter, having been made absolute reveals itself to be contingent."[10] There is a similar contingency operating in Mann's art, of which he is no more aware than was Schoenberg; it is the contingency of the determined form itself, which ceases to have any inherent relationship to the content and becomes mere form.

For these reasons, it would not help merely to change the ending. For example, if Leverkühn's last work had been a failure would Mann's have been a greater success? It is tempting to suppose that the novel would have had a true end if it had concluded truly tragically on irremediable breakdown: if the ring could not be closed, if the bond were to be broken, and if the sphere were shattered. But to suppose that would be to go against the very logic of the work. The end is that which is inherent in the work as a whole, not merely that which takes place in the ending. An art that works with the sphere cannot break it without breaking itself as well. Perhaps it would have been truer if it had sought to break itself from the start, but then it could not have been itself. This work had to end as it did, on that last note from Leverkühn's "Lamentation": "For listen to the end, listen with me: one group of instruments after another retires, and what remains, as the work fades on the air, is the high G of a cello, the last word, the last fainting sound, slowly dying in a pianissimo-fermata" (p. 491). And who is it that cannot hear Leverkühn's last, lost tone changing its meaning and abiding "as a light in the night"? Who would not wish to expire knowing that somehow all is not lost, that even in the end something remains? For Mann music still has its full Orphic power, the power of consolation through reconciliation, ultimately the reconciliation of Man and Nature, and therein his consolation for the fact of death. In music the individual dies reconciled; like Orpheus he can move even death, though not defeat it.[11]

For this Faust is Orpheus; in search of Echo, his Eurydice, his "Lamento" sounds echoing throughout the depths of hell. Nature returns to him his lost echo, sends back to him his voice together with the form of his beloved. For the echo is not merely the "Alas!" of a return to nature of man in his "solitary state" (p. 486); it is also the echo of repetition, of infinite re-iteration, like the waves spreading out from the center of the echo-variations of the "Lamentation," in which "every transformation is itself already the echo of the previous one" (p. 488). Nature will not allow the echo to die away completely, to be extinguished forever; it repeats and retains the human voice, and keeps on giving it back in ever newer transformations. Man in his solitary state is not lost, but in returning to Nature he is assured of his own preservation; he will be repeated transformed, but nevertheless repeated in form, and will come back again and again forever, for his archetype is never lost. Through death and transfiguration in nature Man assumes a natural immortality. That is his "hope beyond hopelessness, the transcendence of despair" (p. 491).

But can literature, modern literature at that, arrogate to itself this Orphic power of music? Can anyone place such trust in music any longer? Can modern Man depend on a musical consolation? To what could it reconcile him: to a Nature that is no longer in any echoing relation with Man, that no longer harmonizes with anything human, that as Mann himself realizes in the ironically named "Marvels of the Universe," the *Symphonia cosmologica* of Leverkühn (p. 274), is a "horrendous physical creation [that] is in no way religiously productive" (p. 272)? In the face of such a reality is not the old consolation of music something of a cheat? Can it console the modern individual in his absolutely solitary state? Can it release him from his solitude? Can there even be any music for such a man?

## SCENE V
## *Faust the Musician*

### I

We began this book with Faust the philosopher and we now end with Faust the composer. There is an inherent logic in that passage, for music is the art of time and Faust is preeminently a figure of time. Every Faust is a time-composition contracted within the pre-set duration of the 24-year day of life, with an agreed-upon opening deed and a predetermined end. Life is given a pre-set form that carries implicit in it a conventional theological meaning. It is against this meter of meaning that the Faust writers have counterpointed their own rhythm of time. Ironically, the question each has had to answer is this: what does a limited human lifetime have to offer and how does it stand up compared to the finality of death and the endlessness of eternity? The question becomes crucial in the ending, at the moment of final reckoning when the account has to be drawn up. This is why the final moment is so decisive in every Faust. This last moment is also "musically" very important, for it determines the sense of time of the whole composition. In deciding what time is, it also decides what music can accomplish in time, for music is the art that realizes time's meaningful potentialities. It follows from this that the end of Faust has to be indicative of the approach of and to time, and that it must involve and be of consequence to music. Music enters at every time. To show this we need only once more reconsider the last moment in each Faust.

In the last hour of Marlowe's *Faustus* time intrudes most insistently in the ticking of a clock. This metrical, mechanical, measurable dimension of time is here for the first time in literature realized as the *Angst* of time. It is the *Angst* of bare and empty time, time that contains nothing but time, that is nothing but abstract time.[1] This claustrophobic metrical beat of time will be repeated over and over in literature and music from *Boris Godounov* to *Wozzeck,* ever more insistently through much of expressionist literature and music—most chillingly in *Erwartung*—to the latest horror film. The *Angst* of time is with us to stay, as time itself, mechanized and organized, is broken up into the instants of the seconds of a clock that echoes mechanically our pulse and heartbeat, beating out the ghostly tattoo of approaching death. In *Faustus* it beats incessantly in that hour "twixt the hours of twelve and one" when "Since first the world's creation did begin such fearful shrieks and cries were never heard" (V.iii). The chaos of noise and time has here broken through that musical order of creation which is set at risk by it. We already know that in the conventional theological sense Faustus—who so loved the pleasures of classical music that he made "blind Homer" sing to him—has forfeited the celestial music of heaven: "(*Music while the throne descends*) Good Angel: Oh, thou hast lost celestial happiness" (V.ii). It is not, however, with the music of celestial harmony that the author tries to contain this chaos of hell, the anguish of time's inexorable tread, the shrieks and cries of horror at its pointless end. Instead, he sets Faustus' agonies within the order of his own art, establishing, as it were, a classical frame in which to contain it. He concludes his work with the classical tag: "Terminat hora diem, Terminat Author opus"—as if the author could complete his work in as calm and orderly a closure as the last hour completes the day. And, by implication, as if Faustus' unruly sufferings could be set within the created order of the work itself. It is to be the classical order practiced with all the punctilious ceremonials of the schools. Faustus is to be received back as a brother in Apollo who came to grief in the world of Christ: "Though Faustus' end be such as every Christian heart laments to think on,/Yet, for he was a scholar once admired.... We'll give his mangled limbs due burial" (V.iii). As these masters of the arts pace slowly off the stage we hear in anticipation the steady, slow beat of a funeral. Faustus is to be ceremoniously interred with order and decorum, and his death is to be contained within the ordered music of art.

It is all unconvincing here, for before us on stage there is still the mangled corpse: "Faustus' limbs all torn asunder by the hand of death."

This refuses to be ordered away; the conflicting sufferings by which Faustus was torn to pieces will not be so easily composed. This funereal music for the passage of Faust is as defunctive as that with which Fortinbras sought to speed Hamlet's passage: "and for his passage, / The soldier's music and the rites of war / Speak loudly for him" (*Hamlet* V.ii). Scholar's music and the rites of art befit Faustus as little as the other kinds become Hamlet.

In Goethe's *Faust* the role of music is not obvious. Goethe's predilections and talents leaned far more toward painting, so it is the visual sense that is extremely well developed in the play—so much so that all too often the play appears to be a series of tableaux. Hence, though music and the dance are often referred to and invoked in the work, it is only at the end, when the time question becomes urgent, that the idea of music implicitly and silently sounds as well. Faust's last words are these: "My highest moment this" (V, "The Great Outer-Court of the Palace"). To which Mephistopheles replies: "This wretched, empty moment at the last, he sought, poor wretch, to grasp and hold it fast. . . . The clock stands still." Here the clock does not merely strike the final hour, it actually stops—"the finger falls"—and with it time disintegrates.

For Goethe the threat of time is not merely, as it is for Marlowe, to keep beating on and on without end; rather, it is that time itself might be empty—and so it would be as if it had never been. Mephistopheles makes this explicit: "Gone, to sheer Nothing, past with null made one." It is in defense against this Mephistophelean reduction of time, which reduces everything else to Nothing, that blind Faust so desperately struggles to keep a firm grasp on his last moment. It is a very complex moment in time, for though it is a present moment, yet it is filled with past recollection and future anticipation; it is at once the moment of death and nothingness, and the moment of fulfillment, the highest moment—a dying moment and also an eternally living moment. How is all this possible in one moment? It is possible if we understand it as a "musical" moment. Goethe writing to his friend the composer Zelter, at the time when he was completing the ending, explained it as follows:

> Fortunately your talent is directed toward the tone, that is, toward the moment. Now since a consistent sequence of moments is itself always a kind of eternity, it has been granted to you always to be constant in the midst of everything transitory, you satisfy thereby both me and Hegel's spirit, insofar as I understand it.[2]

This attainment of the "musical" moment is achieved at some cost, however, for it entails the destruction of the old time-order. The symbol of that in the play is the church bell, the traditional predecessor of the clock. The music of the bell rings through the early scenes in the last act. In the closing speech of the two ancients, Philemon indicates what it means to them: "Let the vesper chimes be tolled." It means something quite different to Faust, who is restless, disturbed by it: "Accursed chime, all solace ending." He does not know why, but "the bell condemns as incomplete, my high estate." Mephistopheles, who understands all too well, explains it to him with the ring of subtle irony: "This clanging is a grief to hear . . . will boom on babe's first bath and on the tomb, contrives that mortal life should seem twixt ding and dong an empty dream." Mephistopheles' spite is in the first place directed against Faust, who is all too unwilling to hear this "knell of passing day." Yet, there is also animus here against the bell itself, which Goethe shares. A lifetime ordered by the music of the bell does become as if it were "an empty dream." The Devil is referring here to an old Christian topos that goes back at least as far as St. John Chrysostom: "Life is as it were a play or a dream." The Christian time-order regulated by the bell makes of a lifetime an unreal interval between ding and dong, birth and death—the larger realities—and this makes of life as it is experienced in time a mere interlude preceding death, the ultimate reality. It is only when Faust, through Mephistopheles, has destroyed the bell that he can free himself from its time order and its reminder of the eternity to come, to affirm the moment here and now as eternal. He dies outside the dispensation of the bell, holding fast his final "wretched, empty moment" in which he finds fulfillment as a man.

Faust's last moment is thus a full moment. The emptiness with which Mephistopheles threatens it, as an eternal emptiness of all time, that threat has not as yet begun to come from inside the moment itself. The fullness of Faust's moment is guaranteed by the ultimate fulfillment of the whole movement of time rising upward and culminating in its completion in the heaven of art. Faust's fulfilled moment is but a single moment in the progressive movement of humanity and all of nature in time. For Goethe, All is gathered up into that End. There is no waste or ultimate loss. In that respect his time is like Hegel's, whom he understood much better than he gave himself credit for.

The "musical" moment has, since Goethe, assumed increasing importance, and it has almost completely displaced the orderly movement of both the Christian and classical-humanist time-orders. Instead of the structurally articulated, rationally extended and spatially laid-out, often symmetrical order of Baroque movement or Classical form, modern music has increasingly sought for the meaningful moment. Since Beethoven it has been expansively working itself up, moving with ever-greater momentum to reach "that glorious moment," and then falling away from it again. At its Romantic crudest the moment is the climax. Beginning with Wagner's *Tristan* prelude, the work itself is but one such climactic moment; in that piece it is the orgasmic moment of sexual consummation in death. In Schoenberg the moment becomes a rapt figure of frozen dread; the expansiveness of time has been contracted into the intensity and density of the moment, as the Devil, paraphrasing Adorno on Schoenberg, expounds to Leverkühn. And as Adorno himself states it, Schoenberg "opposes expansion in time, which has been the basis for the conception of the musical work since the eighteenth century, certainly since Beethoven."[3] Perhaps the briefest, most subtle and compositionally most organized moments are the little movements of Webern. Stockhausen's gargantuan *Momente* is but a modernistic travesty of that procedure. In both of these composers a Christian theological meaning has returned to the moment, very likely mediated by Kierkegaard's philosophy of time. It is not for nothing that Leverkühn is caught reading Kierkegaard when the Devil surprises him with his new proposals for music. It is from Kierkegaard, too, that Heidegger derives the conception of the moment as *Augenblick* that concludes *Sein und Zeit*. Heidegger's moment still has many of the theological connotations of the "still" moment. It is also still within the ambit of the "full" Faustian moment.

The end of the passage of Faust is itself one final moment. Conceived of as a Faustian moment, it receives its last realization in Mann's *Doctor Faustus*. It is the limit of Faust's self-realization. It is also the moment when Faust reaches the utmost of his musical self-consciousness. What is the nature of this self-consciousness? We can study it in an actual composition, for the end of this Faust receives its musical significance in the "Lamentation" of Leverkühn. What is the musical time of this composition? The answer lies in the nature of the composition itself, for as it is meant to be the ultimate fulfillment of the history of Western music, the time of this music comprehends all possible previous musical times. It is one gigantic last moment "rising up until the middle, then descending, in the spirit and inflexion of the Monteverdi *Lamento*" (p. 487), but at the same time it is a moment that moves outward, "broadening out and as it were laying hold on the Cosmos" (p. 485), "certainly non-dynamic, lacking in development, . . . without drama and always the same" (p. 487). This recapitulation of musical time is also one of all historical musical expression (p. 488). The "Confession," which is the verbal analogue to the musical "Lamentation," gives a similar impression of an eclecticism of language in its attempt to sum up all previous styles of German. It, too, is one last present moment that contains within itself the whole movement of the past. It is a last moment before death in which the whole of life is compressed and recapitulated.

The time of the "Lamentation" and "Confession" is itself only a recapitulation of the time of the book as a whole. In it all possible modes of time are brought together and reconciled with each other. In the basic time-figure of the circle all other times are encompassed. The two most important and fundamentally opposed modes of time are Zeitblom's time of linear and ordered progression and Leverkühn's time of retrograde regression. The first comprises all time orders that are humanist and Christian, the second all those that are theologically negative, apocalyptic, and mythic. Leverkühn's time is the "Devil's time," which he is granted by virtue of the bond. It is this time that is referred to in the book as musical time proper, and it is this time, too, that is the time of the eternal moment: the 24 years of musical time the Devil offers is "a work-filled eternity of human life" (p. 249), for "such a time is also an eternity" (p. 248), as the Devil insists. Throughout the book these two time-measures are set in opposition to each other: the linear, chronological character of Zeitblom's narration and the historical period it describes are set constantly at odds with the regressions and retrogressions of Leverkühn's under-world existence and the perverse cultural trends of the times that are reflected in it. It is only at the end that they even themselves out and come together in the time circle that is always the same. Within the circle, time can go forward and backward, can move and be at a standstill. Ultimately that circle is the book itself, which thus embraces and harmonizes all the times of music and literature, of myth and history, of inner and outer, of Devil and God.

This last Faustian fullness of time has now been put in question. Its musical moment is now in doubt. Faust will not find fulfillment in the moment of his end. And it is at that moment that every Faust strives to reconcile and harmonize the conflicting times of his lifetime, so in that respect Mann's time-circle is only the grandiose culmination of an attempt already implicitly there in Marlowe's *Faustus* and well underway in Goethe's *Faust*. In Marlowe, the main conflict is between orthodox, Christian time and what might be called "libertine," humanist time: the former looks to the end and to eternity, the latter is fixed to the moment of present satisfaction. "Libertine" time spends and exhausts itself, its rhythm is that of appetite and passion, the sexual rhythm; its present moment is thus the forever-alternating play of hunger and satiation that can only in the end exhaust itself and wear itself out to death.

In torment alone is it able to prolong itself, for torment does not weary as satisfaction does. And when that torment is the mental anguish of fear, such as the sinner's fear of the Christian end, then it is in principle an endless torment. That is for Marlowe the eternal moment of damnation. In the last moment the libertine and Christian times are locked together in a perversely paradoxical embrace that is the mortal combat of their death struggle. The verbal expression of that conflict is Faustus' prayer for immediate extinction, the obverse of Marlowe's longing for continued torment. The perfunctory Christian-humanist-classical harmony of the time-order of the epilogue does nothing to assuage the anguish of the final unity in contradiction of those times. By contrast, Goethe's *Faust* does in the end ideally reconcile the time-oppositions that had been dramatically in conflict within the play. The past time of Philemon and Baucis, the present time of Lynceus, and the future time of Faust are all unified within the presentness of Faust's last moment: his final vision is that of a human time where "childhood, youth, age shall strive through strenuous years." But, as we know, Goethe is not unmindful of eternity, for in the end the humanist temporality that Faust advocates is, despite everything, brought into unison with the Christian time of eternity. Not only is Faust's last moment an eternal one, but in that moment his spirit embarks on an eternal upward progression that is his salvation. Goethe's Idealism—despite its "pagan" anti-theological critical edge—is an ideal Christian humanism. And so, too, in the end is Mann's idealism, despite its awareness of the horrors of modern Nihilism.

Thus, the end of every Faust is an attempt to give meaning to time through a reconciliation of the conflicting Christian and humanist senses of it. Inherent in the essence of the Faust thematic is the assumption that time, and above all a human lifetime, must have a meaning, for which Faust and the Devil are contenders. Faust is usually the exponent of a positive humanist sense of the here and now of this life, and the Devil, as the upholder of orthodoxy, is there to insist on the claims of the theologically negative hereafter. The need to do dramatic justice to both accompanies a need to reconcile their conflicting claims on time. The thought of Faust contracting with the Devil for a period of time and at the completion of that time having neither lost nor won, been saved or damned, or both, or possibly not even experiencing any final moment, would make nonsense of the whole Faustian theme. That there might be no end, no last moment, or that the last moment of dying might not be an end, that the moment of death might only be a finis, an arbitrary break-off point, neither telos nor eschaton—this is not possible for Faust; that in the face of a death that is no end time might become meaningless—that is a thought no Faust can possibly entertain.

Perhaps a peculiar literary work is conceivable in which the Devil tricks a man into believing that he is Faust, and gets him to take on the role of Faust, only to show him in the end that he is no Faust at all, or not only Faust but someone else as well. But it is very likely that the Devil would not cooperate; for the very presence of the Devil would ward off any such possibility and ensure that despite all its self-reflections *Faust* remains in the end a Christian-humanist drama. Within these terms the radical nothingness of Nihilism cannot be stated because the presence of the Devil as a negativity theologically conceived always implies the absent presence of its positive counterpart. It is true that with each successive Faust that negativity becomes more complex, but it can never break through its own presuppositions. Thus, in Marlowe it is still the very naive negativity of a Devil who is external to and hostile to Man—though there is also the more interesting suggestion that hell is the torment of human life itself. In Goethe there is the predominant sense of the Devil as the negative moment of the dialectic of human progress, acting positively as the necessary gad-fly to spur human endeavor—though there, too, there are other interesting suggestions. In Mann there is even a flirtation with the Devil as Nietzschean Nihilism, but that possibility is not taken very seriously, for the Devil as the basic cosmic principle of duplicity is needed to bond the sphere. Hence, no matter how transformed, the Devil always remains in relation to Faust a theological presence—as Mann's Devil says: "A highly theological business, music—the way sin is, the way I am" (p. 242). Theology, music, sin, and the Devil—do they not somehow go together? A negativity radical enough to do away with the last vestiges of theology and metaphysics would, therefore, also do away with the Devil on whom any Faust must depend. Then, the whole humanist-Christian conflict prevalent in one form or another since the Renaissance-Reformation would also collapse. That would be the real end of Faust. But what about music? Would that, too, go to the Devil?

## II

What does the end of Faust do to music? That would be easy to say if it were possible to accept the Devil's dictum that music is a "theological business." Referring to Kierkegaard, he adds: "He knew and understood my particular relation to this beautiful art—the most Christian of all arts" (p. 242). It follows from this in one simple step that if the Devil is to be no more then music is to be no more. But who would be inclined to accept that kind of an inference on the Devil's word alone? And yet there is something basically correct in the Devil's account of a relationship between music and Christianity, at least as far as the origin of European music goes. Might there not be, then, a relation between Christianity and the end of that music? That must be considered with reference to the end of Faust. If the end of Faust is an attempt to compose time, then the failure of that end must be of profound significance for the time in which music is composed. If time can no longer be rendered musically, then music itself can no longer be. Or is it the other way around—because music cannot be, time cannot be rendered musically? Whichever way it is, the end of Faust seems to bear some relation to the end of music. How can that even be thought of at a time when the air and radio waves are more than ever filled with the sound of music, when there are more notes committed to paper than ever before? But a nagging doubt remains as to whether all this is music of our time, and whether it renders our time musical. If our time is no longer musical, then what kind of a time can it be? But first, what kind of an art is music, anyway, and what is its relation to time?

Music is certainly a most peculiar art. It has been called the youngest of the arts; it has also been called the most profound of the arts. On first hearing, both these claims seem egregiously false, for has there not been music among all people, even the most primitive, and what can be profound in an art deprived of verbal meaning? Yet, there is also a point to these claims that must be explored. Music is ageless, but music as a composed art is relatively recent. It is hardly older than the Christian culture of Western Europe. Nietzsche asks very appositely: "Where does our entire music belong? The ages of classical taste knew nothing to compare with it: it began to blossom when the Renaissance world had attained its evening."[4] Nietzsche had obviously not heard the music of a Machaut or a Dufay, but that only calls for an adjustment to his too-narrow historical perspective, it does not basically alter his main judgment. Medieval music is an amazingly rich art, but it does not go back very far in time. Within the monastic environment of the early Middle Ages the fundamental technical discoveries were made that enabled music to develop to the level of a high art. It was there that a process of rationalization in music began that paralleled the rationalization of work and daily life under the impact of monastic discipline with its offices and hours and other devices for the allocation of time. As Weber points out, of crucial importance, technically speaking, was an exact musical notation, which was developed largely in the monasteries.[5] Elsewhere Weber states that "rational harmonious music, both counterpoint and harmony . . . our chromatics and enharmonics . . . our orchestra . . . all these things are known only in the Occident."[6] But beyond technique, what were the fundamental meanings that enabled medieval Europe to develop its music? To answer that we must look to the meanings of music itself.

As the Devil insists, there is a deep-seated relationship between the possibility of music and metaphysics and theology. Historically speaking, the intellectual basis of music, which precedes the emergence of music as an art in Christian Europe, is metaphysics. Without the intellectual basis of the metaphysics of music that started with Pythagoras, art-music could not have arisen in medieval Europe. Musical harmony and multiple time relationships, so vital to European music, would not have developed without the intellectual stimulus of Platonic, Stoic, and neo-Platonic speculations on harmony and time; without the Aristotelian musical theorizing going back as early as Aristoxenes of Tarantum in the fourth century B.C. and continuing unbroken till Augustine in the fourth century A.D.; without the Boethian speculations on "harmonices mundi" and "musica mundana" at the close of the antique world—all of which passed first into the Arab philosophies of Al Farabi and Avicenna and then into Christian thinking, eventually becoming the cultural commonplace of the "music of the spheres" that lasted till the close of the Renaissance, ending only with Kepler, who still invoked it but also discovered astronomic laws that were to undo it. This metaphysics of music was carried on as part of the intellectual curriculum of the medieval universities in seemingly only a distant rapport with actual musical practices, but it nevertheless provided the generalized meaning of music and endowed it with universal significance and truth practically throughout the history of music.

Certainly, there were major changes in the metaphysics of music, and in its original classical form it does not survive the Renaissance; the last great exponent of it was the Venetian theorist Zarlino, though in an anachronistic way it recurs in Mersenne. The vision of music at the end of the *Merchant of Venice* (V.i), perhaps the last time that it is invoked in great literature, is undercut even in that play itself. Changes in philosophy and science produced a new aesthetic and art of music, first among the Florentine intellectuals of the Camerata with whom the two Galilei, father and son, were associated, and among whom the new science and the new music were developed in close conjunction. In this new rational, epistemological spirit Descartes elaborated his treatise on music, and he was followed by such other scientists as d'Alembert and Euler.

The next major change in the meaning of music took place at the start of the modern period as part of the Faustian transformation, so that one might almost speak of it as the musical Deed of Faust, and the subsequent music one might call Faustian. Theoretically the change was registered in the new attitude to music of the German Idealist writers and thinkers, and practically it occurred in the gigantic musical achievement of Beethoven. Together they represented the first major turning against all the previous rational approaches to music; the very idea of musical order was put in question theoretically and seriously disturbed in musical practice; instead, the dynamism, power, and unconscious affectivity of music were promoted. Such "romantic" new philosophies of music were most significantly developed by Kierkegaard and Schopenhauer. The latter in turn influenced the whole further course of music through his effect on Wagner, who stands on the threshold of contemporary music and even takes the fatal step into its last phase. Nietzsche was already partly aware of the significance of that step, but it is Adorno, on the basis of Schoenberg's music, who has fully understood it. The subsequent history of music can also be very closely associated with developments in philosophy. Thus the rise of positivistic philosophies leaves, of course, no room for any meaning that music might carry, and is directly responsible for the present state of modern music.

Even from this brief account it is evident that the rise of music as an art presupposed the influence of an intellectual "music" as a metaphysical ideal, and its subsequent development was closely bound up with major changes in philosophy. India, the only other culture that came close to developing a musical art, was also a culture that produced philosophies analogous to metaphysics, as well as sciences of mathematics and astronomy. In India, too, music became a theoretical intellectual discipline. What we do not know is to what extent the philosophical and musical developments in India were autonomous and to what extent they were Greek-inspired. We also do not know how Indian theoretical music related to musical practice. Nor is there much known about the influence of the old classical Indian music on the music that we now hear as Indian, though that seems to have been largely derived from Persian and Arabic sources. The Arabs were, of course, closely in touch with the Greek metaphysics of music; Al Farabi, in particular, carried on the tradition of metaphysical speculation on music with genuine relevance to musical practice; he investigated both intervalic and temporal-rhythmic relationships in theory and in practice, referring himself to the music performed in his time.[7] However, nothing seems to have issued out of this work to alter the Arabic musical arts: no new music arose on a philosophic basis. Again, we have little knowledge of why this was so. Nor do we know to what extent Indian musical theory influenced the musical practices of Indonesia—though there is a close connection between the surviving Hinduism and music of Bali—or how Buddhism spread Indian musical ideas to China, Korea, and Japan.

In all these non-European cultures there are remarkable and fascinating musics. And one also finds such among so-called primitive peoples. However, nowhere outside Western Europe is music an art that can rival any of the other major arts. In the Greco-Roman world, despite the presence of a metaphysics of music, the musical art was minor in comparison with the plastic arts, which have rarely been surpassed. Similarly, in China, India, and elsewhere the attainments in the other arts far outstrip in profundity and scope their musics. In none of these cultures is music the fundamental bearer of "truth" and spiritual expression. The significance of music is minor and partial. Only in Western Europe could music assume its high intellectual, spiritual, and emotional role. The difference between this music and the others is so marked that it justifies one in speaking of music as in the last instance a European art, perhaps the European art par excellence.

Only in Europe could music assume an importance which, over whole centuries and throughout large regions, could be greater than that of any other art. One need only think of the role of music in the Low Countries during the fifteenth century or in Italy during the seventeenth or Austria and Germany in the eighteenth and nineteenth centuries. Technical advancement is in itself not a mark of quality, but it is a condition of complexity and therefore indirectly one of importance as well. A technically simpler music could not have carried out all the functions that European music could perform in social, intellectual, and cultural life. In certain periods music was the accompaniment of all life-activities, becoming the constant preoccupation for whole classes and the specialized work of groups of professions. Consequently, a myriad of musical styles and forms were developed that in sheer variety and output dwarf the musical types of all other civilizations combined—even allowing for all the music that was lost due to absence of notation. In Europe music exercised a great influence on all the other arts: the ideal of harmony, which always had its primary locus in music, was of importance for aesthetic theory in general and for the ideal values of every other art. The social, intellectual, and cultural influences of music are equally pronounced, ranging from the role of the motet, mass, and oratorio in religion, opera in social intercourse, and chamber music and the keyboard instruments in personal expression. On these grounds alone one can expect music to have deeply molded the European sense of time.[8]

It would be both misleading and false to identify European civilization with Faust and to make music the Faustian art *tout court,* as Spengler does. Nevertheless, there is a deep-seated correspondence between Faust and music, as we have already noted, through their common concern with time. But it is only in the end that the nexus between them emerges openly and fully and reveals their common fate. Marlowe's *Faustus* comments implicitly on the music of its time, commencing a concern for music that Shakespeare was to carry on from first to last in his dramatic opus; a complex statement on music that we have yet to learn to read with understanding. It certainly marks a crisis of music that the new music starting in Italy then only managed to sidestep, not overcome. The relationship between Goethe's *Faust* and the musical revolution of its time becomes much more apparent—so much so that we can with no impropriety refer to it as the Faustian translation of music. The Faustian transformation is already softly and silently there in Mozart, "whose music so clearly echoes the passage from enlightened late absolutism to the bourgeoisie, a transition deeply akin to Goethe."[9] But in Beethoven the Faustian Deed is loudly and brusquely declared with the violent force of *sforzato* in a clenched fist beating out the theme of heroic destruction. The essential Faustian thematic is there in the music, even in the forms themselves; one might put it that "in the beginning is the Deed" as first subject whose dynamic activity is development through perpetual self-transformation and whose end is a recapitulation. In Beethoven the formal device of the recapitulation takes on much of the meaning that it has in his contemporary, Hegel, and it anticipates the meaning of the recapitulation in Mann. This is the real reason why Mann, who through Leverkühn seeks to "take back the Ninth Symphony," can only recapitulate it, and why Mann's "music," though it avails itself of the technical devices of Schoenberg's music, cannot really express it. The last Faust does not properly understand his relation to music. He has not realized that his end is no "breakthrough" in music but an end to music itself.

Music, like Faust, had been contracted to the end ever since its opening Deed. This finally occurs in Schoenberg's music, "that new—now already older—music in which the subject's suffering sheds the affirmative conventions"; and that is what separates it, as sharply as are the saved from the damned, "from the latest one in which the subject and its suffering hardly have room any more."[10] The latest so-called musical works are "compositions from which the subject withdraws as though ashamed of its own survival, compositions left to the automatisms of construction or chance—these get to the borderline of an unleashed technology that is superfluous beyond the utilitarian world."[11]

As Adorno is well aware, the intellectual and technical means to make music purely technological were already prepared for by the earlier new music; Schoenberg's music was already intellectually constructed and technologically directed, even though in its essence it expressed the most intense subjectivity, the loneliness of the subject under technological domination. Once there occurs "the abdication of the subject, the demolition of subjective meaning," then nothing is left but the intellectual scaffolding of technology. In a similar manner, once it too has lost its basic meaning, the activism expressed in its rhythmic forms, all that is left of Stravinsky's influence is the technology of orchestration and sound sonorities. The activism of massed sound and corps de ballet representing the tribe, the folk, the church, the tradition, which so often overpowered the weak and pitiful individual soul in Stravinsky's music, has disappeared from the similar-sounding spectacles of the latest productions: there is the massed orchestra without the sound, the corps without the ballet—often nothing is left but noisy pyrotechnics.

Only formally and verbally do these pieces deserve the names *music* and *composition*; actually they are neither. There is still music being composed now, but only as a vestigial survival whose future is uncertain. Even so, much of that is only an adaptation of the music of the recent past. New music one hears rarely, if at all. What goes under the name of *new music,* the so-called electronic music, deserves a different title. It is possibly the primitive beginnings of quite another art-form based on sound. Its mode of structuring is far closer to that of cinematic montage than it is to that of music, which derives its structural meaning from the "syntax" of its languages of time and tone, not from the superposition or juxtaposition of textures of raw "interesting" sound. The fact that the conventional instruments of music are also used to produce these sound "spectacles," rather than electronic media alone, does not change their meaning; it only leads to the embarrassing anachronism that musical fragments sometimes emerge accidentally and haphazardly. What is to be the meaning and point of these sound productions, how they are to be used, in conjunction with what other arts—for they can hardly stand on their own—what is to be their mode of performance and reception: all these questions are yet to be answered in theory and practice.

But, then, just as we do not understand the beginning of this new art, neither do we understand the end of the old one. What is the meaning of the end of music? How and why did it come about? For an answer to the latter question we must first look to society. Adorno very pertinaciously remarks in passing that "productive musicality, [which] as an intellectual faculty mankind was late to acquire, is evidently most sensitive to social pressure."[12] He is right on both counts. As we have already seen, music is a very young art-language. It is also one that depends perhaps more than any other on its deliberate cultivation, for it is more artificial and less "natural" than any other—the child has to be specially taught to hear music. It is paradoxical that music, being the most abstract of the arts, the most universal in scope and the least language-like in its meaning, is yet more dependent on meaningful culture and on a very complex social life of feeling than any other art. This is one reason why we find it more difficult to understand the music of past ages or other cultures than to understand their literature or visual arts; thus, for example, medieval music is more difficult than medieval literature or painting or architecture, for no longer being in touch with that whole form of life, and especially with its emotional modes, we can no longer hear a meaning in sounds that we can otherwise quite easily reproduce and listen to. European music generally depends on a very rich verbal culture that cultivates certain complex modes of feeling. And, perhaps, even more specifically, they are the feelings surrounding death, that is, largely Christian feelings, for there is a very close connection between music and death. Music is an art of silence, but not of silence in the absence of speech. As death is present in the midst of life so is music in the midst of language. Music is the art-speech that is furthest removed from verbal speech, yet it is very close to its implicit silences. It is an unspoken spoken that is on the very edge of silence, and so is closest to death.

Perhaps this helps to explain another paradox of music: that though its forms of expression are public, their content can be intensely private. The languages of music are public languages but the voices speaking in those languages are private voices. Each really individual musical composition is a very particular and very private expression of unique feelings. This is one reason why it is impossible to convey those feelings in words. In fact, one of the main impulsions to composing music is to express feelings that cannot be put into words, for only music can plumb depths of meaning that are too deep for words. Frequently those are the depths of the unconscious, and the meaningful feelings that are encountered there need to be expressed in music because they are too particular and disturbing to be said in words. Those silences of one's individual being can only be given voice in music. Thus music is a "speech" that is closest to the silence that is beyond words. And that reveals once more its paradoxical nature, in that it is at once the most universal of art languages, the one easiest to understand because of its abstraction from all particular reality, and at the same time the most esoteric of art-languages, whose meanings are so specific and private that no translation can be offered. It is the most formal and mathematically structured of the languages of perception and also the most intuitive and emotional medium of pure expression. It is at once abstract and particular, public and private, meaningful and meaningless, sensuous and ideal, shallow and deep.

Yet, it is only within publicly practiced musical life and utilizing a common musical language that a composer can give voice to his private thoughts and feelings. This is the main reason why the isolated individual cannot compose music in silence, for himself alone, when he is deprived of the support of a cultural musical milieu. When social conditions are against them, the poet and the painter can go on practicing their arts in isolation far longer than can the composer. The writer inhabiting a "natural" spoken language can develop within it an idiom for himself based on his personal suffering and experience; the painter can distort his "natural" perceptions into a private vision, even though it may be a nightmare of his own; but the composer, not having any such natural starting-point, has nowhere to begin—the feelings he has must remain soundless and unheard. When the social and cultural forms that permit musical meanings to be sensed and emotions to be felt disappear, then the music that depends on them can no longer be sustained in isolation. The very fact that music is such an artificially cultivated art prevents it from growing under adverse conditions, when other arts that have no such requirements, and are therefore hardier, can still survive. Music is the exotic bloom of culture.

Schoenberg, Berg, and Webern carried music deep into privacy, just about as far as it can be taken; it is doubtful whether it can be taken any further. Theirs was a "lonely discourse" in which "the anxiety of the lonely becomes the law of aesthetic formal language."[13] But this they were only able to do under much more favorable cultural conditions than have since prevailed. They wrote at a time when the late Romantics could still express themselves, when the neo-Classics had barely ceased to compose, when there was still so much music in the cultural air that everyone had to breathe it. Now, when that music is incessantly on the air and everyone is oblivious to its background noise, it is far less possible to conceive of even intenser sounds of solitude, a lonelier discourse. And that is what would be required if music were to go on developing, for a music that attempted to fit into any of the prevailing public cultures would inevitably be lost as serious music.

The music that is public and has publicity is, of course, popular music. It is a very lively and thriving culture industry that produces its sound products for mass consumption. On rare occasions it can put out small items that have a distinctive character, charm, and even some nostalgic capacity to move, but by the very conditions of its production, economic and musical, it is precluded from ever being an original expression: it must sell on the mass market and so it must work with preestablished formulae. These formulae are taken from the widest possible diversity of sources—mainly from classical art, for all harmony, rhythm, and orchestration have their locus there, but also from defunct or still surviving genuine folk art, or from more exotic sources such as Negro or Eastern art, and of late it has increasingly borrowed from the avant-garde arts. Necessarily, however, once they have been commercialized these borrowed formulae no longer have the same significance that they had in their original settings, for in order to be sold to a mass public they must be simplified, deprived of any cultivated elaborations, their form reduced to a bare format. Such public requirements make it almost impossible now for a popular composer to produce a real demotic style.

The requirements of salability are also now beginning to dominate the reproduction and performance of art-music itself, which is called "classical" and turned into museum music. And the same pressures operate on avant-garde sound productions, so that these too are drawn into the popular market. The recent success of the so-called *op* and *pop* art styles in avant-garde painting is but the first indication of this trend. There are now similar phenomena within music, and it seems likely that the musical avant-garde will tend to merge into the commercial world, for only there lies hope for success. We may even see the avant-garde become a kind of experimental laboratory or testing-ground for the commercial culture-industry. In such conditions the very idea of a performance must change: the concert, no longer a social occasion for listening, becomes a kind of musical "happening," with the result that "classical" music in performance, pop music, and avant-garde music are merging. For some time we can expect chaos, but eventually within it or beside it something more worthwhile could also develop. It is possible that novel and interesting ways of combining sound material with material drawn from the other arts may begin to shape themselves. The film is already one such mode of *Gesamtkunstwerk* and the model perhaps for many others based on new technologies. These would be new hybrid arts in which sound could play a part. But, of course, sound in some such combinations will no longer be music as we have understood it for the past thousand years. That is now an *opus postumus*. Which modern works enter it and which are now or will be excluded is a moot point of music criticism. Who is the last composer is, of course, as futile a question as who was the first composer.

That music, this uniquely European art, has now reached this impasse is highly symptomatic not only of the fate of Europe but of modern culture and society in general. It is much more than merely the self-liquidation of the bourgeoisie, with whom music was always closely associated. But as Adorno states, it "implies the end of the musical experience of time";[14] and the end of musical time inaugurates an empty time without an end in itself. This ending of musical time is an historical process that music itself carries through. Already in its Expressionistic phase the music of Schoenberg "opposes expansion in time, which has been the basis for the conception of the musical work since the eighteenth century, certainly since Beethoven."[15] Similarly, in the music of Stravinsky and Debussy there occurs a "dissociation of time," "because it avoids the dialectical confrontation with the musical progress of time."[16] In this music "there is no 'end,' the composition ceases as does the picture upon which the viewer turns his back."[17] Similarly, "one of the most outstanding characteristics of Schoenberg's later style is that it no longer permits conclusions; with increasing frequency the closing of a work falls upon the weak beat of the measure; it becomes no more than a breaking-off."[18] Movement and "end" having been abrogated, music becomes "compressed into a moment, [which] is valid as an eruptive revelation of negative experience."[19] But this moment, which was "the seismographic registration of traumatic shock,"[20] could be recorded musically so long as that shock was felt; when the trauma became so overpowering as no longer to be registered, then the moment of shock wore off and it could no longer even be expressed. This is the situation with our so-called new music. What were musical moments in Schoenberg are now sheer instants in the new music, instantaneous fragments of time that allow of no expansion and permit nothing to be sustained. They can only overwhelm with their sheer physicality of sound. This music is the unthinking image of our lifetime, when the experience of the *Angst* of time is all the more menacing as it is quite deliberately suppressed and rarely admitted to. Everybody must succeed in having a good time for fear of being permanently in fear. That is perhaps the real reason why music expressive of *Angst* can no longer be composed: the fear has sunk too deep for conscious expression, and so it can no longer be given its equivalent in musical time.

The end of time in music is simultaneously the end of musical time. No time can now have the shape and form of music. No movement can now unfold as a "musical" development; no moment can have the intense significance of a "musical" moment. It is a time that cannot be given a musical ending any more. It has become too unruly to be composed and brought to a harmonic cadential close. A time without music cannot complete itself or conclude, for it has no end in itself. Its history does not develop, and it knows neither pauses nor finales; it remains inconclusive, suspended in doubt about itself. Yet, this history does not end, either; it is there suspended in time without end, neither starting nor stopping.

Within social entropy, when history does not move, the time of individual lifetimes also stagnates and peters out. It too can have no end. Not even death is any longer an end; it is merely an incidental breaking-off. There is no time now for the slow and painfully protracted business of dying that human beings must carry through in life; hence, nobody can be prepared for that end when it comes, or even know it as the end. It is a time of sheer survival in an existence that is already post-mortem in that it is after any meaning that can be given to death. And because death is now meaningless life is without a real end.

Faust's end, which is no proper death either, also has its exact correlate in music. If we listen closely we can hear the sound of that end, not as a dying fall, falling gently away into darkness and silence—but as an anguished "death chord." "If Beethoven developed a musical essence out of nothingness in order to be able to redefine it as a process of becoming, then Schoenberg in his later works destroys it as something completed."[21] In that statement from Adorno we have the exact musical equivalent of the passage of Faust right down to the very end. The Deed is precisely such a creation of essence out of Nothing, which is then redefined as the becoming of development and Progress. But as that is a contracted Deed, so it must come to its end, when it turns back on itself as something completed and destroys itself. The creative act that extracts essential being out of Nothing turns on itself in a destructive deed that wants to reduce itself back to Nothing again. But what does that mean in terms of the passage of Faust? It means that at the end that passage turns back on itself and undoes itself. Historically it means that Christian humanism, the basis of every Faust, comes to an end; that modern Progress, the basis of the modern Faust, comes to an end; it means that the Nihilism every Faust had so desperately sought to suppress has visibly emerged in history. But that Nihilism is not a new time; it is the old time over again, but this time revealing itself and being realized under the aspect of its nothingness. That is the real meaning of destruction as a process of reduction, the deed whereby the Deed undoes itself.

That other deed by which the Deed undoes itself is not yet fully known to us; it remains nameless, so at best we can speak of it as a "deed without a name." Yet, Faust waits for the sound of it as for his "death chord," for without it he cannot end. And he longs for that release from his endless ends which do not permit him to make an end of himself. Faust can neither break off nor break. He waits for that end to come to him "just as Lulu in the world of total illusion longs for nothing but her murderer and finally finds him in that sound, so does all harmony of unrequited happiness long for its fatal chord as the cipher of fulfillment."[22] Faust's fatal "death chord" will come to him precisely as the cipher of fulfillment that is found in murder. But who is that murderer to be? Who will strike that death blow? Who will do the Deed that undoes all others? And what will that blow sound like? We know already that it is a chord and not a solitary tone. It is not the high G on the cello, held in a long *fermata* "that abides as a light in the night" and is followed by the silence in which its absence still resounds its presence. But what is that silence when Faust speaks no more, the silence of his passage? It is the silence not when the music fades but when it ceases, a silence of the absence of music. It is the silence of a time without music—not a still time, but one "full of sound and fury," of endless noises that are silent because they mean no more.

# PROLOGUE ON THE ENDANGERED EARTH

## I

Our present historic moment commenced in the split-second flash of a thousand suns that plunged all into darkness. In this light Man saw for the first time the real possibility of his own death. This same light has illuminated all our thought since; it is the most concrete consideration, with which all our thinking begins and to which in the end it must return. It is our Alpha and Omega, the one thing needful for our thought. Nothing that is touched by the shadow of this thought remains the same. Neither Man nor Time nor Death itself remains unaltered. All is utterly changed. And there is no ultimate security in anything.

We began this work with that as our first premise and we now return to it in our conclusion. The outstretched body of our argument, however, was the passage of Faust, that world-historic figure of finitude on whose last dramatic Act the curtain has now come down. We have come to the end of our reflections on the passage of Faust, but we have not as yet ended them. How are we to make an end? Standing at the end-point we could be tempted to look back and reflect once again backward on the whole preceding passage of reflection, but to succumb to that would mean to be trapped forever within the infinite mirrors of Faust's self-reflection. Somehow we must strive to break out of his reflective self-preoccupation and recollect ourselves as we are in the present. And this our present is a moment of ending for us as well as for Faust.

It is by no means merely coincidental that the end of the last Faust, that of Thomas Mann, coincides exactly with the onset of our present moment of ending. Both of these moments can be located historically almost at the precise point where the second of the great world wars concluded and there commenced the new cold-war era of awaiting in dread the onset of the last war of all. It might be graphically conveyed that the precise minute of the first explosion of an atomic weapon in war marked the end of Faust and the beginning of our present moment of ending. Of course, that split second in which mankind discovered its own mortality and its capacity for annihilating time as history was only the most visible physical manifestation of the whole historical process of the onset of Nihilism that was coextensive with the passage of Progress. That event itself was not the cause but merely the outstanding symptom of the decisive change in the destiny of Man. It consummated in physical terms the overwhelming incursion of annihilatory Nihilism, which had already established itself in all other dimensions of human life during and prior to the period of the wars. The total domination of men and their soullessness in uniformity, which ensued on the technological mastery of the earth—all this and much besides in the potentialities of annihilation had already been attained before it became physically possible to annihilate mankind as such. This last physical consummation was, nevertheless, the epitome of annihilation, and it itself greatly accelerated the progress of annihilating Nihilism.

Even now, more than thirty years later, we are still situated in the moment of ending inaugurated by the end of the war. Only the danger and ever-present threat of total annihilation encompass us much more so than then, for since then the means of terror have been vastly increased and their utilization and delivery perfected. Compared to this fact nothing that has since happened is worth noting; in relation to this, time has stood still. Politically the world is at a stalemate. The major powers cannot use their real power but can only maneuver inconclusively in the marginal areas still left open for the now-obsolete play of power politics. Economically the limit is being reached in productive expansion as a greater proportion of resources is wasted on armaments and related futilities. Culturally, the inroads made by the propagandistic utilizations of the communications media into the fabric of everyday life are now irreversible. Even the conquest of planetary space, which seems otherwise unprecedented, was itself a by-product of developments in armaments dating back to the last war, and the main effect of it has been to make it even easier to survey and so regulate or devastate the earth. History in this end period is moving toward a standstill, and "this static state compels the incessant and deadly repetition of what has already been accepted."[1] According to Anders, our time is terminal; it has the character not of a developing historical period or transition to another age but of an "intermezzo," an in-between-time, between the dead-line of the first atomic explosion and the dead-end of the final Apocalypse, which is now in the offing.[2] Our only hope is to postpone this end indefinitely, and so stretch out indefinitely this one contracted moment, for our present is a terminal end-moment. In Beckett's metaphor, we are now in the end-game stage of the historic play: all the moves are constrained either toward a checkmate or, as we hope, toward a stalemate. In our Faustian metaphor, the passage of Faust has reached its dead end; it has progressed to the end and come to Nothing.

This is the moment when music stops—not the moment of stillness or silence of words which "after speech reach into the silence," nor "the stillness, as a Chinese jar still moves perpetually in its stillness," the moment of timelessness Eliot could still conceive of within the Christian dispensation of an as-yet-unshattered Logos. If "only by the form, the pattern, can words or music reach the stillness," then when there is no stillness there is no music, and form or order can no longer obtain. In a formless time outside any Logos the only constants are the abstract principles of repetition and chance, the formal principles of change and variation. But instead of the musical free-play of variation-form, such as even Mann could still hope for in *Doctor Faustus,* we now have exact repetitiveness—"the bad infinity of mechanical repetition"[3]—and purely random chance operative in all dimensions of existence. We experience repetitive sameness and standardized uniformity in work and leisure, and what we call freedom and creativity are only licensed random variations. And in this ever-accelerating turmoil of repetition everything changes, everyday life is forever being remodeled; but nothing happens, time does not move, history stands still. And this, too, is a stillness of death, but not—as for Eliot's Christian mystery—a still death wrapt in silence beyond the reach of life; rather, it is a death noisily prevailing in life and making of it an unliving life.

Standing in this deathly present it is possible for us now to look back and see how history came to this dead end, from what starting point it all began and by what passage it arrived at this pass. We can now see Progress as also having been a passage of reduction, a contraction of time to the limit end-point. Ours is the opposite perspective to those who stood at the beginning and hopefully looked ahead: for them time seemed to be opening up and expanding into the prospect of a future without visible end—and if they did foresee some end it was only the telos of fulfillment. From the point of view of the Faustian Deed onward time was all-expansive development, the time of an unlimited Progress. But from our end-point-of-view development was contraction, and Progress was also Nihilism. What they took to be a progressus ad infinitum to us is also a reductio ad absurdum.

It seems that the same passage of time can be seen from its two opposed ends, as though through either end of a telescope: looked at forward, it seems to have an open-ended future; looked at backward, a closed-off end. But these are not merely arbitrary perspectives on time such that one can choose one or other depending on whether one feels like being optimistic or pessimistic. Rather, they are two inherent realities of modern time, two antagonistic meanings contained within the same span of history. One is the hitherto open and visible surface reality of Progress, the time of which was conscious to the historical participants and in the light of which they proceeded to march ahead; the other is the invisible, dark unreality of the time of Nihilism, the unconscious resultant of that very consciousness. The light of Enlightenment cast its own backward shadow. It is only at the present end that the unconscious aspect of modern time is forcing itself into consciousness, though most men do all they can to repress any knowledge of it. Its symptoms are now as unmistakable as are the repetition compulsions of our time. Nihilism, our dark unknowing, is now revealing itself openly in the threat of annihilation, and nobody can shut his eyes to it any longer.

Modern time from the Deed of Faust onward is structured on these two sets of contradictory meanings, which are in effect two kinds of time, one contained within the other. We could speak of it as a dialectical unity in contradiction, for the time of development and the time of reduction are fundamentally identical. But this is not some kind of dialectical synthesis; all it means is that we can translate from one time into the other, carrying out thereby a genuine reinterpretation of meaning and not merely a verbal transference. Thus, what in progressive time is the development of Techno-logy becomes in nihilistic time the reduction of Technocracy; the mediating term of this translation is power over nature (power over nature, seen as the object external to Man the subject, becomes power over human nature internal to Man). Similarly, one can translate from Subjectivity to Subjectlessness: the mediating term here is ownership in privacy (the ownership in privacy of a subjective self becoming the subjectlessness of an ownerless self in privation). And again, Activism translates into In-activity through the mediating term of the pure act divorced from the word and thought (the act in-and-for-itself becomes purely passive). Taken together, these are the aspects of the translation of Progress into Nihilism, or, symbolically speaking, of the passage of Faust into that of Macbeth.

From the larger standpoint of world history, the duality of modern time as well as that of Progress and Nihilism might be seen as the end-products of a comprehensive Western process of Rationalization of the world, in Weber's sense. In its final stages, which define the modern world, Rationalization takes on the appearance of Progress, for it separates and liberates each sphere of society and culture to pursue its own development. Economy, politics, the sciences, individual life, art, and even religion were no longer bound to and unified by any transcendent or fixed Order, whether of theology or metaphysics, and were separated from any inherent connections with each other, and so released to undertake their free development on the principle of continuous activity (the Deed). This new temporalization gave rise to a sense of time as

Development and of history as Progress. But as the process of Rationalization increased, intensified, and moved ever closer to the "iron cage" of modern technocracy, so progressive time appeared more illusory, and gradually a static time-consciousness came uppermost. For rationalizing technocracy subdivides every activity into repeatable operations to the point where it can be pursued as a mechanical process that is, in theory, capable of being automated and carried out by computers. As activity increasingly becomes mere repetitive "computation" it is no longer capable of engendering progressive time and comes to seem to be reducing time to the point of ultimate standstill. At the same time, the overall coherence of these atomized automatic processes, each following its own blind "logic" of computation, is not only destroyed as a sociocultural whole but begins to reveal contradictions that amount to general irrationalities—"civilization as rationalized irrationality."[4] The ultimate irrationality of this incoherent system is that it is now promoting the self-annihilation of civilization, for it seems unable to generate the counter-forces necessary to arrest this process before it reaches its ultimate consummation in total annihilation.

The Faustian Deed which inaugurated the blind onrush of Progress has now become the Macbethan death-dealing "deed without a name." What name could be ascribed to that deed which would make everything nameless? What speech is adequate to that which renders all speech speechless? How can one define this indefinable, or think this unthinkable? As the individual finds it psychically impossible to imagine himself fully dead, for he has to imagine himself as still there in imagining his death, so it is almost conceptually impossible to conceive of the death of everything, for the concepts which we need to conceive it must be thought of as somehow still there when everything else is gone. It is this ultimate horror that "heart cannot conceive, or tongue name it" (*Macbeth* II.iii). As Anders points out, it is precisely because our imagination gives out in conceiving of this horror that we are impotent to do anything about it; because the danger is infinitely great it seems to us utterly unreal, whereas at a much lesser threat to ourselves we would quickly muster all our energies to deal with it.

But it is not just the unimaginable character of the "deed without a name" that paralyzes us; our apathy—we mean here that of mankind in general—comes also from the hypnotic spell of death in the historical guise of annihilating Nihilism. "Absolute negativity is in plain sight and has ceased to surprise anyone. . . . What the sadists in the camps foretold their victims, 'Tomorrow you'll be wiggling skyward as smoke from this chimney,' bespeaks the indifference of each individual life that is the direction of history."[5] The Holocaust that is only recently past bespeaks the one that is yet to come. Ours is a death-dominated terminal moment. In all manner of guises and disguises the manifestations of death are present: death as an endless repetition-compulsion, death as meaninglessness, death as alienation, death as the separation of each single self from its relation to others, death as coldness and lack of feeling in the body, death as despair and total loss of hope in the soul, death as degradation and inhumanity that is beyond help . . . the litany of the names of death tolls endlessly. And even these are the names of death that few properly know, for the ultimate insidiousness of nihilistic death is to render us oblivious to it. It makes us dead to all death, and so to itself. At a time when death is forgotten and almost rendered obsolete, the ever-present working of death is all the more assured. Ours is a *timor mortis* so great that it is afraid to know itself. Fear can go no further than when it is no longer feared.

## II

Having said all there is to be said, what is now to be done? What is to be our deed against the nameless deed of death? In the first place, it can be only the seemingly ineffectual act of Word and Thought; we must think through and speak all the hidden names of death. To call annihilatory death by its proper names is already to expose it and render it visible so that the struggle against it can begin. For us, unlike Macbeth, there must be time for such a word, for if there is not then there will be no time at all, and the "estate of the world will be now undone" (*Macbeth* V.i). The struggle against disguised death is the primary form that the fight for life can now take. It is no longer a search for eternal life, or a contest for the good life, or a striving for the free life; it is now a fight for life itself, for sheer survival.

The fight for survival must begin with thoughts and words but it cannot end there. It must eventually deploy into concrete, practical deeds. It must have a moral and political direction if it is to be effective at all. And so it is mandatory to try to frame imperatives according to which action can be undertaken. Our ground-imperative must be to ensure the survival of Man. The Kantian categorical imperative to treat men as ends in themselves must now be reduced to its ultimate limit, that of avoiding the end of Man. At its most extreme this means ensuring the survival of some men as human beings, but since each man is potentially an individual existent, there is in that the potentiality for the survival of real individuals as well. There are, thus, two basic forms of our categorical imperative calling for the survival of Man: the survival of mankind, which is the utmost extremity, and the more substantial survival of the individual.

Ideally, of course, the two imperatives ought to coincide; but that could only be so on the idealistic premise that mankind is a collection of individuals. However, mankind exists only collectively in a common social being, and though each man is a single being, yet merely as a matter of form is each such also an individual existent: it is more often the case that men are rarely true individuals. One of the main utopian goals of Progress has been precisely to achieve this ideal identity of universal Man and individual man, to transform mankind into self-determining individuals collectively unified in a bond of social solidarity. We can trace this goal from Rousseau through Kant to Marx and beyond; Goethe also shared a version of it. The vision of communist society was the ideal realization of this goal.

But here, too, the negative dialectic of Progress has produced the inverse of this ideal aspiration. Never has the antagonism between the individual and the common collectivity been sharper than at present. Universal Man presses ever more insistently for the denial of individual man as all the agencies of collective mankind suppress the means for the existence of the individual: in the name of society, the nation, the party, the creed or cause, the individual is called upon to surrender himself to the group or mass, to lose his face in the crowd. And this is taking its course at the same time as the human collectivity is itself being effaced by the inhumanity of impersonal technology.

Less than ever before can the interests of mankind be identified with those of the individual; so little have they in common, indeed, that propounding the survival of the individual as a categorical imperative might sound like mere aestheticism. And if it were the case that the collective interest could be ensured by totally disregarding the individual one, if mankind could be saved at the cost of the individual, then indeed that price would have to be paid no matter how regretfully. However, the two opposed interests, though often in conflict with each other, cannot be totally severed. We cannot abandon the individual completely and think thereby to serve mankind. And, in fact, all such communal, folkish, or communistic programs that declared the individual an obsolete historical baggage—as bourgeois egoism, or neurotic ego, or anomic rootlessness—have directly contributed to the disasters of mankind. As is now evident, the interests of mankind are partly dependent on the individual. At the present stage of collective amnesia to the common danger only the individual is capable of voicing the call for the survival of mankind, if for no other reason than because, in fact, as soon as anybody does speak out forcibly enough he is condemned by the collectivity to the solitude of individuality—for no one but a crank can fear what nobody else seems to, and only a madman would see it as threatening himself personally, and try to do something about it.

Nevertheless, it would not only be philosophically mistaken but practically foolish to try to identify completely the two kinds of interests and conjoin the two imperatives again in the unitary formula of the survival of Man *tout court.* In our present world the distance between universality and individuality has widened immeasurably. We must now live with that gulf, and in that sense accept it; we can no longer hope that it may be closed over as it once was in the koinon of the polis, or in the bosom of the church, or in the Gemeinschaft community, or even as in the ranks of the Party. In our time the interests of the individual will all too often conflict with those of mankind, and those of us who strive for individuality will all too frequently have to make painful choices. The choice in any such dilemma must always be weighted on the side of the common good. The individual must often betray his own kind for the sake of others who will not even be capable of understanding his sacrifice. Nevertheless, the imperative for the survival of the individual can be pursued in parallel with that for the survival of mankind even if only as a small minority interest which in the short run might make no difference to the greater interest. It will very much tend to be a solitary endeavor carried on by the few who feel themselves personally impelled to it. And vice versa: working for the greater cause of the collective need not markedly improve the prospects for individual existence. On the contrary, it is likely that the mass action required by the struggle for the survival of mankind will demand an initial sacrifice of individual differences that in some respects will go counter to individual survival.

Considerations of sober realism require a clearheaded and modest appraisal of any expectations to be derived from a linking of the two polarized imperatives. One must look suspiciously on those who promise to attain both a change in the condition of mankind and a liberation of the individual, who expect to achieve both the peace of nations and a moral renewal, both the pacification of existence and the overcoming of one-dimensionality. As a practical stance for the immediate present, instead of seeking to unify the extreme imperatives it were better to separate them, to seek to achieve something independently at both ends. For these are limit-principles that govern the two polarities of Man's being, the most general and the most particular. In the extremity of our present moment it is essential that we aim at the most limited of goals at the extreme limits of being, the goals of sheer survival. The present time does not afford us the luxury of larger ambitions or more expansive hopes; it brings our endeavor down to the barest minimal requirements.

Thus, the two extreme imperatives of survival provide the limit-conditions of a new minimal politics and morality. The basic questions once asked in politics and morals, when human possibilities were so much more open and when Man felt secure, have now in our parlous state to give way to ultimate questions that compel the very rock-bottom of answers. "To be or not to be, that is the question," both for humanity and for the individual. But in neither case must that question be taken in its simplest common-sense sense of choosing to continue to live or to commit suicide. In any case, mankind is not a willing agent, so it has not the capacity for choosing real suicide; since it is not an agent capable of willing its own death, it can merely succumb to a self-created fatality, as Anders has so cogently argued. Nevertheless, "to be or not to be" is the basic unanswerable question for mankind as well, for its continued being has been placed in question. And it is with this question hanging as a sword of Damocles over its head for perpetuity that humanity must develop in response, not an answer which will finally resolve the question one way or the other, but a way of living with the question, of maintaining a questionable existence fraught with the ultimate problematic of being or not-being.

Such are the basic principles for a minimal politics and morality, which will no longer constitute a politics or morality in the classical sense, that is, one setting out the conditions of a good or free society or a virtuous or happy life. Ours are limit-laws covering only the essential minimum. There is much in both moral and political life that they do not embrace, and many worthwhile goals that are intermediary between the two extremes of survival, which we have left out of consideration because they demand much more than this bare minimum. Our two imperatives need not be in conflict with most of the other moral and political values that make up the more ordinary callings, creeds, and causes in which men of different persuasions are still engrossed and to which some are genuinely dedicated. However, insofar as our imperatives have now become primary, and because they serve the most universal interests of all men, they will have to be given priority above the particular ideal interests of any other goals. As Andrei Sakharov has declared: "I believe that the problem of lessening the danger of annihilating humanity in a nuclear war carries an absolute priority over all other considerations."[6]

Such a stance will inevitably lead to conflicts of interest in which only the most level-headed and resolute of men will be willing to grant precedence to the greater interest. Those who are still embroiled in fighting the old evils and upholding the good old causes will be hard put to it to reorient their thinking and feeling so as to realize that these have now become secondary considerations. That few are willing to see the issue of priorities in these terms became apparent in the near-total swing, of the anti-war movement during the last decade, away from opposing nuclear war to opposing neo-colonial wars like those in Vietnam. The latter appeared such an immediate and pressing concern that it almost completely diverted attention from the ultimate concern—a limited evil always appears so much more real than an absolute one. The radical student movement also all too frequently served to sidetrack the concerns of the younger generation away from tangible dangers toward utopian aspirations.

The older moral and political values, beliefs, ideologies, and languages, which we have inherited from the periods prior to the totally endangered world, often stand in the way of any new morality or politics capable of facing up to this danger. Men are suffering from a near-total failure of consciousness, an inability to conceive of or properly imagine their new situation, because their powers of conceptualization and imagination are still so fixated in earlier mentalities. As Anders argues, the moral and political "world" they subjectively inhabit is out of phase with the real world in which they find themselves. This disparity means that their subjective moral and political "world" is itself devalued though it is still adhered to, and that it eventually must come to be experienced as somehow unreal or phony, if not as outright ideology.

This is why it is not so much the old values in themselves that are responsible for our failure of consciousness or conscience but, rather, that they are being maintained in a devalued state. It is a characteristic symptom of Nihilism that something should be maintained without really being upheld. Moral and political Nihilism reveals itself in the lip-service paid to morality and politics without any commitment. And this leads to a pervasive de-politicization and de-moralization that is not the decisive rejection of politics, such as is found in pacifism or anarchism, or denial of morality such as those who are consciously immoral or amoral might practise. De-politicization is inactivity or apathy in politics, the passive acceptance of the prevailing system or the equally passive dreams of overthrowing it. De-moralization is similarly a denial of responsibility; evils occur and injustices are perpetrated that everybody regrets, but nobody feels himself to be responsible for, so nobody is guilty.

This abjuring of guilt and responsibility is perhaps the most insidious stumbling-block to the emergence of a new conscience capable of upholding the imperatives for survival. Nobody feels himself responsible for preparing and maintaining the means of total terror. Everybody who plays his small part in this universal conspiracy feels himself to be merely carrying out his own small mundane job, whose overall effects he cannot oversee, and so he cannot be held accountable for anything that may eventuate. And all of us feel, perhaps correctly but nevertheless culpably, that this situation of being prepared for annihilation is part of an accepted condition about which nothing can be done, that it has become as immutable as a law of nature. Though we know it need not be so, this knowledge makes no difference; we feel it anyway. It is a condition of moral and political denial of conscience that is without precedent in human affairs, for which our traditions of moral and political thinking provide no guidance. Even Kant's thinking, of whose terms we have here temporarily availed ourselves, is otherwise of little relevance, for though we use his terms we cannot mean them fully in his sense. We speak of categorical imperatives, formal principles, limit-laws, etc., but we do so only by metaphorically altering their meaning so that they apply to our altered consciences. In our situation a categorical imperative acts as a law of survival, not an abstract rule of duty; hence, it is also akin to a Hobbesian law of nature.

The real problem for us is not to discover or state these categorical laws of survival, which everybody instinctively knows anyway, but, rather, how to make them operative. The difficulty is not one of knowing what to do but of finding a way to do it. And this once again points to the inherent difference between the way we experience the fundamental moral and political problem and the way such problems were experienced in the past. Before, the problem was always largely one of knowing what to do; rarely was there any insurmountable difficulty in doing what one knew one had to do. Any difficulties that did arise could invariably be ascribed to individual failings—to weakness of will, lack of courage, man's fallen nature. Today we can no longer resort to such escape clauses. It is no longer the case that individuals when presented with the test fail to give of their best, or allow temptation to divert them, for in fact individuals are never presented with such testing occasions. There never arises a critical juncture where they are called upon to choose or refuse. Somehow men find themselves in a situation that seemingly has always been there and so appears unalterable, though they know that it was not there only a short time ago. History, society, the state seem to be operating behind their backs on higher priorities than their own. Thus, conditions have been allowed to arise which though inimical to all men are nevertheless desired and planned for by most men working through their own extra-human agencies. Men are trapped within their own systems. The real problem is how to escape this trap, how to do anything toward that which we all know needs doing and most of us desire to do. If this moral-political problem is insoluble, it is so for reasons never before encountered, which is why no previous system of ethics or politics can be of any guidance to us in this respect. Thus it is that in our time the basic moral-political question "What is to be done?" takes on not only a new urgency but also a new meaning. For we know what has to be done, but we do not know how to go about doing it nor do we know if it can be done at all: we are faced with the necessity of acting in a situation where we do not know whether any action is practically possible.

We can exemplify the workings of this dilemma quite clearly by briefly running through the attempts that have been made to distance or to remove the danger of annihilation, all of which we can at this point say have failed in achieving their primary aim. Since 1945 at least four kinds of endeavor have been launched either to achieve partial disarmament or to safeguard against an accidental outbreak of the holocaust, or ultimately totally to defuse, if not ban, nuclear weapons. At least four distinct types of political body have been involved: attempts made by all the states acting collectively through some supra-national body; attempts by the dominant politicians of the two super-powers in bilateral conferences; attempts by disarmament movements calling on the masses to compel their governments to action; and attempts by colloquia of scientists and technologists seeking to reach an understanding apart from their political masters and to exert their influence on them. None of these endeavors has significantly lessened the danger.[7]

It almost appears as if for the moment all possible approaches have been tried and that all have been found wanting. So what is now to be done? It would be mere futile speculation to try to dream up new schemes in vacuo. For the moment, the only honest answer is to admit that we do not know what else can be done, that, in spite of courageous efforts by individuals and some groups, nothing significant has been achieved, and that in the immediate future, too, we must fear that nothing will be achieved. The longer it is that nothing disastrous happens, the less likely it is that anything will be done to lessen the possibility of disaster, for people become inured to the danger and act as if it had already passed. They behave like the man in the well-known joke who dropped off a skyscraper and was heard to say as he passed the tenth floor: "So far so good." In this respect one must invoke here also Anders' law of psychological inertia: the greater the danger the more unimaginable it is, so the less the fear. The last time people experienced the frisson of annihilation worldwide was during the Cuban missiles crisis, but that was very quickly forgotten, and because it passed so painlessly and so soon, it reinforced the illusory feeling of reassurance. Since then the missiles are even closer overhead, and yet few look up to see if they are coming.

A question mark hangs over mankind: our greatest problem is for us at present an insoluble one. Marx was mistaken in supposing that an age sets itself only such problems as it is capable of solving. Every age has some problems that are insoluble for it and which only another age can overcome. It would be highly characteristic, and therefore not unexpected, that our insoluble problem should be the practical, technological-political one of how to cope with the ultimate fruits of Progress.

The suggestion has been made that since our problem is largely technological, we must look to technology for a solution. Perhaps future advances in defense against nuclear weapons will make obsolete the policy of strategic deterrence and render useless the existing stocks of nuclear weapons. Perhaps future weapons of defense—laser-beam guns, armed satellites, or whatever else is even now being dreamed up on the drawing boards—will in a short time make it impossible for any atomic bomb to reach its target. On this line of thinking, our problem will disappear of its own accord without people having to do anything to counter it; technology will of itself develop its answers to its own problems. Unfortunately, this is wishful thinking, for whatever improvements are made in nuclear defense, it is certain that similar improvements will be made in attack as well. Each side has to ensure that it retains the capacity for massive deterrence, since if one side has this capacity and the other side no longer has it then the balance of terror is lost and the "winning" side can dictate terms to the other. Hence, both sides will do all they can to prevent a situation that is disadvantageous to themselves. Given the nature of present military-political policy, there can be no purely technological solution to the problem of annihilation. And for this policy to change, more than mere technological changes will be required.

Given the full scope and extent of the nuclear problem and its central place in our civilization, it is almost certain that it will not be solved in our lifetime. We can only hope, and some of us might even pray, that in the future it will be solved somehow, in a way perhaps unimaginable to us now, and that nothing disastrous will happen till then. We must bide our time. We cannot conceive what kind of time it will be when the danger no longer threatens, for this time is beyond the ken of our present moment and will constitute a new opening on time itself. It could not be simply another historical age after our own, for the change in the nature of historical time wrought by the present alteration in the status of Man is decisive and irrevocable. The kind of time it might be, when the possibility of the death of Man is there without the ever-present danger of its happening—it is like the vision of the other life, only given us to glimpse through a glass darkly.

For the moment we have to abide in the knowledge that we can do nothing radical enough to be truly effective. And there lies our great ethical paradox: we are enjoined by our basic categorical imperative to do that which we know is at present a practical impossibility. The deliverance of our practical reason is thus at odds with our moral will. Here, too, as in Kant, the will must prevail. We must act as if we could ensure the survival of Man, knowing full well that we cannot, for it is only if we do act on this assumption that we can still maintain ourselves as human beings. By acting for the survival of Man we affirm our humanity. And we hope, in the absence of knowledge, that on this issue, too, as Weber puts it, "man would not have attained the possible unless time and again he had reached out for the impossible."[8]

What is apparent to us even now is that the solution of the problem of the survival of Man cannot be found on its own, for we know that the reason why to us it is now insoluble is that it is deeply immersed in the constitution of our time, bound up with other problematical conditions that are now seemingly unalterable. There is, as we know, a fatal nexus between the greatest danger of all and the need for a feeling of "security," such that when they are threatened with annihilation, men feel themselves secure only when they in turn can annihilate. That is the policy euphemistically known as deterrence. But this "security" does not mean safety; it means the unsecure preservation of the given status quo. And, as we have revealed it, the status quo of the present is the nexus of Progress and Nihilism, and this most men are blindly committed to defending in the specific form or manifestation in which it presents itself to them. For most people, progress is the expanding technological apparatus they believe will guarantee them a better life. At the same time, many are half-aware that this life that Progress gives them is joined in equal measure to a death in annihilation also being prepared for them. It is widely known that as many scientists and technicians work on armaments as work on productive enterprises, and even those who do not know this certainly accept the consequences of it. How many workers would be fearful for their jobs if the arms race were to stop? And that is only the most obvious and generally accepted example of how our progressive way of life is indissolubly linked to a nihilistic way to death.

This is why it would require fundamental changes in people's consciousness and, preceding these, wholesale changes in our system based on Progress before anything could be achieved toward removing the threat of physical annihilation or any of the other obvious symptomatic manifestations of Nihilism. As the means of nuclear annihilation are themselves the products of technology, so the problem of annihilation is only the most salient feature of the problem of Techno-logy as such. The dimensions of this problem are not merely technical or scientific but also industrial, managerial, political, and cultural. It will require restructuring and revising not only relations between men and machines but between men and all their own products and, ultimately, between men and nature. This is why it is not a problem with any immediate present solution, which partly helps to explain why the problem of annihilation also has no present solution.

Even though for the moment there are all these insurmountable difficulties, yet we are obliged to make a start to overcome them. Our imperatives do lead us into action, even when this action is only speech or symbolic action, for to speak is to act—provided that other people can be made to listen. This is where the role of the individual in publicly voicing the common danger is indispensable. Only true individuals are at present capable of openly and fearlessly speaking out for the survival of mankind. Anyone who does so risks incurring, at the very least, the kind of obloquy of the mass media and the authorities who represent and rule the masses that amounts to ostracism from common life and consignment to the prison of isolation.[9] Most men would rather die together than live in disfavor alone, which is why so few are willing to take that risk.

Yet in that role itself there is an appalling paradox which serves to render it anything but heroic. The most vital interest of mankind is at present only of real concern to a small and relatively unorganized minority of individuals, and this fact almost ensures the futility of its pursuit in an imperative form. For anything to be voiced by individuals, who are automatically suspect, is for it to be disqualified. The vast majority have been so conditioned to reject any minority cause that even if their own best interests were thereby being served they would still be inclined to reject it. This is why heroic gestures and denunciatory pronouncements are likely to be counter-productive. The individual who wishes to speak effectively is as much troubled by the difficulty of what to say, and when and to whom to say it, as he is by the difficulty of what to do. Speech in this respect is no easier than action.

Nevertheless, the individual is obliged by his basic imperatives to speak and act even in the absence of any certain belief in his efficacy.

The conviction that it is the only right course and the hope that somehow, at some time, perhaps in ways unknown to himself, it may make a difference must carry him through. The feeling that he both furthers and hinders the interests of mankind will be his most poignant realization of the conjunction and opposition of the two fundamental imperatives: that for the survival of mankind and that for the survival of the individual. Standing out as an individual risks compromising the cause of mankind, but upholding that cause requires standing out as an individual. To this paradox there is no solution except in action.

III

To speak at all the individual must first ensure his own survival, so he has to act on the imperative of survival as an individual quite independently of the imperative for the survival of mankind. But this does not mean that he is acting for his own ends alone. The imperative of survival as an individual is in most respects the opposite of the principle of self-interest, the bourgeois *principium individuationis.* As a matter of historical fact, it is only in an age of rampant self-interest and the prevalence of a corrupt individualism that the individual is faced with the problem of survival. Individualism pursued in the guise of self-interest is really a struggle for identity; it is no longer profit but recognition and power which are at stake. Profit and property, the leading motives of bourgeois individualism, have in our corporate society given way to the trappings of success, to rank, status, and prestige. Since in our society only power can secure identity, the struggle for recognition has become a constant battle for "power after power, that ceaseth only in Death." The ultimate success is obtained by those within whose power it lies to dispose of the fate of mankind by being able to command its annihilation.

The individualistic ego is simply a measure of the need for such an identity and the drive for power necessary to secure it. That hypertrophy of the ego which used to be called egoism—a term still resounding with rational overtones—has now become a psychic pathology that can only be called egomania. To some degree we all suffer from it, and the common expression "going on an ego trip" is the implicit recognition of this. What is now currently known as undergoing an identity-crisis is usually nothing more than a loss of power or the first stirrings of impotency that make people feel their own nothingness. Loss of sexual power is particularly significant, for it is the symbolic form of a loss of ego-power. He who loses his power loses his identity; he literally becomes a non-entity, a nobody, for he has nothing else in himself on which to fall back. Individualism is the absence of any inner entity, and thus is the absence of a real existence.

Individualism is annihilatory, for in his struggle for power the ego-driven individualist lives only by the symbolic death of other egos. As a variant on Canetti's paranoid survivor, the individualist feeds himself fat on the symbolic corpses of his enemies and so gives himself an illusion of substantiality. Demotion, degradation, humiliation, and character assassination are some of the symbolic forms of the "murder" of others. It is in these terms that the permanent battle to the death is carried on in boardrooms, conferences, and other chambers and corridors of power. He who is ambitious has to keep on "murdering" his presumed enemies—that is, anybody who is likely to be a threat to himself—not only to get to the top and stay there but to renew the thrill of power in survival and so vouchsafe his sense of his own existence. We all know who such a person is because to some degree it is always ourselves. Nobody can be above it all.

Who, then, is the individual in an age of rampant individualism? It is he who does not seek an identity on these terms, who can therefore disengage himself from the struggle for success, for recognition and supremacy, sufficiently to develop himself as a real entity. He is the nobody and nothing who is concerned with his own humane existence as an individual. Not engaging in the struggle for power out of an inner necessity, he has no desire to "kill" others; at most he may defend himself from being "killed." To survive in society the individual cannot completely refuse to play the socially sanctioned roles, but he plays them out in full awareness that these are imposed on him. He refuses to acknowledge them as identities, and so shows them up for what they are. If superiors have to be obeyed it is only because they hold powers that it might be suicidal not to acknowledge, not because they are superior, and official inferiors are not for that reason inferior. The firm separation of self and social role is but one of the many strategies of true individual survival.

It is true in principle that there can be no entity without some identity, and that all identity entails recognition, which has to be won even when it is freely given. Ideally, the individual might secure his identity through open and free acknowledgment by his fellows, but such an ideal outcome presupposes a form of society that is no longer in existence—if it ever was. In present society, where there is a pervasive and wholesale struggle for identity through continual competition according to the prescribed rules and where no two people are ever completely free to grant each other acknowledgment or respect, the opposite of the ideal outcome prevails. In such a situation the individual can only affirm his identity by seemingly paradoxically rejecting all other identities offered him. He rejects all bogus identities for the sake of an existence or entity that might under future conditions make possible a real identity. At a time when no such real identity is possible the individual can only exist in an incognito or have a negative identity; his, to borrow a term from Keats, is a purely negative-capability. This is why so often in modern literature the individual is portrayed as the outsider, the criminal or clown, someone on the margin of society.

Anyone who finds himself an individual is already a survivor whose existence is marginal, for he has had somehow to survive the murderous struggle for recognition waged all around him by the power-driven egotistic individualists. To have survived their onslaughts, without either going under or succumbing by being forced to take part in the combat, is in itself a rare achievement which in every case owes much to sheer good luck. And no such survivor ever escapes unimpaired. How much damage—intellectual, moral, psychic, and even physical—he sustains is largely a function of the society in which he finds himself, for some societies are still much more tolerant of the individual than others are. In every case the imperative of individual survival is largely a self-chosen and self-imposed one; in no society is it sanctioned. Thus this imperative of survival is also one that has to be acted on in the face of the impossible. It seems impossible to escape the prevalent struggle for power or the resultant impositions of uniformity and conformity, for anyone who is even suspected of seeking to do so comes to be looked on—not without a degree of unacknowledged envy—as someone who thinks himself "special" and who seems to be taking an unfair advantage. Hence, what the officials do not enforce will be exacted by one's neighbors out of sheer *Schadenfreude*. Individuals have become our social lepers.

No very cogent arguments can any longer be given as to why anyone should wish to uphold the imperative of individual survival, given not only the inescapable penalties of social failure and indignity, or worse, that this incurs, but given also that one can no longer seek succor from the beliefs that upheld the individual in adversity in the past. The orthodox religious stalwarts of implicit trust in God or escape into immortality are no longer available to the modern individual, nor are the traditional humanist supports of undying fame or stoic integrity or rational autonomy or even the moral righteousness of an absolute. In the absence of the old ideals the modern individual has hardly any self-justification. And to the degree that he discovers the purely ideological function now served by these old ideals in their debased form, and so frees himself from them, to that degree he becomes bereft of anything on which to base himself firmly. The individual appears to himself as a self-cancelling anachronism, a survivor from the past who is self-condemned to his own extinction as he realizes the irrelevance of that past from which he derives. Individual existence is thus at present a highly paradoxical predicament, a questionable existence fraught with the basic unanswerable question: to be or not to be. And it is difficult to live as a question mark. There are few precedents to act as guides.

At the inauguration of Western individuality, Socrates, its founding martyr, had pronounced the basic imperative "Know thyself"; now at the end, when the question is of sheer survival as an individual, the imperative for the individual must be restated as "Recollect thyself." Between "knowing," in the classical and largely philosophical sense, and "recollecting," in a sense we are now beginning to try to specify, intervenes the whole history of the individual. There is an extreme difference between these two formulations: instead of seeking to *know*, in the sense of "disclose by intellect or intuition," an inherent ineradicable self, the modern individual must seek to establish a sense of selfhood through a self-recollection that cannot come from knowledge alone but, rather, through a kind of resolution. He who resolves to be an individual undertakes the process of recollecting himself through a taking stock of the past, a gathering together in the present, and a bracing of effort for the future. This is a process that can never be complete and that might be forfeited at any instant, so that no one is ever in a position to say that he has recollected himself, even less so than he might have been in a position to say that he knew himself. Self-recollecting is a temporal endeavor through which self-presence is established, but that self-presence lasts only as long as the sense of the present and of presence is sustained. Like any state of self-balancing, it is precariously poised.

Recollection is a temporal endeavor also in that it seeks to establish a present. The present is not given, but has to be sustained through a hold on duration that will coalesce into a present moment. Without such a hold the present is merely a fleeting interval, an immediate specious present without endurance. Anyone who tries to listen to music intently knows that he has to grasp a full musical moment, for otherwise the music appears merely as discrete fragments of themes, or even totally disjointed as odd sounds. And during the time he is in possession of the musical moment, his own musical present endures as that moment. Something analogous is true of the moment in an individual's lived life or, ultimately, of the historical moment shared by mankind as a whole. In each case the present moment has to be grasped and made to cohere in order for it to endure; otherwise it will scatter and reduce itself to a fleeting nothing.

The reductive process of historical Nihilism on time acts on the present precisely in this way: it narrows the present down to a chaos of evanescent events. In temporal terms this is what it means to say that history is running down, disappearing, or ending—historical time cannot be consolidated into an historical present as it becomes more and more difficult to define the present as a meaningful moment, as saeculum or transition, tradition or destiny, or whatever other way men had of imparting a meaning to their own time for themselves. And what is observed in general on the level of history is itself made up of and reflected in the particular present lives of single men. Men lose their hold on the present moment because of their very absorption in the immediate present, which comes from their drive to rush through it as quickly as possible so as to reach some goal in the future, which when it is attained is made equally illusory. The historical onrush of Progress allows men no enduring present even in their private lives, for whatever they do is directed to future goals. Those who attempt to stem this onrush by an impossible effort to recover a lost past are through their reactionary endeavor also releasing their purchase on the present. This whole temporal reduction expresses "the dawning ahistorical character of a condition in which men experience themselves solely as objects of opaque processes and, torn between sudden shock and sudden forgetfulness, are no longer capable of a sense of temporal continuity."[10]

The present which never endures as a moment is lost, and consequently men lose an awareness of themselves, of their own self-presence. Our previous characterization of the obliviousness of most men to the very tangible dangers surrounding them is symptomatic of a more complex oblivion of the present. With this in mind, as a way of urging the recovery of our own self-presence in the present we propound for the individual the cardinal imperative of "Recollect thyself." One can only hope that eventually such a recollection may become the guiding principle for social life as well. For the individual what is at stake is not merely present time but his very self. This, too, has to be recovered or attained, for just as in listening to a piece of music the self focuses itself in the inner silence of concentration on the musical moment, so, too, in grasping one's present moment one is also attaining to a self as co-present within it. The effort at self-definition is coextensive with that of a definition of present time: "I am" has always to be said in the present tense.

If there is no present, then there can be no past or future. Without a present focus and orientation the history of the past ceases to have any meaning and its truth becomes relative to one's purely accidental standpoint. And the future that has stopped being a projection of present concern is as indifferent as the future course of nature. Truth itself is lost when it has no locus in the present, when men are no longer committed to discovering the one truth by which they can speak, think, and act. Where anything goes and only the marketplace of ideas can adjudicate success and failure, there is neither true nor false; all is permitted and all is believed.

The most urgent task the individual is called on to perform at present is that of recollection. Recollection must be distinguished from mere reflection. The intellectual is the individual who is content to reflect without taking his real self to be involved in his own reflections, without calling himself or his role into question, as if reflection as pure thought were its own self-validation. And just as the thinking individual can no longer be a mere reflective intellectual, so the creative individual can no longer be the artist who simply reflects his surroundings. Art as mimesis of its time is no longer adequate to the recollective task, whether it be the art of the culture industry which "endlessly reduplicates the surface of reality"[11] in a purely mechanical mode of reproduction, or intellectual art that reproduces the bleakness and emptiness of present reality by its own abstract formalism, or any other art that is merely symptomatic of present conditions. Only an art that is aware of its own situation and of its problematic relation to its time might begin to be recollective, but such an art would have to be also capable of thought, and so it would begin to break down the absolute division between artist and thinker. Thinking and art that are not in their opposed ways merely reflective—intellectualizing or mimetic—might begin to approach each other. What such a rapprochement would be like, however, cannot be defined in advance.

Recollection also cannot be defined in advance, for "definitions acquire their full meaning in the course of an historical process,"[12] and we have just arrived at that point in time where we can begin to undertake such a definition. We have arrived at the need for defining recollection at the end of a long passage of mere reflection, largely intellectual. Let there be no mistake about it: this work, as its title proclaims, does not pass beyond reflection. Nevertheless, having arrived at the end of the passage of reflection we are now brought by the passage itself to the point of looking out beyond it. We can begin to get a glimpse of what recollection might be if we try to recollect what this passage of reflection has itself achieved toward this end. Recollecting this must not be a mere re-reflection; it must not re-run the passage and simply repeat it in a summary form. The aim of our recollective thought is to bring the passage of reflection of Faust, that is, of Modernity, up to the present, and make it yield something toward constituting this present moment and affirming our self-presence in it.

Such recollective thought can only proceed in the way opposite to that of traditional philosophy: it cannot seek for universal abstractions, the meta-physical grounds of all Being, but must fix on the salient concrete realities of the present time. The point of departure for a post-metaphysical and, in some senses, post-philosophic thought are the realities that everybody knows about but nobody really knows. These are the phenomena of transcendental present importance, those that determine the consciousness of the time in a way that is unconscious to those subject to them. Atomic weapons and the other key instruments of our technological civilization are among the most important objects for us, as are our modern media and everything that determines our everyday living conditions and the global political situation. Interpreting the real meaning and import of these phenomena is the task of a thought that sees in these concrete realities the real universals of the present. This meaning is not registered in the official languages commonly used to speak about such things. It is, rather, precisely the hidden, secret, silent aspect of these languages, for it is precisely that Other which these languages cover over and suppress from consciousness and so relegate to the sphere of the unconscious—so much so that at present people's unconscious is possibly filled less with sexual or any of the other past taboos than with the current inhibitions against being fully aware of one's real conditions and the terrors and loathings they must inspire.

A mode of thinking that wishes to recollect the present so as to achieve self-recollection must apply itself to eliciting the hidden significance of the dominant realities and so realizing them in its language. Its striving to realize the concrete in language runs parallel to that of modern literature, and, by extension, of the other arts. Literature and the arts are usually first to register the changed meanings in the realities of our time, so thought invariably owes its instigation to such prior realizations. The thinker usually follows where the artist has led the way, but he covers the same ground with a more thorough and systematic attention to its details and its contours. His conceptual tools and techniques are better suited to the kind of study that the literary man is not called upon to undertake, and because his concepts refer back to the whole philosophical or scientific tradition, the thinker is better able to place the meaning of present events in relation to the past. He can recollect the present in the process of recollecting the past and projecting the future as well. But to do this the thinker is called upon to philosophize in the concrete while still relying on the traditions of the abstract. With a degree of poetic license, one might speak of such recollective thinking as a new "metaphysics of the concrete." The example of thinkers such as Adorno and Anders shows how this might be undertaken.

Hence, an artistic element is indispensable for any thought that seeks to direct itself to the concrete presence of things. The modern thinker, like the artist, is also confronted by the problem of communication, which is primarily a problem of language. The difficulties of speaking amid the corruption of all language which forced writers like Kafka, Canetti, and Beckett into the self-enclosed fastness of the hermetic work of art are the same difficulties that forced thinkers like Adorno into a hermetic philosophy. Such a thinker can no longer take himself as the philosopher of the tradition, enunciating perennial truths in a language of clearly defined words. Nor can he appeal to a universality of Reason in overcoming incomprehension, which at present is inevitable, and which he cannot blame on the irrationality of others. In effect, he must give up the ideal of universal comprehension, what Habermas calls "undistorted communication," even among rational men. Like the artist, the thinker must be aware that he is constituting a "language" in the sense of a discourse of his own, and that he has to cope with all the problems incumbent on anyone who wishes to have his language understood, as well as the added difficulty of getting the thoughts expressed in this language accepted as truths. It is only on these conditions that the thinker can hope to develop what Horkheimer has called "independent thought."

Since "the need to lend a voice to suffering is a condition of all truth,"[13] it follows that thought is always bound to language and language in turn is bound to art. If poetry is emotion recollected in tranquillity, thought, too, is a recollection of words for suffering. This entails finding one's own words and gaining a voice. Under present conditions such a voice no longer articulates an individualized mode of speech within a common language, for no language, with the possible exception of the most basic words, has any commonness, and all publicly understood languages are mere ephemeral jargon or languages of publicity. A "voice" cannot even be taken literally as a mode of speech; it will almost invariably have to be a mode of writing, the private form of intercourse among individuals. This written voice is thus bound to constitute a discourse or language of privacy. The source of the thinker's words will, of course, have to be common, deriving from the available stock of terms that itself descends from the once-flourishing common languages, as well as from the currently available jargons. But the discourse conveyed by the thinker's "misuse" of the commonly available language will constitute a speech which, as a language of privacy, will be restricted to those capable of entering into it.

Provided that it is not a formally conceived "private-language" such as the well-known one Wittgenstein outlined, a language of privacy can come to be understood by others. One might put it in general terms that the capacity to understand such a language depends on the possession of that "private experience" on which the language is based. To understand a text couched in a language of privacy one has to share, or be capable of entering into, the meaningful experiences—feelings or thoughts—of the individual whose voice expresses them. And this requires that to a considerable degree one must oneself already be an individual, for he who has a capacity for transforming common suffering into private experiences already has the inner subjectivity of individuality. On the other hand, from the point of view of the writer finding one's voice means creating a language in which the meanings of one's private experiences can be constituted. These meanings are not given prior to the language that expresses them, but neither are they created by the language itself. The language articulates what is already there, not as an altogether unexpressed given but as a meaningful content prearticulated in a clichéd form, that is, in a socially reified or ideological or some other stultified manner. Destroying those clichés, formulae, and stock concepts will be part of the effort to achieve a new articulation and so to constitute another language. The key to this destructive effort will be the articulation of the unspoken, that which is tacitly assumed or suppressed in the old languages, the Silence which, if spoken, will destroy them from inside. The reader comes to understand the new articulation if he can follow this destructive process and, at least during the course of reading, share in it.

At a time of wholesale annihilation, thought must be pushed with ever-greater intensity to this effort of critical destruction. This destruction is directed in the first place against the manifest symptoms of annihilation, but equally so against the tendencies that serve to screen the prevalence of annihilation, such as the residues of traditionalism that try to preserve a false veneer of normality by perpetuating the comforting beliefs that really nothing much has changed—that evil is always only evil no matter in what form it comes, that men are as bad as they have always been, that history is still only a slaughterhouse, and all the negative comforts that tell us that no matter how difficult things seem they will go on as they always have. But destructive thought must also direct itself against the previous great modern destructions of the tradition, for these are now so widely disseminated and debased that they are prone to make us forgetful of the tradition and oblivious of the past as such, and they have become so easily accepted that they can now be presented as if they were themselves a modern counter-tradition. Even the greatest achievements of modernity are now becoming reified and turned into new mythologies which are then used to bolster up and further the prevalent processes of annihilation. Hence, critical thought must turn against the achievements of modern destruction as well; it must negate the negations without hope of any dialectically positive returns.

Destructive modern thought has much in common with destructive modern art. The thinker has much to learn from what the artists have already achieved. Still, there is a basic difference, in that the thinker's activity is conceptual: his is the procedure of constituting and deconstituting concepts, whereas the artist's is symbolic and metaphorical, the formation and deformation of imaginative structures. The difficulties of communicating a conceptual activity are no less, though different, from those of communicating an imaginative one, for it is futile to think of concepts as given rational norms that any rational mind must be able to grasp. To grasp a new concept, a new idea or theory, calls for a quantum jump of the mind comparable to the leap of imagination required to gain insight into a new art form; similarly, the destruction of a concept must be apprehended before it can be understood. Anyone who is indifferent to the problem of communicating thought will invariably not be understood as he would want to be understood. Dialogue and dialectic, the classically sanctioned modes of the communication of ideas, are themselves no longer adequate in "that immense proliferation of private languages which characterize the intellectual life of consumer capitalism."[14] In this situation, shared private experience of thought and suffering remains the basis even of intellectual intercourse.

## IV

Though the mode of recollection of the artist is very different from that of the thinker, yet in the present predicament the main subjects to be recollected are for both the same: Man, Time, and Nothing. Our predicament is precisely the one in which these fundamentals have been irrevocably put in question. The existence of Man has been placed in doubt, both on the universal and on the individual level, and the very belief in Man has been called to account. Time can no longer be assumed to keep on in the flow of its old continuities, history has been ruptured, and temporality itself is threatened with even worse disruption. The nothingness of Nihilism is upon us as death has been sacrilegiously violated, its religious mystery destroyed, its human dignity defaced, until nothing is left but the mere nothingness of annihilation forgetful of itself—the oblivion of the living dead. Macbeth's last words at the end of his passage are a fitting conclusion to this our final reduction of Man, Time, and Nothing:

> To-morrow, and to-morrow, and to-morrow,
> Creeps in this petty pace from day to day,
> To the last syllable of recorded time;
> And all our yesterdays have lighted fools
> The way to dusty death. Out, out, brief candle!
> Life's but a walking shadow, a poor player
> That struts and frets his hour upon the stage,
> And then is heard no more; it is a tale
> Told by an idiot, full of sound and fury,
> Signifying nothing.

Neither in the play nor in our time is this merely a personal condition; it is shared by all, whether they know it or not. As in the Scotland of the play—

> where nothing
> But who knows nothing, is once seen to smile;
> Where sighs and groans and shrieks that rent the air
> Are made, not mark'd; where violent sorrow seems
> A modern ecstasy; the dead man's knell
> Is there scarce ask'd for who;
> (IV.iii)

—so have these words in our time taken on a literal reality and an enormity of scope that even the genius of Shakespeare's imagination could scarcely have conceived. Violent sorrow has indeed become a modern ecstasy, and it, too, is "made, not mark'd."

Murderer or victim or mere onlooker, we have all been brought to the same pass, and from this pass there is no recovery. There is only the slow agony of survival. But in survival men can still choose to perish in oblivion or to sustain themselves in the dignity of recollection. We can still try to recollect what we are, where we are going, and what is our end. Instead of passively succumbing to a fatality, we can actively engage with our fate; instead of allowing our words to degenerate and signify nothing, we can reach out with them to a signification of Nothing; instead of looking blindly ahead to an endlessly, emptily repeating "tomorrow" or back on all our "yesterdays" now gone forever, we can focus on this present moment of ending and sustain it as long as possible. So that Man the walking shadow, the strutting idiot player and cosmic clown, can for the momentary hour of his infirm act recollect himself, come to his senses and know himself.

That, our proper task, is beyond anyone's present power of accomplishment. But we can even now set out something of what it calls for in this epilogue, our own last word. We have attempted to begin a recollection of Man as race and individual and of the present moment of time as our historical predicament. We also began the effort to recollect Nothing in the dominant form in which it presents itself to us as our own Nihilism. To recollect Nothing is to signify it, to speak that Nihilism which is present, hidden within us. For Nihilism is the presence of a silent death that must be exposed if it is not to complete itself in our total annihilation. To speak death is also to realize our own mortality, the new mortality of Man.

To find a voice for this new death is perhaps the most difficult task confronting any recollective effort. Since the religious and humanistic languages of death have become defunct, death has been rendered unspeakable, and so also unknowable. We have forgotten death in the very process of succumbing to it. It has been left to the doctors to give death as a biological process a technical definition, and it has been left to the lawyers to rule on the last wills and testaments of death as a social fact. And death as the experience of the dying has been narrowed down to the brief moment of the end usually hidden out of sight: "So the experience of death is turned into that of the exchange of functionaries . . . death has been fully domesticated. . . . Now it shares the ruin of the socially defunct individual."[15] And, as Adorno is fully aware, this dissolution of death is an historical outcome, "for death comes within the scope of history, and the latter can only be understood through it,"[16] as we have attempted to show.

To speak death, to call it by its proper name, it would be necessary to recollect our own mortality, present in us even while we are alive, and to recollect the mortality of those who are already dead but still living on in us. To recollect our own mortality is to come to experience our own dying, which is inseparable from our living, for as we live so we are also slowly dying. We know our own dying in all those "little deaths" that are to us intimations of mortality—those losses, severances, and negative transformations that signify death to us. Such negative experiences are essential for any lived life; to try to avoid or not to feel them is to render one's life unlived. We also experience dying on a higher symbolic level when we become aware of the silences, gaps, emptinesses in speech, or time, or existence; and without these, too, there could be neither speech nor time nor existence. All these experiences of dying and the very knowledge of mortality cannot be felt or had without a language of death.

The knowledge such a language brings is also necessary in order to acknowledge the death of those who are dead. Without such a language the dead are not truly dead; they might be considered absent or gone or passed away, but not meaningfully dead. It is in the language of the living that the dead, by being properly acknowledged as dead, can be consigned to their secure resting-place in the kingdom of the dead maintained in the life of the living. Thus it is the living who sustain the dead, but only so long as they feel themselves to be sustained by them in turn. "Les morts saisissent les vifs" only because the living in turn hold onto their dead. When that link between the living and the dead is broken, when the living have let go of their dead, then nobody can any longer be pronounced properly dead. How and in what form the living can remember the dead so that they themselves can die in turn is the unexpressed demand calling to us for a response.

In our historical moment, with its ominous threat of the death of Man, the question of death also takes on a new meaning in a higher dimension. It is in our care to safeguard not merely the proper death of the living but that of the whole kingdom of the dead, all those countless dead whom we have carried along throughout our history and whom we even now sustain in ourselves. To be cut off completely from the dead would constitute another kind of death for which we as yet have no name, another form of the death of Man perhaps even more gruesome than physical annihilation—as it were, a total amnesia of the human race. Yet, ultimately, we must also realize that Man is mortal, that sooner or later, in one way or another, mankind will die. And, beyond that, we must acknowledge that everything is mortal, that the earth will disappear, and so will the sun, like all stars, which have "a life of a billion years, then less than a second to die," and it is possible that nature itself, "the universe, has a birth, evolution and death,"[17] that it will be finally swallowed up in the Nothing of its own black holes. There is no immortality or eternity to be found anywhere.

For us, to whom death is so close but so far from our thoughts, there is the recollective task of finding a voice for all these modes of dying.

This is the ultimate form of the Orphic quest: by means of the voice to recover death from oblivion. But now that cannot be the Orphic voice of music. Music, which is speech on the threshold of silence, and so also speech closest to death, has now been stilled. That music has been denied us is a measure of our inability to speak death. Hence, any effort to recollect death will also be an endeavor to recollect the music that is so close to the voice of Silence. For us that recollection will have to be carried out only in words, at a distant remove from music itself.

This work has dedicated itself to beginning a recollection of music in words, to the same endeavor that Thomas Mann undertook in the last *Faust.* Yet, for him music could still act as the formative principle of his world, of the universe as well as of his work, whereas for us music is at an end. This work which strives to recollect music cannot itself be musical. And this points to the self-created paradoxical character of a work reflecting on the passage of Faust, for insofar as it has enacted this passage it has come to its end, but insofar as it is itself constituted by this passage it cannot possibly end it. Is this but the ultimate twist of Faust's self-reflection, that only a Faust could have come to the end of Faust?

## APPENDIX I
## The Story of Faust

Just prior to the start of the Reformation, a sometime scholar and quack-magician calling himself by the ancient Roman name of Faustus appears in sundry places in southern and central Germany.[1] "He came to Basel, and left his quack visiting cards upon humanists and theologians."[2] He is referred to by Philipp von Hutten; Luther and Melanchton speak ill of him. Half a century later a garbled version of extracts from his life together with numerous other accretions from a variety of sources is composed by the printer Spiess in Frankfurt and published as the first chapbook. It very quickly goes through numerous editions and translations. An English translation appears in 1588 within a year of the original, and a ballad in English is sung in the same year. A few years later the first dramatic rendering, that of Marlowe, is brought out, is soon translated into other languages, and becomes known on the continent. Sometime later it is brought back to Germany by strolling English players as a stage-play.

At this point we lose direct touch with Faust—he seems to go underground, though he never completely disappears. He is continually mentioned and written about, he becomes a figure of fun in folk-theatricals, he is played by puppets. During this period Calderón writes a kind of Spanish Faust in his *El Magico Prodigioso.* (Faust is not unrelated to Don Juan, and Goethe certainly drew some of his early inspiration from the seducer as portrayed musically in Mozart's opera.) Out of this relative obscurity Faust reappears in the light of the Enlightenment in a now lost fragment of Lessing. And then almost simultaneously, in the year before the American Revolution, Paul Weidemann, Maler Müller, and the young Goethe write new *Faust*s. Goethe's so-called *UrFaust* is left unpublished; it only appears in a revised version as the *Faust Fragment* in the second year of the French Revolution.

After that Faust is here to stay, and he holds sway during the whole modern age ever more insistently, either in his own name or under an incognito. He embarks on a musical career and appears ofttimes in opera and chorus, most acclaimed in Berlioz's "The Damnation of Faust" and the Chorus Mysticus of Mahler's Eighth Symphony. Under the pseudonym of Ivan Karamazov he makes an appearance in Dostoevski's novel, in league with a modern Devil without knowing it until that Devil himself reveals it to him in a nightmare of madness. Freud undertakes to psychoanalyze him on the basis of an old documented confession from a painter called Christoph Haizmann who trafficked with devils—but who for all that might not really have been a Faust—dating from the mid-seventeenth century.[3]

A real, living Faust who could have benefited from such treatment is the poet Baudelaire, and after him also the poet Rimbaud, who dabbles in poetic magic, in all innocence gives himself over to evil, and finally, knowing himself damned, at the last moment utters that piercing cry of contrition "Un Saison en Enfer," and then abandons his Faustian role for something even more daunting. Following on these French poets another, Valéry, much later characterizes himself in a comic-sardonic vein in the fragments of his *Mon Faust* as "professor-doctor Faustus member of the academy of dead sciences and hero of numerous literary and musical works."[4] Thinkers, too, have been Fausts; Wittgenstein explicitly likens himself, in his loneliness and fear of madness, to Lenau's Faust.[5] In this he also approaches Mann's Faust, the composer Leverkühn. Mann brings Faust home to Germany, though he incorporates much of what Faust has amassed in his foreign travels.

## APPENDIX II
Brief Overview of Acts I–IV of *Faust* Part II

At the end of Act I, Faust snatches at the ghostly form of Helen: it is a modern rape of Helen to cap the classical one. Of course, it cannot succeed—Faust is no Paris. Instead, there is an explosion, pandemonium ensues, and the Devil, who is no longer the Christian Satan in this neo-classical environment, is helpless; he is left to cart Faust's inert body from the stage, muttering wryly about his new folly. Faust's direct, unmediated grasp for the supreme symbol of antique beauty has been premature and had to end in failure. Yet, he had managed all alone to bring her forth from the deepest of all sources, the under-world realm of the Mothers, where "all the forms of Being" both of reality and imagination are gathered. The ghost of Helen is but the culmination of all the shades, shadows, obscurities, luminosities, and illusions of the whole act; it is the most ideal of them all, and the one most difficult to attain, as Mephistopheles complains when Faust first broaches the project: "Think you that Helen comes because you beckon, much as we raised the ghostly paper-guilders?"

The pursuit of "treasures" and "dears" (the German word *Schatz* has both meanings) is the play of appetites on which the society of the emperor's court revolves. The illusory treasury-notes of paper, backed by the security of the unmined gold of the underground, is the best of value that Mephistopheles can give, and, as a later scene shows, it certainly speeds up the circulation of society, stimulating economic life in a Keynesian manner. But for something more worthwhile Faust has to go underground himself. The society of the emperor's court is, of course, delighted with Mephistopheles' scheme, for it is able to satisfy all its vulgar appetites. That society lives by illusions; the motley colors of folly, of masquerade and show are the images in which society reflects on itself. Yet, as Faust had already realized in the first scene of awakening, the pure light of the sun, of light eternal, is not to be looked on or perceived except through the refracted colors of the rainbow, light broken up by the cataract of passionate, tumultuous human striving. This is why Faust on awakening has to plunge into social life and become the showman at court, like Goethe himself as theater-director at his prince's court, but also like Goethe himself as artist in the process of re-creating the life of society as art in this act itself. Hence, both Faust and Goethe reach out for a beauty that is beyond society's aspiration or attainment, the poetic beauty of Helen, beauty in its ultimate form, and show this beauty artistically to an uncomprehending social gaze as the deepest, most profound extension of its own shallower striving for beauty and form incarnate in its idle, amorous play and sexual lust. But Faust as artist in this act can only conjure up this beauty as mere show, an intuited vision thrown up from his inner depths, which he cannot firmly possess. When he tries to come into immediate possession of it and grasp it bodily, it explodes in his hands and disappears. Another two acts will be required before Faust can attain to union with Helen. To do so he has first to follow through the development of beauty in nature and art from its origins to its highest form. But it is his failure to grasp Helen at the end of this act that compels him to the quest of Helen in the next.

In Act II Faust pursues the vision of the birth of Helen, the perfect human form, as it emerges from its origins, evolving from the monstrous shapes embodied in the myths of classical antiquity. This is the quest for ideal form followed back to its origins in its material embodiment in nature. For Goethe the classicist and naturalist, the forms of nature and of classical art are ultimately the same; there is a unity of science and poetry. Hence, in his own art this unity is being realized; the classical Walpurgisnacht is at once a poetic phantasmagoria of the development of the ideal classical myth of Helen and an allegory of the modern scientific theory of the evolution of life out of inanimate material elements. The oneness of the scientific and poetic is the oneness of the True and the Beautiful, as Thales exclaims at the climax of the vision. This journey through nature and the antique neither Faust nor Mephistopheles can undertake unaided. They need the artificial light of the scientific intellect, for only that, through its scholarship, can recover the forms of antiquity and reveal the formations of nature. As Mephistopheles slyly ad-libs: "And we, when all is said and done, depend on creatures we have made" ("Laboratory"). Goethe, too, is ironically commenting on his own dependence on the scientific and classical scholarship of his *epigone*. In the play the scientific intellect is exemplified in Wagner, the student of Faust, and he, in believing he can produce life artificially, only manufactures the disembodied intelligence Homunculus.

It is with Homunculus that the deeper meaning of the act resides, and it is around him that the action revolves. He is the only fit guide for the Faustian expedition into the source of life, for he is himself searching for his own absent origin, since he wants naturally to come into being, to become. He strives for the sexual act, which failed to take place at his engendering. Being intelligence, he is self-consciously aware that he lacks sensual materiality, and as intelligence he strives to be united with his opposite; as mere form, he seeks to be conjunct with matter. Only through that copulation can he start to be. The act in fact concludes when he achieves his consummation with Galatea, prefiguring Faust's marriage with Helen.

The journey of exploration begins with a vision of the most basic strife of the elements, the struggle for survival and supremacy of inchoate forms as a prelude to the battle of life, which is symbolized by the perpetually reenacted ghostly conflict between Pompey and Caesar, a contest that repeats itself on all possible levels of existence. It includes the disputation between the two savants Anaxagoras and Thales, the spontaneous Vulcanist versus the gradualist evolutionist, who uphold the two opposite points of view of the dialectic of origins and transformations: "wie man entstehen und sich verwandeln kann." The journey ends in the vision of the origin of Life through Love, the principle of unification—the opposite to strife—symbolized by Galatea on her chariot-shell riding on the procreative waters like Venus rising from the sea on her oyster-shell. That which Mephistopheles could earlier only see, and participate in through his chase of illusory witches, as an anarchic "dance of Appetite" has in the end become ordered "festive dances" of love. Attracted by this love, suffused in it, Homunculus can finally realize his destiny by commencing to become and to begin the slow evolutionary spiral to Man: climactically he dashes his containing and constraining test-tube glass to pieces in order to embrace Galatea, and so he dies as intelligence, to be absorbed in the procreative ocean, sacrificing himself in love in order to attain to life. It is a distinct premonitory echo of the end of Faust; drawn higher by Love, ultimately Man, too, transcends himself. On another level of the allegory it can be read as signifying the self-sacrifice—that is, its own transcendence—of scientific intelligence, which must be absorbed in love and become poetic before it can be truly creative and conceive of the form of a Helen.

In the next act that sacrifice has been consummated. Helen is there seemingly alive before us; we are in a world of poetry. It is an unreal world of the literary imagination, for the whole act is a phantasmagoria populated by ghosts. But once again it is a developing world. This time we trace through its movement the historical growth of poetic forms, starting with the most severe and noble of classical tragedy and ending with the then-modern poetry of lyricism and elegy. In the center of the act is the symbolic marriage of Helen and Faust: the ideal dream of a classic-Romantic union, which must end in failure. Mephistopheles, in his classical guise as the harridan Phorkyas, is the go-between for this match, about which Helen has had a fearful premonition.

Phorkyas it is, too, who acts as midwife to the fruit of this ideal marriage, the leaping genius Euphorion: the apotheosis of modern poetry, closely resembling Lord Byron. In the splendid career but ultimately tragic fate of Byron, Goethe sees the tragic future of modern poetry, the heir of his own dream of a classic-Romantic synthesis. As it must, this poetic spirit seeks to realize itself in the real world of action. Yet, the action it seeks is the futile one of victory and glory. Death and posthumous fame are its only possible outcome. Euphorion crashes to his death before he can reach the real fight. With that defeat of the hope of success and succession the act dissolves—the shades return to the under-world and the spirits to nature. Poetry that began in the measured perfection of an Apollonian stately tread ends in the orgiastic stamping of a Dionysian bacchanal—a destruction that nevertheless promises a new beginning.

Following this failure, Faust takes up the activity for which his son had striven; he goes to war. For him, though, "the Deed is everything, the Glory naught." Faust is on firmer ground; he literally and literarily comes down to earth at the opening of the next act, stepping down from the cloud of poetic feminine form that had borne him in the air—straight onto a barren, mountainous landscape of unproductive strife. The battle of men in which he engages at first is for him only a means to the real struggle: he conceives of the practical but titanic ambition of war on the ocean, to conquer the very element that had once given Man birth but now limits him to its shores. His mode of action is once again violent, like the earth's volcanic activity when it thrusts up the mountains. But that is a necessary prelude: a partial success is his, for by participating in the futile war of the rival emperors he succeeds in winning as his fiefdom the barren strand—that thin line between the elements that is the place where amphibian Man must toil to secure his habitation. Faust's achievement is dubious, being without long-standing legal title and threatened with usurpation by the traditional authority of the church acting through the legitimate emperor whom Faust had restored.

Unfortunately, in this act Goethe's own artistic achievement is also dubious, and much of the act consists in rather heavy-handed satire on the late revolutionary upheavals and Napoleonic wars and the more recent attempted restoration of the Ancien Régime. Nevertheless, the act does develop further the dialectical progression of the play as a whole. The catastrophic principle, the principle of violence, by which Faust had so far lived, being true to his name and to his Devil, is in this, the penultimate act, subjected to its most searching criticism, prior to its final abandonment in the last act. For just as sheer volcanic violence cannot create a habitable world, so sheer military violence cannot produce the treasures of life or hold a kingdom together. But the struggle to win treasure and rob kingdoms is as persistent as the subterranean working of volcanoes; it is the upthrusts of human greed that have recourse to violence. Wars are futile but inevitable, productive life must go on despite them. Life only begins when these violent activities have subsided and the earth has settled back to its own subtle creative labors of building up and breaking down. It is on this note of expectation that the last act of real activity is about to begin.

# NOTES

PRELUDE

1. The outstanding contemporary exponent of the dramatic metaphor is, of course, Kenneth Burke, who has developed a "dramatistic" method "from the analysis of drama" which "treats language and thought primarily as modes of action." *A Grammar of Motives* (Berkeley: University of California Press, 1969), p. xxii. A recent, fruitful use of the model of drama, applied in this case to the history of political theory, is Norman Jacobson's *Pride and Solace* (Berkeley: University of California Press, 1978).

EPILOGUE IN HEAVEN

1. "La Technique Considérée en tant que Système," *Etudes Philosophiques* 2 (1976): 154–57. (My translation.)
2. William Wordsworth, "Preface to the Lyrical Ballads," pp. 129–30, quoted in Gerald L. Bruns, *Modern Poetry and the Idea of Language* (New Haven: Yale University Press, 1978), p. 51.
3. Samuel Johnson, from "A Review of Soame Jenyns' *A Free Inquiry into the Nature and Origin of Evil*," in *Rasselas, Poems and Selected Prose,* ed. Bertrand H. Bronson (New York: Holt, Rinehart and Winston, 1952), p. 197.
4. Ibid., pp. 204–5.
5. *Beyond the Pleasure Principle,* in *The Complete Psychological Works of Sigmund Freud,* Vol. XVIII, trans. J. Strachey (London: Hogarth, 1968), p. 42.
6. Ibid., pp. 38–39.
7. *Civilization and Its Discontents,* in *The Complete Psychological Works of Sigmund Freud,* Vol. XXI, trans. J. Strachey (London: Hogarth, 1973), p. 145.
8. Michel Montaigne, ch. XIX, "That to Philosophise is to Learn How to Die," in John Florio's *Translation of Montaigne's Essayes,* Vol. I (Oxford: Oxford University Press World's Classics, 1910), p. 89.
9. Quoted in Karl Löwith, *From Hegel to Nietzsche,* trans. David E. Green (London: Constable, 1965), p. 288.
10. Theodor Adorno, *Minima Moralia,* trans. E. F. N. Jephcott (London: NLB, 1974), p. 17.
11. Ibid., p. 148.
12. Franz Kafka, *The Diaries,* ed. Max Brod, trans. Joseph Kresh and Martin Greenberg (London: Secker and Warburg, 1948), entry for October 19, 1921.
13. Walter Benjamin, letter to Gerhard Scholem, April 17, 1931, quoted in *Illuminations,* ed. Hannah Arendt (London: Collins/Fontana, 1970), p. 19.
14. Czeslaw Milosz, "A Song on the End of the World," *Post-War Polish Poetry* (Baltimore: Penguin, 1970), pp. 60–61.
15. Cf. Elias Canetti, *Crowds and Power,* trans. Carol Stewart (Baltimore: Penguin, 1973), Epilogue.
16. Alfred Alvarez, *Under Pressure: The Writer in Society: Eastern Europe and the U.S.A.* (Baltimore: Penguin, 1965), p. 27.
17. Jacques Derrida, "The Ends of Man," in *Philosophy and Phenomenological Research* XXX (1969–1970): 57.
18. Theodor Adorno, *Philosophy of Modern Music,* trans. A. G. Mitchell and W. V. Bloomster (London: Sheed and Ward, 1973), p. 132.

19. Alfred Weber, *Farewell to European History,* trans. R. F. C. Hull (London: Kegan Paul, Trench, Trubner, 1947), p. 29.
20. Cf. Jill Redner, "The World's Body Anatomised: A Study of Shakespeare's Destructive Languages" (unpublished manuscript).

ACT I FAUST THE PHILOSOPHER
Scene I. *Word, Thought, and Deed*

1. *Faust,* trans. Philip Wayne (Baltimore: Penguin Classics, 1962), Part I, "Faust's Study," p. 71. Wayne's translation will be employed throughout this book except where otherwise indicated.
2. Malcolm Lowry, author of *Under the Volcano*; see *Selected Letters,* ed. Harvey Breit and M. Bonner Lowry (London: Cape, 1967), p. 76.
3. Cf. Thomas Mann, "Goethe's Faust," in *Essays,* trans. H. T. Lowe-Porter (New York: Vintage Books, 1957), p. 22.
4. *Farewell to European History.*
5. Goethe was, of course, by no means alone in this. Most of the poets and philosophers and some scientists of this crucial period carried through an analogous translation of the Logos into the Deed. For example, Coleridge states that "Reason, Proportion, communicable intelligibility, intelligent and communicant, the Word—which last expression strikes me as the profoundest and most comprehensive Energy of the human Mind, if it be not in some distinct sense energma Theoparadoton. . . . The moment we conceive of the divine energy, that moment we co-conceive the Logos." Here he is in effect carrying through the Faustian translation but in a much more literal and theologically obscurantist fashion than does Goethe. Cf. *The Notebooks of Samuel Taylor Coleridge,* ed. Kathleen Coburn, quoted in Bruns, *Modern Poetry and the Idea of Language,* pp. 52–53.
6. An ancient theme going back to Ovid and Apuleius (I owe this point to John Pocock).
7. F. W. Nietzsche, *Thus Spake Zarathustra,* trans. A. Tille (London: Everyman, 1950), p. 275.
8. Erich Heller, *The Disinherited Mind* (Baltimore: Penguin, 1961), p. 104.
9. Martin Heidegger, "What Is Metaphysics?" in *Existence and Being,* ed. and trans. W. Brock (Chicago: Henry Regnery Co., 1970), p. 355.
10. Paul Ricoeur, *Freud and Philosophy,* trans. Denis Savage (New Haven: Yale University Press, 1970), p. 3.
11. Ibid., p. 27.
12. Michel Foucault, *The Order of Things* (London: Tavistock, 1970), p. 304.
13. Ibid., p. 289.
14. George Steiner, *After Babel* (Oxford: Oxford University Press, 1975). On Hamann see p. 76; Herder, p. 78; and Humboldt, p. 81.
15. Foucault, *The Order of Things,* p. 290.
16. Foucault, "History, Discourse and Discontinuity," trans. Anthony M. Nazzaro, in *Esprit,* p. 237.

17. Ibid., p. 240.
18. For a short critique of Foucault see my "The Ends of Science and Philosophy: An Essay in the Sociology of Knowledge and Rationality," (Forthcoming).
19. Werner Marx, *Heidegger and the Tradition,* trans. Theodore Kisiel and Murray Greene (Evanston, Ill.: Northwestern University Press, 1971), p. 9.
20. Ibid., p. 212.
21. Cf. Horst Stuke, *Philosophie der Tat* (Stuttgart: E. Klatt, 1963).
22. *Philosophy of Mind,* trans. W. Wallace (Oxford: Clarendon Press, 1971), "Mind Subjective," sec. 458, pp. 213–15. This is a signal instance of Hegel's failure to understand the reconception of language that his friend Humboldt, whom he quotes, was carrying out. On Hegel's approach to language in general see Daniel J. Cook, *Language in the Philosophy of Hegel* (The Hague: Mouton, 1973), in particular ch. VII, on the spoken word as the Logos.
23. Cf. J. P. Eckermann, *Conversations with Goethe,* trans. John Oxenford (London: Everyman, 1970), p. 384.
24. Engels, "On Historical Materialism," in *Marx and Engels,* ed. L. S. Feuer (New York: Doubleday, 1959), p. 51.
25. Marx and Engels, *German Ideology,* in *Writings of the Young Marx,* ed. Guddat and Easton (New York: Doubleday, 1967), p. 409.
26. *Theses on Feuerbach,* ibid., p. 400.
27. *German Ideology,* ibid., p. 421.
28. *Theses on Feuerbach,* ibid., sixth thesis, p. 402.
29. *German Ideology,* ibid., p. 421.
30. *Grundrisse,* trans. D. McLellan (London: Paladin, 1973), pp. 27–28.
31. Cf. my "The Ends of Science and Philosophy," ch. III.
32. *Grundrisse,* p. 28.
33. *The Order of Things,* p. 305.
34. *Will to Power,* ed. Walter Kaufmann (New York: Vintage, 1968), Sec. 522, p. 283.
35. Heller, *The Disinherited Mind,* p. 105.
36. *Vermischte Bemerkungen,* ed. G. H. von Wright (Oxford: Blackwell, 1977), p. 65.
37. Ibid., p. 90.
38. *Philosophical Investigations,* trans. E. Anscombe (Oxford: Blackwell, 1953), Sec. 23.
39. *Philosophical Investigations,* p. 226.
40. *Philosophical Investigations,* Sec. 19.
41. *On Certainty,* trans. E. Anscombe (Oxford: Blackwell, 1969), Sec. 344.
42. *Foundations of Mathematics,* trans. E. Anscombe (Oxford: Blackwell, 1964), p. 57.
43. Trans. R. Rhees, in *The Human World* (May–August 1974): 157; cf. also *Vermischte Bemerkungen,* p. 43.
44. *Vermischte Bemerkungen,* p. 43.
45. Ibid., p. 22. As for Sraffa, we know a little more of his influence because of the unique tribute Wittgenstein pays to him as having been the major instigation through which he freed himself of the

Positivism of the *Tractatus* philosophy and went on to the thought of the *Philosophical Investigations.* It is here that Wittgenstein's relation to Marx can be "genealogically" traced, for we know that Piero Sraffa, the outstanding Cambridge economist, was in the days when he knew Wittgenstein the close friend and follower of Gramsci, the Italian Marxist theorist. It is perhaps not too farfetched to believe that Wittgenstein's relation to Nietzsche could similarly be traced through Spengler. Unfortunately, an intellectual biography of Wittgenstein is still lacking.

46. Stanley Rosen, *Nihilism* (New Haven: Yale University Press, 1970), p. 10.
47. James Demske, *Being, Man and Death* (Lexington: University Press of Kentucky, 1970), p. 132.
48. Ibid., p. 181.
49. Cf. "Hölderlin's Dichtung," quoted in ibid., p. 128.
50. Demske, *Being, Man and Death,* p. 128.
51. Heidegger elaborates this terminology in *What Is Called Thinking?,* trans. J. Glenn Gray (New York: Harper and Row, 1968), pp. 138–47.
52. "Vom Wesen der Wahrheit," in *Existence and Being,* p. 308.
53. Demske, *Being, Man and Death,* p. 145.
54. Ibid., p. 181.
55. "The Origin of the Work of Art," in *Poetry, Language, Thought,* trans. A. Hofstadter (New York: Harper and Row, 1971), p. 73.
56. "Hölderlin and the Essence of Poetry," in *Existence and Being,* pp. 277–79.
57. Ibid., p. 281.
58. Ibid.
59. Cf. William J. Richardson, *Heidegger: Through Phenomenology to Thought* (The Hague: Nijhoff, 1963), p. 625.
60. "Spengler after the Decline," in *Prisms,* trans. S. and S. Weber (London: Neville Spearman, 1967), p. 53.
61. *Being, Man and Death,* p. 193.
62. *Philosophical Investigations,* Sec. 109.
63. Ibid., Sec. 124.
64. Ibid., Sec. 126.
65. Cf. W. Marx, *Heidegger and the Tradition,* p. 229.

Scene II. *Word, Thought, and Deed—once again*

1. *Vermischte Bemerkungen,* p. 22.
2. "Science as a Vocation," in *From Max Weber,* ed. H. H. Gerth and C. W. Mills (London: Routledge and Kegan Paul, 1970), p. 141.
3. *Will to Power,* p. 291.
4. These categories have analogues in the metaphysical ones of unity, verity, and goodness (*omne ens est unum, verum e bonum*), as well as in the Positivist ones of the logical, empirical, and evaluative.
5. *L'Activité Rationaliste de la Physique Contemporaine* (Paris: Presses Universitaires, 1951), p. 7.
6. *The History of Nature* (Chicago: Chicago University Press, 1949), p. 71.
7. *Philosophical Investigations,* Sec. 339.

8. *The Order of Things,* p. 328.
9. *Tractatus Logico-Philosophicus,* trans. D. F. Pears and B. F. McGuinness (London: Routledge and Kegan Paul, 1961), Sec. 5.64.
10. Cf. P. Engelmann, *Letters from Ludwig Wittgenstein,* trans. L. Furtmüller (Oxford: Blackwell, 1967), p. 114.
11. *Philosophical Investigations,* Sec. 23.
12. Ferdinand de Saussure, "Course in General Linguistics," in *The Structuralists from Marx to Lévi-Strauss,* ed. R. and F. De George (New York: Doubleday Anchor, 1972), p. 70.
13. Ibid., p. 71.
14. Norman Malcolm, *A Memoir* (Oxford: Oxford University Press, 1958), p. 93.
15. *Vermischte Bemerkungen,* p. 141.
16. *Foundations of Mathematics,* p. 194.
17. Ibid., p. 190.
18. Cf. *Vermischte Bemerkungen,* p. 163: his incredible answer to the question "Has philosophy made no progress?"
19. *Philosophical Investigations,* p. 230.
20. Ibid., Sec. 415.
21. The word *development* radically changed its meaning toward the end of the eighteenth century; having previously meant *unfolding* or *unfurling,* it came to mean *actively bringing out something latent.* The chemistry of Lavoisier and the biology of Lamarck were also influential in this change of meaning, as Jack Lindsay points out.
22. "What Are Poets For?," *Poetry, Language, Thought,* p. 132.
23. Ibid.
24. "The Origin of the Work of Art," p. 74.
25. "Hölderlin and the Essence of Poetry," p. 281.
26. *Introduction to Metaphysics,* trans. Ralph Manheim (New York: Doubleday Anchor, 1961), p. 44.
27. *Philosophical Investigations,* Sec. 371.
28. *Existence and Being,* p. 283.
29. "The Origin of the Work of Art," p. 74.

ACT II MAN, TIME, AND NOTHING

Scene I. *Dialectics of the Deed (quasi una fantasia)*

1. Goethe, "One and All," *Selected Verse,* trans. David Luke (Baltimore: Penguin Poets, 1964), p. 275.
2. Cf. Preface to the *Critique of Pure Reason,* trans. N. Kemp Smith (London: Macmillan, 1958).
3. For a fuller exposition see my "The Ends of Science and Philosophy."
4. *Dialectic of Enlightenment,* trans. John Cumming (London: Allen Lane, 1973), p. 231.
5. *Negative Dialectics,* trans. E. B. Ashton (London: Routledge and Kegan Paul, 1973), p. 5.
6. Ibid.
7. *Philosophical Investigations,* Sec. 119.
8. Quoted in Ernest Becker, *The Denial of Death* (New York: Free Press, 1973), p. 255.
9. *The Order of Things,* p. 317.

10. Sam Dolgoff, ed., *Bakunin on Anarchy* (London: Allen and Unwin, 1973), p. 308.
11. Cf. Heidegger, *Being and Time,* trans. J. Macquarie and E. Robinson (New York: Harper and Row, 1962), pp. 98–100.
12. Dolgoff, *Bakunin on Anarchy,* p. 57.
13. Cf. Foucault, *The Birth of the Clinic,* trans. A. M. Sheridan Smith (London: Tavistock, 1973), ch. 8.
14. *Dialectic of Enlightenment,* pp. 233–34.
15. *Crowds and Power,* p. 255.
16. *Contribution to a Critique of the Philosophy of Right of Hegel,* trans. A. Jolin and J. O'Malley (Cambridge: Cambridge University Press, 1970), p. 137.
17. Louis Althusser and Etienne Balibar, *Lire Capital,* Tome II (Paris: Maspero, 1965), p. 291.
18. *The Order of Things,* pp. 341–42.
19. Ibid., p. 342.
20. Ibid.
21. Louis Althusser, *For Marx,* trans. Ben Brewster (Baltimore: Penguin, 1969), p. 219.
22. Quoted in *After Babel,* p. 82.
23. Cf. Jacques Derrida, "The Ends of Man."
24. "Remarks on Frazer's *The Golden Bough,*" *Synthese* 17 (1967).
25. *The Order of Things,* p. 333.
26. *Thus Spake Zarathustra,* Introductory Discourse, p. 5.
27. Cf. *Will to Power,* Sec. 866, p. 463.
28. See David Roberts, "The Sense of an Ending: Apocalyptic Perspectives in the 20th-Century German Novel," *Orbis Litterarum* (1977). The discussion in this article is of the endings in Heinrich Mann's *Der Untertan,* Thomas Mann's *Dr. Faustus,* Broch's *Die Schlafwandler,* and Canetti's *Die Blendung.*
29. *The Phenomenology of Mind,* trans. J. B. Baillie (London: Allen and Unwin, 1910), p. 83. In what might be seen as a dig at Goethe, Hegel begins this paragraph with these words: "The exaltation of so-called Nature at the expense of thought misconceived leads. . . ."
30. *Philosophy of History,* trans. J. Sibree (New York: Dover, 1956), p. 72.
31. *Conversations with Goethe,* p. 244.
32. "Metamorphose der Pflanzen," in Goethe, *Selected Verse,* pp. 147–51.
33. Ibid.
34. Eckermann, *Conversations with Goethe,* p. 35.
35. *Faust Part II,* trans. Bayard Taylor (New York: Modern Library, 1930), p. 4.
36. Eckerman, op. cit., p. 287.
37. Cf. *Being and Time,* Division II, Secs. V, VI.
38. Claude Lévi-Strauss, *The Savage Mind* (Chicago: University of Chicago Press, 1966), p. 263.
39. Ibid., p. 262.
40. *The Order of Things,* p. 369.

41. Louis Althusser and Etienne Balibar, *Reading Capital,* trans. Ben Brewster (London: NLB, 1970), p. 94.
42. Ibid., p. 96.
43. Ibid., p. 97.
44. Ibid., p. 99.
45. Ibid., p. 104.
46. M. Foucault, *L'Ordre du Discours,* inaugural lecture delivered at the College de France, February 12, 1970 (Paris: Editions Gallimard, 1971). Translated in *Social Science Information* X (1971): 24.
47. *Reading Capital,* p. 101.
48. Ibid., p. 103.
49. Nietzsche, *Will to Power,* p. 12.

Scene II. *The Language of Nihilism*

1. Quoted in Stuke, *Philosophie der Tat,* p. 231. (My translation.)
2. Löwith, *From Hegel to Nietzsche,* p. 449.
3. Maurice Blanchot puts this metaphor very graphically. See his "La Littérature et le Droit à la Mort," quoted in Maurice Nadeau, *The French Novel since the War,* trans. A. M. Sheridan Smith (New York: Grove Press, 1967), pp. 171–72.
4. Cf. *Will to Power,* Sec. 12, p. 13.
5. For the sake of logicians and linguists it is perhaps necessary to emphasize that there are no rules, decision procedures, or even firmly delineated criteria for distinguishing between nonsense and absurdity. But that is no shortcoming of the two concepts in question, for despite all the efforts and claims of recent research in this direction there are as yet no such procedures for distinguishing sense and nonsense, either. Nor can there be any, for sense is a non-rule-governed matter of understanding and judgment. No rules would ever be adequate for deciding that the sentence "Colorless green ideas sleep furiously" is nonsense but that the equally peculiar sentence "Annihilating all that's made to a green thought in a green shade" makes perfect and very profound sense. The latter is, of course, a line from Marvell's great poem "The Garden." What it states, which can only be apparent to those who can read and understand poetry, is that the human mind exercises an annihilating action on natural things, and in the process comes to reduce itself to those things. This short and inadequate paraphrase would itself be nonsense to a positivistically-minded linguist, which only proves that his mind too has that power of annihilating sense to which Marvell refers. And this is the subject under consideration.
6. Cf. "The Ends of Man," p. 55.
7. Bernard S. Myers, *Expressionism: A Generation in Revolt* (London: Thames and Hudson, 1963), p. 9.
8. *Philosophy of Modern Music,* trans. A. G. Mitchell and W. V. Bloomster (London: Sheed and Ward, 1973), p. 118.
9. Ibid., p. 42.
10. *Beyond Good and Evil,* trans. M. Cowan (Chicago: University of Chicago Press, 1955), p. 46.
11. See the two Anatomy Lessons, of Dr. Tulp and Dr. Deyman.

12. Theodor Adorno, *The Aging of Modern Music,* quoted in George Lukacs, *Realism in Our Time* (New York: Harper and Row, 1964), p. 37.
13. For reduction in science see "The Ends of Science and Philosophy."
14. See "Epilogue in Heaven."
15. Quoted in Dieter Arendt, *Nihilismus* (Cologne: Jacob Hegner, 1970), from the introduction. (My translation.)
16. Ibid., p. 34.
17. Ibid.
18. Ibid., p. 36.
19. *Faksimileausgabe,* ed. Heinz Nicolai (Stuttgart: Sammlung Metzler, 1977). I owe the reference to David Roberts.
20. Ibid., p. 123.
21. Quoted in D. Arendt, *Nihilismus,* p. 13.
22. Quoted in ibid., p. 21.
23. Quoted in ibid., p. 60.
24. *Negative Dialectics,* p. 381.
25. *Genealogy of Morals,* trans. F. Golffing (New York: Doubleday Anchor, 1956), p. 209.
26. D. Arendt, *Nihilismus,* p. 82.
27. *Jargon of Authenticity,* trans. K. Tarnowski and F. Will (London: Routledge and Kegan Paul, 1973), p. 35.
28. "Letter to Jünger," in *The Question of Being,* trans. William Kluback and Jean T. Wilde (London: Vision, 1959), p. 85.
29. Ibid., p. 103.
30. Ibid., pp. 108–9.

ACT III THE DEED IN DEED

Scene I. *The Origins of the Deed*

1. Cf. Hannah Arendt, *The Human Condition* (Chicago: University of Chicago Press, 1958), ch. 5.
2. Cf. inaugural lecture delivered in Frankfurt, 1965, in *Knowledge and Human Interests,* trans. J. J. Shapiro (London: Heinemann, 1973).
3. Sergio Cotta, "Homme et Nature," in *Etudes Philosophiques* (April–June 1976): 175. (My translation.)
4. Ibid., p. 176.
5. A. Weber, *Farewell to European History,* p. 60.
6. "The Social Psychology of the World Religions," *From Max Weber,* p. 280.
7. Cf. *Oeuvres Complètes,* ed. Lewinter (Paris: Club Français du Livre, 1969), vol. II, p. 349.
8. H. Arendt, *The Human Condition,* p. 301.
9. Albert Camus, *The Rebel,* trans. Anthony Bowen (Baltimore: Penguin, 1962), p. 32.
10. "The Madman," *The Joyful Wisdom,* trans. Thomas Common (New York: Ungar, 1960), Sec. 125, p. 169.

Scene II. *The Equivocations of Progress*

1. Adorno, *Philosophy of Modern Music,* p. 14.
2. Nietzsche, *Will to Power,* Plan XV, p. 141.

3. *Dialectics of Enlightenment*, p. 154.
4. *Philosophy of Modern Music*, p. 15.
5. Max Weber, *Religion of China*, trans. H. Gerth (New York: Free Press, 1964), p. 248.
6. "Science as a Vocation," in *From Max Weber*, p. 140.
7. Ibid.
8. Ibid.
9. Ibid.
10. Walter Benjamin, *Illuminations*, trans. Harry Zohn (London: Collins/Fontana, 1973), Sec. XIII, p. 263.
11. "Science as a Vocation," in *From Max Weber*, p. 155.
12. Ibid., p. 139.
13. Habermas, *Knowledge and Human Interests*, p. 309.
14. *Etudes Philosophiques* (April–June 1976): 152.
15. George Lukacs, *Realism in Our Time: Literature and the Class Struggle* (New York: Harper and Row, 1964), p. 27.
16. Cf. ibid., pp. 21–25.
17. Walter Benjamin, *Charles Baudelaire: A Lyric Poet in the Era of High Capitalism*, trans. Harry Zohn (London: NLB, 1973), p. 98.
18. *Will to Power*, Sec. 943, p. 497.
19. Ibid., Sec. 944, p. 498.
20. Stanley Cavell, *The World Viewed* (New York: Viking, 1971), pp. 40–41.
21. "Science as a Vocation," p. 149.
22. Ibid., p. 148.
23. Ibid., p. 147.
24. *Prisms*, p. 59.

ACT IV THE END OF FAUST

Scene II. *Dr. John Faustus—the first Faust*

1. Wilbur Sanders, *The Dramatist and the Received Idea* (Cambridge: Cambridge University Press, 1968), p. 233.
2. Ibid., p. 242.

Scene III. *Heinrich Faust—the middle Faust*

1. *Selected Verse*, p. 197.
2. *Faust*, trans. W. Kaufmann (New York: Doubleday Anchor, 1962), p. 493.
3. *Selected Verse*, p. 277.
4. Cf. *Goethe's Faust: Kommentiert von Erich Trunz* (Hamburg: Christian Wegner, 1963), p. 497.
5. *Selected Verse*, p. 154.
6. E. Heller, *The Disinherited Mind*, p. 256.

Scene IV. *Adrian Leverkühn—the last Faust*

1. *Doctor Faustus*, trans. H. T. Lowe-Porter (New York: Vintage Books, 1971), p. 478. All subsequent references to this work will be marked by page numbers in the text.
2. Thomas Mann, *The Tales of Jacob*, trans. H. T. Lowe-Porter (London: Sphere Books, 1968), p. 162.

3. Mann has almost certainly followed Freud's analysis of a surviving documentary confession of a pseudo-Faust: "A Seventeenth-Century Demonological Neurosis: The Story of Christoph Haizmann the Painter," in *The Complete Psychological Works of Sigmund Freud,* Vol. XIX, trans. J. Strachey (London: Hogarth, 1961), pp. 73–100.
4. Ibid., p. 85.
5. Ibid., p. 83.
6. Ibid., p. 90.
7. *Prisms,* pp. 171–72.
8. *Prisms,* p. 172.
9. *Prisms,* pp. 169–70.
10. *Prisms,* p. 168.
11. Cf. Adorno, *Philosophy of Modern Music,* pp. 128–29.

Scene V. *Faust the Musician*

1. Cf. Adorno, *Introduction to the Sociology of Music,* trans. E. B. Ashton (New York: Seabury, 1976), p. 47.
2. Letter to Zelter, March 11, 1832, in *Goethes Briefe,* Vol. IV (Hamburg: Christian Wegner, 1967), p. 477.
3. *Philosophy of Modern Music,* p. 37.
4. *Will to Power,* Sec. 842, p. 444.
5. Cf. *The Rational and Social Foundations of Music,* trans. Martindale, Riedel, and Neuwirth (Carbondale: Southern Illinois University Press, 1958), p. 83.
6. Author's Introduction, *The Protestant Ethic and the Spirit of Capitalism,* trans. Talcott Parsons (London: Allen and Unwin, 1967), p. 15.
7. Cf. Eric Emery, *Temps et Musique* (Lausanne: L'Age d'Homme, 1975), p. 270.
8. Considerations of this kind give some credence to Spengler's thesis of the expressive role of music for his so-called Faustian cultural "soul" of Europe. However, that contains some wild and irresponsible extrapolations, even apart from the very questionable premise of the Faustian "soul" itself.
9. Adorno, *Introduction to the Sociology of Music,* p. 69.
10. Ibid., p. 180.
11. Ibid., pp. 181–82.
12. Ibid., p. 160.
13. Adorno, *Philosophy of Modern Music,* p. 43.
14. Ibid., p. 82.
15. Ibid., p. 37.
16. Ibid., p. 187.
17. Ibid., p. 188.
18. Ibid., p. 65 n. 29.
19. Ibid., p. 37.
20. Ibid., p. 42.
21. Ibid., p. 77.
22. Ibid., p. 82. The reference is, of course, to Berg's opera *Lulu.*

## PROLOGUE ON THE ENDANGERED EARTH

1. Adorno, *Prisms,* p. 58.
2. Cf. Günther Anders, *Endzeit und Zeitenende* (Munich: Beck, 1972), p. 203.
3. Max Horkheimer, *The Eclipse of Reason* (New York: Seabury, 1974), p. 134.
4. Ibid., p. 94.
5. Adorno, *Negative Dialectics,* p. 362.
6. *Trialogue* (February 1979).
7. Cf. H. and J. Redner, *An-atomy of the World* (Melbourne: Collins/Fontana, forthcoming).
8. Cf. "Politics as a Vocation," in *From Max Weber,* p. 128.
9. In the interval between the completion of the manuscript and the publication of this book a mass peace movement has arisen in Western Europe, alleviating some of the practical difficulties of criticism and protest, at least for the time being.
10. Adorno, *Prisms,* p. 55.
11. Horkheimer, *The Eclipse of Reason,* p. 142.
12. Ibid., p. 165.
13. Adorno, *Negative Dialectics,* pp. 17–18.
14. Frederic Jameson, *Yale French Studies* (New Haven: Yale University Press, 1977), p. 309.
15. *Minima Moralia,* p. 232.
16. Ibid., p. 231.
17. In the words of Remo Ruffini, a leading astrophysicist, reported in *The Age* (Melbourne), November 12, 1978.

## APPENDIX I. THE STORY OF FAUST

1. For a more extensive treatment of the early life of Faust the reader is referred to the *Faust-Bibliographie,* ed. Hans Henning (Berlin: Aufbau, 1966), the first part of which, covering the literature only till 1790, lists over 3,000 titles. See also Paul A. Bates, *Faust: Sources, Works, Criticism* (New York: Harcourt Brace, 1969).
2. Mann, "Goethe's Faust," p. 18.
3. Freud, "A Seventeenth-Century Demonological Neurosis."
4. "Lust, La Demoiselle de Cristal" (Paris: Gallimard, 1946), Act I, Scene I, p. 22.
5. Cf. *Vermischte Bemerkungen,* p. 103.

# INDEX

Designer: Marian O'Brien
Compositor: Innovative Media, Inc.
Text: VIP Sabon
Display: Phototypositor Sabon
Printer: Thomson-Shore, Inc.
Binder: John H. Dekker & Sons